HARLAXTON MEDIEVAL STUDIES

VOLUME SEVENTEEN

RECORDING MEDIEVAL LIVES

HARLAXTON MEDIEVAL STUDIES

1. ORMROD, W. M. (ed.), *England in the Thirteenth Century*, Proceedings of the 1989 Symposium (1991).

2. HICKS, Carola (ed.), *England in the Eleventh Century*, Proceedings of the 1990 Symposium (1992).

3. ROGERS, Nicholas (ed.), *England in the Fourteenth Century*, Proceedings of the 1991 Symposium (1993).

4. ROGERS, Nicholas (ed.), *England in the Fifteenth Century*, Proceedings of the 1992 Symposium (1994).

5. THOMPSON, Benjamin (ed.), *The Reign of Henry VII*, Proceedings of the 1993 Symposium (1995).

6. THOMPSON, Benjamin (ed.), *Monasteries and Society in Medieval Britain*, Proceedings of the 1994 Symposium (1999).

7. STRICKLAND, Matthew (ed.), *Armies, Chivalry and Warfare in Medieval Britain and France*, Proceedings of the 1995 Symposium (1998).

8. MITCHELL, John (ed., with Matthew Moran), *England and the Continent in the Middle Ages. Studies in Memory of Andrew Martindale*, Proceedings of the 1996 Symposium (2000).

9. EALES, Richard and TYAS, Shaun (eds), *Family and Dynasty in Late Medieval England*, Proceedings of the 1997 Symposium (2003)

10. BACKHOUSE, Janet (ed.), *The Medieval English Cathedral. Papers in Honour of Pamela Tudor-Craig*, Proceedings of the 1998 Symposium (2003).

11. BARRON, Caroline M. and STRATFORD, Jenny (eds), *The Church and Learning in Later Medieval Society. Essays in Honour of R. B. Dobson*, Proceedings of the 1999 Symposium (2002).

12. MORGAN, Nigel (ed.), *Prophecy, Apocalypse and the Day of Doom,* Proceedings of the 2000 Symposium (2004).

13. STRATFORD, Jenny (ed.), *The Lancastrian Court*, Proceedings of the 2001 Symposium (2003).

14. BURGESS, Clive and DUFFY, Eamon (eds), *The Parish in Late Medieval England*, Proceedings of the 2002 Symposium (2006).

15. HORDEN, Peregrine (ed.), *Freedom of Movement in the Middle Ages*, Proceedings of the 2003 Symposium (2007).

16. DAVIES, Matthew and PRESCOTT, Andrew (eds), *London and the Kingdom. Essays in Honour of Caroline M. Barron*, Proceedings of the 2004 Symposium (2008).

17. BOFFEY, Julia and DAVIS, Virginia (eds), *Recording Medieval Lives*, Proceedings of the 2005 Symposium (2009).

18. CHERRY, John and PAYNE, Ann (eds), *Signs and Symbols. Essays in Memory of Janet Backhouse*, Proceedings of the 2006 Symposium (2009).

HARLAXTON MEDIEVAL STUDIES, XVII

RECORDING MEDIEVAL LIVES

Proceedings of the
2005 Harlaxton Symposium

Edited by
Julia Boffey
and
Virginia Davis

SHAUN TYAS
DONINGTON
2009

© The Contributors
Published in 2009 by
SHAUN TYAS
(an imprint of 'Paul Watkins')
1 High Street
Donington
Lincolnshire
PE11 4TA

ISBN
1 900289 954 (ten digits)
978 1 900289 955 (thirteen digits)

Typeset and designed from the discs of the authors
by Shaun Tyas

This publication was assisted by a grant
from the Isobel Thornley Bequest Fund.

Printed in Great Britain by the MPG Books Group,
Bodmin and King's Lynn

CONTENTS

LIST OF CONTRIBUTORS

Caroline Barron	Royal Holloway, University of London
Julia Boffey	Queen Mary University of London
Mishtooni Bose	Christ Church, Oxford
Janet Burton	University of Wales, Lampeter
Virginia Davis	Queen Mary University of London
A. S. G. Edwards	De Montfort University
Christopher Fletcher	Lille, France
David J. King	University of East Anglia
Pamela King	Bristol University
David Lepine	University of Exeter
Richard A. Linenthal	Bernard Quaritch Ltd
William Marx	University of Wales, Lampeter
Carol M. Meale	Bristol University
Susan Powell	University of Salford
Pamela Robinson	School of Advanced Study. University of London
Nicholas Rogers	Sidney Sussex College, Cambridge
Henry Summerson	Oxford Holinshed Project
Anne F. Sutton	Mercers' Company
Pamela Tudor-Craig	Society of Antiquaries, London
Shaun Tyas	Independent Publisher
Livia Visser-Fuchs	Baarn, The Netherlands.

LIST OF PLATES

1 (Barron) A marginal illustration by the scribe, found in the registered copy of Salter's will, showing Salter's executor holding a money bag and preparing to hand over bequests to the five children (three men and two girls) of Robert and Elizabeth Symonds. John Symonds, who was to act on behalf of his brothers and sisters is named. TNA PROB/11/42a fol. 103v (copyright: The National Archives)

2 (Barron) A marginal illustration by the scribe, found in the registered copy of Salter's will, showing the six glasses and the earthenware bottle with a funnel belonging to it, together with Salter's urinal glass and case, and a drinking 'cruse' (bottle) of earthenware, which Salter bequeathed to John Busshope, the parish clerk of St Nicholas Acon. TNA PROB/11/42a fol. 104v (copyright: The National Archives)

3 (Barron) The first page of Thomas Salter's original will, drawn up 31 August 1558, showing the heading 'Jesus aductor meus' and the side headings 'The Wax Chandeler' and 'The Salters almesmen'. Salter decided that it should be the curate of St Michael Cornhill, rather than of St Nicholas Acon in Lombard Street, who was to accompany his body to the burial in St Magnus' church, and this alteration can be seen in line 21. TNA PROB/10/38 fol. 1 (copyright: The National Archives)

4 (Barron) The fourth page of Thomas Salter's will showing where Salter ceased to write the will himself and it was continued in the hand of the notary, Thomas Bradforth, who is also the first witness. The two smudged marks (one a cross) at the end of the will may be the marks made by Thomas Salter when he was no longer able to write. TNA PROB/10/38 fol. 4 (copyright: The National Archives)

5 (Barron) Thomas Salter's letter to Thomas Cromwell, dated 7 August 1534. The letter is written by Salter himself: the distinctive handwriting can be identified again when Salter drew up his own will twenty-four years later (see Illustration 3). TNA SP1/85 (copyright: The National Archives)

6 (P. King) The tomb of Ralph Woodford, Ashby Folville (copyright: Meg Twycross)

7 (P. King) The tomb of Ralph Woodford, Ashby Folville (detail) (copyright: Meg Twycross)

8 (P. King) The tomb of Ralph Woodford, Ashby Folville (detail) (copyright: Meg Twycross)

9 (P. King) The arms of Ralph Woodford, Ashby Folville (copyright: Meg Twycross)

MAPS AND FIGURES

PREFACE

Speakers at the 22nd Harlaxton Symposium in 2005 were invited to explore the variety of forms in which medieval lives were recorded, and some of the many considerations which determined how such records were prompted or shaped. Among the papers offered were some which used diverse sources of evidence to reconstruct the lives of individuals, and others which tackled the questions prompted by particular forms of evidence, whether chronicles, wills, manuscript images, seal matrices or brasses. The conference considered both individual lives and the value of a prosopographical approach to understanding the late Middle Ages. At the heart of our discussions was the challenge of writing medieval biography.

Biography has been somewhat disdained by medievalists in recent decades, particularly in the second half of the twentieth century when the study of the medieval past became increasingly influenced by approaches taken from the social sciences. If biography was indeed – according to Disraeli's *Contarini Fleming* – 'life without theory', then its unpopularity was unsurprising.[1] K. B. McFarlane summarised the situation when he wrote that the historian cannot honestly write biographical history: given the nature of surviving records, human motives are hard to excavate, and the historian's province is rather 'the growth of social organisations, of civilisation, of ideas'.[2]

Recent published debates, however, such as those generated by the essays about methodology in *Writing Medieval Biography, 700–1250* (2006), suggest that the pendulum may be swinging the other way.[3] The challenges are undoubted: evidence is indeed fragmentary, and medievalists are faced with the difficulty of writing about individual inner lives without many of the written sources available for more recent periods – in particular those constituted by diaries, private correspondence, memoirs and reflections. Even apparently personal documents from the Middle Ages, such as wills, are often seriously formulaic. It is not easy to deduce motives from actions alone or to reconstruct individual interests simply from surviving personal possessions. Yet it is not impossible. The

---

[1]   Benjamin Disraeli, *Contarini Fleming* (London, 1832), part I, chapter 23, quoted from *The Bradenham Edition of the Novels and Tales of Benjamin Disraeli, 1st Earl of Beconsfield, Volume IV* (Edinburgh, 1927), p. 110.

[2]   K. B. McFarlane, *The Nobility of Later Medieval England* (Oxford, 1973), p. ix.

[3]   David Bates, Julia C. Crick and Sarah Hamilton (eds), *Writing Medieval Biography, 700–1250: Essays in Honour of Professor Frank Barlow* (Woodbridge, 2006).

records of medieval lives can be made to speak to a twenty-first-century society, as the papers at this conference demonstrate; and they can speak in ways which both enhance understanding of the lives of particular individuals, and illustrate wider concerns pertaining to selfhood and the methodologies by which it may be investigated and defined. Our hope is that the nineteen papers published here will help to stimulate further work on the range of sources available to medievalists in the twenty-first century who wish to understand the past through the singularity of its inhabitants.

We would like to express our gratitude first and foremost to the speakers at the symposium, who have displayed extraordinary patience with the editors of this volume, and to the participants who joined in the conversations there. For support of various kinds we are very grateful to The Harlaxton Committee, particularly its former chairman Professor Barrie Dobson and its current chairman Professor Caroline Barron; to the Committee's successive secretaries Dr Eleanor Quinton and Mr Christian Steer; and to Dr Shaun Tyas, who has put so much energy and care into the production of this volume.

This publication was assisted by a grant from the Isobel Thornley Bequest Fund.

Julia Boffey
Virginia Davis

Rethinking Medieval People: the Experience of the DNB[1]

HENRY SUMMERSON

The *Oxford Dictionary of National Biography* contains the lives of many medieval people; if for present purposes the word 'medieval' is taken to embrace those subjects active between the middle of the fifth century and the end of the fifteenth, then in the *Dictionary* which appeared in September 2004 there are notices of 4,729 people contained in 3,600 articles. (Online releases up to the end of 2007 have included lives of a further seventy-nine medieval subjects within seventy-five articles.) The composition of a work of reference like the *DNB* inevitably involves making choices; in this case, double choices. For behind the new edition stands its progenitor, the *Dictionary of National Biography from the earliest times to 1900*, edited by Leslie Stephen (1832–1904) and Sidney Lee (1859–1926), which first appeared in sixty-three quarterly volumes between 1885 and 1900. Invoking the same criteria as above, that first *DNB* contained 2,912 articles on medieval subjects, involving a total of 3,092 people. Its successor, containing notices of 1,637 more medieval subjects than the Victorian *Dictionary* – an increase of about fifty-three per cent – emerged from processes which included a dialogue with a predecessor that was not so much supplanted as adapted and reshaped. This process did not involve dropping anyone covered by the first edi-

[i] The fundamental sources for this article are *The Oxford Dictionary of National Biography*, ed. H. C. G. Matthew and Brian Harrison (Oxford, 2004), published both in sixty printed volumes and online, and *The Dictionary of National Biography*, ed. Leslie Stephen and Sidney Lee, cited here in the revised and consolidated version that was issued in twenty-two volumes in 1908–9. Statistics derive from the preliminaries to both old and new editions. Also cited is Sir Sidney Lee's Leslie Stephen lecture, *Principles of Biography* (Cambridge, 1911). Some of the points made here were previously discussed in H. Summerson, 'Problems of Medieval Biography: Revising DNB', *Medieval Prosopography* 17 (1996), 197–222. In addition to the scholars named in the article text, I should like to make grateful acknowledgment of the contribution of all those who wrote or revised articles on medieval subjects for the 2004 edition, and not least that of my colleague in the work of editing medieval entries, Dr Marios Costambeys, and also to pay tribute to the masterly leadership provided by Barbara Harvey, as Consultant Editor for the pre-1500 area within the project as a whole. For those wishing to offer comments, suggestions or corrections, *Oxford DNB* can be contacted either through its website, www.oxforddnb.com, or by telephone, at 01865 355010.

tion – all the latter's full subjects and subsidiary subjects (in *DNB*-speak co-subjects) are still there. But decisions had to be made firstly how those existing subjects should be treated, and secondly what new subjects should be chosen to stand alongside them, by their presence reflecting the developments and changes brought about by the medieval scholarship of the intervening century.

This paper reviews both aspects of the collective task, and deliberately does so from a position under the shadow cast by the first edition. Its title is '*re*-thinking medieval people', and so in discussing the ways whereby the new edition came into being, it also tries to assess the intellectual attitudes and historical priorities which created the medieval contents of the old one, and to compare them with those of the generations that followed it. And since the first edition left sadly little documentary record of the debates and decisions which lay behind its creation, this must largely be remedied by reference to the contents of the old *DNB*.

In thinking about Victorian attitudes to biography, it is convenient to start with Thomas Carlyle. 'Universal History, the history of what man has accomplished in this world, is at bottom the History of the Great Men who have worked here', he had declared in 1840. Later writers had modified Carlyle's dogmatism, but in 1911 Sir Sidney Lee, as second editor of the *DNB* honouring his predecessor by giving the Leslie Stephen lecture in Cambridge, could still pronounce that 'A fit biographic theme is, in the Aristotelian phrase, a career which is "serious, complete, and of a certain magnitude"', and he elaborated upon the issue of magnitude by stating that 'Actions, however beneficent or honourable, which are accomplished or are capable of accomplishment by many thousands of persons, are actions of mediocrity, and lack the dimension which justifies the biographer's notice'. From such statements it may be deduced that at the heart of the old *Dictionary* there lay a sort of pragmatic individualism, a belief that people matter because it is ultimately what they do as individuals – Lee denounced 'life and times' history, saying that it could be 'classed neither with right history nor with right biography' – that generates social development, whether good or bad. The first edition of the *DNB* had found space for disreputables and malefactors, and this was in keeping with Lee's claim that 'True biography is no handmaid of ethical instruction'. These attitudes fostered a conviction of the utility of biography, and help to explain the treatment of the subjects chosen for inclusion in the old *Dictionary*. However long ago they lived, they were basically like ourselves, and could be explicated through straightforward narratives, leavened by appropriate anecdotes, and with limited interpretative comment – the latter was unnecessary because people's actions explained themselves, and did so in terms of a morality which, where medieval subjects were concerned, the Victorians deduced principally from chronicles and saints' lives, and found so congenial that they largely ignored the biases and purposes of the sources in which they discovered it.

There were two fundamental principles which people being considered for inclusion in the first edition of the *DNB* had to satisfy. The first was to be dead –

no problems there for medieval subjects (with the possible exception of King Arthur). And the second was to have been notable, though to have been merely notorious would suffice. For large reference works dealing with the distant past, there is an abiding temptation to extend the second principle to embrace those who were neither notable nor notorious, but simply known. To this temptation the old *Dictionary* clearly sometimes yielded. Hence the inclusion of large numbers of theologians and writers for no better reason, it would appear, than that they and their works were recorded by the Tudor bio-bibliographers John Leland and John Bale, and of lawyers because they had been included in his mid-nineteenth-century multi-volumed *Judges of England* (1848–64) by Edward Foss. Heredity gave the landowning classes a head-start in the pursuit of commemoration, which the old *DNB* sometimes duly conferred without, it may appear, always considering sufficiently whether those it honoured had actually done anything to deserve it.

Progressing from these generalities, this article will now look at a small sample of articles from the old *Dictionary*, and offer comments on how, and why, their authors treated their subjects in the way they did. It will then briefly scrutinise what seem to be the principal historiographical developments between the generation that produced the first edition of the *DNB* and the one that compiled its successor, before returning to the sample, this time to look at the new articles on the same subjects, and to draw attention to the most important differences between old and new, in the light of those developments. In the online version of the *Dictionary*, it may be useful to know, any reader can do the same, since every article brings with it access to its predecessor. And by way of conclusion there is a brief survey of the men and women who have been added to the *DNB*, the people who became subjects of articles for the first time in 2004, and about the way they have been treated. In deference to the theme of the symposium, as well as to the constraints of time and space, what follows is confined almost entirely to England, and to the period between the late thirteenth century and the end of the fifteenth.

James Gairdner (1828–1912) was one of the older writers who made up the 653 contributors to the first edition of the *DNB*. A distinguished editor of documents, he is described in his own article as a man of 'unswerving Conservatism' and as one unable to keep his personal prejudices out of his historical writing. This certainly comes across in his entry on John Ball (d. 1381), which presents its subject as nothing better than a demagogue, a man endlessly in trouble with the authorities and implacably hostile to the existing order. Apart from two references to David Wilkins's *Concilia* and (surprisingly) an unprinted patent roll, its sources are entirely chronicles, whose possible bias Gairdner did not investigate, presumably because it was akin to his own. Context is woefully lacking – the poll tax is not even mentioned, rather the Peasants' Revolt is presented as an outburst of anarchic egalitarianism. In Gairdner's words, 'The project was clearly to set up a new order of things founded on social equality – a theory which in the whole history of the middle ages appears for the first and last time in this movement.'. It would be interesting to know what Leslie Stephen thought when this landed on his desk. Culturally Stephen was a strong liberal, and he also disliked literary effusiveness of any kind; in Lee's words 'He was always impatient of rhetoric, of sentimentality, of floridity in life or literature…'. Perhaps the fact that Gairdner was older than himself, and writing about a period with which he was unfamiliar, stayed the editor's controlling hand, though it is worth noticing that it seems to have taken some time for the *Dictionary*, which was published in quarterly instalments and in alphabetical sequence, to settle to an acceptable quality of utterance. The general standard of articles from 'C' onwards is consistently higher than those for 'A' and 'B', as contributors like W. S. Tregellas (1831–94), author of a bizarre and useless entry on the Cornish benefactor Thomasine Percyvale (d. 1512), either retired or were weeded out – Tregellas wrote about twenty-five entries under 'A' and 'B', one under 'C', but nothing after volume XIII (1888). The entry on Percyvale (made even more of a curiosity by the decision to enter her, contrary to usual *DNB* practice, under an eccentric spelling of her maiden name of Bonaventura, rather than under her married name) is an exercise in pure antiquarianism, a mixture of legend and facts that were mostly recycled from Richard Carew's *Survey of Cornwall* (1602), while also drawing upon works of doubtful usefulness like R. S. Hawker's *Footprints of former men in far Cornwall* (1870), inaccurately cited. Tregellas upon Percyvale not only provides a good example of an article so badly presented as actually to obscure its subject's merits, but also serves as a reminder that the old *Dictionary*, despite its apparently monolithic quality, did in fact gain strength during its long gestation.

T. F. Tout (1855–1929) joined the editorial team while work was in progress upon 'B'; among those who enlisted later were C. L. Kingsford (1862–1926) and James Tait (1863–1944), who were both enlisted under 'G'. Kingsford was the author of a short article on John Orum (b. in or before 1364, d. 1436), described as vice-chancellor of Oxford University, which was presumably the reason for his inclusion, that and his authorship of surviving sermons on the Apocalypse. In accordance with what was clearly house policy (one that was extended to all writers, of all kinds), no attempt was made to analyse the contents of the sermons, and Kingsford clearly had difficulties in reconstructing anything resembling a life story, providing instead only the bare outline of a career, in terms of benefices and offices held. In all likelihood no more was demanded of him. The old *Dictionary* took a close interest throughout in what were once called the ancient universities, and it seems probable that entries like this one (and there were many) were intended to furnish a sort of prosopography *avant la lettre*, all illustrating the achievements and rewards that came with a university training. There could be no doubt, by contrast, of the eligibility of William Canynges (1402–74), the famous Bristol merchant, memorialised by William Hunt (1842–1931), who with 582 articles, running from 'Ad' to 'Wu', was by far the longest-serving and highest-scoring of all the medieval contributors. Drawing on a family history and on Bristol sources published and unpublished, this comes far closer to a coherent biographical narrative than any of the articles described so far. Hunt records Canynges's family background, his role in civic and national affairs, and the ecclesiastical turn his life took in its final years. What he is far less clear about is the sources of Canynges's wealth, with only two brief references to his engaging in trade. Perhaps Hunt, whose own *DNB* article tells us that he was conservative in politics, subscribed to the prevailing view that gentlemen did not discuss money matters, but it seems just as likely that at a time when economic history was still in its infancy, he was simply not technically equipped to discuss Canynges's commercial enterprises. The same explanation may apply to Hunt's vagueness about urban government, so that, for instance, he refers in passing to Canynges's role in making 'certain rules for the government of the society of merchants' without saying what these were. Quite possibly he did not know whether they were important or not – his article appeared eight years before the publication in 1894 of Alice Stopford Green's *Town Life in the Fifteenth Century*, which might have helped him – and therefore decided that he had done his duty by mentioning them. But the result is to give the entry a curiously uneven texture, as it moves from precision to abstraction and back again.

In writing about Canynges, Hunt was a generalist doing his best on unfamiliar ground. Nobody, by contrast, could have been better qualified than Robert Steele, a specialist in the history of medieval science, to tackle the fifteenth-century alchemist George Ripley (d. c. 1490). In many ways Steele did a good job, using manuscript and printed sources both to provide a summary of the life and to list the surviving writings. His problem was if anything the opposite of Hunt's, in that he knew too much about his subject and fell into obscurity through incidental references to matters likely to baffle most readers, however clear they were to the author. Many readers, informed that 'Ripley was probably the first to popularise the works of Raymond Lully, which were translated into Latin in 1445, and exerted great influence in England on the alchemical revival', will ask 'what alchemical revival?', and some may ask 'who was Raymond Lully?' as well. Probably Steele could have provided the context necessary to make his subject accessible to a wider readership, but perhaps the reservations felt by Lee (who was now editor) towards 'life and times' history stood in his way, with the result that here he ended up writing as a specialist for the benefit of his scholarly peers. It may not be just coincidence that this was the only article he wrote for the *Dictionary*.

The examples chosen so far have all been short articles, but it seems appropriate to end this brief taster of entries from old *DNB* with one of the longer ones, T. F. Tout on King Henry IV (1366–1413). Tout was probably the most distinguished of the substantial medieval contributors to the *Dictionary* (the qualifying phrase is necessary because F. W. Maitland wrote four articles), contributing 237 entries. In terms of sheer knowledge, especially of chronicle sources, both English and continental, this article is most impressive, and Tout knew the printed record sources – parliament rolls, privy council proceedings, Rymer's *Foedera* and the like – equally well. But he was not yet the man who transformed the understanding of medieval English administration, and he was heavily influenced by the writings of William Stubbs. The result is an account which is detailed to the point of relentlessness concerning the political events in Henry's life, particularly in the years around 1399, but less assured in its handling of the issues which lay behind the conflicts and controversies of his reign, notably crown finance and the royal household. The use of Stubbsian phraseology – expressions like 'the Beauforts and the constitutional party' recur – may have been intended to act as a sort of shorthand for the political context which editorial policy precluded – 'it is the art of the biographer sternly to subordinate his scenery to his actors', in Lee's equally stern words. If that was indeed Tout's strategy, one can only question its success, the entry's focus on the *king* being all too often so close as to obscure the development of his *reign*. And Tout could also be exasperatingly non-committal on precisely those points where the reader may feel the need of a firm opinion, for instance on Henry's intentions in returning to England in 1399. Perhaps the discussion of controversial issues, like the provision of more than minimal context, lay under an editorial ban, as straying too far from the path of true biography.

A king, a scholar-priest, a rebel, a merchant, an alchemist and a local benefactor, all were treated in ways which reflected both editorial policy and authorial personality, and based upon scholarship which ranged from antiquarianism to a considerable depth of learning – any historian today who showed Tout's mastery of late medieval chronicles, extending to the writings of Juvenal des Ursins and the compilations of the *Scriptores rerum Prussicarum*, would be deservedly admired. Nevertheless, in considering the principal differences in historical scholarship between the generations which produced the two editions of the *DNB*, there can be no escaping the bedrock upon which all those differences rest, the huge increase in factual knowledge which the intervening century has produced. Time does not allow a detailed analysis of this process; suffice it to say that the continuing work of what was then the Public Record Office, supplemented by the efforts of national societies like the Camden Society, the Canterbury and York Society and the Selden Society, supplemented by county record societies and by what one may call record publications like the *Victoria County History*, have put a vast amount of additional primary source material into circulation, providing the means to transform every aspect of medieval English history. When to that is added the amount of archival research that medievalists now routinely do, in the National Archives, the British Library, and record offices and collections all over the country, and indeed outside it, it becomes obvious that we simply know far more than Tout, Gairdner and their contemporaries did, about a far wider range of activities – the publication of inquisitions *post mortem*, for instance, has transformed our understanding of late medieval landowning society.

In some cases increased knowledge has led directly to historiographical development, as with the growth of administrative and institutional history. In the case of economic and social history, on the other hand, it seems rather to have facilitated an advance that had already begun, but had been hampered by insufficient data. The connection between knowledge and its exploitation is not in fact always straightforward. The one may lead directly to the other, or it may simply make it possible, as external factors make such a development seem desirable. It seems unlikely, for instance, that advances in the understanding of medieval science had no connection with the massive development of the natural sciences during the twentieth century, still less that the relatively recent growth of women's history can be dissevered from contemporaneous feminist movements. And the impact of Marxism during the twentieth century can hardly have failed to stimulate an interest in ideas and ideologies as motivating forces in people's lives, something the pragmatically-inclined Victorians were inclined to overlook. The new plethora of information may well have tempted historians down the unfamiliar, and potentially hazardous, paths created by the development of psychology, offering the chance of a deeper understanding of human beings, biography's raw material. Rather more certainly, it has enabled both the detailed criticism of existing sources like chronicles, and the emergence of new techniques for its own analysis, notably prosopography, which has among other things both encouraged and facilitated a due sensitivity to local and regional issues. A deeper understanding, and knowledge, of how institutions work, and of the relations between those who operate them; an appreciation of the role of economic considerations in determining the conduct of both public and private affairs; an awareness of relations between men and women, and of the potential complexity of both – these are just some of the more powerful weapons which the last hundred years have added to the medievalist's armoury, and whose use we may expect to find reflected in the new edition of the *DNB*.

Going back to the sample articles discussed above, a comparison of the old with the new does indeed show a substantial change in factual content, to the latter's advantage, but that is only where the differences start. One of the most significant lies not only in the personalities but also in the skills of the people who have written the new entries. Dr Andrew Prescott, writing about John Ball, has the authority that comes from being an experienced authority in the relevant field. 653 contributors wrote the articles which made up the first edition of the *DNB*, nearly 10,000 its successor. The latter is overwhelmingly the work of specialists, the former largely the achievement of men of wide learning and culture, often with specialised skills, but often also writing about people a long way off their usual academic tracks – Gairdner on Ball is a good example. Comparing his article with Prescott's, apart from the latter's enhanced detail and accuracy, not to mention his awareness of the 1381 poll tax, the new entry gains from greater sensitivity to geography – we read of Kentish and Essex insurgents, rather than a generalised 'insurrection of Wat Tyler' – from a much more sophisticated analysis of the relationship between the doctrines of Wyclif and the preaching of Ball, and an awareness of what Prescott describes as 'the radical Christian egalitarianism that constituted much of the ideology of the rebels.' Ball is no longer a sort of demonic flash in a revolutionary pan, but instead a spokesman for forces rarely in a position to make their voices heard.

Great though the differences between them are, the old and new articles on John Ball are at least recognisably about the same person. With Thomasine Percy-vale this is only barely the case. In Dr Matthew Davies's new entry almost every-thing in the old one turns out to be wrong, including the legend of Thomasine's peasant origins – in fact she came of a gentry family. Clearly correcting factual inac-curacy has to be a priority for a project like the *Oxford DNB*, but amending con-ceptual error is hardly less important. The greatest defect in the brief original entry was the inadequacy of its account of Thomasine's position in London, which was after all the source of the wealth behind her benefactions. To help remedy this, not only are there now brief accounts of her first two husbands, unnamed by Tregellas, but her third and most important husband, Sir John Percyvale, has become a co-subject in his wife's article. As a result it is possible to see Thomasine as a landowner and businesswoman, and in her founding a grammar school in Cornwall, acting as Sir John had earlier done in Cheshire. The nuts and bolts of the foundation, too, are exposed, revealing what sort of levers, personal as well as administrative, had to be pulled to make the ground secure for a foundation of this kind – a royal licence, the cooperation of the Merchant Taylors' Company, the local support of her kinsman, John Dinham of Lifton, all were needed. At a personal level, Thomasine comes across as a woman of interestingly divided loyalties; in her will she made bequests to her remaining kinsfolk in Cornwall, yet she chose to be buried beside Sir John in St Mary Woolnoth, London.

In the case of John Orum, greater factual knowledge has again enabled a con-tributor, this time Dr David Lepine, to fill gaps and create a clear narrative. Orum's links with Wells become less puzzling once it is shown that he started his career there, as a vicar-choral of the cathedral and probably a member of a city family. Kingsford had also been unable to show how Orum started his way up the ladder of ecclesiastical preferment, perhaps unsurprisingly – the concept of patronage in its 'McFarlanite' sense appears to have been wholly unfamiliar to the contributors to the old *Dictionary*. By contrast, a passing reference to Orum's 'gaining access to royal patronage' at Oxford is all that is now needed to explain his advancement in that informally constituted career structure which for historians of late medieval England has become part of their mental furniture. It also, incidentally, draws attention to the role of the universities in providing a pool of talent for the crown to draw upon. But even more telling is Dr Lepine's account of Orum's writ-ings, which, taken together with his book ownership and his recorded activity against heresy, show him as a representative figure, exemplifying the particular sort of uprightness that the early-fifteenth-century church wanted. Educated, orthodox, a known preacher, he can now be seen in the round as just the sort of man who could expect promotion in the church of his day, and consequently received it.

The differences between the old and new articles on William Canynges are partly ones of presentation, though the form this takes is in itself significant. Breaking up his account into clearly differentiated paragraphs enables Dr Clive Burgess to bring out the different strands in Canynges's career – family background, commercial interests, role in civic affairs and national politics, the religious turn his life took in his last years – with a clarity that eluded Hunt, who ran all these elements together within a basically chronological narrative. But Hunt suffered from the additional disability of being often in no position to tell what *was* significant about Canynges's life, whereas Burgess is able, for instance, to appreciate the importance, and the rarity, of Canynges's diverting his capital into ships, and so into carrying the goods of others rather than his own, and in the process he shows that the information about those ships provided by William Worcestre can probably be trusted, something Hunt strongly doubted. Similarly when Burgess writes that 'the effort that Canynges devoted to Bristol's government is remarkable', he can do so with confidence because the development of urban history during the twentieth century had been such as to make it possible to distinguish the ordinary from the extraordinary in the history of a town like Bristol. Hunt could not have known whether what Canynges did was remarkable or not. The foreground in the life of Canynges is now clear not only because Burgess knows, and can deploy, the relevant facts, but also because the background is now clear as well.

Similarly Dr Anthony Gross benefits from his understanding of the background, local and national, to the career of George Ripley, elucidating his dealings with the Nevilles in Ripley's native Yorkshire, and also with King Edward IV – the significance of the latter to Ripley's career was completely missed by Steele in the old *DNB*. But like Lepine discussing Orum, Gross also shows the advantages to be gained from familiarity with his subject's works, which enables him to place Ripley within the development of alchemy, both before and after his own time, extending, indeed, into the late seventeenth century, and in the process he goes some way towards explaining the legendary reputation that Ripley acquired – fumes from his laboratory were said to have provoked complaints from the people of Bridlington, and he was alleged to have used his alchemical arts to make gold worth £100,000 a year for the Hospitallers of Rhodes.

As far as Henry IV is concerned, considerations of space make it necessary to avoid comparisons, and to concentrate instead on an aspect of historiography that the first edition hardly considered but that the new edition of the *Dictionary* is very much concerned about, on a small scale with someone like Ripley, and on a much larger one with major subjects like King Henry, namely issues of reputation, historiography and assessment. The article on Henry IV, by the late Professor A. L.

Brown and Dr Henry Summerson, closes with three discrete sections headed 'Personality', 'Historiography' and 'Assessment'. Tout in the first edition devoted a single short paragraph to the first of these, along with a couple of sentences on Henry's physical appearance, but provided no equivalent to the other two sections. But as with the new edition of the *DNB* itself, we now see a person's life as made up of many layers, while where someone's reputation is concerned we no longer perceive it as coming into being once and for all, but rather as built up in strata of interpretation.

A number of the factors that have enriched the historian's vocabulary in the past century can be perceived in the *Oxford DNB's* assessment of Henry IV. What might be called psychologising lies behind references to his policy of 'deliberate self-concealment', and to the possibility that a sense of humour 'provided release from self-imposed constraints'; his concern for appearances reflects the recent development of court history; while the contrast drawn between his public image and his private qualities may well owe something to the preoccupations of journalism. A discussion of the historiography of a major figure like Henry IV was from the outset required by the *Dictionary's* editorial policy, itself moved by the now-general belief that the historian who does *not* criticise his sources, does *not* point to their prejudices, inconsistencies and disagreements, is failing in his duty. Thus by comparing the conclusions of Thomas Walsingham (favourable) and Adam Usk (negative) it becomes possible to show that problems of interpretation exist, in a way that the protocols of the first edition prevented Tout from doing. Henry's association with the persecution of Lollards, brought out by John Foxe, can then be shown to have deepened the hostile colours transmitted by Usk, which were in turn fed by Raphael Holinshed into the plays of William Shakespeare. Shakespeare humanised King Henry, later historians from Hume to Stubbs anachronised him, through a preoccupation with what they called constitutional principles that was very much in keeping with their attitudes towards the politics of their own times, and that was still *en courant* when Tout wrote his entry for the old *DNB*. Stubbs's viewpoint was denounced by K. B. McFarlane, but the final assessment in the new article questions whether McFarlane may not have been too quick to condemn it, suggesting instead that Stubbs had appreciated that Henry's kingship had aspired to the same consensual quality (another expression now very much in fashion) as that now attributed to the reign of Edward III. In the light of this possibility – although other conclusions are shown to be possible – the article concludes by taking a generally favourable position on Henry IV and his reign.

When its articles offer judgmental conclusions in this way, the *Oxford DNB* is consciously stepping off the monumental plinth on which posterity has set its predecessor, and it has in fact been criticised in some quarters for doing so. Undeniably there are risks involved, not least that of incurring the sort of inbuilt obsolescence that may result from the *Dictionary's* having deliberately set itself within the very historiographical processes it records. If any mitigation is needed, it can be pleaded that few scholars now subscribe to the doctrine that complete impartiality is possible for the historian – even the most dryly factual narrative still reflects, through its choices and emphases, something of the personality and concerns of the man or woman who wrote it. The very fact that the *DNB* is a collection of signed memoirs, each one containing an individual appraisal of its subject, works to the same end. It is also possible that a well-turned conclusion may provide the reader with guidance and enjoyment, together with an understanding of the intellectual and historical developments that underlie them.

This article concludes with some reflections upon a different sort of choices, the new subjects that have been added to the *DNB* in the edition of 2004. Many require no explanation, since they are exactly the same sort of people who made up the first edition, from which they were for some reason omitted. It may seem odd that no space was found then for Thomas Beauchamp, eleventh earl of Warwick, one of the founder members of the Garter, or for Henry Holland, second duke of Exeter, one of the stormiest petrels of the Wars of the Roses, or for the hermit John of Farne, or for William Bingham, founder of Christ's College, Cambridge, or for Marmaduke Huby, the last great abbot of Fountains, and it cannot seem strange that space should be found for them now, among so many people like themselves who were already included. Others, however, have been added in response to the widening of the scope of historical endeavour referred to earlier. Two of the fields that have expanded most are those of economic and social history and of science. In the former the new subjects include a number of Londoners, as was inevitable. But they also, in response to an effort throughout the entire *Dictionary* to modify the first edition's perceived metropolitan bias, include a number of merchants from other towns; hence the presence of Richard Embleton of Newcastle, John Hawley, 'merchant, pirate and administrator' of Dartmouth, Hugh Fastolf of Yarmouth and Mark le Fayre of Winchester. That geographical widening has in fact extended beyond Britain, to embrace a number of foreigners who came to play a significant role in British life, whether as participants or observers. This is a characteristic of the entire *Dictionary*, in response to the opportunities presented by the open-endedness of its title, to define the word 'National' in terms which extend beyond those who happened only to be born or to die in Britain. And so the merchants have also been reinforced by men like Gerhard von Wesel from Cologne, Gabriel Corbet from Venice, and William Servat from Cahors. As for the scientists, they have been more often reinforced by native Englishmen, in keeping with the growing awareness of England's contribution to late medieval science, in a number of fields, including medicine, optics and kinematics. As a result there are now more articles on physicians, surgeons, astronomers and astrologers (including the Italian William Parron, who having foretold a life of eighty or ninety years for Elizabeth of York, left the country under a cloud shortly afterwards, when the queen died aged thirty-seven), and an entry on the fourteenth-century clockmakers Roger and Laurence Stoke.

There has been a determined effort to increase the number of women in the *DNB*, one extending across the entire *Dictionary*. As far as late medieval England is concerned this has brought in ladies of all ranks of society. Thus at the very top there are now articles on the redoubtable Lady Joan Beaufort, the much less alarming Marie de St Pol, foundress of Pembroke College, Cambridge, and a number of other women who mostly made their mark as dowagers; the thrice-married Alice Chaucer, for instance. But of no less interest are women like the Yorkshire anchoresses Margaret Kirkby and Emma Raughton, the London prison reformer Agnes Forster, and Alice Chestre of Bristol, a cloth exporter and benefactor who in Clive Burgess's words 'seems particularly to have come into her own after the death of her husband'. The ranks of foreigners have been expanded by the inclusion of several reporters and chroniclers, including Dominic Mancini, Jean Waurin and Jean Froissart, as well as the papal diplomat Piero da Monte, the soldier Jean de Grailly, captal de Buch (another founder member of the Garter), and the Cologne artist Hermann Scheerre. A number of the new subjects are simply one-offs, people of unique achievement who fall into no category; these include Sir Geoffrey Langley, Edward I's envoy to the ilkhan of Persia, the Bristol merchant and Atlantic explorer Thomas Croft, who possibly sighted America before Columbus, and John Tate, the first British paper-maker. Some new subjects have an essentially symbolic value – hence the addition of George and Andrew to make up the roster of British national saints. A few people have been included because they are so well-known through literary or artistic associations that it seemed to form part of our wider service to the public to record them; hence, for instance, articles on Sir Edward Dallingridge, builder of Bodiam Castle, Edward Grimston, the beneficiary of a famous portrait by Petrus Christus in the National Gallery, and Thomas Paycocke of Coggeshall, subject of one of Eileen Power's *Medieval Lives* – none of these men was negligible, but none was likely to achieve inclusion on the basis of personal achievement alone. And in a tiny number of cases the limits of biography have been stretched to include people whose identities have to be deduced entirely from their actions or remains, since their names have been lost – these include the music theorist 'Anonymous IV', and above all the late-fourteenth-century 'Gawain Poet'.

A number of the developments discussed above – for instance greater awareness of economic and social factors, more attention to local and regional concerns, appreciation of the significance of patronage – are brought together in perhaps the most important of the innovations which characterise the new addition of the *DNB*, namely its articles on families and groups. From these it is possible to see how people were held together by lateral as well as vertical links, their lives set within a cross-weave of connections of all kinds. Four of the medieval group entries are devoted solely to women – Lollard women, Women medical practitioners, Women traders and artisans in York and in London – and show how in these particular contexts they acted and conducted their lives, lives which are usually insufficiently detailed to justify individual entries. Sidney Lee might have objected that the background was in danger of submerging the ostensible subjects, but when they are presented together in this way these articles shed valuable light upon lives and occupations that would otherwise usually be left in the shadows cast by men. The family entries serve the same purpose, presenting both men and women within a positive cat's-cradle of contexts – political, economic, social and cultural, as well as dynastic. The entry on the Cobham family provides a panoptic survey of the gentry and lesser nobility of Surrey and Kent, especially in the fourteenth century, with their marriages and interconnections. Three separate lineages are presented, with a full array of cross-references, some to local grandees, others to some of the great men of the realm, to Sir John Oldcastle, Ralph Neville, first earl of Westmorland, and even to Humphrey of Gloucester, son, brother and uncle of successive kings. A further innovation within the *Oxford DNB* is the provision of likenesses. The brass of John Cobham, second Lord Cobham of Cobham, that illustrates the article on his family is one of a famous collection in Cobham collegiate church. It adds to the visual appeal of the article, and also to the range of its content, as a demonstration of the pride of rank and achievement shown to posterity by the Cobham family – a reminder that a portrait can serve other purposes besides bequeathing a likeness to posterity. The painting of John, duke of Bedford, in his book of hours may be a truthful image of its subject, but it is also a visible expression of his activities as an artistic patron and collector, a side of his life on which William Hunt was completely silent in old *DNB*, but which is now authoritatively handled by Dr Jenny Stratford.

Rethinking the late medieval lives in the *DNB* has involved much more than the addition of details and the correction of errors, important though both activities are, rather producing the new edition has entailed as far as possible the complete reconstruction of people's lives, in response to the many new perspectives that the intervening century has opened up. And since further perspectives will certainly emerge, just as mistakes and omissions will certainly come to light, so this process will continue, as it is intended that the project will also. It is all part of the process of continuing development which has transformed the *DNB* from the monument bequeathed to us by the Victorians into, it may be hoped, an exercise in *living* history.

Documenting the Lives of Medieval Nuns

JANET BURTON

It has been something of a commonplace to describe medieval nunneries as poorly documented, and this was at one time used to explain their absence from historical scholarship. Happily the last twenty years or so have seen a surge in studies of women religious, and as historians have combed sources other than the admittedly exiguous records surviving from nunnery archives they have succeeded in placing female monasticism firmly on the map, allowing women to be perceived as participants in the vibrant religious life of the period. Marilyn Oliva's study of East Anglian nunneries, for instance, has shown that there is much to be learned about the social origins of nuns, and about the pattern of administration and office holding.[1] The northern nunneries have been characterized as numerous – some twenty-five in Yorkshire and a handful between the Tees and the Scottish border – yet small and poor. To late medieval female monasticism in this region Eileen Power gave a rather bad press: from her study prioresses emerge as aristocratic women ill-suited to the religious life, with little ability to govern without the help of men, and nuns as quarrelsome and lacking in vocation.[2] I have discussed aspects of the governance of northern nunneries and their prioresses elsewhere.[3] In this paper I want to ask another question: how much can we know of medieval nuns, of individual lives within the religious community and within the broader community in which medieval nunneries were located? Can we construct any kind of picture, or do we have to accept that these women's lives are poorly documented, and that if – to borrow Sally Thompson's memorable phrase – medieval nunneries 'had no history',[4] still less did the women who lived in them?

---

[1] Marilyn Oliva, *The Convent and the Community in the Diocese of Norwich from 1350 to 1540* (Woodbridge, 1994).

[2] Eileen Power, *Medieval English Nunneries, c. 1275–1535* (Cambridge, 1922).

[3] See my papers 'Cloistered Women and Male Authority: power and authority in Yorkshire nunneries in the later middle ages', in *Thirteenth-Century England X: Proceedings of the Durham Conference 2003*, eds Michael Prestwich, Richard Britnell and Robin Frame (Woodbridge, 2005), pp. 155–65, and 'The Chariot of Aminadab and the Yorkshire Nunnery of Swine', in *Pragmatic Utopias: Ideals and Communities, 1200–1630*, eds R. Horrox and S. Rees Jones (Cambridge, 2001), pp. 26–42.

[4] Sally Thompson, 'Why English Nunneries had no History. A Study of the Problems of English Nunneries founded after the Conquest', in *Distant Echoes: Medieval Religious*

The approach that I have taken in this paper is to consider the kind of picture that can be built up of nuns' origins and their lives and careers, and the environment in which they lived, based first of all on the study of two nunneries, Nun Appleton and Nun Monkton. Nun Appleton, lying near the confluence of the rivers Ouse and Wharfe, was founded between 1148 and 1154 by Alice of St Quintin in association with her son, Robert, for the soul of her first husband, Robert son of Fulk. Nun Monkton, to the north-west of York and located where the rivers Ouse and Nidd meet, was founded around the same time as Nun Appleton by William and Juetta de Arches, uncle and aunt of Alice of St Quintin.[5]

The names of the nuns of these two nunneries start to reveal a geographical pattern of recruitment. In January 1308 Archbishop Greenfield wrote to the prioress of Nun Appleton allowing her to accept as a sister of the house Agnes of Saxton.[6] Saxton lies north-north-west of Sherburn in Elmet, about five miles to the west of the priory. Two years earlier in May 1306 Greenfield had appointed Roger of Saxton, rector of Aberford, about three miles west of Saxton, *custos* of Nun Appleton. Roger is recorded in this post in 1307, when his accounts as *custos* were to be audited by four named individuals, and in 1311, when he released to the prioress and nuns 20 marks that they had given him as a bond for the good behaviour of one of their number.[7] It is tempting to suggest a family connection between Agnes and Roger, particularly as Greenfield's letter urging Agnes's entry also mentions the facilities provided at the priory for its *custos*: he was to eat 'each day in the chamber assigned to him unless by chance the prioress should be eating in her chamber by reason of guests visiting' and then 'the *custos* may be able to keep company with her'.[8] Agnes of York – and there were probably at least two nuns of

---

Women, I, eds J. A. Nichols and L. T. Shank (Kalamazoo: Cistercian Publications, 1984), pp. 131–49. See also her *Women Religious: the Founding of English Nunneries after the Norman Conquest* (Oxford, 1991), pp. 1–15.

5   On the foundation of the priories of Nun Monkton and Nun Appleton, see Janet Burton, *The Monastic Order in Yorkshire 1069–1215*, Cambridge Studies in Medieval Life and Thought, fourth series, 40 (Cambridge, 1999), pp. 132–4 and 141–2. For a short history of Nun Appleton see Marjorie J. Harrison, *The Nunnery of Nun Appleton*, University of York, Borthwick Paper, 98 (York, 2001). Between 1143 and 1154 a third foundation associated with the Arches family was made. This was Nunkeeling, established by Agnes de Arches, William's sister and Alice's mother, for the soul of her second husband, Herbert of St Quintin (d. 1129), and her sons Walter and Alan.

6   *The Register of William Greenfield, Lord Archbishop of York 1306–1315*, eds William Brown and A. Hamilton Thompson, 5 vols, Surtees Society 145, 149, 151–3 (1931–40), II, 47.

7   Ibid., pp. 2, 40, 111. On the latter occasion Roger also had a bond for an annual pension of 60s. and hay from three acres of meadow.

8   Ibid., p. 47: 'in camera sua eidem assignata comederet omni die, nisi forte priorissa in camera sua commederet racione extraneorum et tunc idem custos eidem comitivam facere poterit'.

Nun Appleton by that name – and Elizabeth of Holbeck (near Leeds), were also apparently fairly local recruits.[9] Matilda (Maud) of Bossall's name suggests that she came from a little further afield, about ten miles north-east of the city of York. She occurs in 1308 when she was sent to Basedale on the North Yorkshire Moors to do penance for misdemeanors which were uncovered in the course of a visitation; Maud, whose offences included disobedience, obstinacy, rebellion, disturbing the peace of the community and causing a scandal, was to take with her no vessels (*jocalia*) or other utensils (*utensilia*) that might be called her own.[10] Matilda of Ripon, another apostate nun, who occurs in 1309 and 1311,[11] Joan of Scarborough (1335),[12] and Katherine of Huggate (who occurs in February 1246/7)[13] also apparently hailed from further away.

Other evidence points us in the direction of family or social origins. Joan de Normanville was confirmed as prioress of Nun Appleton in 1303 and occurs in 1306.[14] Another nun with this family name appears as prioress: this is Isabel, who was elected in 1320.[15] Just a year or so earlier the archbishop of York had forbidden admission of more than two or three nuns of the same family.[16] This is an injunction repeated from time to time, that clearly indicates the clustering of members of the same secular family within the monastic one. This gives us another glimpse into the nature of these female communities: houses which drew recruits

[9] Ibid., p. 219, for record of Agnes as an apostate to be readmitted to Nun Appleton in 1315. See F. Donald Logan, *Runaway Religious in Medieval England c. 1240–1540*, Cambridge Studies in Medieval Life and Thought, fourth series, 32 (1996), p. 263. For the election of Elizabeth as prioress in 1316 see *Reg. Greenfield*, V, 250, and *Heads of Religious Houses. England and Wales, II, 1216–1377*, eds David M. Smith and Vera C. M. London (Cambridge, 2001), p. 592.

[10] *Reg. Greenfield*, II, 44–7. Basedale was to receive payment of 9*d.* per week for Maud's maintenance. Her penance was to follow the convent into the choir, cloister, refectory and dormitory, unless prevented by illness or other legitimate cause; she was to have no opportunity to go outside the monastery; on Friday she was to fast on bread, vegetables and ale; she was to say the psalter each month.

[11] On Matilda see *Reg. Greenfield*, II, 74, 111. She is noted in Logan, *Runaway Religious*, p. 263.

[12] For Joan see York, Borthwick Institute, Register 9A (Reg. Melton), fol. 247r (old fol. 202r).

[13] York, Borthwick Institute, Register 10 (Reg. Zouche), fol. 14v.

[14] *The Register of Thomas Corbridge, Lord Archbishop of York 1300–1304*, ed. William Brown and A. Hamilton Thompson, 2 vols, Surtees Society, 138, 141 (1925–8), I, 82; Smith and London, *Heads of Religious Houses*, II, 592.

[15] York, Borthwick Institute, Register 9A (Reg. Melton), fol. 173v; David Smith notes that the next recorded prioress after Isabel, Sybil de Normanville, may be the same woman as Isabel: Smith and London, *Heads of Religious Houses*, II, 592.

[16] York, Borthwick Institute, Register 9A (Reg. Melton), fol. 161r (old fol. 131r). The visitation injunctions are summarized in *The Victoria History of the Counties of England: A History of Yorkshire*, III, ed. William Page (1913, rpt London, 1974), pp. 171–2.

from the locality and where available places might be limited could see pressures building and factions forming.[17] The last subprioress of the house before its closure was another Normanville (Normavel), Eleanor, who is named in the pension list of the house as prioress. Claire Cross has identified her as the sister of William Normavel, esquire, of Kildwick in the East Riding, who bequeathed her 26s. 8d. in his will of 1520.[18] There was an enduring connection between Nun Appleton and the local knightly family of Ryther, and this can be traced right back to the foundation, when William of Ryther witnessed the foundation charter.[19] Ryther lies just across the river from Nun Appleton on the south bank of the Wharfe and members of the family were benefactors of the priory.[20] They also, apparently, produced some of its prioresses. Agnes of Ryther was evidently prioress in the

[17]   For a similar clustering at Swine, see Burton, 'Chariot of Aminadab', p. 30.

[18]   *Monks, Friars and Nuns in Sixteenth Century Yorkshire*, eds Claire Cross and Noreen Vickers, Yorkshire Archaeological Society Record Series, 150 (1995 for 1991 and 1992), p. 581. In 1538 the prioress of Nun Appleton, Anne [Agnes] Langton, who had held the office since 1507, received licence for the convent to continue even though the valuation of £73 9s. 10d. was well below the £200 required. She was prioress when the house was surrendered on 5 December 1539, but as she died before March 1540 it was the name of Eleanor Normavel [Normabell], formerly subprioress, that appears on the pension list as that of the prioress. There was a total of 19 nuns but this number included Agnes Aslaby and Elizabeth Parker, who transferred from Ellerton Priory on its closure, and Jane Fairfax, who came from Sinningthwaite (ibid., pp. 580–4). There is no pension list from Nun Monkton (see ibid., pp. 538–9).

[19]   *Early Yorkshire Charters*, I–III, ed. W. Farrer (Edinburgh, 1914–16), IV–XII, ed. C. T. Clay, Yorkshire Archaeological Society Record Series, extra series (1935–65), I, no. 541; W. Dugdale, *Monasticon Anglicanum*, ed. J. Caley, H. Ellis and B. Bandinel, 6 vols in 8 (London, 1817–30), V, 652–3.

[20]   Another William, possibly William's grandson, granted the nuns the church of Ryther, which was confirmed to the priory by King John (Dugdale, *Monasticon Anglicanum*, V, 652–3). William was succeeded by his younger brother, also called William, who granted the nuns a yearly rent of five marks from the church in return for a quitclaim of the advowson (Farrer, *Early Yorkshire Charters*, III, 303). A court case of 1294 between Henry, parson of Ryther, and the prioress of Nun Appleton refers to an agreement reached between her predecessor, Maud, and William of Ryther, in the time of Richard I, concerning the advowson (*The Register of John le Romeyn, Lord Archbishop of York, 1286–1296*, ed. W. Brown, 2 vols, Surtees Society, 123, 128 (1913–17), I, xxiii). A later Sir William Ryther married c. 1280 Lucy daughter of John de Ros, son of Robert de Ros, lord of Helmsley, and in 1299 received a barony by writ. He was still living in 1309. For the family see *The Complete Peerage*, ed. G. E. Cockayne, revised edn V. Gibbs, H. A. Doubleday et al., 13 vols in 14 (London, 1910–98), XI, 6–11. Sir Ralph Ryther of Ryther, in his will dated 26 March 1520 and proved on 26 April of the same year, left 10s. to the nuns to pray for his soul; in 1527 his son, Thomas, bequeathed 26s. 8d. to the nuns, and to Joan Gower, evidently a nun of Nun Appleton, above her share of the money a further 15s.; Thomas's will was proved on 25 September 1528: *Testamenta Eboracensia*, ed. J. Raine and J. W. Clay, 6 vols, Surtees Society, 4, 30, 45, 53, 79, 106 (1836–1902), V, 125–7 (Ralph), and 225–30 (Thomas). See also V, 192 and VI, 37.

fifteenth century.[21] Joan of Ryther occurs as prioress in the 1450s and 1460s.[22] She was admitted to the York guild of Corpus Christi in 1467,[23] and was executor of the will of John Lytham (Lathom) in 1470.[24]

Evidence for other Yorkshire nunneries, among them Nun Monkton, reveals the same kind of patterns. We have evidence of the geographical origins of nuns of Nun Monkton in places such as Tholthorpe, connections with local benefactors, such as the family of Cornbrough, and social origins, notably links with the families of Fairfax and Goldesburgh.[25] The entry into Nun Monkton of Helen Fairfax, daughter of Richard Fairfax 'squire and one time lord of Walton' (Walton near Wetherby, a few miles south of the priory) in 1430 was arranged by her father. Richard enfeoffed four nephews with property in Walton and Follifoot (near Harrogate) 'so that my daughter Helen be made a nun of the house of Nun Monkton and that my feoffees grant an annual rent of 40s. issuing from the manors of Follifoot and Acaster Malbis for the term of the life of the said Helen to the time that she be a nun'. They were then to pay 19 marks for making her a nun.[26] They evidently did so, and in 1445 she was admitted to the York guild of Corpus Christi.[27]

21 F. Drake, *Eboracum or The History and Antiquities of the City of York* (York, 1736), p. 386, noted a grave slab, taken from the priory and at that time located in Bolton Percy church, the inscription of which reads: '+ Orate pro anima Agnetis de Ryther quondam priorisse hujus monasterii ... xxiii que obit primo die mensis Martii MCCCC ... cujus anime propitietur Deus': 'Pray for the soul of Agnes of Ryther, formerly prioress of this monastery ... 23 who died on the first day of March in 14...'. Drake also described, as present on the tomb, the arms of the family of Ryther, and his note (a) indicates that the slab was taken out of the nunnery chapel, and was used 'to stop water at a miln' until removed and placed in Bolton Percy church by his 'worthy friend' Rev. T. Lamplugh.

22 The cartulary of the Benedictine priory of Monk Bretton contains documents emanating from the court of Joan Ryther, prioress of Nun Appleton, held at Worsborough in 1458 and 1471: *Abstracts of the Chartularies of the Priory of Monkbretton*, ed. J. W. Walker, Yorkshire Archaeological Society Record Series, 66 (1924), pp. 134–6.

23 *The Register of the Guild of Corpus Christi in the City of York*, ed. Robert H. Skaife, Surtees Society, 57 (1872), p. 68.

24 *Testamenta Eboracensia*, III, 173–8; she was presumably the unnamed prioress to whom in 1462 Sir William Lascelles bequeathed his better decorated belt: *Testamenta Eboracensia*, II, 255–6.

25 Charters of the Cornbrough family for Nun Monkton are to be found among the archives of Alnwick Castle (Northumberland), X series, II, 6, boxes 16, 36, 37. See also Janet Burton, *The Yorkshire Nunneries in the Twelfth and Thirteenth Centuries*, Borthwick Paper, 56 (York, 1979), p. 13. For Fairfax recruits see Janet Burton, 'Yorkshire Nunneries in the Middle Ages: recruitment and resources', in *Government, Religion and Society in Northern England 1000–1700*, eds John C. Appleby and Paul Dalton (Stroud, 1997), pp. 104–16 (p. 108). Joan Goldesburgh was admitted to the guild of Corpus Christi in 1484: *Register of Corpus Christi*, p. 116.

26 London, BL, Add. Charter 1782; *VCH Yorkshire*, III, 123.

27 *Register of Corpus Christi*, p. 44. Other Nun Monkton nuns admitted to the guild were

Another Nun Monkton recruit whose entry was accompanied by a payment was Elizabeth Sewerby. The will of her aunt, also called Elizabeth Sewerby, left Elizabeth £6 13s. 4d. 'if she shall become a nun' (si facta fuerit monialis); her probate inventory indicates that Elizabeth's executors had paid the 'customary expenses' for making her niece a nun: the 'customary fee' of £3 demanded from a new entrant, £3 13s. 7½d. for her habit and bed, £3 11s. 4d. for entertaining her friends, and 2s. to John Homilton – these last two expenses were incurred on the occasion of her profession.[28]

There are also indications of the kinds of contacts with the local community that nuns continued to enjoy or to cultivate after they entered religion. The will of John of Woodhouse, former rector of Sutton on Derwent in the East Riding suggests a close connection with Nun Appleton, and in particular a nun named Alice Conyers. To her and to another nun Agnes of York, he left fifteen marks and 20s. respectively, and to Isabella of Ryther he left 13s. 4d. He also left to Alice Conyers one long chest standing next to his bed in York, one goblet of maplewood with an image of St Michael on the base, and one goblet of silver which he, John, had of the gift of Alice. This goblet had on its base a hand holding a falcon. Alice was charged along with his executors, to see that his last requests for commemoration were carried out.[29] Among other wills to mention nuns of Nun Appleton the most notable is that of John Lytham (Lathom), canon of Beverley, who in 1470 left his body to be buried in the priory church of Nun Appleton in the chapel before the altar of St John the Baptist.[30] He left money for the performance of masses and for the fabric of the church, including £26 13s. 4d. for a new roof (ad facturam novi tecti in eadem ecclesia). To the priory, and in particular to its prioress Joan of Ryther he left an array of plate, beds, bolsters, coverlets, tapestry work, and gowns. He founded a chantry in the priory and supplied for the use of his chaplain there a portable breviary, two chalices, a paxboard (paxebrede),[31] and a missal accord-

Katherine, daughter of Avice Thorlthorpe, widow, with whom she was admitted in 1418/19, Joan Rosell (1440/41), Margaret Delarever (1445), Isabella Wilsthorpe (1457), Mariota, Margaret Pickering and Margaret Watir, prioress (1473) and Edenne Nevell (1475). Nuns of Nun Appleton were Joan Mooreton (1455), Joan Byrstall and Elizabeth Byrdhere (1469): ibid., pp. 20, 38, 43, 57, 61, 70, 73, 92, 93.

28 Testamenta Eboracensia, III, 161–8 (especially p.165). I discuss further instances of entry fees and their implications in 'Recruitment and Resources', pp. 109–10.

29 Testamenta Eboracensia, I, 14–19.

30 Ibid., III, 173–8, discussed by Harrison, Nunnery of Nun Appleton, pp. 13–14; on Lytham see R. T. W. McDermid, Beverley Minster Fasti, Yorkshire Archaeological Society Record Series, 149 (1993 for 1990), p. 86.

31 From pax, 'a plaque made of wood, metal, glass, etc, often decorated with a representation of Christ's passion or other religious subject, which is passed among the congregation after the priest has given it the kiss of peace during the celebration of the mass': see Middle English Dictionary, ed. H. Kurath et al. (Ann Arbor, 1954–2001), pax, n. (a).

ing to the use of York. He also remembered the sub-prioress Isabella Burdet and Margaret Davy, the prioress's servant. Prioress Joan of Ryther was one of his three executors and residuary legatees. Further wills reveal connections enjoyed by the nuns: Joan Pickering, nun of Nun Monkton, was left 40s. by her brother, Sir Richard Pickering of Oswaldkirk, in 1441, and 6s. 8d. by her brother in law, Thomas Palmes of Naburn, in 1443.[32]

The will of John Lytham gives us some indication of the furnishing and physical setting of priory buildings, and wills may also mention the books that were bequeathed to nunneries or individual nuns. In Nun Monkton's case the library was supplemented with the legacy of *librum meum vocatum Vice and Vertues* ('my book called Vices and Virtues') from Anne (Agnes) Stapleton, widow of Brian Stapleton of Carlton,[33] and 'a book in English *De Vita Domini Nostri Jesu Christi*' left by Thomas Hornby, chaplain, to nun Elizabeth Sewerby in 1486.[34] John Marshall left to Nun Appleton a *Legenda Aurea* as well as a vestment of 'chamelet' ('chamlett').[35] Other material bequests included those items bequeathed by John de Thorp, canon of York in 1346 when he requested burial in the priory church next to Prioress Alice de Thorp: blue cloth for making garments, and two silver candelabra for his burial.[36] Further bequests were the two silk clothes coloured red and green for the high altar at Nun Monkton, along with 100s., granted by Stephen Scrope, archdeacon of Richmond, in 1418.[37]

The evidence of wills is significant in another way, in that it indicates that while some priories and some families shared close ties, recruitment was often spread across different houses. John Fairfax, rector of Prescot in Lancashire, left a legacy to his sister, Margaret, the prioress of Nun Monkton,[38] who in a visitation of 1397

---

[32] After the death of his wife, Alice, Thomas Palmes added a codicil bequeathing 20s. to the prioress and convent. For these wills see *Testamenta Eboracensia*, II, 30–1, 82.

[33] *North Country Wills, 1383 to 1558*, ed. J. T. Clay, Surtees Society, 116 (1908), pp. 48–9. David Bell (*What Nuns Read: Books and Libraries in Medieval English Nunneries*, Cistercian Studies Series, 158 (Kalamazoo, 1995), p. 157), notes this as the English translation of 'Somme le Roi' of Frère Laurent d'Orléans. Agnes also bequeathed to the abbess of Denny (Cambridgeshire) 'a book *de Frensshe*', to the nuns of Sinningthwaite 'librum meum vocatum *Bonaventure*', to the nuns of Arthington 'librum meum vocatum *Prik of Conscience*', and to the nuns of Esholt 'librum meum vocatum *Chastisyng of goddeschildern*'.

[34] *Testamenta Eboracensia*, III, 165.

[35] Ibid., V, 192. The *Middle English Dictionary* defines chamelet as 'some kind of costly fabric from the Near East': chamelet, n.

[36] Ibid., I, 31–2. A John de Thorp contested the prebend of Barnby in 1349: see John de Neve, *Fasti Ecclesiae Anglicanae 1300–1541*, VI: Northern Province, compiled by B. Jones (London, 1963), p. 31.

[37] *Testamenta Eboracensia*, I, 385–9.

[38] Ibid., I, 186–90. When Margaret of Wilsthorpe, who was elected prioress of Nun Monkton in 1365, died in 1376 (Smith and London, *Heads of Religious Houses*, II, 595) both

came under fire for her non-nun like dress and behaviour.[39] But he also remembered two other sisters, Mary and Alice, who were nuns of Sempringham.[40] Yet another reminder that not all nuns of the same family entered the same convent is provided by the will of Agnes de Percehay, who left her body to be buried next to that of her husband, Walter, in the Gilbertine priory of Malton, and legacies to two daughters; one, the (unnamed) prioress of Yedingham received 2 robes with mantles and 40s., and the other Agnes, nun of Watton, received 40s.[41] So the picture of small and poorly endowed nunneries recruiting from the immediate locality is something of an over simplification.

It might be argued that the kind of evidence that is brought together here is too sporadic and scattered to build up a picture of the lives of individual nuns except in the few cases of those who are extremely well documented. But the evidence is sufficient to be able to build up a group biography of the Yorkshire nuns. Indeed there are occasions when entire communities are recorded. In February 1397 a visitation named the seven nuns then residing at Arden Priory near Hawnby on the North Yorkshire Moors.[42] Six of them gave evidence as to the state of the

---

Isabel Neville and Margaret Fairfax were candidates, and Isabel was elected by ten votes to two, out of fifteen nuns who were entitled to vote. Margaret Fairfax succeeded Isabel as prioress. See A. Hamilton Thompson, 'The Registers of the Archdeaconry of Richmond, 1361–1442', *Yorkshire Archaeological Journal*, 25 (1920), 129–268 (especially no. 32 (p. 171), and no. 114 (p. 183)). John Fairfax, who was the younger son of William Fairfax of Walton near York, occurs as rector of Prescot in 1375; his successor took up his post on 25 June 1393: *VCH Lancashire*, III, 341. In 5 Richard II (22 June 1381 × 21 June 1382) as rector of Prescot he and the parson of Wensley received licence to grant to the nuns of Nun Monkton land in Naburn, and the advowson of St George, Fishergate, York: PRO, E326/3522.

39   For the visitation of 1397 by Thomas Dalby, archdeacon of Richmond, see Hamilton Thompson, 'Registers of the Archdeaconry of Richmond', no. 209 (pp. 196–7). The complaints against her were (i) that she wore furs and silk veils, (ii) that she also held the office of bursar and had sold a large amount of timber, (iii) that she was too frequently in the company of John Monkton, and supped with him in her chamber. She wore inappropriate dress in choir, contrary to the ancient custom of the priory. She too readily received back nuns who had lapsed into fornication and allowed nuns to receive presents from friends 'for their maintenance'. John Monkton was mentioned a second time, as playing dice ('ad tabulas') with the prioress and drinking in her chamber. The injunctions forbade John and three other men (named, including the chaplain) from having conversation with the nuns except in the presence of two senior nuns, and silks and furs were forbidden.

40   Margaret Cotum, also mentioned in John Fairfax's will was the next prioress after Margaret Fairfax. She died on 15 September 1421, and Matilda of Goldesburgh was elected prioress: Hamilton Thompson, 'Registers of the Archdeaconry of Richmond', no. 278 (p. 205).

41   *Testamenta Eboracensia*, I, 53–4 (will proved 26 February 1349).

42   York, Borthwick Institute, Register 5A (Sede Vacante Register), fols 228r–229r; summarized in *VCH Yorkshire*, III, 114–5.

priory and the conduct of its prioress. The seventh nun, Eleanor, had been elected as prioress of the community in 1392 on the resignation of her predecessor, whose name is not recorded. At the visitation five years later she stated that she was 26 years of age when she was elected, placing her date of birth around 1366. We also have snapshots of communities when a full list of nuns is given at an election, as at Keldholme in 1497. Eight nuns, including Katherine of Anlaby who had resigned as head of the community, requested the archbishop to provide as prioress Eliza-beth Davell, who at the time held that office at Basedale.[43] Eighteen nuns, includ-ing the former prioress Emma of Walkeringham elected Margaret Dawtry (also called 'de Alta Ripa') as prioress of Wilberfoss in 1310, and we have in this evidence a picture of the pattern of office holding, with the names of the subprioress, two sacrists, two cellarers, precentrix, and guest mistress.[44]

This paper will end briefly with a snapshot of the lives of the nuns of Rosedale in the early fourteenth century. Although the prioress was unnamed in an archiepiscopal letter of 1306, she can be identified as Mary de Ros by the content of that letter, which allowed her to visit her father, Sir William Ros of Ingman-thorpe (near Harrogate), twice a year.[45] In 23 August 1310 Mary was ordered to render her accounts for audit, following allegations made against her, and by 28 September she had resigned 'feeling herself powerless in government and in the discharge of her office' (*se ad regimen et curam sui officii senciens impoten-tem*).[46] Her successor and fellow nun of Rosedale, Joan of Pickering (about ten miles south of the priory), was confirmed on 12 January 1311, twelve days after Joan had brought the archbishop news of Mary's death and he had issued licence for an election.[47] Joan of Pickering had been through an unhappy period. In 1308 she was appointed by Archbishop Greenfield to be prioress of Keldholme, only seven or eight miles from Rosedale following a few fraught years of disputed elec-tions when successive nuns of Keldholme were elected and resigned. However, the nuns of Keldholme had refused to accept Joan. The archbishop was forced to visit the priory in person and disperse four rebel nuns to other nunneries.[48] It may have been with some relief that Joan resigned in 1309, and one can only hope that

---

[43] *The Register of Thomas Rotherham, Archbishop of York, 1480–1500*, I, ed. Eric E. Barker, Canterbury and York Society, 69 (1976), p. 152. Two days later the election of Agnes Thomlynson as prioress of Basedale was confirmed: ibid.

[44] *Reg. Greenfield*, III, 177–8; ibid., II, 127, notes that the Dawtry family held the patron-age of Full Sutton church in the deanery of Harthill.

[45] *Reg. Greenfield*, III, 12–13.

[46] Ibid., 56–7.

[47] Ibid., 58. On 18 January royal assent to the election was issued, the patronage being in the hands of the king by reason of the minority of Thomas Wake, patron of the house: *Cal. Patent Rolls 1307–1313*, p. 302; Smith and London, *Heads of Religious Houses*, II, 602.

[48] For this episode see Burton, 'Cloistered Women and Male Authority', pp. 160–2.

her experience as prioress at Rosedale was somewhat happier. In 1319 the unnamed prioress of Rosedale – possibly still Joan – was ordered by Archbishop Melton to accept as a nun Beatrice of Kirkby, and two years later a further licence was issued to accept the (unnamed) daughter of John of Dalton, bailiff of Pickering, if she was suitable.[49] In 1322 we hear of another Rosedale nun, when in May Melton wrote to the prioress of Handale near Whitby instructing her to receive Isabel Daiville, nun of Rosedale, to do penance following her apostasy and in June he instructed the prioress of Rosedale to send Isabel thence.[50] We cannot identify Isabel with certainty, but she may have been related to the branch of the Daiville family that held a tenancy of the Honour of Mowbray in Kilburn. An important member of the family was Sir John de Daiville, chief justice and keeper of the forests north of Trent, 1257–61, who died in 1291.[51] Apparently less successful was his son, another John, who sold his lands in Kilburn and Hood in 1319 and his manor of Thornton on the Hill in 1322 – the year in which Isabel apostasized. It would be interesting to see if any connection between the two can be traced. Isabel was not the only nun at about this time to leave her convent; and the spate of apostasy may have been connected with the Scottish raids that occurred at this time, and so disrupted conventual life. In November 1322, just a few months after Isabel's departure, because of the damage done to their house by the Scots, Archbishop Melton dispersed the nuns of Rosedale, as he did those of Moxby and the canons of Marton. He sent Alice of Rippinghale to Nunburnholme, Avelina de Brus to Sinningthwaite, Margaret of Langtoft (East Riding) to Thicket, and Joan Crovel to Wykeham. If Elena Daiville, who was sent with letters of the queen to do penance at Hampole, right down in the south of the county, is to be identified with Isabel, then her stay at Handale had been brief.[52] There is no mention here of the

[49] *The Register of William Melton, Archbishop of York, 1317–1340*, eds R. M. T. Hill, D. Robinson, R. Brocklesby, and T. C. B. Timmins, 5 vols, Canterbury and York Society, 70, 71, 76, 85, 93 (1977–2002), II, 34, 73.

[50] Ibid., 77–9.

[51] The family of Daiville was originally enfeoffed of lands in Kilburn of the Honour of Mowbray: *Charters of the Honour of Mowbray 1107–1191*, ed. D. E. Greenway, British Academy Records of Social and Economic History, new series, 1 (London, 1972), p. xxxiv. Sir John de Daiville of Egmanton (Nottinghamshire) and Adlingfleet, Kilburn and Thornton on the Hill (Yorkshire), was a chief justice and keeper of the king's forests north of the Trent. He died in 1291 (C. T. Clay, *Early Yorkshire Families*, Yorkshire Archaeological Society Record Series, 135 (1973), p. 24). His son, John, who was underage in 1295, sold the manors of Kilburn and Hood in 1319 to the earl of Lancaster, and that of Thornton to John Elleker in 1322. He died in 1326. The transactions were completed by his son, Robert, in 1330 and 1331. Robert was succeeded by his son, John, who died without issue in 1351. His heir was his brother, Robert Daiville of Adlingfleet, clerk, who in 1369 was succeeded by his three sisters. See *Complete Peerage*, IV, 130–34 (Deiville).

[52] *Reg. Melton*, II, 84. For Moxby and Marton, see ibid., pp. 83–4. For a full discussion of the Rosedale and Moxby dispersals see Burton, 'Cloistered Women', pp. 160–62.

two women whom the prioress was licensed to accept a few years earlier, but in 1323 Melton ordered the prioress of the reassembled convent to receive back Joan, daughter of John of Pickering, who claimed to have been unjustly expelled.[53] Careful sifting of the records has been able to reveal something of the composition and nature of the community at Rosedale over this twenty year period.

It is not unusual to read that communities of religious women – and by extension the women themselves – are poorly documented and have gone largely unrecorded. However the investigation of a range of evidence is able to challenge those statements and indeed challenge other assessments of northern nunneries. Far from being consistently small, some nunneries were at least of a size comparable with the houses of regular canons. It seems that in terms of geography the Yorkshire nunneries may have recruited from a wider area than commonly supposed, while retaining those close links with local families that from time to time resulted in the clustering of members of the same secular family within the monastic one. Further research may reveal more of the social origins of nuns. Something can be said of the pattern of office holding within female communities, and the movement of women from one house to take up the reins of power in another. Wills in particular are revealing of the connections between female religious and the local community, and of the physical environment within which these women lived and worshipped. They also suggest the high regard in which many of them were held.

---

[52]   *Reg. Melton*, II, 88–9.

'The Noiseless Tenor of their Way'?:
The Lives of the Late Medieval Higher Clergy

DAVID LEPINE

A great work of medieval biography might almost be an oxymoron, such are the difficulties of writing medieval lives. Indeed, it is legitimate to question the extent to which medieval biography can be written. What biographical tradition has developed is largely confined to monarchs, magnates and bishops, and a handful of others. Despite the new Oxford Dictionary of National Biography, medievalists have largely been excluded from the great British passion for biography. It seems that medieval people, like the inhabitants of Gray's country churchyard, are condemned to obscurity, to be village-Hampdens keeping the 'noiseless tenor of their way'. The traditional view is that medieval lives cannot be reconstructed because there simply is not enough evidence. Shortcomings in the evidence pose two major problems. First, there are often large gaps, blanks where nothing is known, even basic details that might seem fundamental to biography such as dates of birth and death, and family relationships. Second, the nature of the surviving evidence, particularly the lack of personal documents such as letters, precludes much consideration of an individual's personality, motives, thoughts and feelings, discussion of which has to remain at best speculative.

While acknowledging the problems of writing medieval biography, the aim of this paper is to challenge some of the assumptions behind this rather pessimistic view. In fact, we know more than we think we know. If individual biographies of medieval people are problematic, then prosopography, collective biography, offers a way forward when dealing with groups.[1] Prosopographers might perhaps be dismissed as 'snappers up of unconsidered trifles', but prosopography is an important and valuable tool in reconstructing medieval lives because it gets round many of the evidential problems of writing individual biographies. It works best for relatively small and clearly defined groups. While evidence for much of a single medieval life rarely survives, sources for many if not most aspects can be found from a group of individuals from which a representative collective biography can

---

[1]   L. Stone, 'Prosopography', *Daedalus*, 100 (1971), pp. 46–73, is still an important discussion, though with perhaps undue reliance on a quantitative approach; see also N. Bulst and J-P. Genet, *Medieval Lives and the Historian: Studies in Medieval Prosopography*, (Kalamazoo, 1986) and the journal *Medieval Prosopography*.

be written. For medievalists important raw materials already exist for some groups, including MPs, Oxford and Cambridge graduates and cathedral canons.[2]

The latter are the subject of this paper. The late medieval higher clergy can best be defined as those who rose above the level of resident parish clergy but did not reach the heights of the episcopal bench. Educated and frequently in ecclesiastical or royal service, they occupied the upper levels of the Church, the canonries of cathedral and collegiate churches and the wealthier rectories, usually in plurality. They have often been seen through stereotypes, both contemporary and modern. The contemporary one, reinforced by Protestant reformers, is the rapacious pluralist. Foremost among them was the notorious Bogo de Clare, who collected more than thirty benefices.[3] More recently they have been accused of having the smug complacency of the Barchester Close. Modern historians have largely discarded both stereotypes but are in danger of creating a new one for the early twenty-first century, the administrative careerist. This sees the higher clergy as the ambitious and successful high fliers of their day, on the 'fast track' of the late medieval Church.

The evidence for the lives the late medieval higher clergy, like that for other medieval individuals, is problematic but surprisingly full. Because the administrative records of the Church have survived most abundantly, we know a lot about the benefices and offices they held, and their career patterns are relatively easy to reconstruct. Even so, some of the most basic details of a life such as dates of birth and death are often unknown. In general it is their early life that is least known. Fortunately some of this can be pieced together from the details of their adult life. Approximate dates of birth can be calculated from ordination and career details as can general geographical origins by diocese, but family and social origins are more opaque, especially for those of relatively humble birth. We are on much stronger ground once clerics enter adulthood, that is the later stages of their university education, their graduation, often in higher degrees, benefices, and royal and ecclesiastical service. Even so, this is only half the picture. It has little to say about a very important part of their lives, their religious vocation and spiritual life. For this we are heavily dependent on their wills and post mortem provision for their souls, which, despite their great detail and usefulness, are not a reliable guide to their religious lives during their lifetimes.

What do the higher clergy say about themselves and what evidence is there of this? Letters and other personal documents are extremely rare and consequently

[2]   See A. B. Emden's biographical registers of the universities of Oxford and Cambridge, the revised versions of J. Le Neve's *Fasti Ecclesiae Anglicanae 1300–1541*, 12 vols (London, 1962–7) and J. S. Roskell et al., *The History of Parliament: The House of Commons 1386–1421*, 4 vols (Stroud, 1993).

[3]   M. Altschul, *A Baronial Family in Medieval England: The Clares 1217–1314* (Baltimore, 1965), pp. 176–87.

of little help. However, their general attitude was boldly set out by Roger Otery in 1366. In his reply to the pluralist return that year he declared that he lived an honest and upright life and had many years experience diligently engaged in temporal and spiritual affairs, especially the correcting and reforming of morals. Furthermore, he went on, canon law taught that a good, industrious and learned priest could faithfully look after two or even ten churches just as well as one, whether he was resident or non-resident, provided that he lived well and spent well.[4] A similar optimistic view can be found in the cathedral chronicle at Lichfield which praises the late fifteenth century resident canons for their learning and generosity and considers them an ornament to the Church.[5] A different type of formal statement of how the higher clergy saw themselves, or more accurately how they wished others to see them, can be found on their tombs. Richard Rudhale's splendid if mutilated brass in Hereford Cathedral proclaims his status, wealth and devotion. His academic status, as *magister*, and doctor of canon law, is stated in the inscription and his portrait, which shows him wearing his doctor's cap. The inscription sets out his status within the Church, as papal sub-collector, archdeacon of Hereford and canon residentiary. His wealth is reflected in the rich vestments he is wearing, an elaborate decorated cope and a fur amice. His devotion is evident in the eight saints depicted in the canopy on his brass, among them two local Hereford saints, Ethelbert and Thomas Cantilupe, and the three Latin couplets at its foot appealing to Christ's holy passion to heal his soul.[6]

Others were less charitable. The contemporary stereotype is set out in Ottobuono's Constitution in 1268 which describes pluralists as "walking shamelessly in the ways of vanity and lying delusions, necessarily neglect[ing] the wretched souls which they have received".[7] Ottobuono might almost have had his near contemporary Bogo de Clare in mind. Even in his lifetime Bogo attracted widespread condemnation, notably in Archbishop Pecham's damning pun that he was not a rector but ravager of churches.[8] The Paston letters give a rare glimpse of an ambitious cleric 'on the make'. Philip Lepyate (d. 1488) ended his days as an apparently respectable resident canon at Lincoln, but in the 1460s he had a questionable

4   *Registrum Simonis de Langham, Cantuariensis archiepiscopi [1366–8]*, ed. A. C. Wood, Canterbury and York Society [CYS], 53 (London, 1956), 44.
5   H. Wharton, *Anglia Sacra*, 2 vols (London, 1691), i, 454.; M. Greenslade, *The Staffordshire Historians*, Staffordshire Record Society, 4th Series 11 (1982), 8–9.
6   A. J. Winnington-Ingram, *Monumental Brasses in Hereford Cathedral*, 3rd edn (Hereford, 1972), p. 17; S. Badham, 'The Brasses and Other Minor Monuments', in *Hereford Cathedral: A History*, eds G. Aylmer and J. Tiller (London, 2000), pp. 334–5.
7   A. H. Thompson, 'Pluralism in the Medieval Church; with Notes on Pluralists in the Diocese of Lincoln, 1366', *Associated Architectural and Archaeological Reports and Papers*, 33 (1921–2), 44.
8   *Registrum Epistolarum fratris Johannis Peckham, archiepiscopi Cantuariensis*, ed. C. Trice Martin, Rolls Series, 3 vols (London, 1882–5), i, 371–2.

period in the service of the duke of Suffolk.[9] The letters reveal him aggressively pursuing Suffolk's interests in a dispute with the Pastons over the manors of Drayton and Hellesdon, and intimidating the tenants there. In May 1465, at the head of an armed retinue, he seized possessions and threatened violence, warning that the duke had more men than Daubeny, a Paston servant, had hairs on his head. There was a further confrontation in July when Lepyate with 300 men went to Hellesdon to serve writs on Paston's supporters. Only the presence of Sir John Paston with his own force prevented a violent affray. Margaret Paston considered him to be of "ryotous and evyll dysposicyon".[10] Given this side of his character, it is perhaps not surprising that his executors were able to place over £620 in cash in the treasury at Lincoln for safe keeping on his death in August 1488.[11] However, not all contemporaries were hostile. Richard Hooker, a Protestant historian of Exeter, remembered the resident canons of the 1530s with affection and wrote warmly of their learning, hospitality and preaching.[12]

The remainder of this paper will use a prosopographical approach to explore what is known of both the material and spiritual lives of the higher clergy and go beyond the false dichotomy often presented between the learned, devout administrator and the ambitious and worldly cleric, to uncover a more complex and paradoxical mixture of the two. The origins, education and careers of the higher clergy have long been well-established and will only be briefly touched on here. Typically they were born into landowning and upper burgess families, had access to a university education and were geographically mobile in the course of their careers. They formed the mainstay of ecclesiastical and royal administration for which they were well rewarded with benefices, the income from which enabled them to live comfortable lives. To give just one example, Edmund Ryall, a canon of Hereford, is unremarkably typical of the higher clergy as a whole. A member of a Worcestershire gentry family, birth gave him two advantages: access to university study at Oxford, from where he had graduated as a bachelor of civil law by 1393, and his first benefice, Nafford, Worcestershire. From 1408 to 1425 he served successive bishops of Hereford in diocesan administration which he combined with residence at Hereford cathedral until his death there in 1428.[13]

First their material lives. Perhaps the most striking feature of the material lives of the higher clergy is their wealth and the aristocratic lifestyle this supported. The sheer ubiquity of plate and cash listed in their wills and inventories can make them

---

9   A. B. Emden, *A Biographical Register of the University of Oxford to A.D. 1500*, 3 vols (Oxford, 1957–9) [*BRUO*], ii, 1196.

10   *Paston Letters and Papers of the Fifteenth Century*, ed. N. Davis, 2 vols (Oxford, 1971–6), i, 294–7.

11   Lincolnshire Archives Office [LAO], Dean and Chapter [D&C] A/3/1, f. 57.

12   N. I. Orme, *Exeter Cathedral as it Was* (Exeter, 1986), pp. 93–4.

13   *BRUO*, iii, 1614.

appear shockingly rich. Few were as fabulously wealthy as Walter Sherrington, chancellor of the duchy of Lancaster and residentiary of St Paul's, who at his death in 1449 left over £3200 in cash in an iron chest in the cathedral vestry.[14] But probate records show that estates of between £300 and £1000 were not uncommon. Such wealth enabled them to acquire extensive collections of plate and other luxury goods. Even William Kexby's relatively modest estate, valued at £150, contained three silver-gilt pieces and a dozen silver spoons.[15] Dean Henry Mamsfield (d. 1328) had a dozen silver-gilt cups worth £20 and thirty silver dishes with saucers worth £40 at Lincoln.[16] Luxury is also evident in the textiles that made their houses comfortable: tapestries, curtains, cushions, bedding and table linen. Much of it was high quality, made from expensive cloths in fine colours, and was embroidered. The higher clergy cut striking figures when not attending divine office. They dressed fashionably and luxuriously, often in scarlet. Thomas Cotte of Lincoln (d. 1384) had a best robe of sanguine worth £8 and another murrey coloured worth £4 in his wardrobe.[17] William Smith, archdeacon of Winchester and keeper of the hanaper (d. 1514), took care to keep up appearances court, buying studs for his black velvet girdle, and six long points of silk for the sleeves of his doublet.[18] On a more practical note Dean Mamsfield's wardrobe also included protection against the damp and cold of a Lincoln winter: boots, galoshes, socks, stockings, mittens, and fur lined caps.[19]

Almost every aspect of their material and daily life reflected their status and wealth. Conspicuous consumption and liberality were expected of them. Resident canons lived in substantial stone houses modelled on rural manor houses. There was space for them in cathedral closes which was not generally available in an urban setting.[20] Fine examples survive at Exeter, Lincoln and Salisbury. The importance of the provision of open and generous hospitality is reflected in the size of the hall and range of ancillary rooms, buttery, pantry, kitchen, larder, bakehouse and brewhouse, together with rooms for guests. The deanery hall at Salisbury was large enough to accommodate the twenty-six foot principal table.[21] There was also usually a chapel and private rooms, chamber, parlour and study. Larger houses had gatehouses and new fashionable accoutrements such as the fifteenth-century

[14]   London, Guildhall Library, MS 25,121/2073.
[15]   *Probate Inventories of the York Diocese 1350–1500*, eds P. M. Stell and L. Hampson (York, 1998), p. 57.
[16]   LAO, D&C Dii/60/3/9.
[17]   LAO, D&C Dvi/13/1.
[18]   *BRUO*, iii, 1721–2; Westminster Abbey Muniments [WAM] 5474, f. 23.
[19]   LAO, D&C Dii/60/3/9.
[20]   For a general discussion of this see D. N. Lepine, *A Brotherhood of Canons Serving God* (Woodbridge, 1995), pp. 114–23.
[21]   Royal Commission on the Historical Monuments of England [RCHME], *Salisbury: The Houses of the Close* (London, 1993), p. 212.

trend at Lincoln for oriel windows. While the exteriors and ground plans of canons' houses are clear, interiors are rarely described and have to be pieced together from inventories. The partial description of the subdeanery at Lincoln contained in the will of John Carelton (d. 1405) is a rare exception. Reading like a fifteenth-century estate agent's particulars, it lists a large Flanders chest standing in front of the east window in the chamber, an adjustable desk and another round one in the study, another desk next to the bed in the inner chamber and another hanging desk in the small oratory. In the hall there was a table for cups, a long, broad table in the west part and a sideboard for bowls and ewers in the centre.[22] The rural houses of the higher clergy, prebendal manors and rectories, were similar but seem to have been on a slightly smaller scale. The prebendal manor house at Nass-ington, Northamptonshire, is one of the few to have survived. It was built in the thirteenth century and remodelled in the fifteenth, probably by a notorious dean of Lincoln, John Mackworth, who is known to have resided there.[23]

Resident canons at cathedrals had a reputation for generous hospitality which was at least acknowledged as well as berated by their critics. The diet accounts of Archdeacon William Smith for three months from December 1491 to March 1492 are unique, the only surviving ones for a member of the higher clergy, albeit one on the verge of the episcopal bench; he was bishop-elect of Lichfield at the time.[24] Smith's table matched those of the lay aristocracy and the Benedictine monks of Westminster. During the three months the accounts cover he spent £33 on food. Almost half of this was for meat and fish, £18 and £8 respectively. Mutton, veal, ham, pork, lamb and beef (in order of quantity) were the staple meats, supplemented with rabbit and birds such as plover and woodcock. Fish was eaten on Fridays and Saturdays as well as during Lent: mainly salmon, whiting, haddock, gurnard and eels (also in order of quantity). Bread was bought in large quantities. Dairy produce consisted of eggs, butter, milk and cream, but not much cheese. The fruit eaten was mostly dried, such as dates, currants and prunes, which were bought most weeks. Apples and pears were the only fresh fruit and no vegetables were bought. Sugar was consumed on a large scale. Other spices, pepper, saffron, ginger, cinnamon, cloves and mace were used more sparingly but still purchased weekly. Beer and wine were drunk in large quantities. Smith's wealth and status enabled him to live more extravagantly than most of the higher clergy but even the humble chaplains of Munden's chantry in Dorset had a recognisably similar diet.[25]

22   LAO, D&C A/2/29, ff. 19v–20.
23   RCHME, An Inventory of the Historical Monuments of the County of Northampton, 6 vols (London, 1975–84), vi, 123–5; A. H. Thompson, The English Clergy (Oxford, 1947), p. 94.
24   WAM 5474.
25   C. Dyer, Standards of Living in the Later Middle Ages (Cambridge, 1989), pp. 55–70; C. M. Woolgar, The Great Household in Late Medieval England (London, 1999), chap-

The lives of many of the higher clergy, even in the later middle ages, were peripatetic. They moved in the course of their careers and travelled extensively while carrying out their duties in ecclesiastical and royal service. The extent of their travel is revealed in the household accounts of Robert de Kareville, treasurer of Salisbury, for the year 1256–7.[26] These detail where he was every day that year and show that he rarely stayed more than three weeks continuously in any one place. Most of his travelling was done in the service of the bishop of Winchester, whom he served as official. He was frequently at Winchester and the episcopal manors of Farnham and Hursley, Hampshire, and it was probably in this connection that he made five journeys to London that year as well as visits to Canterbury, Southampton and the Isle of Wight. He was an occasional visitor to Salisbury but a regular one to his rectory of Enford, Wiltshire. From the fifteenth century onwards the higher clergy were probably less peripatetic but their life on the road continued and is reflected in Richard Tollet's very generous bequest of £30 in 1528, to repair three stretches of road in Devon each of which was en route to one of his benefices from Exeter, where he was a resident canon.[27] Because of their peripatetic lives the stable was an essential part of the households of the higher clergy and most contained several horses. The short will Ranulph Pole drew up in 1538 is mainly taken up with his horses.[28] It lists and describes nine, four of them by name. Does this reveal a sixteenth-century hunting parson? His family background – he was a member of a gentry family, the Poles of Netherpool, Cheshire – seems to confirm this.[29] Yet a closer scrutiny of his will provides a cautionary note about the usefulness of wills, particularly their completeness. All nine horses were amblers, slow riding horses, requiring little skill in horsemanship, the sort comfortable for long journeys, rather than faster trotting horses suitable for hunting. The undue emphasis on horses in his will is because he had left other instructions for his executors both verbal and written. The horses were perhaps all that was left to dispose of.

Family relationships are amongst the hardest elements of a life to reconstruct for the medieval period. Even the most basic facts needed to draw up a family tree are often missing and the nature of the relationships between family members is usually impossible to discover. Occasionally there are some clues. Some hints of their complexity emerge from the will of Richard Delves, a resident canon of Lichfield who died in 1527.[30] There is evidence of family warmth. One of the two alter-

---

ter 6; *A Small Household of the Fifteenth Century*, ed. K. L. Wood-Legh (Manchester, 1955).
26 Salisbury Cathedral Archives, Press III Treasurer's Roll.
27 The roads from Exeter to Crediton, Exeter to Cullompton and Ashburton to Plymouth (The National Archives [TNA], PROB 11/22, f. 270).
28 TNA, PROB 11/27, f. 130.
29 G. Ormerod, *The History of the County Palatine and City of Chester*, 2 vols, 2nd edn (London, 1882), II part ii, pp. 421, 423.
30 Lichfield Joint Record Office [LJRO], D30/2/1/4, ff. 43v–46v. For Delves see J. Le Neve,

native burial places he requested was the chapel of St Mary Widdenbury, Cheshire, with his parents and he bequeathed two long broaches to a nephew, Thomas Butler, as heirlooms. Another nephew, Harry Delves, sent him a mattress during his last illness. Yet there also seem to have been family tensions. Bequests to both nephews were hedged with exhortations and conditions as though he was expecting difficulties from them. Thomas Butler was to be 'loving and kind to my executors and help them in my right against any that might wrong them, and not to vex or trouble them in no manner wise for if he do then I will that the said bequest stand void and of non effect'. Harry Delves' condition was that 'neither he nor any man or woman in his name or by his procurement do vex or trouble or cause to be troubled my executors, instead he patiently help them or the bequest shall stand void'. While precautions against negligent executors, sanctions against troublesome legatees and alternative provisions to cover a range of eventualities are a commonplace of late medieval wills, it is unusual for such stern warnings to be made against family members.

The material lives of the higher clergy can be reconstructed with relative ease but their religious and spiritual lives are a more difficult and comparatively neglected area of study. In the light of their successful careers and comfortable lifestyles it has frequently been assumed that their spiritual lives were routine or of marginal importance, that their religious vocation was less important than career advancement with all the implicit moral criticism this carries. Often busy with administrative or secular duties, they were rarely resident parish clergy engaged in the daily pastoral round. This impression is reinforced by their belief that there was no contradiction between wealth, worldly success and a religious vocation. Historians face two further problems when considering the religious lives of the higher clergy. First, it is rare to find explicit expressions of their personal devotion. This is partly because there was no need: it was self-evident and taken for granted. Few like John Taylor (d. 1492), a noted theologian and preacher, have left behind a motto summing up their beliefs. His was 'Let me not glory in anything but the cross'.[31] For the majority of individuals it was only when drawing up their wills, and not always then, that they explicitly set out their beliefs. A clearer idea of their personal devotion can be gained from their possessions and actions, in particular the often extensive provisions made for their souls. The second and largely insoluble problem is how to measure the quality of their belief. How can historians distin-

---

Fasti Ecclesiae Anglicanae 1300–1541, vol. 10: *Coventry and Lichfield Diocese*, ed. B. Jones (London, 1964), pp. 24, 51, 57 and *Calendar of Papal Letters* [*CPL*] (London, 1893–1955), 13 part ii, 829. For his residence at Lichfield from 1502 until his death see LJRO, D30/2/1/3, f. 60 *et seq.* and LJRO, D30/2/1/4 *passim*.

[31]   N. I. Orme, 'St Michael and his Mount', *Journal of the Royal Institution of Cornwall*, New Series 10 part i (1986–7), 32–43.

guish between genuine piety and time serving conformity?

Wills, for all their uncertainties and shortcomings, are a very important source for the personal devotion of the higher clergy, both through invocations and in the provisions made for their souls. Though the bulk of surviving invocations are brief, formulaic and of limited interest, the exceptions can be considered clear expressions of faith, especially from such a literate and well-educated group. A conventional late medieval piety emerges from the many surviving wills of the higher clergy with familiar themes emphasised: a fear of judgement resulting in great urgency and anxiety for the health of the soul, a Christocentric approach that emphasised Christ's redeeming passion, appeals for the intercession of saints, and frequently an awareness of the unworthiness and sinfulness of the testator. Fear of what John Plente called the 'terrible day of judgement' led to great care and attention being paid to provisions for the health of their souls.[32] These provisions were the most conspicuous expression of their piety and have the advantage of being well documented. The higher clergy made a massive financial investment to escape the pains of purgatory, devoting a large proportion of their considerable wealth to it. In the case of Nicholas Sturgeon, composer and royal clerk, it was 'all my worldly goodes'.[33] Unlike the laity, who were required by canon law to assign a third of their possessions to their wives and a further third to their children, they could devote the bulk of their estates to their souls. Indeed, the provisions the higher clergy made for their souls can be considered a late medieval form of progressive taxation. Through them a substantial proportion of their wealth, much of it originating from the most lucrative benefices in the English church, was redistributed to the 'clerical proletariat' and poor praying for them.

Two principal but related types of provision were made: masses and almsgiving. Masses, especially those said for named individuals, were considered the most efficacious. Consequently there was a wholesale multiplication on a scale that can seem obsessive, mechanical and mechanistic in the early twenty-first century. The higher clergy could afford hundreds, thousands, and sometimes tens of thousands of masses. Chantries and obits, both permanent and temporary, were founded, trentals and masses said, and chaplains employed. In addition to establishing a chantry in Salisbury cathedral, John Frankes (d. 1438), a chancery clerk and master of the rolls, instructed his executors to spend £100 on masses for his soul 'immediately and without delay after my death'. Not content with these arrangements, he appended to his will the text of special prayers he had written mentioning his name to ensure he secured the full benefits of the masses said.[34] Such

---

[32] TNA, PROB 11/7, ff. 55v–56.

[33] *The Fifty Earliest English Wills in the Court of Probate 1387–1439*, ed. F. J. Furnivall, Early English Texts Society o. s., 78 (1882), 131–4.

[34] *The Register of Henry Chichele, Archbishop of Canterbury, 1413–43*, ed. E. F. Jacobs, 4 vols, CYS 42, 45–7 (London, 1943–7), ii, 591–5.

prayers were commonly specified in chantry foundations. Spiritual benefits were also sought through the ringing of bells, lighting of candles, saying of psalters, and the activities of fraternities. Almsgiving was widely and often generously practised. It also brought spiritual benefits, intended primarily, as it was, to solicit prayers from the recipient for the donor. However, we are left with an important question. Were these provisions a deathbed panic as the reality of an eternity in the pains of purgatory approached or the culmination of lifetime's devotion? Or put more simply, how religious were the higher clergy during their lifetimes?

While there are no easy answers to such questions quite a strong case can be put forward for a genuine religious vocation and piety. Though it is hard to quantify, at least some of the higher clergy took their liturgical duties seriously and attended mass and the divine offices regularly on a daily basis. Daily attendance at mass and one other office was a requirement of residence at most cathedrals. Surviving accounts at some cathedrals, notably Exeter and Hereford, record attendance by canons at particular services. At Hereford a core of residentiaries attended 300 or more masses a year.[35] At Exeter some went to more than the minimum number of offices. Throughout the fourteenth and fifteenth centuries significant numbers of resident canons regularly attended obits. It might be argued that this was financially induced. Whilst this cannot be entirely discounted, the small payments received for attending obits, typically a few pence, at most one or two shillings, were not a significant part of their income and it is therefore unlikely they attended primarily for financial advantage.[36] The regular presence of ten or more canons at the funerals of the poor at the beginning of the fourteenth century, when payments ranged from $\frac{1}{4}d$. to $1d$., was even less financially motivated. Presumably it was concern for her soul that motivated eleven canons including the dean to attend the funeral of Joan the seamstress in February 1306 rather than the $\frac{1}{2}d$. each received.[37] It was a charitable act; burial of the dead was the seventh work of mercy. However, against this there is evidence, especially from collegiate churches, of lax standards and the perfunctory performance of duties. Among the many faults exposed by Bishop Alnwick's visitation of New College Leicester in 1440 were a failure by canons to say mass more than once a week and to get up for matins, with canons saying 'I know how much [money] I shall lose: I had rather lose it than get up'.[38]

---

[35] Hereford Cathedral Archives, R475–576.

[36] In the early 1360s quarterly incomes from obit attendance amounted to between 2s. and 4s., occasionally rising to between 6 and 7s. (Devon Record Office, Exeter Cathedral Archives, D&C 3766, ff. 90v–103v).

[37] *Death and Memory in Medieval Exeter*, eds D. N. Lepine and N. I. Orme, Devon and Cornwall Record Society, New Series 47 (Exeter, 2003), 272–311, 286.

[38] *Visitations of Religious Houses in the Diocese of Lincoln*, ed. A. H. Thompson, 3 vols, CYS 17, 24, 33 (London, 1915–27), ii, 190.

An impression of genuine piety is reinforced by the fact that the higher clergy were rich in what might be called the material culture of devotion: their chapels, vestments, liturgical books and equipment and devotional objects. Their houses usually had private chapels which inventories show were well equipped with vestments, altar linen and vessels, often silver or gilt, and other equipment together with service books. Houses without chapels might have a portable altar. William Duffield's house at Cawood, Yorkshire, did not have a chapel but contained a 'table with high trestles for the celebration of masses'.[39] Even the most apparently worldly careerists had a few liturgical and devotional books. Walter Sherrington, forty years a senior royal civil servant, but resident at St Paul's for the last nine years of his life, though not a graduate, gave twenty-three books to its library which his great wealth had funded. These comprised mainly educational and pastoral works. The former included standard works, Papias' dictionary, a Catholicon, and grammar books, but also a volume of classical Latin containing works by Cicero, Seneca and Virgil. Among the pastoral works were glosses on the psalter, a *Reportorii moralis sive dictionarii*, and popular handbooks, the *Pupilla oculi*, a *Speculum curatorum* and a *Speculum peccatoris*.[40] Possession of devotional objects has left fewer traces, but inventories often list images and rosaries, though rarely relics; William Melton's chapel at York contained 'a litle clothe staned with Christe, Marie and John', an image of Our Lady and a 'paynted clothe staned with Christe and ii thefes'.[41]

Their devotion was also expressed in their full engagement in the popular devotional trends of the late medieval period, among them the cult of saints, pilgrimage, and fraternities. Robert Kareville was an early promoter of the cult of St Edmund of Abingdon (d. 1240), his predecessor as treasurer of Salisbury. In 1251, only four year's after St Edmund's canonisation, he built a chapel dedicated to him at Figheldean, Wiltshire, one of the treasurer's estates.[42] William Lochard's devotion was to St George whose cult at Hereford cathedral he augmented by founding a chantry in St George's chapel there. St George was a fitting patron saint for a clerk of the king's chapel and canon of Windsor.[43] Countless other examples could be given. Though there are few records of individuals going on pilgrimage, the higher clergy shared the late medieval enthusiasm for it. We only know about Thomas Candour's pilgrimage to Rome in September 1475 because he made his will en route at Dover before he crossed the channel.[44] The higher clergy were

[39] *Probate Inventories York*, p. 205.
[40] London, British Library, Cotton Charters XIII.11.
[41] *York Clergy Wills 1520–1600: I Minster Clergy*, ed. C. Cross, Borthwick Texts and Calendars 10 (York, 1984), 12.
[42] *Calendar of Close Rolls 1247–51*, p. 455.
[43] TNA, PROB 11/3, ff. 202v–203; S. L. Ollard, *Fasti Wyndsoriensis: the Deans and Canons of Windsor* (Windsor, 1950), p. 82; *Calendar of Patent Rolls [CPR] 1436–41*, p. 549.
[44] TNA, PROB 11/6, ff. 253–4.

active participants in fraternities as members, founders and promoters; Thomas Heywood, dean of Lichfield, founded a fraternity of Jesus and St Anne in the cathedral there in 1487.[45] Walter Sherrington cast his membership wide, in London to St Bartholomew's Priory, St Helen's Nunnery, the Franciscans and Dominicans, the Taylors and the parish fraternities of St Lawrence Jewry and St Dunstan, and further afield to Colchester, Leicester and Coventry.[46]

The pastoral contribution of the higher clergy is a more controversial aspect of their lives. It mainly consisted of diocesan administration, and for a handful, preaching. As we have seen, they were rarely resident in their parishes (though I am not sure quite how true that assertion is) and this has led to some harsh judgements against them. If their pastoral contribution were to be judged solely on their parochial cure of souls it would indeed be meagre. However, diocesan administration often had a substantial pastoral component, especially the exercise of spiritual jurisdiction in the lower ecclesiastical courts. These dealt with cases of sexuality, marriage, testamentary business, defamation, debt and what might be called Christian discipline. The complexity and scarcity of the surviving records of these courts have rendered this work almost invisible. Yet there are occasional glimpses of it. In his capacity as dean Thomas Heywood exercised a close pastoral supervision of the citizens of Lichfield.[47] Confounding the venal stereotype, Richard Rudhale was a conscientious archdeacon who took his duties seriously. The cathedral library at Hereford still has some of his carefully annotated law books, among them up to date Italian commentaries on canon law.[48] Both William Doune and William Nassington might appear typical fourteenth-century diocesan administrators, the former at Lincoln and Worcester and the latter at Exeter, York and Salisbury, yet Doune wrote a notable pastoral handbook, the *Memoriale Presbiterorum* and Nassington a devotional treatise, the *Speculum Vitae*.[49] We should beware assuming that diocesan administrators were mere quill pushers.

In their moral lives few members of the higher clergy were out and out scoundrels, though this may partly be a reflection their status. They were less likely to be charged with offences than lesser clergy. Cathedral minor clergy by contrast appear unruly, truculent recidivists addicted to drinking, gambling and fornicating. Of course there were some individual cases, mostly of fornication. Few were

[45] A. J. Kettle, 'City and Close: Lichfield in the Century before the Reformation', in *The Church and Pre-Reformation Society*, eds C. Barron and C. Harper-Bill (Woodbridge, 1985), p. 163.

[46] Lambeth Palace Library, Register of Archbishop Stafford, ff. 170v–171v.

[47] Kettle, 'City and Close', pp. 164–9.

[48] D. N. Lepine, 'A Long Way from University: Cathedral Canons and Learning at Hereford in the Fifteenth Century', in *The Church and Learning in Late Medieval Society*, eds C. Barron and J. Stratford, Harlaxton Medieval Studies, xi (Donington, 2002), pp. 191–5.

[49] M. Haren, *Sin and Society in Fourteenth Century England: A Study of the Memoriale Presbitorum* (Oxford, 2000), pp. 39–44, 57–9, 190–216.

as serious as the case of Master John Day, canon of New College Leicester, who was described as a 'common roamer in the town and haunter of taverns' and was convicted of sodomy and deprived of his canonry in 1440.[50] Some of the higher clergy, especially deans, seem to have been particularly prone to the sin of pride. Henry Mamsfield, dean of Lincoln, is best known today for the scale of his vanity evident in the twenty-four donor portraits in the windows he gave to Merton College chapel, Oxford c. 1294.[51] In 1422 the York chapter complained that the former dean, John Prophete, behaved more like a bishop or archbishop than a dean in the way he celebrated mass and gave blessings in the minster.[52]

There was a paradox of wealth and piety at the heart of the lives of the late medieval higher clergy who saw no contradiction between the two. This paradox is particularly evident in the case of Richard Ravenser, archdeacon of Lincoln (d. 1386) whose life shows that, despite the difficulties, medieval biography can be written. At first glance Richard Ravenser might be thought the archetypal clerical civil servant and worldly careerist, an impression amply confirmed by the details of his royal service, benefices and material possessions. Yet he did have what might be called a religious life that included a special interest in hospitals for the poor. Though he never reached the bench of bishops, there can be little doubt that Ravenser had a very successful career.[53] At his death his wardrobe contained the trappings of its success: liveries not only of the king and queen but the archbishop of Canterbury and the bishop of Lincoln.[54] His forty-year royal career owed much of its success to his origins. Probably born in the mid or late 1320s, his family originated in the now lost coastal settlement of Ravenspur in the East Riding of Yorkshire, hence his toponym. He was a kinsman, probably a nephew, of Archbishop Thoresby of York and thereby a member of a powerful clerical affinity, the so-called 'Yorkshire clerks' that dominated royal administration for much of the fourteenth century. It was doubtless through these connections that he entered royal service, where he first appears in the records in 1343 as the attorney of Queen Philippa. He rose steadily through the chancery, where he was a master for twenty-four years, keeper of the hanaper from 1357 to 1379, and still active in December 1384. His financial skills were particularly highly valued; he served successive queens as treasurer or receiver, unravelling their tangled finances.

---

50   *Lincoln Visitations*, pp. 191, 194–5.
51   R. Marks, *Stained Glass in England during the Middle Ages* (London, 1993), p. 16.
52   York Minster Library, L2 (3)a, f. 122.
53   R. McDermid, *Beverley Minster Fasti*, Yorkshire Archaeological Society Record Series 149 (1993), 50–1; B. Wilkinson, *The Chancery under Edward III* (Manchester, 1929), pp. 170–1; A. H. Thompson, 'The Registers of the Archdeaconry of Richmond, 1361–1442', *Yorkshire Archaeological Journal*, 25 (1920), 251–3; *Memorials of Beverley Minster*, ed. A. F. Leach, 2 vols, Surtees Society [SS], 98, 108 (1898–1903), ii, pp. lxvi–lxix.
54   LAO, D&C Dvi/13/2, ff. 8v–9, 15v.

The reward for such faithful service was a string of lucrative benefices as well as a substantial income from fees and other perks of office. Beginning with the relatively modest rectory of Anderby, Lincolnshire, in 1349, valued at £10 in the 1291 *Taxatio*, he built up a substantial collection of benefices using a combination of royal patronage and judicious exchanges.[55] Contrary to the stereotype, he was unexpectedly scrupulous in his observation of canon law on pluralism. Most of his benefices were prebends in cathedral and collegiate churches which were without cure of souls and could be held in plurality. He held benefices with cure of souls one at a time. This did not prevent him amassing a huge income from his benefices, most of which came from the mastership of St Leonard's Hospital, York, valued at £367 17s. 9 ½d., and the archdeaconry of Lincoln, valued at £350.[56] From 1363 his annual income was over £460 a year and at its peak from 1371 nearly £900.[57] Ravenser's income from royal office is almost impossible to quantify but would have been substantial.[58] The only visible part is his money lending, a widespread and accepted perk of office. In one year alone, 1358, he made fourteen loans totalling over £400.[59] His wealth is amply reflected in his possessions listed in the lengthy inventory drawn up by his executors.[60] It reveals the luxurious and comfortable lifestyle we have already seen. The quality and sheer quantity of Ravenser's luxury goods stand out; the silk curtains and hangings of his bed, a coverlet of red carde lined with silk and ermine worth 40s.; an extensive collection of furs, among them a dozen pieces of miniver, and no less than 350 pieces of plate (250 of them dishes, saucers and spoons). He had three principal residences, a house in the suburbs of London, probably Westminster, known as Ravenser's Inn, a house in the close at Lincoln (1378–86) and one at Stretton, Lincolnshire.[61]

While Ravenser's personality and character cannot really be known, it is possible to comment on what kind of impression he made. An energetic, talented and shrewd man of business, especially in financial matters, he seems to have been a strong and forceful individual. Bishop Buckingham of Lincoln was no match for him in a dispute over episcopal and archidiaconal jurisdiction.[62] In 1368, immedi-

[55] *Taxatio Ecclesiastica Angliae et Walliae Auctoritate Nicholai IV c. 1291*, eds T. Astle, S. Ayscough and J. Caley (Record Commission, 1802), p. 59.

[56] *Valor Ecclesiasticus*, ed. J. Caley, 6 vols (Record Commission, 1810–34), v, 17; *CPL*, iv, 367.

[57] In 1363 his Lincoln prebend was valued at £36 and his Beverley canonry £57 (*Taxatio* p. 56; *Beverley Fasti* p. 2) and in 1371 the free chapel of Tickhill £26 and his York prebend £46 (*Taxatio* pp. 298–9).

[58] M. Richardson, *The Medieval Chancery under Henry V*, List and Index Society Special Series 30 (1999), 38–49.

[59] Wilkinson, *Chancery under Edward III*, p. 170.

[60] LAO, D&C Dvi/13/2, ff. 6v–16.

[61] *CPR 1374–7*, p. 80; S. Jones, K. Major, J. Varley, *Survey of Ancient Houses in Lincoln*, 4 vols (Lincoln, 1984–96), ii, 84; LAO D&C Dvi/13/2, f. 12.

ately after he became archdeacon of Lincoln, Ravenser secured a significant victory over the rights of episcopal officials in the archdeaconry and it was not until after Ravenser's death that the bishop recovered his rights. However, the dispute did not sour relations between the two and the archdeacon continued to receive Buckingham's livery. Ravenser's dispute in 1381 with Archbishop Neville of York, whom he described as his 'mortal enemy', was much more bitter. It arose from Neville's conflict with Beverley Minster, where he was a canon. Ravenser led the chapter's resistance and bore the brunt of the archbishop's anger for which he was deprived of both his Beverley and York prebends with a resulting loss in income of £100 a year.[63] Ravenser was capable of winning good opinions. A royal encomium of 1366 speaks of his 'honest and faithful service to the king ... abstaining from injuries to anyone'.[64] At Beverley he was regarded as an industrious provost who managed the chapter resources 'profitably and laudably'.[65] On a more personal note his brother John Ravenser described him as *magistri mei carissimi*.[66]

But could such a successful and worldly career be combined with a religious vocation and genuine piety? Our misgivings about combining great wealth and a Christian life were not shared by the late medieval higher clergy. While some aspects of Ravenser's devotion, his books, private chapel and the provisions of his will are unremarkably typical of late medieval trends, his interest in hospitals and almsgiving shows more individuality and is strong evidence of his piety. His library was relatively small and not very distinguished, comprising mainly of the standard legal texts and commentaries on them needed for his archidiaconal duties, and two devotional works, a book of the seven penitential psalms glossed in French and a little book of devotional stories.[67] His private chapels at London and Stretton were richly appointed; the former was notable for the quality of its liturgical books, a new *portiforium* with musical notation valued at £10 and a large missal valued at £13 6s. 8d.[68] His will broadly reflects current devotional trends in its patronage of friars and nuns rather than older established monastic houses. What is more unusual is the extent of his patronage of anchorites and recluses. There were not just one or two individual bequests but comprehensive support for those in his locality, 2s. for each one in Lincolnshire and Yorkshire, 3s. 4d. for each one

[62]   C. Morris, 'The Ravenser Composition', *Lincolnshire Architectural and Archaeological Society Reports and Papers*, New Series 10 (1963), pp. 24–39.

[63]   R. B. Dobson, 'Beverley in Conflict: Archbishop Alexander Neville and the Minster Clergy, 1381–8', in *Medieval Art and Architecture in the East Riding of Yorkshire*, ed. C. Wilson, British Archaeological Association 9 (1989), 149–64.

[64]   *CPR 1364–8*, p. 225.

[65]   *CPR 1370–4*, p. 125.

[66]   *Early Lincoln Wills 1280–1547*, ed. A. Gibson (Lincoln, 1888), p. 69.

[67]   LAO, D&C Dvi/13/2, f. 9.

[68]   Ibid., f. 9v.

in York and larger gifts to two named individuals.[69]

What makes Richard Ravenser unusual is his almsgiving and interest in hospitals for the poor. This was a long-standing interest and is the strongest evidence of his genuine piety. He seems to have been a diligent master of St Leonard's Hospital York rather than an absentee content to enjoy the substantial income. In 1384 he successfully resisted an attempt to use the hospital to maintain a royal nominee, insisting that it had been founded to support the bedridden.[70] He was a generous benefactor, granting in 1377 an endowment to fund an extra weekly loaf for every pauper and in 1380 an additional income of sixteen marks a year.[71] In his will he was equally generous, bequeathing 3s. 4d. to every pauper in the infirmary and every chorister, 13s. 4d. to each brother and 6s. 8d. to each sister.[72] Ravenser was also a benefactor of hospitals in three other places he was closely connected with, Beverley, Hull and Lincoln. At Beverley he initially planned to found a new hospital for twelve poor men but instead, in 1378, decided to support an additional twelve at St Nicholas Hospital there.[73] At Hull he was co-founder of Selby's Hospital with his brother, Robert de Selby. The hospital was founded in 1375 for twelve poor men and received further endowments from him in 1376 and 1380.[74] At Lincoln he in effect re-founded St Giles Hospital in 1380, changing its nature by making closer links with cathedral. His original plan to found a *mansionem* in Great Stretton, Lincolnshire, was abandoned in favour of supporting St Giles Hospital. Ravenser's gift of the manor of Great Stretton was to provide ½d. daily to twelve poor inmates and a clothing allowance. Preference was to be given to 'needy ministers and servants of the cathedral and canons who were not able to work', to be nominated by Ravenser and his successors as archdeacon of Lincoln.[75] Ravenser's charity suggests it would be unwise to assume that clerical royal servants had a broadly secular outlook and little sense of religious vocation.

In conclusion, far from having a 'noiseless tenor' Ravenser and the rest of the later medieval high clergy have collectively left ample evidence of their lives, if not their personalities and characters. Undoubtedly successful and wealthy, they combined a comfortable aristocratic lifestyle and a religious vocation. Most were con-

---

[69]   LAO, Register XII (Register of Bishop Buckingham), ff. 326–7.
[70]   *CPR 1381–5*, p. 366.
[71]   *CPR 1377–81*, pp. 31, 482.
[72]   See note 66.
[73]   *CPR 1377–81*, pp. 112, 259; *Victoria County History [VCH], Yorkshire East Riding*, vi, ed. K. J. Allison (Oxford, 1989), pp. 182–3.
[74]   *CPR 1374–7*, pp. 167, 258; *CPR 1377–81*, pp. 561–2; *Cartularium Prioratus de Gyseburne, Ebor. Dioeceseos, Ordinis S. Augustini, Fundati A. D. MCXIX*, ed. W. Brown, 2 vols, SS 87, 89 (1889–94), ii, 267–9, 276–7; W. Dugdale, *Monasticon Anglicanum* (London, 1655–73), vi, part i, 275; *VCH Yorkshire*, iii, ed. W. Page (London, 1913), 313.
[75]   *CPR 1377–81*, p. 556; *CPR 1381–5*, pp. 412–13; *VCH Lincolnshire*, ii, ed. W. Page (London, 1906), 233.

scientious and had a genuine piety and the best like Thomas Heywood, were learned, devout and generous. To return to Thomas Gray 'Let not [History] mock their useful toil'.

Fifteenth-Century Mercers and the Written Word: Mercers and their Scribes and Scriveners

ANNE F. SUTTON

A fifteenth-century London mercer, who followed the ancient trade of mercery, dealt in silk, if he could afford it; he made his real money from linen imported from the Low Countries and Germany; he bought and sold miscellaneous small goods that included such items as books and dress accessories; he also specialised in worsted piece-goods, that is bedding, curtains and clothing lengths. A mercer's household made accessories of silk and linen, such as ribbons, laces, fringe and tassels. By about 1380 richer mercers dominated the native import of linen into London from the Low Countries and they increasingly dominated the native export of English cloth through London. To all intents and purposes, the Mercers ran the adventurers of London, the most powerful sub-group of the Merchant Adventurers of England, in the fifteenth century. The Mercers' Company of London therefore contained a wide range of wealth, from newly fledged freemen and shopkeepers to great merchants, but affluence was the norm. There were always several aldermen in their ranks and a regular supply of mercer mayors. Men of this status would have employed a permanent household scribe or secretary, besides a household chaplain. Mercers therefore usually had more prestige, wealth and power than scribes, scriveners, writers of the court letter or public notaries, as well as any man in the book-trade from stationer down. This is emphasised by the tax lists of the London companies of the fifteenth century: in 1488, for example, the Mercers paid £740, the Scriveners £25 and the Stationers £20. The Mercers were a mercantile company, the others were largely 'handy crafty' men, as one scrivener put it.[1] Mercers were therefore the patrons in this relationship. Nor is it surprising that it was a mercer – William Caxton – not a scrivener or stationer who had the means to launch printing in the English language. Mercers provide the main documents for this study and they provide the London location.

Most mercers lived in the central parishes and wards of the city: especially those north of Cheapside up to and around Guildhall such as St Laurence Jewry, St Stephen Coleman Street, St Michael Bassishaw, St Mary Aldermanbury and St Mary Magdalen Milk Street. Their area of business was the main shopping street

---

[1] C. P. Christianson, *A Directory of London Stationers and Book Artisans 1300–1500* (New York, 1990), p. 38. And see John Parker's will, below.

of the city, Cheapside, and the Mercery stretched along Cheapside between St Mary le Bow to opposite what is now Mercers' Hall, and south to an east–west line that included Pancras Lane. Mercers' Hall was part of the complex of buildings that made up the hospital of St Thomas of Acre, the great church which counterpoised St Paul's at the other end of Cheapside. St Thomas's played a large part in local life and sheltered both text writers and scriveners touting for business among other tradesmen, in the same way as St Paul's. It also ran a school for its choristers and fee-paying boys.[2] Just as the area of St Paul's, its churchyard, and Paternoster Row in particular, was the area of the book-trades and of the Stationers' Company, the other end of Cheapside round St Thomas's can be defined as the area of the Scriveners' Company, the legal writers of the court letter who worked mainly on the documents of lawyers and businessmen, and who had firmly separated their craft from the booktrade in 1373. The company's use of premises at St Thomas of Acre for meetings is well-known; they also met at the best inns nearby, such as the 'Cardinal's Hat' in Lombard Street, or at the great house of one of their wardens such as that of Henry Woodcock in Bucklersbury.[3] Woodcock was secondary of the Poultry Compter, an important but unsavoury institution a little further to the east of St Thomas's. It was one of the two prisons of the two sheriffs of London and Middlesex; their court held its sessions at Guildhall but the compters of Bread Street and Poultry were their administrative headquarters. Few mercers had no experience of the compters as litigants over debts and few scriveners did not know their value as a source of work.

Mercers of London were educated, literate and numerate, though their abilities and interests varied. Most merely kept business accounts, made a living and dictated their wills, but all of them used these skills to record their lives; few did not employ a scrivener or scribe at some point, and inevitably they used the men of their own locality. There are four main sources of written record for their lives, all of which involved personal absorption in the written word. First there were the books of accounts and multifarious subsidiary documents, bills and obligations of their mercantile life. Secondly, the leases, grants and acquittances they made and

2   C. P. Christianson, 'A Community of Book Artisans in Chaucer's London', *Viator*, 20 (1989), 209–10, his 'Early London Bookbinders and Parchmeners', *The Book Collector* 1985, 43–44, and his *Directory*, pp. 18–21, 32–3. *Memorials of London and London Life in the XIIIth, XIVth and XVth Centuries*, ed. H. T. Riley (London, 1868), p. 113 and n. For scribes in St Thomas's, A. F. Sutton, 'The Hospital of St Thomas of Acre of London: the Search for Patronage, Liturgical Improvement, and a School, under Master John Neel, 1420–63', *The Late Medieval English College*, eds C. Burgess and M. Heale (Woodbridge, 2008), 199–229, esp. pp. 200–01 and n. 2.

3   For Woodcock see below. For the emergence of these two companies, Christianson, *Directory*, Introduction, *Scriveners' Company Common Paper, 1357–1628*, ed. F. W. Steer, London Record Society 4 (1968), pp. vii–x, and his *A History of the Worshipful Company of Scriveners* (London and Chichester, 1973), pp. 1–11.

had to preserve regarding their real estate, which will not be considered here. Thirdly, there were the books they owned for the acquisition of knowledge, for the practice of religion or for recreation, which would have been acquired new or secondhand from members of the booktrade, writers of the text-letter or from stationers, the greater men of the trade who were dealers and who conferred their name on the company that came to represent all the bookcrafts from 1403; these are reserved for discussion another time. Fourthly, there were the documents which underpin the first two, their wills, in which they set out their life in terms of bequests to family and friends and took care of their souls. This paper relies on the records of the mercers' mercantile life and on their wills, for which in the fifteenth century it was the norm for mercers to employ a scrivener to write in the correct form.[4]

Mercers themselves wrote many of the documents they used every day – accounts, memoranda, letters – but they also employed scribes, scriveners, writers of court hand, clerks, notaries public, attorneys, secretaries, and sometimes lawyers much higher up the legal scale, to write or translate more formal documents for them. The abilities of mercers were as varied as those of the scribes they employed. In the top rank were the adventurers or overseas merchants who knew two or more languages with varying competence for the purposes of trade. The lowest level of mercantile competence would have consisted of the *lingua franca* of the cross-channel trade between England and the Low Countries, and certainly no sophisticated or literary expertise. Few of them developed the translator's skills of a Caxton, but Caxton was by no means the only mercer fluent in four languages – English, Dutch, French and Latin – nor was he the only one with diplomatic skills employed by the kings of England.[5] A scribe employed by any of these men would have needed at least the same level of skill as his employer. A mercer who stayed in England and only distributed goods to provincial markets, in contrast, only required the basic skills that recorded day to day expenses, income, and some knowledge of how to set up the documents in a credit transaction.

All merchants were expected to keep certain books for business purposes, and there is no doubt that they did keep them. No account books survive for a fifteenth-century London mercer, but they were endlessly referred to in court cases. What a merchant was *expected* to keep was set out by Jan Ympyn, a merchant of Antwerp in the early 1540s in his 'teach-yourself accounting' manual, which covered the principals of double-entry book-keeping. He repeated much older guidelines as well as Italian sources and attached elaborate exempla of the accounts he

---

4   Commissary Court of London, Guildhall Library (hereafter GL), London, MS 9171; Prerogative Court of Canterbury, The National Archives, PROB 11; Husting Court of the City of London, Corporation of London Records Office (CLRO), HR.

5   A. F. Sutton, *The Mercery of London: Trade, Goods and People, 1130–1578* (Aldershot, 2005), pp. 302–15.

described.[6] The names and number of books kept varied with the size of business and their names varied from one language, probably from one city, to another, and with the passage of time. Some were mentioned in fifteenth-century English lawsuits, and William Caxton was well aware of similar books in the 1480s. Ympyn's Antwerp had long been the favourite trading place for London mercers, and at no time should it be assumed that London merchants lagged behind the practices of their fellow merchants across the channel.

Ympyn's Chapters 3 and 23 set out in brief all the main books required and he discussed each in detail in their own place.[7] The 'great book' or double-entry ledger was by far the largest of all at 300 folios, with its index known as the register, and does not concern us here. The main books were as follows:

> Firste it is nedefull to make a litle long boke to write in the charges of houshold ... Also another long boke wherin shalbe written all small expences of marchandise, as cariage and so furthe, because the principall boke shall not be troubled nor bloted therwith, the whiche costes shalbe somoned every moneth or every mart and set into the Jonall. And yet a litle long boke wherin the Cassier shall daily write what that he laieth out parcell meale as he paieth it or receiveth it ....

A 'Memoriall boke' was for 'all maner of thynges that daily doth happen', payments, receipts, delivery of bills, wages, carriage, etc. It could be kept by the merchant, his wife or servants and was to be written up directly after the event recorded, and it was essential for any man 'troubled with greate affaires ... as in a compaignie or felow ship' with different matters managed by different persons, the master, his wife or factor.[8] 'And if it be one that sendeth muche wares into diverse countrees then must he kepe a boke of the contentes of every packe and bale and their Numero and what marke thei are marked withall', maintained by the factor concerned. Another 'smaller' book recorded the daily retail sales of a shop,

---

6 Jan Ympyn Christoffels, *Nieuwe instructie ende bewijs der looffelijcker consten des rekenboecks, 1543*, facsimile Scolar Press (London, 1979); French translation published by his widow Anne Swinters, *Nouvelle instruction et remonstration de la tres excellente science du livre de compte ...* (Antwerp, 1547). An English translation by an unknown person was printed 1547 and survived in one copy in Estonia (whereabouts now unknown), of which the treatise (not the exempla) was published by P. de Waal, 'De Englesche vertaling van Jan Ympyn's *Nieuwe Instructie*', *Economisch-Historisch Jaarboek*, 18 (1934), 1–58. And see R. De Roover, *Jan Ympyn. Essai historique et technique sur le premier traité flamand de compatabilité (1543)* (Antwerp, 1928, repr. 1946), and his 'Een en ander over Jan Ympyn Christoffels den schrijver van de eerste Nederlandsche handleiding over het koopmansboekhouden', *Tijdschrift voor Geschiedenis*, 52 (1937), 163–79. I am indebted to Livia Visser-Fuchs for assistance with the Dutch.

7 The translations generally accord well but there are oddities in the English version of ch. 23. All quotations are from chs 3, 23, Waal, pp. 19–20, 49–50; modern usage of u and v has been adopted.

8 Ch. 4 expands on this book (Waal, pp. 20–21).

and was often kept by the merchant's apprentice, wife, maid servant or factor, who served in the shop, over whom Ympyn advised the master keep strict watch.[9]

Most important for those interested in more consciously literate and composed texts than in accounts – apart from the potentially interesting Memorial Book – was what the English translator rendered as, 'Another square boke wherin shalbe written the copy of letters and suche other thynges, and therupon shal ye write: The copies of letters, etc.' Between the Memorial Book and this square book, it is clear that Ympyn expected the merchant to jot down memoranda of events and send news to his correspondents,[10] for business depended on news of the change of kings, changes in laws which affected trade, storms and loss of goods, etc, as the surviving letters of the Hanse towns, for example, testify. Merchants also needed to remember things 'For men have not Angels wittes, but maie forget'.[11] In other words records of events were considered part of merchants' daily work – and what might start as a newsletter could end up embedded in what modern historians call 'chronicles'. Over 150 years earlier Chaucer had called merchants the 'fathers of tidings and tales' simply because their very business depended on news from other cities and countries.[12] In 1482 Caxton deplored that 'there can not be founden in these dayes but fewe that wryte in theyr regystres such thynges as dayly happen and falle ...'; he recorded his fruitless search in his epilogue at the end of Book 7 of Higden's *Polychronicon* to explain the inadequacies of his continuation up to 1460.[13] Perhaps Londoners had simply failed to keep such registers as Caxton said; perhaps each generation destroyed their predecessors' books of business.

There is no doubt that mercers of London kept accounts. The safety of a man's soul and its passage through purgatory depended on the payment of his debts, a regular injunction laid upon all executors in a man's will, and the executors' ability to perform this duty depended upon their having reliable account books to refer to. John Boton, one of the few mercers who wrote out his own will in the fifteenth century said that his debts must be paid 'whiche dettes ye shall fynde in my boke of accomptes'. John Trussbut desired that reasonable satisfaction be made for his offences over selling goods testified to by entries in his 'journal'.[14] John Ellis relied on his books and bills to reveal to his wife and sole executor all the debts owed to him under obligations and statutes staple. Sir John Stokton specifically referred to his book of debts in order to pardon a man a debt, and Alderman John Fisher referred to his 'boke of dettours';[15] while Stephen Gibson remitted to James

---

[9] For the management of a retail shop, Ch. 15 (Waal, pp. 35–9).

[10] Dutch: *een tamelijck groot boeck aen een ghenayt en viercant.*

[11] Waal, p. 21.

[12] *The Man of Law's Tale*, lines 129–30.

[13] N. F. Blake (ed.), *Caxton's Own Prose* (London, 1973), p. 132.

[14] Boton: PROB 11/5, f. 43v (1464). Trussbut: PROB 11/3, ff. 211–12v, esp. f. 211v (1439).

[15] Ellis: PROB 11/10, f. 153r–v, esp. f. 153v (1494). Stokton: PROB 11/6, ff. 71v–75, esp. f.

Yarford the third penny of all the debts owed to him on condition Yarford 'make up my perfite rekenyng at Cales of all my bookes in London'.[16] These books were equally essential to the successful pursuit of legal cases: in 1479 Roger Basford's 'bokes of rekenyng' and Thomas Rivers' books are referred to during disputes settled within the Mercers' Company, and in 1498 the dispute between John Burton and Thomas Quadring referred to their books.[17] Sir Ralph Verney's large green journal was a main source in a suit waged against his chief executor, and extracts survive.[18] The brothers and partners, John and Thomas Warren, shared a merchant's mark and an account book which ended up in chancery. 'Greffs, clayme and misrekenyng' between mercers and their factors were commonplace and frequently settled by reference to the books maintained by the parties.[19] Jan Ympyn noted that 'negligence of kepyng of bokes hath caused more striefe in lawe and variance of children and frendes then any one thyng in the world: Servantes and factors have undone their Masters, riche men hath sodenly become beggers ...'.[20]

Apart from the myriad business books maintained by individual mercers in the fifteenth century, of which not a jot remains, there were the books maintained by the Mercers' Company, for the worship of their chapel and the day to day business of the company. Of these a fraction survives. There were current accounts, fair copies of the previous years' main accounts of the three senior wardens, and from 1442 separate renter wardens' accounts concerned with the company's landed estate. There were the rolls of members' names which recorded their seniority and dates of entry into the liveried class.[21] In 1436 William Haxey contributed 6s. 6d. for twelve quires of parchment for a new Ordinance Book, and the company had it bound by a stationer (unnamed) for 2s. 9½d. By 1453 annual paper 'pamphlets', as they were called, of the minutes or acts of court meetings were kept in English by the beadle. A great book of evidences existed for Whittington's lands marked 'C' and another for John Abbot's estate; in 1487 there was mention of a 'great book of deeds', and by 1519 there was a cartulary of John Colet's estate. By 1527 a 'book of testaments' of benefactors was maintained, and the literary and book-minded John Coke had begun a 'register' of members.[22] The company also had reference

72v (proved 1473). Fisher: PROB 11/7, ff. 140v–42, esp. f. 141v (1485).

16   PROB 11/8, f. 314v–15v, esp. f. 315 (made 1485).

17   *Acts of Court of the Mercers' Company 1453–1527* (hereafter *AC 1453–1527*), ed. L. Lyel and F. Watney (Cambridge, 1936), pp. 113, 134, 656.

18   Verney: PRO, Chancery Proceedings, C 1/230/53. The 'journal' was part of the double-entry system (Chs 8–9; Waal, pp. 55–7). Verney's wealth suggests his journal was of the type described by Ympyn.

19   Warren: C 1/34/1–2. Shore against Salford, *AC 1453–1527*, pp. 66–7 (quotation, p. 66); Shelly and Ryver against Wyndout, ibid., pp. 133–4.

20   Waal, p. 58.

21   Mercers' Company (hereafter MC), Wardens' Accounts 1348, 1390–1464 (hereafter WA), ff. 138, 149.

22   WA, f. 126 (1436). Sutton, *Mercery of London*, pp. 172–81, 521–2.

books: two quires containing the 'divers liberties granted to the citizens of London' at a cost of 8s. 4d., and a book of twenty quires containing the statutes of the realm.[23]

Those mercers who made a career of company office cut their teeth on the demanding post of renter warden, who had to supervise the collection of rents, repairs to the company's property and all the attendant problems of tenants. He and the rentgatherer and beadle would have kept rough accounts and these had to be audited. The other three wardens had greater experience, of whom the most senior was an alderman and increasingly called the master; each had their own duties for which he accounted. An outside scrivener was employed to make a fair copy of all the final and audited accounts of the year's business if the company beadle did not do it. In their capacity as leaders of the London adventurers the Mercers made use of royal secretaries or Guildhall clerks to draft letters to illustrious correspondents abroad, from the duke and duchess of Burgundy down, or to set out a bill to the English parliament. In the Low Countries, where the Adventurers had their headquarters, the governor of the Adventurers, of whom Caxton is the most famous, could not have operated without a permanent clerk.

The company employed the best clerks available for the task in hand, and not only hand-writing skills were demanded but also the ability to write elegant or effective English, French, Latin or Dutch. At the other end of the spectrum individual and ordinary mercers made use of run-of-the-mill scriveners who touted for business in a local church or their shop if they had one – but they turn up less regularly in the surviving records.[24] Let us first consider the men employed by the company itself. Employed is the key word, for though some employees were 'decayed' mercers who had fallen on hard times – and it must be remembered often well-versed in record-keeping – others were trained scribes who did piece-work as paid menials. Only a few of these men went on to better things: John Stodeley, scrivener, who became an MP, or the sixteenth-century clerk of the company, John Coke, who moved into a crown office at Westminster.[25]

The company's common servant is first mentioned in the accounts of 1348, and one man was probably all that was needed to do the wardens' bidding, summon men to meetings, keep the hall, and maintain simple accounts. As yet the company had no landed estate. By 1390 he was known as the beadle and scribal duties were beginning to be more burdensome. The first known beadle was William Willesdon (by 1390–1406), almost certainly a 'decayed' mercer, for in 1384 he can be glimpsed as one of several mercers disciplined for speaking against the mayor and aldermen.[26] The salary was £2 12s. a year with clothing and some

---

[23] WA, f. 188v (1456–7).

[24] Compare booktrade, Christianson, *Directory*, pp. 30–32.

[25] *The Commons 1422–1504*: Stodeley; I am grateful to the History of Parliament Trust for permission to cite this. For Coke, Sutton, *Mercery of London*, pp. 387–8.

rewards, raised to £3 18s. in 1411–12. He was responsible for collecting rents from the company's estate until an under-beadle or rentgatherer joined the staff in or before 1422–3 at £2 with 3s. 4d. costs.[27] Anglo-French remained the language of the Mercers' accounts until 1458–59, although English had broken out earlier and undoubtedly had become the norm for subordinate accounts before that date. Who turned the final or audited account into Anglo-French is not certain. Outside scriveners were regularly employed to make the fair copy, but mercers with such skills might be used for secrecy: Martin Kelom copied the 1376 ordinances in 1404 and received the usual fee for such work, 3s. 4d.; he was later renterwarden, 1413–14.[28] Some well-known scriveners were employed briefly: John Stodeley, famous for composing a surviving newsletter and a warden of the Scriveners in 1446 as well as an MP, wrote up the accounts 1439–41; and Robert Bale, another warden of the Scriveners (1450), wrote the fair accounts 1443–49, drafted awards and indentures, transposed French or Flemish into English, and was rewarded for his advice as well as compositional skills.[29] For letters to go overseas one of the king's secretaries, such as Gervase le Vulre, might be approached, or the clerk of Dr Thomas Kent, clerk of the king's council, a long-standing friend of the Mercers.[30]

It is certain that the company servant or beadle had writing skills: for example Beadle William Rumbold is known to have written up the annual accounts for 1438–9. The development of the job and title of 'clerk' can be credited to the efforts of Beadle Richard Box. By 1456 he had managed to exclude outside scriveners from the annual accounts for the benefit of the 'secretenes del mistier' – it was worth 6s. 8d. a year to him. Box appears to have been a new broom: he kept the common roll (list of members) up to date, and did one-off jobs, such as 'collecting together and writing up the old and new ordinances and divers other bills enrolled by divers persons of this company' in 1456–7. Box's successor, John Pierson, was the first to be appointed with the title of 'clerk', possibly after a term as beadle when Box was pensioned off in 1463 or 1464.[31] Although we lack any personal statement by these beadles and clerks – none left surviving wills – there is

26 *Calendar of Plea and Memoranda Rolls of the City of London 1323–1482* (hereafter *CPMR*), eds A. H. Thomas and P. E. Jones, 6 vols (Cambridge, 1926–61), *1381–1412*, p. 64.
27 Lists of clerks and beadles by Jean Imray and Anne Sutton at MC. *AC 1453–1527*, pp. 50–51.
28 WA, f. 39. Sutton, *Mercery of London*, p. 168.
29 Sutton, 'Robert Bale', *English Manuscript Studies* 14 (2008), pp. 184–6. The copying process explains many trivial errors of date, omission, etc., in the records.
30 Sutton, *Mercery of London*, pp. 251–2, 254, 258, 306.
31 WA 1456–7, f. 188v. *AC 1453–1527*, pp. 658–60. MC, Renterwarden's Accounts 1463–64, f. 47, has Box as an almsman, but compare 1465 (*AC 1453–1527*, p. 281) when Box is still beadle (these acts are misdated and should read 1465). The precise terms of Box and Pierson are difficult to establish; Pierson was admitted to the company in 1469 and died 1498.

little doubt they were much like civic officials of the rank of yeoman or serjeant as regards education and skills, aspirations and consequence.[32]

* * *

For one task at least almost all mercers had to employ a professional scrivener or legal writer, a writer of the court letter. The will was the last written document of a man or woman's life. The examination of 227 commissary court of London and prerogative court of Canterbury wills of mercers, their widows and one daughter, between 1400 and 1499, shows that only six mercers wrote their own wills,[33] and though some must have drafted them on paper or referred to earlier wills made to take care of the dangers of overseas travel, most mercers only collected their thoughts in anticipation of imminent death. They therefore called in a professional scrivener or clerk or cleric of some sort to their deathbed, a search that was conducted necessarily close to the testator's home. Only six scrivener-writers of wills were specifically referred to by name in these wills. Others were concealed among the seventeen scriveners listed as witnesses, as proving the will by their oath, or among the nine who received a small bequest (see table). As mere piece-workers, they were not important enough to warrant mention: it is known, for example, that Robert Bale, scrivener, wrote the wills of Sir William Estfeld and Robert Large, both mayors, and Alderman William Melreth, but this was not mentioned.[34] The evidence of the wills endorses the lowliness of station enjoyed by the average scrivener – his main use was as a witness to the will. Payment for writing a will is equally elusive but Robert Geoffrey left John Carmadyn, clerk of the Bread Street Compter, £3 for him and his children, which included the price of writing his will in 1508.[35] Other payments mentioned in this paper will show scriveners could be well paid, especially if they did more than merely compose the will.

Some scriveners counted as friends and close associates of mercers. Twelve can be found acting as mercers' executors or supervisors: William Grove, an executor of the estate of Richard Whittington, benefactor extraordinary of the city who had single-handed turned the Mercers into the wealthiest company of London; or William Clon who had to do most of the work of Ellis Davy's will in 1456 and received £5.[36] That eminent scrivener, John Stodeley, acted for the equally eminent ex-governor of the Adventurers, Thomas Dunton, in 1460.[37] A trawl of the

32 A. F. Sutton, 'Civic Livery in Medieval London: the Serjeants', *Costume*, 29 (1995), 12–24, esp. pp. 21–2.

33 William Fleet 1444; Robert Baron 1448 (a CC and a PCC will); John Boton 1464; William Bufford 1481; Robert Hallum 1453; Richard Claver 1456. See above n. 4.

34 Sutton, 'Robert Bale', p. 186: he was required as witness in all these cases.

35 PROB 11/16, f. 22r–v. Before 1400 payments, Christianson, 'A Community', p. 213.

36 Davy: PROB 11/4, ff. 28v–29.

37 Dunton: PROB 11/4, ff. 147v–49; Dr Thomas Kent, secretary of the king's council, was Dunton's supervisor, and Thomas Fraunces, clerk and keeper of Guildhall, received 10 mks. Sutton, *Mercery of London*, p. 306. Stodeley, see above.

Table 1: Scribes in the Wills of Mercers, 1400–99

Mercers who write own wills	General use of lawyers or officials	General use of priests	Use of public notaries	Scribes as witnesses	Scribes as executor or supervisor	Scribes specified as the will writer	Scribes as legates	Total references to scribes	Total wills of Mercers, widows and daughters	
4	6	4	2	4	5	4	3	16	84	CC
2	6	6	7	13	7	2	6	30	143	PCC
6	12	10	9	17	12	6	9	46	227	
				7	3			not known	43	HR

Table 2: Parishes of Testators Referring to Scribes in the Mercery Area

Lawrence Old Jewry	Mary Mag. Milk Street	Michael Bassishaw	Mary Aldermanbury	Olave Old Jewry; Stephen Coleman St.	St Pancras	Stephen Walbrook; Antonin	Mary le Bow	All Hallows Honeylane	11 Parishes outside this area	Total
13	5	4	3	2	2	3	2	1	11	46

forty-three mercer wills proved before the court of Husting, 1400 to 1499, adds another seven scribes who were called to witness wills, among whom some were probably also the writers.[38]

The mercers mostly employed scriveners, members of the legal writers' fraternity, for their wills and more formal property deeds and business documents such as bills obligatory or contracts. Most of the tasks demanded of them were mundane and learnt during an apprenticeship which would have reflected the practice of the city's courts and emphasised the London way of doing things. They needed reference books: some they inherited, others they bought or made. Formularies or books of precedents set out the form and phrasing of documents: leases, wills, obligations, conveyances and quitclaims in Latin, or even love letters and proposals of marriage. John Vale's Book falls partly into this category with an emphasis on items in English and of interest to laymen, but as its compiler was a man working within someone else's household and not in his own shop it lacks the urgency and focus of a working man's compilation.[39] Robert Leget, a scrivener used by the mercer, Henry Logan, as a witness and possibly the writer of his will,

[38] The registration process of wills proved before the court of Husting makes more consistent reference to witnesses, but does not always give them designations. All mercer Husting wills have been counted: several of these duplicate a will before PCC or CC; and several mercers made multiple wills for the purposes of land transactions.

[39] *The Politics of Fifteenth Century England: John Vale's Book*, eds M. L. Kekewich, C. Richmond, A. F. Sutton, L. Visser-Fuchs and J. L. Watts (Stroud, 1995), esp. ff. 16–70v.

left his own books of precedents compiled during a thirty-year-long career (1462–93), to those who would find them most useful, his apprentices:[40] his 'thike boke of presydentis with yalowe coveryng and my name writtin uppon the same coveryng' and his 'bokys of presidentis of the gadering of diverrse featis not set in order which boke is reverd within old keveryng of parchemen'. The contrast between these work-books and those to be found in a stationer's shop is marked. The latter was full of examples of books and shorter texts, the subjects varying with the stationer's specialities, waiting to be copied for clients or already copied if the text was short and popular. The messy, serviceable *exempla* books of John Multon are a case in point.[41] The two companies of stationers and scriveners had pronounced differences – Thomas Froddesham was allowed to translate from the Textwriters to the Scriveners in 1439 because of those differences.[42] There survive no early records of the Stationers' Company but there is an early register of the Scriveners with the declarations of members as they were admitted to the company – 'As there is no evidence to the contrary, it must be assumed that the declarations were written by the persons making them'.[43] Scriveners were expected to append their names to the documents they created or copied, many of them were public notaries whose very name and mark authenticated documents, and many documents survive to show they did append their names: their value was as witnesses. This was a status not shared with the bookmakers. Scrivening and bookmaking had pronounced differences and their practitioners were well aware of them, however much they were closely related by the basic skill of writing. Poorer practitioners of both crafts would have needed to take what piece-work they could find; members of either company might have skills learned in the royal departments of chancery or privy seal rather than by simple apprenticeship with a member;[44] and both companies had members who sought security by taking on regular employment with another citizen, a civic office or a school.[45] Both companies benefited from the presence of a few top men of the city in their ranks, but probably that was especially true of the Scriveners, whose legal expertise gave them an entry to well-paid work.[46]

There is space here to recreate the lives of two scriveners who worked for mer-

---

[40] Admitted to Scriveners 1462, *Common Paper*, p. 22. GL, MS 9171/8, f. 58r–v; he had a *Gestis Romanorum*. Christianson, *Directory*, pp. 120–21.

[41] *John Vale's Book* (see n. 39), pp. 107–10.

[42] Compare Bylton's stock, Christianson, *Directory*, pp. 81–2; Froddesham, p. 108; for the tightening up of regulation, pp. 22–3.

[43] *Common Paper*, p. xiv.

[44] Steer, *A History*, pp. 3–4. Christianson, *Directory*, p. 41.

[45] Below: Woodcock. Christianson, *Directory*, p. 28.

[46] G. Pollard, 'The Company of Stationers before 1557', *The Library*, 4th ser. 18 (1937), 13. Christianson, 'Bookbinders', 47. The advent of printing may have made it possible for stationers to make serious money.

cers, both long lived and one a city official. John Parker was the scrivener most frequently mentioned in mercer wills between 1471 and 1494: six times in wills proved before the ecclesiastical courts and once before Husting.[47] His fifty-year career was successful but over-burdened with troubles according to his report. He subscribed to the ordinances of the Scriveners in 1442, was clerk of works for London Bridge in the 1440s and 1450s, and was well established in his own business by 1467 when he witnessed with the common clerk, William Dunthorn – and probably wrote – the Husting will of John Andrew which set up Thomas Chalton's chantry;[48] in 1471 he attracted a generous payment of £10 from Thomas Rich who asked him to make a reckoning of the estates of Thomas's father, Richard, and of Thomas himself, in order to ensure that Thomas's responsibilities for his father's soul were completed after his own death; Parker was then to make copies of his calculations for Thomas's executors and certain clerics.[49] Parker was therefore a man of administrative ability, providing invaluable service to families and individuals.[50] His appointment as an executor, with a fee of £20, by Alderman John Fisher in 1485 is additional proof of his talents,[51] as is his role as a feoffee, alongside the common clerk of the city, of Thomas Hill the wealthy grocer and mayor who died in 1485.[52] Otherwise he witnessed the wills of the mercers, Ralph Kemp (1485), William Pratte, the friend of Caxton (1486), and John Reynold (1492), and the mercer widow, Margaret Agmondesham (1494), all of which he may have drawn up and written.[53] He lived in St Mary Colechurch parish, possibly on the corner of Cheapside and Ironmonger Lane by 1486,[54] and much of his trade came from this area. His origins are not discernible – the only place outside London mentioned in his will was Morden, Surrey – but he was not without contacts with the provinces: for example he prosecuted a scrivener of Clare, Suffolk, for 40s. in 1484.[55]

---

[47] Compare Richard Lindsey (5 refs) and John Stodeley (2). For Lindsey, Sutton, 'Hospital of St John of Acre' (see n. 2), pp. 215–16, 221 n. 112.

[48] *Common Paper*, p. 22. C. P. Christianson, *Memorials of the Book Trade of Medieval London. The Archives of Old London Bridge* (Cambridge and Woodbridge, 1987), p. 35. Andrew: CLRO, HR 203 (15).

[49] Parker is not in Richard's will; Thomas's will, PROB 11/6, f. 147r–v; made 1471 when Thomas died but not proved until 1475.

[50] E.g. in 1474 he was a surety for the estate of orphans, *Calendar of the Letter Books of the City of London, L*, ed. R. R. Sharpe (London, 1912), p. 114.

[51] Fisher: PROB 11/7, ff. 140v–42.

[52] D. Keene and V. Harding, *Historical Gazetteer of London before the Great Fire*, vol. 1, *Cheapside* (Cambridge, 1987) (hereafter K&H), 145/36A (pp. 785–6 in single-space printout), in 1480s.

[53] Kemp: PROB 11/6, ff. 244–45. Pratte: PROB 11/7, f. 192r–v. Reynold: PROB 11/9, ff. 96–98v. Agmondesham: PROB 11/10, ff. 44v–45v.

[54] K&H, 105/13–15 (p. 470).

[55] Robert Clerk, PRO, Plea Roll, Common Pleas, CP 40/890, 472.

His fellow scriveners recognised his quality by electing him a warden in 1481,[56] and it is further attested by the success of at least one of his apprentices, Morgan Williams, the public notary.[57] John Parker died neither content nor rich, however, according to the will which he wrote himself in English in 1493 when he was in his seventies. He called himself scrivener and public notary, and the 'elder' to distinguish himself from his scrivener son, and chose the saints of his local parish churches as the special recipients of his soul: 'swete saint Marie' and 'marters' Laurence, Katherine, Thomas Becket, and 'the swete' St Michael 'provost of Paridys'. He chose to be buried in St Thomas of Acre, the patron of his small, first floor parish church of St Mary Colechurch already over-crowded with the dead. He remembered local fraternities of St Katherine and St Margaret and the Scriveners' common box, but his bequests were few and small. He blamed his three adult children for his poverty as

> right chargeable and costlewe unto me aswele while they were of their tendre ages as sithen they cam to theyr lauful ages by dyverse and many sondry meanes, I being but a pore handy crafty man and have borne gret losses and charges dyverse tymes in my dayes and now in grete age not so lusty to labour for my lyving as I was in my yonge and florisshing daies ....

He left them each God's blessing and his own and 40s. on condition none of them troubled his executors or his wife. He also had two children who were still minors 'and have put me as yet to no further charge of cost than naturall and paternal love hath it required'. The residue of his estate went to 'Johanne my true and wel-beloved wife, she to do hire own voluntary wil and fre disposicion therwith'.[58] If Parker ever engaged in literary pursuits or copied literary texts they have yet to be found and identified – he had a career which can be likened to that of a modern family solicitor – but he has left one composition in the English language behind him at least.

More eminent was Henry Woodcock who operated for most of his career from the Poultry Compter, a thriving centre from which mercers might draw a man with writing skills.[59] It was the business hub for many men in legal employment, ranging from humble scriveners to the up and coming lawyer destined to be recorder of the city and a royal justice, who represented plaintiffs, defendants, prisoners,

---

[56] *Common Paper*, p. 12.

[57] *Common Paper*, p. 13, and see p. 24; it is not clear whether Morgan was the apprentice of John Parker the father or son.

[58] His son and namesake subscribed the ordinances 1494, *Common Paper*, p. 24. PROB 11/10, ff. 106v–07; made 1 June 1493 and proved 8 Oct. 1494; executors: Robert Harryson clerk and the widow, Joan.

[59] E.g. John Rede, clerk of the paper in a Compter, probably the Poultry, by Sept. 1452 when he received a gift of goods and chattels from the young William Caxton, A. F. Sutton, 'Caxton was a Mercer', *England in the Fifteenth Century*, ed. N. Rogers, Harlaxton Medieval Studies, iv (Stamford, 1994), p. 122 and n. 12.

debtors or creditors. A compter was a cross between a modern police-station and court-house, although the actual court sessions were held at Guildhall where the undersheriff was the judge.[60] The senior man of the clerical staff was the secondary, followed by the clerk of the paper, and four to six clerks whose numbers the city tried regularly to control.[61] Compter officials were greatly valued by the mayor and aldermen and especially the sheriffs whom they served more directly: the goldsmith and past mayor, Sir John Shaa, gave Secondary Woodcock a ring weighing an ounce of gold, and Woodock was equally useful to Robert Tate and his brother, Sir John Tate, both mercers, aldermen and past mayors, performing 'dyvers other labours and wrytynges' as well as acting as the supervisor of Sir John's will.[62]

Henry Woodcock subscribed to the ordinances of the Scriveners in 1471,[63] and his early career followed a similar course to that of Parker: he was feoffee of John Parys pewterer in 1474; his oath proved the will of Dame Alice Wiche in 1476; and he was an executor of one of John Donne's wills in the same year.[64] He had 'arrived' by the time he was a warden of the Scriveners, with John Moorcock, in 1478; he served again in 1490 with Edmund Tasburgh, his clerk of the paper,[65] and in 1498 he was senior warden again. During his term the Scriveners' Company met in his great place on the north side of Bucklersbury and the subjects discussed can be taken to reflect his concerns. Most important was the decision to scrutinise the expertise of apprentices in grammar; any boy who failed was to be sent to grammar school and his master admonished. They were

> to be competently erudite and lerned in the bokes of pervula, gendres, declynysons, preterites and supynes, equivox and sinonimes.[66]

Such competence was essential to any scrivener seeking the security of a post in the compters or Guildhall. It is not surprising that a secondary of a compter should have advocated this regulation and overseen its acceptance, and Woodcock's own will of 1516 proves the sophistication of his Latin.

[60] R. B. Pugh, *Imprisonment in Medieval England* (Cambridge, 1968), pp. 109–11, 185–91.
[61] In 1486 Woodcock was secondary and Edmund Tasburgh the clerk of the paper, with 6 clerks, *L*, p. 236.
[62] Shaa: Woodcock's will below. A. F. Sutton, *A Merchant Family of Coventry, London and Calais: The Tates, c. 1450–1515* (London, 1998), pp. 33, 43 n. 6, 51, 62.
[63] *Common Paper*, p. 23.
[64] *CPMR 1458–82*, pp. 83–5, 101. CLRO, HR 213 (37). In 1499 Woodcock and John Rede, notary, and one of his regular associates at the compter, witnessed the will of Thomas Wyndout mercer, PROB 11/12, ff. 28v–29. In 1500 he was an executor of the serjeant at law, Richard Heigham (who had also bought land in Ilford from him), *The Visitation of the County of Suffolke by William Hervey*, ed. J. J. Howard, 2 vols (London, 1876), vol. 2, pp. 254–6.
[65] *Common Paper*, pp. 12, 13.
[66] 12 Jan. 1498, *Common Paper*, pp. x–xi, 49–52. Steer, *History*, p. 11 nn. 14–17.

He described himself as *scriptor lettere curialis*; he did not refer to his post of secondary.[67] Unsurprisingly the will is in Latin, but there are many personal touches and the details of his landed estate alone prove how successful a London scrivener could become; it also reveals that Woodcock, like Parker, had a troublesome son and heir. Several clauses prove his piety: he was to be buried in his tiny parish church of St Benet Sherhog, across the Poultry from the compter, in the place beneath the tomb of Jesus Christ, in other words the Easter Sepulchre of the church. His burial and month-mind were to be 'honest' in the sound mercantile tradition of the *Book of Good Manners*,[68] *absque aliquo vestito nigro de novo dando vel fiendo, et absque pompa vel ulla solempnitate fiendo*. He established a one-year chantry for himself, his family dead and a few others.[69] He had a special devotion for St Mary Magdalen and possessed a silver-gilt and enamel covered cup made in the form of the saint's box of ointment (*ad simulitudine pixidis beate Marie Magdalene*). He possessed a fragment of the True Cross enclosed in a gold cross decorated with pearls and the signs of the Five Wounds, on which were written the words 'Here is hidden part of the True Wood which brings Salvation' (*meam crucem de auro cum quinque vulneribus domini nostri Iesu Christi super eandem operatis ac cum quattour perulis eidem cruce fixatis et una alia magna perula ad eandem pendentem super quam quidem crucem taliter scriptum est 'veri salutiferi pars hic est abdita ligni'*). His devotion to the cult of the Five Wounds was also expressed by his bequest of five nobles to five persons in their honour. Another devotional possession was a gold ring made in imitation of a rosary (*ad simulitudinem unius paris precum*).

He remembered the poor prisoners in his compter with 40*s*., and the Scriveners' Company with £20. His only surviving son, George, was the main heir – receiving the great place on Bucklersbury and substantial property in Kent and Surrey – but the provision for George's wife and the fact that George was not an executor, indicate that Henry did not think that his son treated his wife as he should.[70] Henry's daughter, Elizabeth, and her daughter, received bequests, and Elizabeth's husband, Hugh Reading, was an executor. One of his most interesting bequests went to Dame Elizabeth Reed, widow of Sir Bartholomew, goldsmith and once mayor. He gave her a choice between his alabaster table designed to stand on an altar – unfortunately no subject is given – and his hand-written vellum manuscript of the 'Pilgrimage of the Soul' (*librum meum in pargameno scriptum tractantem de peregrinacione anime*). Had he written it himself as a pious relaxation from legal forms?

---

67   All following details from will: PROB 11/18, ff. 102r–v; proved 22 Feb. 1516.
68   Sutton, 'Caxton was a Mercer', pp. 141–6.
69   See also his additional will, *Calendar of Wills Proved in the Court of Husting* (hereafter *CWH*), ed. R. R. Sharpe, 2 vols (London, 1889–90), vol. 2, p. 622.
70   *CWH*, vol. 2, p. 622. George died 1522, *CWH*, vol. 2, p. 629, and duplicate PROB 11/18, f. 24r–v.

It seems that mercers expected their scribes, scriveners and clerks to be at least as competent as themselves in languages and accounts. Many of these employees remained unknown and poorly rewarded, but some became masters of successful businesses in the legal 'solicitor's' line. It was difficult to rise above humble beginnings and maintain a good position. There was, however, a great variety of opportunity for a young man of some talent, good professional training and some application, setting out in the craft of scrivener in London or a large provincial city. Robert Bale benefited from schooling at Bury St Edmunds and a good professional grounding in a variety of scripts, he wrote accounts for the Mercers, he acquired acquaintance with some notable lawyers, but he still needed to take whatever piece-work offered and find a wife of property. John Vale was another migrant from Bury St Edmunds, but he took immediate employ with a London merchant and purchased a lifetime's security by loyal service. The busy and long-lived Geoffrey Sperlyng became common clerk of Norwich after acting as an administrator of Sir John Fastolf,[71] and had a career as exemplary as that of Henry Woodcock who died full of years and wealth as secondary of the London Poultry Compter. All these men can also be found using their professional writing skills to copy books of one sort or another: Robert Bale copied the *Musica Ecclesiastica* by Thomas à Kempis in 1469, almost certainly for a client, and thereby trespassed on the preserves of the booktrade; John Vale found time to copy in his everyday working script many types of text into an ordinary parchment-covered book, creating a cross between a formulary and a commonplace book, intended solely for his own use; Geoffrey Sperlyng took time to transcribe the *Canterbury Tales* presumably for his own entertainment and relaxation; and Henry Woodcock perhaps exercised his piety by copying the 'Pilgrimage of the Soul'. But most scriveners, like those employed by mercers, just read, lent, borrowed and discussed books, and left their making and copying to the bookcraft fraternity. The books scriveners were really concerned to write and maintain were the books of their own business. Apart from the formularies already mentioned, these were notebooks recording their daily work – conveyances, obligations or wills – as they did it. These notebooks were the equivalent of the mercers' journals. One survives for an unknown scrivener of Bury St Edmunds in the 1460s and another for an unknown scrivener of London who dealt with many mercers in the 1440s and '50s but failed to record his name.[72]

---

[71] R. Beadle, 'Geoffrey Spirleng (c.1426–c.1494): a Scribe of the *Canterbury Tales* in his Time', *Of the Making of Books: Medieval Manuscripts, Their Scribes and Readers. Essays Presented to M. B. Parkes*, eds P. R. Robinson and R. Zim (Aldershot, 1997), pp. 117–46.

[72] Bale, Sutton, 'Robert Bale', pp. 180–206; Vale: *Vale's Book*, pp. 103–12; Spirleng see n. 71 above. A. E. B. Owen, 'A Scrivener's Notebook from Bury St Edmunds', *Archives* 14 (1979), 16–22 (now Cambridge University Library, Add. 7318); and BL, MS Royal 17.B. XXVII.

The variety of their work comes into focus and the comparative low status of the scrivener and writer of court letter, although this article has emphasised some high-flyers. Perhaps these are the most important facts discovered. Most scriveners were rendered invisible by their low status – they were too insignificant to be named even in the documents they were paid to compose or copy, as the accounts and wills of mercers prove. Most were as insignificant as the modern typist (female) – they resemble the 'temps' in particular, for they had no security of employment unless they took a post with a wealthy merchant like a John Vale and earned a job for life with loyalty. The tendency of modern commentators is to accord the medieval scribe (male) a status higher than that of the modern typist (female) because they were men, and this can be misleading. These average scriveners were like the book-scribes whom Professor Pearsall has recently described as copying with care, accuracy and occasional ingenuity but 'no more effort of thought than is immediately necessary'.[73] They were average and insignificant. Only special talents, as a penman, composer of legal documents or administrator, enabled such a man to become a well-paid servant of a great mercer, a sought-after legal consultant, or an honoured city official.

[73]   D. Pearsall, 'The Organisation of the Latin Apparatus of Gower's *Confessio Amantis*: the Scribes and Their Problems', *The Medieval Book and a Modern Collector: Essays in Honour of Toshiyuki Takamiya*, eds T. Matsuda, R. A. Linenthal and J. Scahill (Woodbridge, 2004), p. 112.

Thomas Gascoigne's Biographies

MISHTOONI BOSE

Between 1434 and 1457, Thomas Gascoigne (1403–58), Doctor of Theology and Chancellor of the University of Oxford, compiled his longest work, the *Liber Veritatum*.[1] Although its closest generic affiliations are with the *compilatio* and the *distinctio*, this work, now extant in only one copy and filling two folio volumes of nearly seven hundred pages each, could be regarded not only as a theological dictionary, but also as a 'Dictionary of National Biography' for late-medieval England, so plentiful are its vignettes of contemporary and other figures of historical importance. These include 'pungent descriptions of notables such as bishops Wykeham, Beaufort, Waynflete, and Pecok' as well as John Wyclif, Thomas Arundel, George Neville, Henry VI and, no less significantly, Gascoigne himself.[2] But as becomes clear from his repeated and hostile treatment of Reginald Pecock, the ultimately disgraced bishop of Chichester, and of Pecock's patron, William de la Pole, duke of Suffolk, these are partial, carefully-selected portraits in which Gascoigne has vested a high degree of anti-Lancastrian animus. Biography and autobiography are

[1] The *Liber Veritatum* is extant as Oxford, Lincoln College, MSS. Lat. 117 and 118. Passages quoted here are taken from *Loci e Libro Veritatum. Passages selected from Gascoigne's Theological Dictionary Illustrating the Condition of Church and State 1403–1458*, ed. James E. Thorold Rogers (Oxford, 1881) – henceforth 'Rogers, *Loci*'. Unless otherwise acknowledged, all translations from Gascoigne are my own. I am grateful to the President and Fellows of Magdalen College, Oxford, and to the Bodleian Library, for permission to quote from manuscripts in their respective collections, and I am particularly grateful to Mrs. Hilary Pattison and to Dr Christine Ferdinand for facilitating access to Magdalen College, Oxford, MS 93 (compiled by John Dygoun and containing Gascoigne's life of St. Jerome). On Gascoigne, see Christine von Nolcken, 'Gascoigne, Thomas', in *Oxford Dictionary of National Biography*, 60 vols (Oxford: Oxford University Press, 2004), 21: 587–9; A. B. Emden, *A Biographical Register of the University of Oxford to A.D. 1500* (Oxford, 1989), pp. 745–8; Winifred Pronger, 'Thomas Gascoigne', *English Historical Review* 53 (1938), 606–26 (I): 54 (1939), 20–37 (II). On his place in intellectual life, see R. M. Ball, *Thomas Gascoigne, Libraries and Scholarship* (Cambridge, 2006) and 'The Opponents of Bishop Pecok', *Journal of Ecclesiastical History* 48 (1997), 230–62; Jeremy Catto, 'Theology after Wycliffism', in *The History of the University of Oxford, vol. 2: Late Medieval Oxford*, eds J. I. Catto and Ralph Evans (Oxford, 1992) pp. 263–80 (especially 271–2, 274).

[2] Douglas Wurtele, 'The Penitence of Geoffrey Chaucer', *Viator* 11 (1980), 335–59 (343–4).

threaded continuously through the *Liber* and elsewhere in Gascoigne's remaining works, and his repeated self-naming far exceeds that of medieval vernacular writers from Chrétien de Troyes and Christine de Pizan to William Langland and Thomas Hoccleve. He also exhibits the sensibility of a chronicler, and, where possible, of an assiduous eye-witness and oral historian, priding himself on having secured biographical testimonies from men such as John Orle, Pecock's chaplain. A codicologist and zealous patristics scholar as well as an eye-witness, he is equally zealous in noting down where and when he sees particular works, such as those of Scotus or Grosseteste, from which he transcribes so assiduously. It was as a repository of records of contemporary events that the *Liber* was valued by its nineteenth-century editor, Thorold Rogers. But Rogers' assertion that 'there is little to interest any reader in the merely theological part of the work' is utterly misleading.[3] The 'theological part' – indeed, the theological perspective – is inseparable from Gascoigne's interpretation of contemporary events and persons, both in the *Liber* and elsewhere in his writings. In this essay, therefore, I will concentrate, firstly, on elucidating the importance of biography and autobiography in expressing Gascoigne's distinctive clerical subjectivity; and, secondly, on placing that subjectivity in its immediate historical context.[4]

First, however, it is necessary to address the genre and organisational principles of the *Liber*. Gascoigne has produced a book that does not fit any of the generic labels – chronicle, preaching manual, dictionary – that might legitimately be attached to it. The *Liber* is thematically paratactic: contemporary events and scriptural exegesis are yoked together without any attempts being made to prioritise them; the heading *episcopus*, for example, contains material that, without warning, swerves into what might initially be read as digressions into the biography of one notably transgressive bishop (Pecock) whose case was hardly typical. Nevertheless, the organising principles of the work were derived from long-established scholastic practices. As R. M. Ball notes, it has many of the characteristics of a private commonplace book, but its creativity is descended from that of the *distinctio* and the *compilatio*.[5] These two expressions of Gascoigne's creativity were obliquely noted by Winifred Pronger, who observed that 'the fact of the material [in the *Liber*] being second-hand is not nearly so important as the fact that the selection of it is plainly deliberate. [Gascoigne's] position is that of a critic.'[6] In the first place, the book is a collection of *distinctiones* such as might be used by a preacher, and is thus an appropriate choice of genre for one to whom the neces-

---

3   Rogers, *Loci*, vii.
4   Some of the issues addressed in this essay are briefly adumbrated in Mishtooni Bose, 'The Opponents of John Wyclif', in *A Companion to John Wyclif*, ed. Ian Levy (Leiden, 2006), 407–55 (450–53).
5   Ball, *Thomas Gascoigne*, p. 4.
6   'Thomas Gascoigne', II. 33.

sity of preaching was paramount.[7] Christina von Nolcken in the *DNB* describes it as 'a preachers' aid, the *Dictionarium theologicum*, or *Veritates collectae ex s. scriptura et aliorum sanctorum scriptis in modum tabulae alphabeticae*, also known as the *Liber Veritatum*'. As she goes on to explain, the distinctive characteristic of this lengthy book is its organisation of often passionately subjective and (as exemplified in the treatment of figures as diverse as Arundel and Pecock) repetitive materials under the apparently dispassionate headings of the medieval *tabula*: the book is, she notes, 'a collection of theological excerpts under alphabetically (or roughly alphabetically) arranged headings accompanied by a good deal of moral, topical, and often autobiographical commentary of [Gascoigne's] own'. More tellingly still, she notes that the book 'differs from similar predecessors above all in the extent to which it reflects the personality of its compiler; it is indeed because Gascoigne so determinedly wrote himself into the work that much of the information available about him exists'. Elsewhere in this entry, she refers to the book as 'his highly personal *Dictionarium*' and expands on the extent to which Gascoigne seems to have possessed no ordinary degree of authorial self-consciousness:

> Contemporary or near contemporary sigla draw attention to Gascoigne's unusually personal commentary [in the *Liber*]; it is tempting to regard these as being ultimately the work of the compiler, and as originating, at least in part, in Gascoigne's desire to bequeath a lasting version of himself to posterity.

Distinctive it certainly is, but Gascoigne's creativity is, at least in part, a natural culmination of, rather than a notable deviation from, medieval scholastic practices. The alphabetical collection of *distinctiones*, analytical dissertations on the different senses and interpretations of seminal theological keywords, had long been a genre that permitted juxtapositions of the particular and the universal, insisting upon the interpretation of various incidental features of quotidian life according to the moral and eschatological imperatives imposed by the prospect of eternity. The Bodleian Library alone provides several examples of *distinctio*-collections, such as Bodley 4, *Distinctiones theologicae* (or *Summa de virtutibus et vitiis*), written on parchment in the fourteenth century; MS 41 (*Distinctiones theologicae, alphabetice dispositae*) also written in the fourteenth century; and MS 474. This last is a *Speculum laycorum* consisting of an alphabetical list of topics such as virtues and vices, sacraments and other essential elements of the religious life

---

[7]   On *distinctiones*, see Mary H. Rouse and Richard H. Rouse, 'Biblical Distinctions in the Thirteenth Century', *Archives d'Histoire Doctrinale et Littéraire du Moyen Âge* 49 (1974), 27–37 and 'Statim invenire: Schools, Preachers, and New Attitudes to the Page', in *Authentic Witnesses. Approaches to Medieval Texts and Manuscripts* (Notre Dame, Indiana, 1991), pp. 191–219 (first published in 1982); Robert J. Karris, 'St. Bonaventure's Use of *Distinctiones*: His Independence of and Dependence on Hugh of St. Cher', *Franciscan Studies* 60 (2002), 209–50 (p. 210).

(*De amore dei & eius causis; De amore mundi & eius fallaciis*, and so on). Woven into this collection, however, are anecdotes identified with particular Oxfordshire locations, such as one set in the church of St. Mary Magdalen in 1356 (134r), and the more widely-known legend of St. Augustine of Canterbury's visit to Combe (49r–50r) which John Lydgate would later put into poetry. The enterprising mentality that incorporates local anecdotes and legends in discussions of excommunication or penitence is not so far removed from Gascoigne's in the *Liber*, and does much to explain the clerical, and specifically Oxonian, predecessor cultures that ultimately produced him.

Nevertheless, while the *distinctio*-collection for preachers is a useful generic point of departure for the *Liber*, examples of the genre such as these scarcely account for Gascoigne's peculiarly energetic exploitation of its possibilities for both *copia* and associative logic. In addition to having affiliations with long-established scholarly genres, therefore, the *Liber* is also indicative of a new late-medieval mentality that would give rise to free-standing treatises on particular topics. Daniel Hobbins has located this process in a broader context, interpreting the growth of the autonomous tract as the chief medium through which late-medieval 'public intellectuals' disseminated their ideas.[8] Gascoigne was, if anything, a 'private' intellectual who does not easily fit even into a modern historiographical category that includes writers as diverse, and even antithetical, as John Wyclif and Jean Gerson. There is, rather, a latent tension between the private and public dimensions of the *Liber*. It occupies an uncertain point at the intersection of private and public spheres, its quasi-objective framework interacting provocatively with its singularly subjective content. This is part of the larger tension at work in the life of one who, on the one hand, sequestered himself for the most part at Oxford, and appears to have been far more adventurous in his pursuit of books than he may have been in the quest for benefices, but who also repeatedly sought to project a distinctive, critical and insistently *engagé* persona in his writings. While the immediate purpose and intended readership of the *Liber* may be inferred indirectly from what can be reconstructed of Gascoigne's compilatory and other literate practices, an example such as the following dramatic anecdote from the end of his life makes absolutely explicit his keen sense of the book's potential for fixing cultural memory. Here this central tension in Gascoigne's life and writing – between scholarly introversion and reformist extraversion – comes fully into focus:

> O how great are your works, Lord God! In this year of Jesus Christ 1457, [in which] you caused many men in England to die by shedding blood through their bones, nostrils, eyes, nails, joints ... namely, in those parts of the body by which they had used horribly to swear oaths – that is, by the eyes, face, side, blood and precious

---

8   'The Schoolman as Public Intellectual: Jean Gerson and the Late Medieval Tract', *American Historical Review* 108 (2003), 1308–37.

heart of Christ, and by the nail-wounds in Christ's hands and feet – from which body-parts many men, in that year of Our Lord's incarnation, shed blood, as *I, author of this book, or manuscript, of collected truths, in the form of a table, know, and have written for the memory of those to come...* (italics mine).[9]

Gascoigne functions here as a castigatory eye-witness with unequivocally public ambitions for his compilation. We will see later in this essay how the recording of lives both ancient and modern was intended to enable him to play this self-appointed, quasi-prophetic role.

Although Gascoigne's compulsive orientation towards the recording of lives has not received sustained scholarly attention, Christina von Nolcken in the *DNB* rightly emphasizes that this was an essential component of his intellectual temperament. She describes him engagingly as 'a medieval schoolman who loved gossip'. The temptation when writing about Gascoigne, however, is to be lured into presenting him merely on such terms, and thus to reproduce a catena of anecdotes in the style of the *Liber*, with special emphasis, perhaps, on the more lurid examples, such a notorious account and moralistic interpretation of the shrivelling of John of Gaunt's genitals after his death.[10] The Gaunt episode is hardly an isolated case. From the perspective of literary history, the anti-Lancastrian orientation of the *Liber* is equally evident in an anecdote ascribing to Chaucer a plangent retraction in which the poet laments, in a manner that inadvertently recalls his hapless Criseyde, his inability to safeguard his posthumous reputation:

> [Chaucer] before his death often cried out, 'Woe is me, woe is me, because I will not be able now to call back or do away with those things that I wickedly wrote about the wicked and truly disgraceful love of men for women, but they will still continue to pass from person to person willy-nilly.[11]

---

9 'O quam magna sunt opera tua, Domine Deus! Hoc anno Xti Jesu 1457, in quo fecisti plurimos homines mori in Anglia emittendo sanguinem per os, per nares, per oculos, per ungues, per juncturas ... scilicet in illis partibus corporis per quas horribiliter jurare consueverant: scilicet per oculos Xti, per faciem Xti, per latera Xti, per sanguinem Xti, per cor Xti preciosum, per clavos Xti in suis manibus et pedibus; in quibus partibus homines plurimi tum illo anno dominicae incarnacionis sanguinem emiserunt, ut ego autor hujus libri, seu scripti, de veritatibus collectis, secundum formam tabulae, novi et pro memoria futurorum haec scripsi ...' (*Loci*, p. 12).

10 This anecdote (printed in Rogers, *Loci*, pp. 136f) has been most recently and conveniently reproduced and discussed in Michael Vaughan, 'Personal Politics and Thomas Gascoigne's Account of Chaucer's Death', *Medium Aevum* 75 (2006), 103–22 (pp. 109, 119–20).

11 'Ante mortem suam saepe clamavit, 've mihi, ve mihi quia revocare nec destruere iam potero illa quae male scripsi de malo et turpissimo amore hominum ad mulieres sed iam de homine in hominem continuabuntur, velim, nolim:' Vaughan, 'Personal Politics', pp. 103, 118 (punctuation of Latin mine; English translation by Vaughan). Vaughan's discussion supersedes Wurtele, 'The Penitence of Geoffrey Chaucer'. Vaughan's broader subject is Gascoigne's hostility to the network of Lancastrians that

From the perspective of ecclesiastical history, moreover, Gascoigne's anti-Lancastrianism finds a focus in his resentment of Thomas Arundel, archbishop of Canterbury. The animus against Arundel is an important and recurrent element in the *Liber*, as two nearly-identical excerpts make clear:

> [T]hat archbishop, who was the cause whereby few or none at all might preach without a licence from a diocesan or metropolitan bishop (for which great prices are exacted, and sums of money given to the bishop) had an obstruction in his throat a while before his death because of a bone lodged there, which he couldn't swallow or spit out; and thus he died from it …. Thus, when the word of God had been thus fettered, the same archbishop Arundel was so struck down in the throat that he was never again able either to swallow or speak, right up until his death; and thus he who had silenced the word of God had his own speech silenced when he wished very much to speak before his death.[12]

Although it is true that Gascoigne's writings are everywhere marked by 'a leading preoccupation' with the 'widespread propagation of orthodox teaching', his voluble disapproval of Arundel's strident brand of religious orthodoxy (which had been most forcefully enunciated in ecclesiastical legislation necessitating the licensing of preachers) brings sharply into focus the nuanced and flexible character of religious life in late-medieval England.[13] The anti-Lancastrianism of which this anti-Arundel obsession is one further example is not confined to the *Liber*, moreover, since Gascoigne elsewhere redacted a notably partisan narrative about the 'martyrdom' under Henry IV of Richard Scrope, archbishop of York, in 1405.[14]

---

included Thomas Chaucer, son of the poet and also de la Pole's father-in-law through the latter's marriage to Alice Chaucer. See also James Dean, 'Chaucer's Repentance: a Likely Story', *Chaucer Review* 24 (1989–90), 64–76; Olive Sayce, 'Chaucer's "Retractions": the Conclusion of the Canterbury Tales and its Place in Literary Tradition', *Medium Aevum* 40 (1971), 230–48. For the Lancastrian dimension of Chaucer's posthumous reputation, see also John M. Bowers, *Chaucer and Langland. The Antagonistic Tradition* (Notre Dame, Indiana, 2007), pp. 183–90.

[12] '[I]lle archiepiscopus, qui causa fuit quod pauci vel nulli praedicarent sine licencia diocesani vel metropolitani, pro qua jam magnae preces fiunt, et eciam pecuniae dantur episcopo, obtrusus fuit diu ante mortem suam in gutture per os descendens in guttur suum, quod numquam potuit deglutire, nec expellere, et sic ex illo moriebatur… … et sic verbo Dei tunc sic alligato, idem archiepiscopus Arundel ita percussus in gutture fuit, quod numquam usque ad mortem suam potuit deglutire nec loqui, et sic, qui verbum Dei lingua sua suspendit, in lingua sua ligatus fuit quando loqui maxime ante mortem optavit:' Rogers, *Loci*, pp. 180–1.

[13] Catto, *History of the University of Oxford*, p. 260. On Arundel's *Provincial Constitutions* (1407–9), the legislation to which Gascoigne objects in this vignette, see Ian Forrest, *The Detection of Heresy in Late Medieval England* (Oxford, 2005), pp. 67–8.

[14] Gascoigne's versions of Scrope's execution appear in the following manuscripts: Oxford, Bodleian Library, MS James 23, ff. 31–2; Oxford, Lincoln College, MS Lat. 54, ff. 17v–18r; and, most substantially, Oxford, Bodleian Library, MS Auct. D. 4.5, ff. 99–107. This last account has been printed in Rogers, *Loci*, pp. 225–9.

Once again, a Lancastrian is punished by sudden and extreme physical decay, as the king succumbs to a precipitate attack of leprosy following his condemnation of Scrope (an element of the narrative that appears to have been narrated to Gascoigne by an eye-witness, Stephen Cobingham).[15] Moreover, despite the self-consciously hagiographic character of this *vita*, surely what particularly commended this particular narrative to Gascoigne, over and above its Yorkshire provenance, is its enumeration of the particular reformist measures in both secular and ecclesiastical spheres that had been advocated by the heroic archbishop, not least the insistence that the King keep his promise to free the English Church from an excessive burden of taxation.[16]

Pronger, focusing on the 'personal bias' of the *Liber*, concluded that 'Gascoigne's denunciations of abuses are now interesting chiefly from an autobiographical point of view. He is not impartial nor is his evidence complete'.[17] This makes him, from her point of view, little more than a faulty historian. But to interpret his autobiographical sensibility as reductive and intellectually parochial is to misread the functioning of that sensibility as part of a distinctive scholastic temperament in which rhetoric is inseparable from the writing and the interpretation of history.[18] Gascoigne's compulsion to locate himself in close relation to what he commemorates functions firstly as a basic verification principle, as is shown, for example, in Oxford, Bodleian Library, MS Lat. theol. e. 33. This is a compilation of Gascoigne's notes on St Bridget of Sweden, to whose cult he was devoted, and on various other theological topics, in an idiom consonant with that of the *Liber*. On

---

[15]   MS Auct. D. 4.5, f. 101r; *Loci*, p. 228.

[16]   The version printed as 'Miscellanea Relating to the Martyrdom of Archbishop Scrope', ed. James Raine, in *Historians of the Church of York*, Rolls Series 71 (London, 1886), II, 304–11, has been studied most extensively by Stephen K. Wright, who has concluded that the account in Oxford, Bodleian Library MS Auct. D. 4.5, although printed in Rogers, *Loci*, did not originate with Gascoigne and is most probably his slightly adapted version of a narrative by Clement Maidstone, a Trinitarian friar ('Provenance and Manuscript Tradition of the Martyrium Ricardi Archiepiscopi', *Manuscripta* 28 (1984), 92–102). Nevertheless Ball (*Thomas Gascoigne*, 29) maintains that Gascoigne supplied Maidstone with the account of Scrope's death, and at present I agree with this. Wright analyses the literary and rhetorical dimensions of the account of Scrope in 'Paradigmatic Ambiguity in Monastic Hagiography: The Case of Clement Maidstone's *Martyrium Ricardi Archiepiscopi*', *Studia Monastica* 28 (1986), 311–42; and on Scrope now see the essays in *Richard Scrope. Archbishop, Rebel, Martyr*, ed. P. J. P. Goldberg (Donington, 2007).

[17]   'Thomas Gascoigne', II.29.

[18]   For a general appraisal of the characteristics of the genres we now call 'biography' and 'autobiography' in this period, see Jay Rubenstein, 'Biography and Autobiography in the Middle Ages', in *Writing Medieval History*, ed. Nancy Partner (London, 2005), pp. 22–41. Rubenstein concentrates on the early Middle Ages, but his remarks are more broadly pertinent: in particular the incidental 'autobiographical moments' that he finds in early medieval works also feature in Gascoigne's writings (26).

ff. 40–41, autobiographical notes are inserted paratactically into the text, with Gascoigne characteristically segueing seamlessly from critical, bibliographical and codicological observations to an insistent self-inscription that almost includes an epitaph:

> Thus my Lord of Lincoln, Doctor Robert Grosseteste on the Psalter of David, on Psalm 68 in his own exposition, written with his own hand, and thus he wrote on the Psalter up until Psalm 100 inclusive, and this work of his, written thus in his own hand, saw I, Thomas Gascoigne, son and heir of Richard Gascoigne, sometime lord of the manor of Hunslet in the diocese of York; and this work of my Lord of Lincoln, which he wrote in his own hand [is] at Oxford among the Friars Minor, and registered in the convent library … and in the year of our Lord 1445 I saw this work and then wrote this. In the year of Jesus Christ one thousand four hundred and x, died Thomas Gascoigne, called to be a priest and doctor of Theology, born in the county of York in the year 1403, son and heir of Richard Gascoigne, sometime lord of the manor of Hunslet in that same county.[19]

As Christina von Nolcken points out, this is further evidence that Gascoigne wanted 'to create … a version of himself': here, with dramatic self-consciousness, he 'even writes in his own obit, leaving a space for the year in which this would take place'. The narrative thus moves inwards, narrowing in its focus from Grosseteste and his theological insights to Gascoigne as codicologist, then to Gascoigne's background and finally to his anticipated death. By contrast, another vignette works outwards, starting with Gascoigne himself and his immediate environment and working up into a celebration of the repelling of the Ottoman army at the Battle of Belgrade in 1456. This not only situates the particularities of Gascoigne's life within the broader and dramatic picture of contemporary European history, but also enables him to conclude with some criticism of the episcopacy that is, as we shall see, a typical focus of many of his anecdotes:

> And Thomas Gascoigne, of the diocese of York, called to be a doctor of Theology in Oxford, know these things and heard them in Oxford, and saw them in the letters of the aforesaid nobleman [John Hunyadi], decorated with the seal of his coat of arms, and preached a sermon in the presence of the university, in a general procession there, with the *Te Deum* sung in its entirety, in the church of the Blessed

---

[19] 'Hec dominus lincolniensis doctor robertus grosseteste super psalterium david super psalmum 68 in exposicione sua propria et propria manu sua scripta et sic scripsit super psalterium usque ad psalmum 100 inclusive et hoc opus suum sic scriptum manu sua propria vidi ego Thomas Gascoigne filius et heres ricardi Gascoigne domini quondam manorii de hunsslet eboracensis diocesis et hoc opus domini lincolniensis quod propria manu sua scripsit et oxonie inter fratres minores et registratus in libraria conventus … et anno Christi 1445 hoc opus vidi et hoc tunc scripsi. Anno iesu Christi millesimo xxxx [*gap inserted for date of Gascoigne's death*] obit Thomas Gascoigne vocatus sacerdos & doctor theologie natus in comitatu eboraci 1403 anno Christi, filius & heres quondam ricardi Gascoigne domini manorii de hunsslet in eodem comitatu quondam.'

Frideswide, virgin; and I neither know nor have heard that the bishops of England preached sermons of divine praise for this great divine miracle, but if these bishops have been silent, the stones will cry out – that is to say, ordinary Christian folk will say 'Let every spirit praise the Lord forever'.[20]

Typical of Gascoigne is the dilation of the narrative to accommodate two very different manifestations of religious orthodoxy: that orchestrated by Hunyadi abroad in his opposition to the Turks and that spontaneously articulated by the simple 'stones' of the English church. Caught in the middle, as ever in a Gascoigne anecdote, is a retrograde episcopacy suspected of neglecting its homiletic duties. Thus it is not merely appropriate but absolutely necessary to read the *Liber* as a created text (that is, as a compilation of subjective truths); and the most important motive underlying this compulsive recourse to biographical and autobiographical details – often amounting to no more than brief character-sketches or fragments, rather than fully-fledged, rhetorically sophisticated *vitae* – is a reformist temperament that is as much a part of Gascoigne's intellectual character as was his predilection for patristic scholarship (indeed, as will be seen in the case of his life of St Jerome, these two dimensions were interrelated). His relentlessly critical view of the contemporary English church is crystallised in an autobiographical vignette that is, typically for Gascoigne, plausible at best, but compelling in any case. Once again, consideration of Grosseteste (who haunted the English reformist imagination in the fifteenth century as vividly as he had impressed Wyclif's supporters in an earlier generation) leads Gascoigne to melancholy reflection on the contrast between that bishop's time and his own:

> Things are not now as they were then [*i.e. in Grosseteste's day*]. When Henry VI spoke to me at his castle in Windsor and asked me 'Dr. Gascoigne, why aren't you a bishop?', I told him, 'Lord, I tell you, the state of things in England these days is such that if I wanted to make money hand over fist, I would rather be a good shoemaker than the most learned academic in England;' for as God is my witness, I would rather that many good preachers of God's word multiplied among the English people than [have] all the worldly goods of the richest man in England.[21]

---

[20]   'Et praedicta novit Thomas Gascoigne, Eboracensis diocesis, vocatus doctor Theologiae Oxoniae, qui haec audivit in Oxonia, et vidit in literis praedicti comitis, sigillo armorum suorum sigillatis, et fecit sermonem coram Universitate Oxoniae, in processione ibi generali, cantato ibi 'Te Deum laudamus' usque ad finem, in ecclesia beatae Frideswidae virginis, et non novi nec audivi quod Episcopi Angliae praedicaverunt materiam divinae laudis pro hoc magno miraculo divino, sed si hi episcopi tacuerint, lapides clamabunt, i.e. simplices Xtiani dicent, "omnis spiritus laudet Dominum semper"': Rogers, *Loci*, p. 9.

[21]   '[N]on est nunc sicut tunc fuit; nam Henrico vj[to] dicente et quaerente a me apud Castrum suum Wyndsore: 'Quare', inquit rex, 'non estis vos, doctor Gascoyne, episcopus?' et ego respondi sibi, 'Domine, dico vobis, si cuperem esse pecuniarum multarum fidelem adquisitorem, mallem esse bonus sutor quam scientissimus doctor in Anglia, existente statu in Anglia ut est modernis temporibus; 'testis enim est michi Deus, quod

Liber Veritatum it may have been entitled, but, as this anecdote reveals, the work amounts to much more even than a compilation of subjective truths. Rather, its usefulness for modern scholars is its manipulation of biographical detail in the service of reforming polemic, the latter usually centring on the necessity of improvements in pastoral care or the need for more, and better, preachers. The insistent subjectivity of Gascoigne's writings, as shown in his multiple biographies and autobiographies, is not incidental, haphazard or merely compulsive, but the measured outcome and expression of a vehement and scarcely unique concern with contemporary clerical practices and the possibilities of ecclesiastical reformation along practical, manageable lines. One further example will suffice to establish this: Gascoigne's plangent note on John Stafford, who became archbishop of Canterbury in 1443. The Church is 'desolate', he insists, since it no longer rules over vices by the operation of virtues, by the manifestation of new miracles, and by the communication and dissemination of knowledge. Now, he asserts, lead has been substituted for gold, and in place of the saints of former days the church has given birth to fatuous idiots. He writes about Stafford's life as 'one example among many' of this decadence, pointing out that Stafford was the offspring of an adulterous union and asserting that he in turn had sons and daughters with a nun and had benefited from promotion to the archiepiscopate by papal *fiat* rather than by legitimate election.[22]

I have already stated that Gascoigne's work is situated provocatively on the borders between private and public life, intra- and extramural worlds, since one of the central paradoxes of the *Liber* is the extent to which it looks outward, at events both national and international, contemporary and historical, while nevertheless providing little evidence to suggest that it exerted much influence in Gascoigne's time or afterwards. But this paradox leads us to the nexus of Gascoigne's intellectual and devotional lives: his close temperamental affiliation with St Jerome, another writer in whose life public ambitions and ascetic introversion were complexly interwoven and who is, as Ball has shown, by far the most frequently-cited *auctor* in the *Liber*.[23] Ball has commented that the *Vita Sancti Jeronimi*, now extant in a manuscript written by John Dygoun of Syon, is notably bibliographic.[24] At every stage in his account of the saint's life, Gascoigne identifies his sources, which include Vincent of Beauvais' lengthy account of the saint's life in the *Speculum historiale* and John Andreas' *Jerominianum*. But Gascoigne's primary

---

mallem bonos et plures praedicatores verbi Dei in populo Angliae multiplicari quam omnes divicias temporales quae sunt cum ditissimo homine Angliae': ibid., pp. 176–7.

22 Oxford, Bodleian Library, MS Auct. D. 4.5, f. 104r; Rogers, *Loci*, p. 231.

23 'The Opponents of Bishop Pecok', 262. Gascoigne's life of St Jerome is in Oxford, Magdalen College, MS 93, ff. 226, 233r–236v.

24 Ball points out that this account, written by 1444/5, is 'a scholar's life – no beating his breast with a stone, and no lion' (*Thomas Gascoigne*, p. 7).

sources are Jerome's representations of his life in his epistles and prefaces, and in such works as *De viris illustribus*, as well as one of the lives recorded in turn by Jerome, the *Vita Malchi*, through which the saint was able to commend and promulgate ascetic values and practices as embodied in the life of Malchus. Gascoigne's favourite sources from Jerome are the famous epistles *ad Eustochium* (*Audi Filia*), and *ad Asellam* (*Si tibi putem*), and he also cites the epistles *ad Geruchiam* and *ad Vigilantium* among others. The perspectives of modern Jerome scholars are particularly valuable in illuminating Gascoigne's willing collaboration in Jerome's own self-promotion. Richard J. Goodrich has asserted that 'Jerome existed largely as an image built up in the minds of his readers' and that he devoted an extraordinary amount of effort to 'crafting, projecting and defending his image through his writings.'[25] This goes some way towards explaining his attraction for Gascoigne who, while in no way as prolific, systematic or charismatic as Jerome, nevertheless found in the saint's evocations of the ascetic life and castigation of contemporary priests a compelling combination of preoccupations that spoke directly to his own institutional and pastoral anxieties. In his *vita*, Gascoigne takes care to emphasise the extent to which Jerome was hated by heretics and negligent priests alike, leaving the attentive reader to infer his own thoughts about possible relationships between those two groups, and thus about the validity of Jerome as a prototype for an ascetically- and pastorally-inclined late-medieval reformer.[26] Stefan Rebenich has noted that 'for more than 1,600 years, scholars have been deceived by the picture of the learned ascetic in his barren cell in the *solitudo Syriae Chalcidis*'.[27] Rather than simply abandoning Gascoigne to the massed ranks of the haplessly deceived, however, we might choose instead to notice that, however inauthentic it may have been, this Hieronymian persona was eminently useful in furthering Gascoigne's own polemical purposes, and how assiduously, indeed, relentlessly, pragmatic he was in crafting a *vita* through which his own ascetic ideals could be authoritatively embodied. Jerome was not merely an eremitic exemplum for Gascoigne; he had also provided sustained exegesis of the scriptural books of prophecy through which Gascoigne sought to attack contemporary ecclesiastical abuses. Thus, when Ball states that Gascoigne is 'overwhelmingly Hieronymian', this must be understood not merely as a scholarly predilection but

---

[25] 'Vir Maxime Catholicus: Sulpicius Severus' Use and Abuse of Jerome in the *Dialogi*', *Journal of Ecclesiastical History* 58 (2007), 189–210 (pp. 189–90).

[26] 'Oderunt eum heretici quia eos inpugnare non desinit. Oderunt eum clerici quia vita eorum infectatur crimina. Sed plane eum boni homines admirantur & diligunt' (Oxford, Magdalen College MS 93, f. 235r).

[27] *Jerome* (London and New York, 2002), p. 40. Jerome's use of the epistolary form in the artful crafting of his eremitical and ascetic persona is further explored in Andrew Cain, 'Vox Clamantis in Deserto: Rhetoric, Reproach, and the Forging of Ascetic Authority in Jerome's Letters from the Syrian Desert', *Journal of Theological Studies* 57 (2006), 500–25.

as a close temperamental affinity. In the *Liber*, Gascoigne uses both Jerome and the voices of the scriptural prophets as mouthpieces through which to ventriloquise his castigation and critique.[28]

By contrast, the extent of Gascoigne's polemical resourcefulness may be further appreciated through a later and very different biographical vignette, as assertively contemporary as the life of Jerome was, at least in certain respects, antiquarian. The contemporary narrative is a miracle story in honour of St Bridget of Sweden. Gascoigne's keen interest in her cult is evident from extensive notes and anecdotes in several of his extant works.[29] In the *Liber*, St Bridget features most dramatically in a story concerning her power over the demons that afflicted Richard Tenant, Junior Proctor in Oxford in 1434 and Principal of Little Black Hall from 1444 possibly until 1452, the year in which he suffered temporary demonic possession and died from this trauma, as Gascoigne relates:[30]

> The most blessed Mary is always a source of terror to demons, as the dreadful battle-line of fortresses is to weak combatants. A similar observation might be made about any saint through whose merits and prayers a demon is led out of a person possessed. I know of recent cases like this at Oxford, c. 1450, and c. 1452. Some men were praying to Saint Bridget, formerly a widow and princess of Sweden. A man subjected to serious mental distress by terror and anxiety sent by Satan was suddenly liberated from severe mental anguish by the blessed Bridget appearing to him in a mental vision or as a glittering [physical] apparition, and consoling him with mental words. I also know that once, in Oxford, one master Richard Tenant was frequently and horribly tormented, possessed by an evil spirit (or spirits), because he kept on crying out, 'I am damned! And the judgment has been given: "Depart from me, ye accursed, into everlasting fire!" God is nothing but a devil!'. He repeated this publicly, in the presence of many, with me saying to him, 'In the name of Jesus Christ – if only you could say this – "Jesus Christ! God and man! Have mercy on me"'. He repeatedly responded to me by saying, 'I *can't* say it'; and then, although his lips were closed, he cried out the same words again in the same horrible way: 'I am damned, I am damned, God is nothing but a devil!' Various men were standing nearby, and at the instigation of one of them, prayed to St Bridget, the spouse of Christ; at this, the aforesaid master Richard Tenant was set free from the clutches of the demons, and repeated, 'O Lord Jesus Christ, have mercy on me'. He added: 'I was badly disturbed', and after that he repeatedly kissed the

---

[28] Ball, *Thomas Gascoigne*, p. 7. I explore the relationships between prophecy and reform in Gascoigne's writing more fully in 'Complaint, Prophecy and Pastoral Care in the Fifteenth Century: Thomas Gascoigne's *Liber Veritatum*' (forthcoming).

[29] See also Ball, *Thomas Gascoigne*, pp. 28–9.

[30] Gascoigne asserts that he included this anecdote in a life of St Bridget that he wrote for the nuns of Syon, but, as Pronger points out, this anecdote is missing from the Middle English life printed by Pynson in 1516 ('Thomas Gascoigne', I.625). On Tenant, whose connection with the York diocese might in part account for Gascoigne's interest in him, see Emden, *BRUO*, pp. 1854–5, which records 26th May 1452 as the day of his death.

image of Jesus Christ crucified for us; then he repeated in my hearing, 'St Bridget, pray for us'. He received the sacraments of the church two days after his liberation and died on Friday; and he was interred in Oxford, on the Vigils of Pentecost, in the church of the most holy Mary, ever virgin. I have written up this narrative more fully in the life of the same St Bridget, and have translated that life from Latin into English for the sisters and brothers of the order of the Holy Saviour in the monastery of Syon, in the diocese of London. This woman Bridget, therefore, the holy spouse of Christ, caused a great disturbance in the house of the prince of darkness.[31]

This is a complete contrast, and complement, to the life of St Jerome. Where that was bibliographical, and even bibliophilic, in character, a library-bound product of hard reading and scholarly synthesis, the miracle story is presented as a fresh piece of oral history readily assimilable within vernacular devotional culture. To consider these two narratives together is to appreciate the breadth of Gascoigne's religious sensibility and his pragmatic mastery of both scholarly and extramural discursive modes.[32]

[31] 'Semper enim beatissima Maria est terribilis daemonibus, sicut est terribilis castrorum acies debilibus pugnatoribus; consimiliter potest dici de quolibet sancto, cujus meritis et precibus ducitur daemon a possesso; sicut nuper novi Oxoniae, circa annum Domino m° cccc° l°, et circa annum Domini mo cccc° lij°, quando hominibus orantibus ad Sanctam Brigittam viduam quondam, et principissam Sueciae, novi virum graviter mentaliter vexatum horrore et timore per Sathanam immisso, quem novi tunc subito liberatum ab illa magna vexatione mentali, beata Brigitta sibi in mentali visione aut specie fulgenti apparente et cum verbis mentalibus eum consolante. Item, novi tunc Oxoniae quondam magistrum Ricardum Tenant, qui horribiliter et saepissime vexatus est, possessus a maligno spiritu, vel a malignis spiritibus, quia semper longo tempore clamavit, 'Ego sum dampnatus! Et sententia est data, Ite, maledicti, in ignem aeternum!' 'Nullus est Deus nisi dyabolus!' et hoc saepissime dixit publice coram pluribus, et me dicente sibi, 'In nomine Jesu Xti, dicatis, Jesu Xte! Deus et homo! Miserere mei.' Ipse michi saepe respondebat, dicens, 'Non possum hoc dicere;' et tunc, clausis labiis suis, similiter statim iterum verba praedicta horribiliter clamavit, dicens. 'Ego sum dampnatus, ego sum dampnatus, non est Deus nisi dyabolus!' et circumstantibus diversis hominibus, et ex motione unius ad Sanctam Brigittam sponsam Xti orantibus, praedictus magister Ricardus Tenant liberatus fuit de manibus daemonum, et dixit saepe, 'O Domine Jesu Xte! Miserere mei.' 'Ego', inquit, 'fui male vexatus;' et postea saepe osculatus est ymaginem Xti Jesu crucifixi pro nobis; et postea saepe, me audiente, 'Sancta Brigitta! Ora pro nobis;' et receptis sacramentis ecclesiae infra biduum post suam liberationem mortuus est, in die Veneris, et in vigilia Pentecostis Oxoniae sepultus in ecclesia sanctissimae Mariae semper virginis; quam historiam scripsi latius in vita ejusdem Sanctae Brigitte, quam vitam ego transtuli de Latino in Anglicum, sororibus et monialibus de ordine Sancti Salvatoris in monasterio Syon, Londiniensis diocesi. Haec ergo mulier, sancta sponsa Xti Brigitta, magnam fecit confusionem in domo principis tenebrarum.' (Rogers, *Loci*, pp. 139–40; emphasis mine).

[32] On the context of devotion to St. Bridget in England during this period, see Roger Ellis, '"Flores ad Fabricandam ... Coronam": An Investigation into the Uses of the Revelations of St. Bridget of Sweden in Fifteenth-Century England', *Medium Aevum* 51

There is, therefore, a more than sufficient critical imperative for regarding the *Liber* not as a problematic 'source', but as a creatively compiled text, and the dividend afforded by such a shift in perspective is that it enables us to be more attentive to the provocative interplay in Gascoigne's writing between eternal and quotidian temporalities. This dual focus is hardly unique to him: rather, it is part of the long-established cultural heritage of Christian writers accustomed to rapidly adjusting between the claims of the temporal and the eternal. But Gascoigne's having written and having thought in this way in mid-fifteenth-century England tells us something very important about the particular possibilities of intellectual life, no less than about the flexible resources of religious orthodoxy, during that period. Jeremy Catto has placed Gascoigne among a small but significant group of Oxford theologians who attempted to think resourcefully about the relationships between theology and pastoral care in the decades after the Wycliffite controversies.[33] Catto's account brings together Gascoigne and his *bête noire*, Pecock, as diverse but related examples of reformist creativity. This is persuasive, since, despite his avowed detestation of Pecock, Gascoigne's *Liber* could legitimately be viewed as the Latin correlative of Pecock's vernacular project: both contain elements of self-dislosure and this complicated (though it does not invalidate) the 'public' usefulness of such writings, albeit in very different ways. Nevertheless, important distinctions remain between them, and not merely the fact that Gascoigne's strongly patristic temperament is radically at odds with Pecock's scepticism about the ability of patristic *auctores* to resolve tensions in contemporary religious life. Gascoigne is as obviously part of a general reformist culture as was that earlier generation of former Wycliffites who channelled their reforming energies constructively at the Council of Constance and elsewhere. (Richard Fleming, who ordained him in 1427, is a forceful reminder of the ambiguities of earlier generations in this respect – a year after ordaining Gascoigne, he would consign Wyclif's ashes to the River Swift, in fulfilment of a decree from Constance that his predecessor, Philip Repingdon, had not carried out).[34] He remains a powerful and inexplicably under-exploited witness to the extent to which it remained possible to think cogently, vigorously and unapologetically about ecclesiastical reform well after the Wycliffite controversies had subsided, and his writings vividly illustrate

---

(1982), 163–86. The similarities between devotion to St. Jerome and to St Bridget are well brought out in George R. Kaiser, 'St. Jerome and the Brigittines: Visions of the Afterlife in Fifteenth-Century England', in *England in the Fifteenth Century. Proceedings of the 1986 Harlaxton Symposium*, ed. Daniel Williams (Woodbridge: Boydell, 1987), 143–52.

[33] Catto, 'Theology after Wycliffism'.

[34] On this generation, see Jeremy Catto, 'Fellows and Helpers: The Religious Identity of the Followers of Wyclif', in *The Medieval Church: Universities, Heresy, and the Religious Life*. Studies in Church History, Subsidia 11, eds Peter Biller and Barrie Dobson (Woodbridge, 1999), pp. 141–62.

the polychromatic nature of fifteenth-century religious orthodoxy. As Ball has meticulously shown, Gascoigne's visits to libraries and his distinctive bibliographic sensibility show that it was possible, albeit with some difficulty, to pursue a patristically-inclined intellectual life in England during the first half of the fifteenth century. The *Liber* and Gascoigne's other writings also show that the result of these journeys was the honing of a particular scholastic form of creativity in which the recorded life was a vital resource to think with, both devotionally and polemically.

Recording a Dynasty:
Verse Chronicles of the House of Percy

A. S. G. EDWARDS

The shaping of an individual history in written form can demonstrate a variety of strategies of a broadly ideological kind, exemplary of various philosophical or personal tendencies that can impose an intelligible shape on the available materials. To construct an account of a dynasty raises broader problems. These may entail locating the individual and local circumstances within a wider sense of the movement of history itself. Event and fact need to be connected to a larger sense of destiny that transcends the personal to situate it in relation to what we can broadly term the political on a local and/or a national level.

These generalizations have as their particular focus one such attempt to compose a dynastic history, the English verse chronicle accounts of the Percy family that were written in the early sixteenth century. The Percies were an appropriate subject for such memorialization. After its post-Conquest arrival in England the family swiftly established itself as one of the most powerful northern families, its members linked by ties of marriage to other important regional magnates, and acting as patrons of local institutions and protectors of the northern borders.[1] Their eminence seems to have led to more than one attempt to celebrate the Percy family's achievements, each conditioned seemingly by rather different pressures. Some of these can be loosely categorized as literary, like the ballads of *The Battle of Otterburn* or *Chevy Chase* in which Percies figured triumphantly.[2] Others, like John Hardyng's *Chronicle*, seem more concerned to provide political justification for the family's actions (Hardyng had served in the Percy household).[3] And there are responses that seek to set the family in wider historical perspectives. It is with these responses that I am concerned, as reflected in the various forms of the verse chronicle that has been most often termed 'the discent of the lordis percies.' The textual and representational complexities of these forms, hitherto unexplored, offer some insight into the problems of recording medieval lives of public men.

---

[1] For a recent account of the medieval Percies see Alexander Rose, *Kings in the North: The House of Percy in British History* (London, 2002).

[2] For editions of these poems see O. Arngart, *Two English Border Ballads: The Battle of Otterburn, The Hunting of the Cheviot* (Lund, 1973).

[3] See *The Chronicle of John Hardyng*, ed. H. S. Ellis (London, 1812), pp. 352–3.

What is probably the earliest form of this chronicle survives uniquely in Alnwick Castle 79, an early-sixteenth-century roll.[4] This was professionally produced, copied by a trained scribe, and carefully decorated, with an illuminated border and initial at the start of the text; in the outer margin is a series of roundels depicting the Kings of England from William the Conqueror to Henry VIII (with two roundels each for Henry V and VI); in the inner margin is a series of shields depicting various quarterings of Percy arms. The text of this elaborate roll comprises 329 lines in 47 rhyme royal stanzas. It offers a form of historical writing, the purpose of which is outlined in a concluding stanza:

> In this Roole ȝe þᵗ schall herr reede
> Beholde and considere þe noble discent
> Of þis vᵗʰ Erle marke it well in dede
> His progenitours in mynde if ȝe will imprent
> It schall apper cler and also euident
> Off the grettest blode he is commyn ȝe can tell
> Off þe Merches Lancaster and Arundell.

The impulses here were clearly primarily genealogical; the aim is to provide an account of the descent of the Percy line from its beginnings to the present. This roll presents a formally coherent and metrically consistent, relatively succinct record of Percy family history. It traces the origins of the Percies from pre-Conquest Normandy down to the sixteenth century, in clear chronological sequence, recording fairly systematically, where appropriate, details of marriage, progeny and place of death, as in this typical passage:

> Withowt ischew decessyd William primogenitus
> And Iohn the seconde sonne as I vndirstonde
> Wherfor yonge Henry Perse which was gracius
> As trew inheritor succedid all þe londe
> Awnwyke so cam fyrst to þis thrid Henry hande
> He maryd to his wyffe as cronicle doth tell
> Elenor doghter to therle of Arundell
>
> This lady Elynor was constant and sadd
> Gude godly and vertuous honorable and wyse
> And by this lorde Henry fair ischew sche hadd
> At Semar a chapell full well sche dyd devyse
> And it causyd to be beildyd in ryght gudly wyse
> This Henry third at last cam into þe fate
> At Fontaneȝ tofor high alter he lyeth intumulate
>
> The iiiiᵗʰ Henry Perse his soun and heyr was
> He was at Durham battell the captayn principall
> By kynge Edward thrid fauour grett thinges he did purchase

---

4   I have edited this chronicle in 'A Verse Chronicle of the House of Percy,' *Studies in Philology*, 105 (2008), 226–44.

He reparyd Avonwyke castell and mayd it more substantiall
A lady he maryed Ydone the booke dothe hir call
The lorde Clyfford daughter by whome hadde he
Myche gudly ischewe of grett nobilyte.

In general, the account seems to strive to be enumerative, to record familial chronology, rather than to overtly proclaim the political significance of the Percies. Such a distinction is, of course, oversimplistic. The record of powerful alliances through marriage, of the acquisition of estates and of military achievements, cumulatively provides the narrative with its own implicit affirmation of Percy status and power.

Such status and power are presented in the chronicle largely within a regional context, that of a northern dynasty. Only in the rarest of circumstances is the history of the Percies situated in any wider political or historical spheres. This stance, at times, must have presented some difficulties to the chronicler, particularly in his account of Henry Percy, first earl of Northumberland (1341–1408). Henry, of course, thrust himself into the broader course of history by his serial betrayal, first of Richard II, in 1399, and then of his successor, Henry IV, twice, in 1403 and 1405, in the first instance with the assistance of his son, Hotspur.

The challenge of putting any positive spin on this multiple treachery is one that the chronicler avoids by the dual expedients of falsehood and evasion. His strategy is, in part, to affirm the first Earl's loyalty to Richard II: 'This Henry to kynge Richarde secound was a trew knyght | To be trew to his maister it accordyth to right | In his maister's qwarell at the last was he slayn ...'. The account shows an understandable determination to ignore the facts: the first lord Percy died in February 1408 at Bramham Moor, attempting yet another act of rebellion against Henry IV. The chronicler would have been hard pressed to develop his claim that Henry Percy was defending Richard II's 'qwarell' nearly a decade after his death, and wisely he does not try. Indeed, no direct mention is made of either Henry IV or V; the chronicle passes on hurriedly from any mention of the reign of Richard II straight to Henry VI, overleaping this embarrassing phase in the Percy family history. In this instance, dynastic history requires the elision of wider political history.

The only other moment when the equilibrium of the narrative is disturbed is a little later, during the reign of Henry VII. This is not the only work to commemorate the death of Henry Percy, fourth earl, murdered by the citizens of Thirsk in April 1489 as he attempted to collect taxes for the king. But the poet's indignation prompts him into uncharacteristic *exclamatio*:

O horryble myscheff o most cruell crime
In our days not seen so detestable a thinge
Ther own natural lord þe common₃ so murderynge
He gudly commandyng them in þe kynges nayme
To doo þer dewte and kepe þamselfe fro blame

Here, of course, he can safely take the moral high ground. Indeed, the chronicler's response has a ring of sincerity to it. Perhaps he had actually known the murdered earl. But his response is also located within a sense of the affront to local order: '... so detestable a thinge | Ther own natural lord þe common₃ so murderynge.' It is as much the violation of proper regional fealties as the crime itself that seems to excite his indignation.[5]

What is presented in the chronicle in Alnwick 79 is a celebration of family history and achievement. The poet proclaims that 'the perse₃ in þer actes baith bein right glorius | ... In prouince of Yorkeschire they have bein full gracius.' The narrative is, in its overall effect, directed to the development of this theme of local glorification, to setting the sequence of lives of the Percies in their regional contexts.

If this roll were the only form of 'the discent of the lordis percies' that had survived, the author would be entitled to a modest place in early modern English literary history, and historical writing, as the creator of a unique form of Middle English verse writing, the chronicle of a noble house; he creates an account that is succinct and coherent, an appropriate memorialization of a long-established noble family. But the poet was to be denied his own secure niche in the house of fame. For there also survives another version of the Percy chronicle, ascribed to one William Peeris. The two versions of the chronicle have never been clearly discriminated, but those forms associated with 'Peeris' can be clearly distinguished in a number of respects.

Before describing these differences it may be appropriate to say something about the very little that is known about Peeris himself. William Peeris has only rarely excited the interest of posterity. Such meagre facts as are establishable about his life have been admirably marshalled by Henry Summerson in the *Oxford Dictionary of National Biography*, and I gratefully acknowledge my debt to his researches.[6] Peeris seems to have flourished in the 1520s, as a member of the household of Henry, 5th earl of Northumberland. He is characterized in the manuscripts I will discuss as 'clerke and preste secretarye to the right nobill Erle henry the v. Erle of Northumberlande', although some of the later manuscripts omit the word 'priest'. The term 'priest secretary' seems to signify no more than that he was an educated cleric employed in some undetermined administrative role in Percy's household.

Peeris' only claim on history's attention rests on his achievements as a verse chronicler. It is possible that he may have written other verse. The records of Bev-

5   For analysis of the factors that contributed to the fourth earl's murder see M. A. Hicks, 'Dynastic Change and Northern Society: The Career of the Fourth Earl of Northumberland, 1470–89,' *Northern History*, 14 (1978), 78–107.

6   Henry Summerson, 'Peeris, William (*fl.* c. 1520)', *Oxford Dictionary of National Biography*, Oxford University Press, Sept 2004; online edn, May 2006 [http://0-www.oxforddnb.com.catalogue.ulrls.lon.ac.uk:80/view/article/21771, accessed 7 Aug 2008].

erley Corporation attest that in 1519–20 one William Peeris was paid for making alterations the town's Corpus Christi play. He is described in these records as a poet. Peeris' work for Beverley has not survived.[7] The only verse that can be attributed to him are those manuscripts of the 'the discent of the lordis percies' that credit him as author.

Some broad generalizations are possible about the nature of the version of the Percy chronicle associated with Peeris' name. This form was more than twice the length of the original design, over seven hundred lines. The opening stanzas of the longer version do correspond quite closely to the earlier one and there are points throughout where occasional passages or parts of stanzas appear that bear some verbal correspondence to passages in the shorter form of the text. For example, the account of the death of the 4th earl at the hands of his aggrieved tenants (quoted above) is retained in its entirety. But there are few extensive parallels and some striking differences. The shorter version, for example, places the Percy's origins with the 'Grandysons lorde$_3$ de Sauoye' and takes the etymology of their name from the fact that they fought on the Grandisons' behalf in Persia. The Peeris version claims they come from 'the contrye of Denmarke and Norway.'[8] It credits lord Geoffrey Percy with establishing the family in England, a distinction in the earlier version credits to Lord William Percy.

The differences between the two versions are not simply quantitative or informational. They address themselves most directly to the luckless reader in the question of verse form. The author of the original demonstrated a workmanlike competence in his consistent use of rhyme royal. The later version demonstrates, in all the manuscripts, a degree of insouciance as to the formal constraints of verse. Indeed, the stanzas at times extend to eight, nine, ten or eleven lines; on occasions they are only six lines. And the only aspect of the verse that has any claims to regularity is the consistency with which the shape of the pentameter line is flouted, at times to create effects of teeth-gritting awfulness.

This is the only version of the Percy chronicles to achieve print. It was published in an obscure antiquarian series in Newcastle in 1845 from an imperfect version of the text.[9] It is on the basis of this version that a historian has recently praised Peeris' poem as 'a vividly poetical history of the early Percys'.[10] It is not. Even if one were to disregard its demonstration of the author's quite appalling incapacity as a versifier, the preoccupation with the minutiae of noble genealogy and the tone of

---

[7] See Summerson, 'William Peeris'.

[8] Throughout, all quotations from the longer version of the chronicle are taken from BL Royal 18 D. II, fols 186–95.

[9] By J. B[lesley] in *Reprints of Rare Tracts and Imprints of Antient Manuscripts &c Chiefly Illustrative of the History of the Northern Counties*. Vol. 1: Biographical (Newcastle, 1845), pp. [9]–43.

[10] Alexander Rose, *Kings in the North*, p. 17.

steadfast sycophancy, combined with the not infrequent incoherence of the text, would provide ample grounds for disqualifying Peeris' chronicle from any claim to be 'poetical'.

Nor does it have very many grounds on which it can be held to be historical. It may seem a little strange to emphasize this since one of the other distinctive aspects of the longer version is its insistence on its own historical authority. It goes out of its way to draw attention to its own documentary basis by citing a number of specific authorities, something the shorter version does not do. Some of these are local sources that cannot now be verified. Peeris mentions, for example, 'bookes of Whitby wheryn the names of abbottes of Whitby regestred be' and 'euy-dens & dedis vnder seale which I haue sene & lokide vpoun'. With such authori-ties one might be disposed to grant Peeris the benefit of the doubt. But this version also names particular works. These include 'the secunde booke of William Malmesbury' cited on at least six occasions; 'Henry of Huntyngdoun ... his iii^de booke', Higden's *Polychronicon*, cited at least twice and 'Nicholaus de regibus anglie' as well as other less precisely specified sources: 'the fraynche cronykles', 'the saide cronykles of Normandy', 'the saide annuall bookes of Normandy.' Such sources are clearly intended to suggest a range of reading appropriate to a diligent historian. But they, like much else in the longer version of Peeris' work, do not stand scrutiny. None of them turn out to have any direct bearing at all on the house of Percy. They are authenticating gestures rather than precise documentation. This is not history but a form of historiographical smokescreen.

It is not, however, altogether empty gesture. It is possible to discern some dif-ferences in narrative emphasis that suggest some form of controlling design to this longer narrative. I have already touched on the Percies' involvement in the arrival of Henry, earl of Derby in the north of England in 1399, a matter that the short ver-sion sought to avoid discussing. In the longer version this episode is treated very differently:

> The said Henry of Darbie after he was entered into this lande
> At Doncaster in the whyte freeris was sworne on the sacramente
> To the said vii^th Henry the firste erle of Northumberlande
> And to the lorde Percie his eldeste sonne beinge ther presente
> With his vncle the erle of Worcester that he wold be contente
> His owne inheritance onlie to clame
> Wich was the dukedame of Lancaster wich of right he shold optane
> And not to vsurpe the crowne vpon his prynce kinge Rychard
> But sone after was periured and of his othe had no regarde
>
> For his wrongfull delinge and pariurie
> As policronicon in his lyfe dothe planlie expresse
> God punished him right sore and grevoslie
> For after he had taken the crowne vpon him wrongefullie
> Immedietlie striken he was with the contagius siknes

Of lepre wich is a diseas remediles
The bodie of the said erle of Northumberlande in Yorke minster doth lie
At the right hand of the hige awtor right honorable.

Here we find a form of pro-Percy propaganda carefully nurtured from the mid-fifteenth century, most notably by John Hardyng, in which the Percies become the trusting dupes of the usurping king.[11] The Percies are on the side of the angels, assigned a state 'right honorable' in York Minster while Henry suffers a vile death from leprosy, punished by God 'right sore and grevoslie' because he seized the crown 'wrongefullie.'

Another indication of the overt political purpose of the longer chronicle can be in a lengthy interpolation that is also not present in the shorter version. This recounts a dispute over jurisdiction, about royal claims to payments from the abbey at Whitby, a house founded by the Percies. It is concerned with the alleged malfeasance of Serlo, second prior of the abbey of Whitby, who is accused in this version of contriving by 'crafte' and 'males' to pay money to the crown, initially ten pounds but 'wich now is rased to more large somme', all on the basis of documents which Serlo is alleged to have forged. The authority of 'aunciente monumentes of trewe remembrance' is invoked to affirm the legitimacy of Percy claims to these monies.

> Notwithstandinge this first Erle Percie the second prior of Whitbie afterward
> Was first that woulde haue wrongide his blode from the defendinge
> And foundershipe of the Abbay to his dutie hauinge no regarde
> God pardon his soule for he purposed a dampnable thinge
> And when this serke cold not defete his brother of his right by wronge surmysynge
> By crafte he devysed and by males out founde
> To cause his house to pay to the king x pound
> At everie vocation wich now is rased to more large somme
> And bringeth in variance to the house and causith it in gret damadge to ronne
>
> No man may lett a religious place
> To yeve or lende what the liskit afforcithe but a smale
> But be it litle or muche or shall require the case
> The founders right tytle it hurtethe nothinge all
> For when the said Serle prior of Whitbie had lade his trappes all
> Yet God in his power wold not suffer it for to lie
> To defende the right of of the foundershipe from his brother lord William Percie
>
> In the monasterie of Whitbie olde recordes be
> And aunciente monumentes of trewe remembrance

---

[11] For discussion of the Percies' role in Richard's deposition and the attendant strategies of justification see J. W. Bean, 'Henry IV and the Percies,' *History*, 44 (1959), 212–27 and Andy King, '"They have the Hertes of the People by North": Northumberland, the Percies and Henry IV, 1399–1408,' in *Henry IV: The Establishment of the Regime, 1399–1406*, eds Gwilym Dodd and Douglas Biggs (York, 2003), pp. 139–57.

That after the dissease of lord William Percie
A controversi was and also a variance
Betwene Serle Percie wich was the seconde priore of Whitbie and had the gouer-
    nance
Of the said Abbay and the lord Alane the firste founder of the said monasterie and
    his nevew
Wherevpon a wronge tytle the said Serle forgede out newe

To intytle the kinge as founder was the said priors entente
Howbeit the Percie tytle is iust playne and euident
For his wrongefull dedis God haue him sore punyshmente
For a longe tyme or he departed great petie it was to see
With a contageus cankar rufullie vexed was he

After he had great repentance in his consciens he knewe
That lorde William Percie was the founder rightful trew
For by evidens and dedes vnder seale wich I have seen and loked vpon
The iust tytle of the foundacion appereth obiection may be none
And also the syet of the place standethe n the percis ground
Whearvpon the saide lorde William Percie his abbay first did found.

Like the later justification of the Percys' role in the usurpation of Richard II this passage suggests some attempt to situate and justify the family in relation to royal power and authority. Here, once again, chronicle merges into propaganda that seeks to establish the credible authoritative tradition that underpins the claims of the Percy family to their proper jurisdiction and attendant financial benefits. Once again, the account of the history of the family is shaped by political self-justification.

If the desire for such self-justification gives a pattern, if not a shape, to William Peeris' longer version of the Percy chronicle, it does not resolve some of the obvious questions this version poses. Particularly hard to grasp are the reasons for the collapse of metrical and narrative coherence as the work was expanded, and the larger motives that made it necessary to attempt such extensive reworking. No obvious answers present themselves to these obvious questions. But they do prompt a dim but insistent suspicion. Did William Peeris really write the shorter version of the chronicle associated with his name? Could his powers as versifier have failed so abruptly, or did Peeris attempt to rework someone else's altogether more competent verse account of the family? It is not a question that admits of a clear or confident answer, but there is some evidence that seems to bear on the relationship between Peeris' work and what may have preceded it. It occurs in a transcript by the seventeenth-century antiquary Roger Dodsworth in what is now MS Bodley Dodsworth 50. This is a copy of a manuscript of Peeris' chronicle that does not now survive, described by Dodsworth in some detail.[12] He goes on to

---

[12]   'Here followith yᵉ coppy of an ould parchment booke ... It is in folio & conteines | eight
    leaues of parchment whereof the first | word is (here) & the first lettre (H) | is a greate

quote what is apparently its prefatory heading: 'Here beginneth the Prologue of this litle treaties | followinge wch is ye discent of the Lord Percies | made & compiled briefely by mee Wm Peeris' (fol. 119). The syntax is admittedly ambiguous but it seems to seek to make a distinction between the authorship of the Prologue, which, as I have said, corresponds closely in both the shorter and the longer forms of the text, and the rest of the work for which Peeris seems to claim authorship. It is clear that the longer version achieved an enduring popularity that led to it being copied in at least six manuscripts over the course of a century. These manuscripts, all in codex form, range in date from the early sixteenth to the mid-seventeenth centuries. Three are at Alnwick Castle, the seat of the Duke of Northumberland, manuscripts 82, 521, 522; one is on the British Library, Royal 18. D. II; one in the Bodleian, Dodsworth 50, discussed above; and one in the Beinecke Library at Yale University, Osborn fa.19. The evidence of Dodsworth 50, a seventeenth-century transcript, suggests there were once others. In their number they evidence an insistent desire, seemingly within the Percy family and its circles, to preserve this record of the family's achievements.[13]

The apparent efforts to multiply copies of Peeris' work pose the obvious question: why? Presumably copies, some quite elaborate, could only have been produced through the encouragement of the fifth earl. What prompted him to encourage the circulation of such a work by a member of his household?

The answer may lie in the uneasy position of Henry Algernon Percy, (1478–1527), the fifth earl, after the death of his father. The fourth earl, it should be noted, had enjoyed an equivocal national political status because of his passivity at the battle of Bosworth in 1485, where he supported neither the defeated Richard III nor the future Henry VII. The family's power lessened during Henry's reign even before the fourth earl's murder.[14] After it Henry Algernon Percy was effectively marginalized and enjoyed no significant role in the politics of the time. His life was lived on the margins of power.[15]

In such an environment it would be natural to seek to affirm the family's traditions of service and achievement both among the family's retainers and possibly elsewhere. The different forms of the Percy chronicle provide a tangible record of the family's history and achievements at a time when their status was under threat. These circumstances might have made it seem appropriate for someone else to

---

Red le*tt*re & is in length from | ye first line to the seauenth Line' (fol. 119).

[13] Three of the manuscripts remain at Alnwick and Royal 18. D. II has Percy associations. I have been unable to establish the provenance of either the Dodsworth or the Beinecke maunscripts.

[14] See further M. Reiss, 'A Power in the North? The Percies in the Fifteenth Century,' *Historical Journal*, 19 (1976), 501–09.

[15] M. E. James, 'The Murder at Cock Lodge, 28 April, 1489,' *Durham University Journal*, 57 (1965), p. 87: 'The fifth earl was never the provincial satrap his father had been but was excluded from major office all his life.'

seek to expand the original chronicle, to seek to invest it with greater bulk and greater appearance of authority.

But the ineptitude of the Peeris version mirrors the wider futility of the attempt. The fifth earl did nothing to arrest this process of decline. He was succeeded by his eldest son, Henry Percy (1502?–1537): the 'Unthrifty' earl, whose death together with the execution of Henry's brother Thomas in the aftermath of the Pilgrimage of Grace led to the loss and attainder of the family's estates in 1537.[16] The attempt at poetic self-aggrandisement did nothing to check the family's decline. It becomes an epitaph, not a celebration.

Nonetheless, the Percy family's interest in their verse chronicles suggests a sense of the potential of the written word that forms one aspect of a larger preoccupation in the recording of their history. This preoccupation is reflected elsewhere in an illustrated Middle English prose chronicle of the Percy family in Bodley Rolls 5 (SC 2986).[17] British Library, Royal 18. D. II includes, in addition to Peeris' chronicle and other poems associated with various Percy family houses, John Skelton's poem on the murder of Henry Percy, 4th earl of Northumberland, which survives uniquely in it, and which was seemingly commissioned from him by the Percies.[18] This elaborately produced manuscript is one reminder of the interest the family took in the early sixteenth century in demonstrating its possession of manuscripts of historical works, in verse, directly linked to the family itself. Another example of this interest is Bodleian Library Arch. Selden. B. 10 (SC 3356), a copy of John Hardyng's fifteenth-century verse *Chronicle*, a work of pronounced Percy sympathies (Hardyng had been, as I have noted, a Percy retainer), that also contains the added arms of the 5th earl of Northumberland.[19] He clearly inherited his interests from his father, the 4th Earl, who had himself owned another large work of vernacular poetic history, British Library Royal 18. D. V, a copy of Lydgate's *Fall*

[16] See further R. W. Hoyle, 'Henry Percy, sixth earl of Northumberland and the fall of the house of Percy in 1537,' in *The Tudor Nobility*, ed. G. W. Bernard (Manchester, 1992), 180–211.

[17] For description and discussion see E. D. Kennedy, *Chronicles and Other Historical Writings, A Manual of the Writings in Middle English*, vol. 8 (Hamden, Conn., 1989), pp. 2677–8.

[18] On Royal 18. D. II see M. E. James, *A Tudor Magnate and the Tudor State: Henry Fifth Earl of Northumberland*, Borthwick Paper 30 (York, 1966), pp. 33–9. For a description see G. F. Warner & J. P. Gilson, *Catalogue of Western Manuscripts in the Old Royal and King's Collections*, 4 vols (London, 1921–5), II, 308–10; the Percy arms are on fol. 162, at the end of Lydgate's *Siege of Thebes*.

[19] See Otto Pächt & J. J. G. Alexander, *Illuminated Manuscripts in the Bodleian Library Oxford III: British, Irish, and Icelandic Schools* (Oxford, 1973), no. 1117. and M. B. Parkes, *English Cursive Book Hands 1250–1500*, 2nd edn (London, 1979), p. 15, pl. 15 (ii). For a recent study of this manuscript see Alexandra Gillespie, '"The proverbes yet do last": Lydgate, the Fifth Earl of Northumberland, and Tudor Miscellanies from Print to Manuscript', *Yearbook of English Studies*, 33 (2003), 215–32.

of Princes, which includes his arms,[20] as well as a manuscript of Chaucer's *Canterbury Tales* now at Petworth House.[21] Evidently for the Percy family at this period poetry and history possessed some importance that seems to have prompted emulative impulses.[22]

The Percy chronicles stands apart from these other manuscripts or writings. As I have already noted, these are the only English verse chronicles of the history of a noble household. As such they gesture towards an attempt to give poetic form to dynastic ambition. The verse Percy chronicles demonstrate how the writing of household history becomes revisionist history, amplifying and readjusting the Percies' relationship to local and national events, presumably according to different senses of political exigency and self-justification. The attempt, for all its manifest imperfections of execution, seems worth noting.

---

[20] For description see H. Bergen (ed.), *Lydgate's Fall of Princes*, Part IV, Early English Text Society, extra series, no. CCXIV (London, 1927), pp. 27–8. The Percy arms are on fol. 216vb.

[21] For description see N. R. Ker & A. J. Piper, *Medieval Manuscripts in British Libraries IV: Paisley–York* (Oxford, 1992), p. 179.

[22] In the case of the fifth earl this interest may have extended into other aspects of contemporary literature. His household seems, at one time, to have included a 'maker of interludes' and he may have sponsored the interlude *Youth*; see further, *Two Tudor Interludes The Interlude of Youth Hick Scorner*, ed. Ian Lancashire (Manchester, 1980), pp. 27–9.

Charles VI and Richard II: Inconstant Youths

CHRISTOPHER FLETCHER

The characters of Charles VI and Richard II have long fascinated historians. Their unstable personalities have seemed to be emblematic of the mixture of extremes which Johan Huizinga ascribed to this period in the history of Europe.[1] Charles VI is a tragic figure, whose early signs of chivalric vigour never reach fulfilment in adult campaigns, but are instead reduced to absurdity with the recurrent attacks of insanity which began in the early 1390s.[2] His childlike tractability in the hands of his uncles or his father's former servants passes quickly into vacuous pliability in the hands of faction.[3] Richard II's personality, meanwhile, has been ascribed a vital explanatory role in each successive interpretation of the politics of his reign. Whether the troubles of Richard's reign are seen to derive from the king's foreign policy, his political ideas or his use of patronage, the traditional view of his character – unchivalric, prodigal and authoritarian – is always invoked in one form or another to explain why he chose to pursue the dangerous policies in question.[4]

Concerned by the clearly tendentious nature of contemporary comment on the personalities of these two kings, writers in an empirical historical tradition have gone to the archives, using record material to test the validity of the remarks made by contemporary chroniclers and literary writers.[5] In the case of Richard II, this has made it possible to discard some of the conventional traits which have tra-

---

[1] J. Huizinga, *The Autumn of the Middle Ages*, trans. R. J. Payton and U. Mammitzch (Chicago, 1996).

[2] B. Guénée, *La folie de Charles VI: Roi Bien-Aimé* (Paris, 2004), pp. 8, 58–9; F. Autrand, *Charles VI: La folie du roi* (Paris, 1986), pp. 31–3; J. B. Henneman, *Olivier de Clisson and Political Society under Charles V and Charles VI* (Philadelphia, 1996), pp. 104–5, 142.

[3] Henneman, *Olivier de Clisson*, p. 130; R. Vaughan, *Philip the Bold* (London, 1962), pp. 39–58, esp. pp. 41–4.

[4] C. Fletcher, *Richard II: Manhood, Youth and Politics, 1377–99* (Oxford, 2008), pp. 7–12.

[5] See e.g. G. B. Stow, 'Chronicles versus Records: The Character of Richard II' in J. S. Hamilton and P. Bradley (eds), *Documenting the Past: Essays in Medieval History Presented to G. P. Cuttino* (Woodbridge, 1989), pp. 85–94; N. Saul, *Richard II* (New Haven and London, 1997), esp. pp. 435–68; G. O. Sayles, 'King Richard II of England: A Fresh Look', *Proceedings of the American Philosophical Society*, 115 (1971), 28–31; Sayles, 'Richard II in 1381 and 1399', *EHR*, 94 (1979), 291–300.

ditionally been ascribed him – that he was uninterested in hunting, for example, or that he was physically unsuited for chivalric pursuits – but until recently the tendency has been merely to present a more nuanced version of the older picture, rather than to propose a radically new view of the king.[6] In a comparable fashion, the character of Charles VI as portrayed in recent historiography is not so very different from that found in the work of Jean Froissart, the monk of St Denis or Christine de Pizan. Perhaps because historians have been less concerned with Charles's sane personality than with his madness, even the most sophisticated recent work tends to accept the account presented by these contemporary writers when they portray a king gifted for chivalric pursuits, but somewhat tainted by the sins of the flesh.[7] Richard II's character has been more controversial, but in the end historians' views have tended to resolve into positive or negative attitudes towards this king's traditional reputation.[8] It is thus perhaps not surprising that when, in 1981, James Sherborne compared Froissart's portrayal of Charles and of Richard, he concluded that in both cases this famously inventive chronicler was fundamentally right, even if he made up the details.[9]

Trained in a tradition of source criticism, political historians have had a troubled relationship with established topoi in their sources for the character of these two kings. It has been difficult to avoid oscillating between a rejection of the use of established themes as merely conventional, and an acceptance of tropes in attenuated form.[10] Although literary scholars have done much which should help historians to understand the significance of the remarks of contemporary chroniclers, notably by analysing the rhetorical themes which inspired contemporaries to portray these kings in a particular way, this analysis has tended to remain restricted to considering these works, notably Froissart's *Chroniques*, as texts in a network of other similar texts, rather than as part of a wider social world.[11] Historians have yet to take the next step, reintegrating these insights into their interpretations of the political society of these years.[12] As a result, there is still room for

---

[6]   See e.g. Stow, 'Chronicles versus Records', p. 168; V. H. Galbraith, 'A New Life of Richard II', *History*, 26 (1942), 223–39 and the comments in C. Fletcher, 'Manhood and Politics in the Reign of Richard II', *Past and Present*, 189 (2005), 3–39, pp. 29–31.

[7]   Guénée, *La folie de Charles VI*, pp. 8, 138–40.

[8]   For a positive account see C. Barron, 'The Art of Kingship. Richard II, 1377–99', *History Today*, 35 (1985), 30–37; Barron, 'The Deposition of Richard II', in *Politics and Crisis in Fourteenth-Century England*, eds J. Taylor and W. Childs (Gloucester, 1990), pp. 132–49; and the response of N. Saul, 'Richard II: Author of his Own Downfall?', *History Today*, 49 (1999), 36–41.

[9]   J. Sherborne, 'Charles VI and Richard II' repr. in *War, Politics and Culture in Fourteenth Century England*, ed. A. Tuck (London, 1994), pp. 155–70.

[10] M. Aston, 'Richard II and the Wars of the Roses' in *The Reign of Richard II*, eds C. Barron and F. R. H. du Boulay (London, 1971), pp. 280–317, at pp. 316–17.

[11] See esp. P. Ainsworth, *Jean Froissart and the Fabric of History* (Oxford, 1990).

[12] For a similar division in the the treatment of a rather different kind of text, see J. L.

a comparison of the way Charles VI and Richard II were portrayed by their con-temporaries, one which takes account of the use of certain tropes and themes, but which is focused on the political societies of these two kingdoms at the turn of the fourteenth century. Hopefully this will make it possible to consider the social and political import of their account of the characters of these kings, without being forced into a binary choice between accepting them as the simple truth, or reject-ing them entirely.

The first step in any such inquiry must be to put contemporary portrayals of these two kings back into the context of the particular political circumstances of their reigns. Both Richard II and Charles VI came to the throne young, at the ages of 10 and 12 respectively. They did so within a few years of each other, in 1377 and 1380. In each case, no formal regency was established. Instead, it was agreed to continue as if each king was in full control of the government of his kingdom. In England a series of permanent councils of greater or lesser formality were established to reg-ulate government, to compensate for the king's youth and to ensure that he was well brought up in his tender age.[13] In both kingdoms, the king's uncles played a prominent part as his principal counsellors in his youth. Whilst in France this was formally established, with the uncles appointed as royal councillors, in England the arrangement was looser.[14] First, formal 'continual councils', and subsequently the king's notional rule with his chief officials, masked the real influence of his uncles, and foremost amongst them John of Gaunt, duke of Lancaster, alongside other less clearly identifiable influences in the royal household, notably the former followers of Richard's father, the Black Prince.[15] In France, it was more clearly Philip the Bold, duke of Burgundy, whose keeping of the king's person put him in the role of 'father' figure, even as this role was contested by the former advisers of Charles V.[16] In neither kingdom did these arrangements meet with universal approval. Partly as a result of their contestable legitimacy, and partly because of underlying socio-economic pressures, both England and France faced tax revolts and vocal criticism of the way that taxes were raised and spent in the early 1380s.

Watts, 'The Policie in Christen Remes': Bishop Russell's Parliamentary Sermons of 1483–84' in G. W. Bernard and S. J. Gunn (eds), *Authority and Consent in Tudor Eng-land: Essays Presented to C. S. L. Davies* (Aldershot, 2002), pp. 33–60.

[13] A. Tuck, *Richard II and the English Nobility* (London, 1973), pp. 33–8; A. Goodman, *John of Gaunt* (Harlow, 1992), pp. 70–3; Saul, *Richard II*, pp. 38–9; Fletcher, *Richard II*, pp. 74–96.

[14] Autrand, *Charles VI*, pp. 13–19; Vaughan, *Philip the Bold*, pp. 39–42; Henneman, *Olivier de Clisson*, pp. 103–19.

[15] C. Given-Wilson, *The Royal Household and the King's Affinity: Service, Politics and Finance in England, 1360–1413* (New Haven and London, 1986), pp. 160–67, 175–83; Fletcher, *Richard II*, pp. 76–8.

[16] Autrand, *Charles VI*, p. 177; Henneman, *Olivier de Clisson*, pp. 107–8, 123–4.

These upheavals made the control of the king during his youth – and thus the control of the purse strings – a still more sensitive issue than it would have been in less disturbed times.[17]

At length, both kings became increasingly impatient with this state of affairs. As Charles and Richard entered their late teens and early twenties, each attempted to shrug off the domination of his uncles and of appointed councillors. At this point, however, their fates diverged. Richard's attempts to destroy those who would restrain him ended in disaster with defeat in battle and the exile or judicial murder of his supporters.[18] Charles VI's four-year reforming personal rule in alliance with his father's former officials, known as the *marmousets*, came to an end with his first bouts of insanity.[19]

The present paper is not primarily concerned with Richard II, since I have considered him at length elsewhere. It focuses instead on the insights which come to the fore when contemporary accounts of the character of Charles VI are reconsidered in the light of a re-examination of Richard II's reputation. At the risk of repeating what has already been said, however, it should be helpful to sketch out briefly an outline of this account of the king. The conventional picture of Richard II's personality is composed of types taken from late medieval moral stereotypes, mainly concerning the characteristics of adult males, women and youths.[20] Yet this does not mean, as one might be tempted to deduce, that this view of the king's personality is of no use in understanding the politics of this reign, a mere arbitrary collection of conventional types. The types chosen are anything but arbitrary, but in order to understand their precise significance for the politics of the reign, these stereotypes need to be reinserted into the traditions which inform them. In particular, the impression that Richard was temperamentally opposed to war or distant from chivalric culture derives primarily from a misreading of contemporary topoi in terms of the modern associations of masculinity and effeminacy, rather than in terms of medieval commonplace associations of youth and manhood.

The aim of this essay is to consider how very similar stereotypes could be used to compose such different images of the two kings. Both were portrayed as exhibiting characteristics associated with the psychology and even the physiology of young men, but in ways which produced very different results. I would suggest

---

[17]   Autrand, *Charles VI*, pp. 69–119; Henneman, *Olivier de Clisson*, pp. 105–7; L. Mirot, *Les insurrections urbaines au debut du règne de Charles VI (1380–1383)* (Paris, 1906); Saul, *Richard II*, pp. 56–82; J. J. N. Palmer, *England, France and Christendom, 1377–99* (London, 1972), pp. 1–14; C. Fletcher, 'Corruption at Court? Crisis and the Theme of *Luxuria* in England and France, c. 1340–1422' in *The Court as Stage: England and the Low Countries in the Later Middle Ages*, eds S. Gunn and A. Janse (Woodbridge, 2006), pp. 28–38, esp. pp. 30–31; Fletcher, *Richard II*, pp. 74–150.

[18]   Fletcher, *Richard II*, esp. pp. 151–75.

[19]   Henneman, *Olivier de Clisson*, pp. 120–71; Autrand, *Charles VI*, pp. 189–213, 304–18.

[20]   Fletcher, 'Manhood and politics', pp. 3–25; Fletcher, *Richard II*, pp. 1–73.

that the differences are not simply a consequence of their contrasting personalities. Instead, we are dealing with a rather different phenomenon – a process involving genuine observations of events, but which is influenced by a traditional palette of themes. The final result is ultimately determined neither by these kings' characters nor by commonplace ideas, but by the particular balance of power and sequence of events on each side of the Channel.

Let us now turn in detail to contemporary perceptions of the character of these two kings. At the outset, it is important to note that contemporaries did not conceive of the personalities of Charles VI and Richard II as purely psychological phenomena, confined to a world of the mind distinct from that of the body. Drawing no such Cartesian division, they conceived of the kings' characters as an aspect of their bodily constitutions.

In the case of Charles VI, this comes out most clearly in contemporary medical explanations of his illness. Charles VI had his first public attack of 'frenesie' in the August heat of 1392, riding to war in Brittany.[21] According to Jean Froissart, as soon as Guillaume de Harcigny, the famous doctor of Laon, heard of the king's illness he immediately knew what the problem was.[22] Froissart reports that the eminent doctor, who 'believed he knew well enough the complexion of the king' and the circumstances of his first symptoms proclaimed:

> This illness has come to the king from *tourble* [i.e. trouble, agitation, stirring up].
> He takes too much from the moisture of the mother.[23]

Froissart asserts that de Harcigny, summoned to the king's bedside, concluded that the king had been seized by 'weakness of the head and by incidence of *tourble*,' and set to work on appropriate therapy for his recovery.[24] When, some months later, Charles had indeed recovered, the good doctor returned home. In doing so, he left the following general prescription for the king:

> From now on, make sure he does not become angry nor melancholy; since he is
> not yet firm in all his spirits, but little by little he will firm up…[25]

---

[21] The word is Froissart's; the monk of St. Denis carefully avoids the implication that Charles was 'fou'. See Guénée, *La folie de Charles VI*, pp. 23–34.

[22] Jean Froissart, *Œuvres*, ed. M. le baron Kervyn de Lettenhove (Brussels, 1867–77) [hereafter *Froissart*], vol. xv, p. 48. Translations are my own.

[23] *Froissart*, xv, p. 49: 'Ceste maladie est venue au roy de tourble. Il tient trop de la moisteur de la mère.' Cf. A. J. Greimas, *Dictionnaire de l'ancien français: Le Moyen Âge* (Paris, 1995), s.v. 'torble'.

[24] Ibid., p. 50: 'le roy l'avoit conchue et prise par foiblesse de chief et par incidence de tourble'.

[25] Ibid., p. 77: 'D'ores-en-avant on le garde de courrouchier et mérancolier; car encoires n'est-il pas bien ferme de tous ses esperits, mais petit à petit il se affermera, et joyes et déduits, oubliances et dépors par raison luy sont plus prouffitables que autres choses.'

The king was not to be exposed to excessive distractions, and was to avoid all burdensome duties, in particular the effort of taking counsel,

> since he still has and will still have for this season a head which is weak and tender and all disturbed, and it is true, for he has been struck and stirred up with a very serious illness.[26]

Historians, when they have considered contemporary diagnoses of Charles's illness, have – understandably enough – tended to analyse them in terms of the reliability of the evidence they give concerning the true medical ontology of Charles VI's madness.[27] Bernard Guénée has noted the improbability of the famous doctor Guillaume de Harcigny, then in his eighties, making his way at speed from his home at Laon, and replacing the imposing array of doctors from the princely and royal entourages who already surrounded the king.[28] Guénée suggests that it is more likely that de Harcigny was consulted later in the year, when the king was in that region. This seems a not unreasonable suggestion. But it should also be noted that, although this version of events does detract from Froissart's testimony concerning the circumstances of Charles VI's first illness, it does not diminish the value of his account of the state of medical opinion before Harcigny's death in the following year. Froissart is absolutely correct in asserting that doctors prescribed peace, quiet and removal from the court as the best therapy for the king, much to the chagrin of both Charles and his courtiers.[29] Yet Guénée, following earlier commentators, gives relatively short shrift to this account of medical analysis of the king's condition. Froissart's assertion concerning 'the moisture of the mother' is taken to be a reference to a condition which the king inherited from his mother, Jeanne de Bourbon. She also seems to have 'lost her good sense and good memory' in 1373.[30] This, along with Froissart's reference to the king being 'weak in the head' (*la teste du roy qui estoit foible*) are taken to be examples of the chronicler's contempt for the Valois king, and his pleasure in raking over old scandals, to be contrasted with the tactful evasions of the monk of St Denis.[31]

In fact, there is more to Froissart's account of Charles's illness than meets the eye. Although it is not immediately apparent from a casual reading, Guillaume de

---

[26]   Ibid., p. 78: '...car encoires a-il et aura tout ceste saison le chief foible et tendre et tost esmeu, et c'est raison, car il a esté batu et fourmené de très-dure maladie.'

[27]   G. Dodu, 'La Folie de Charles VI', *Revue historique*, 150 (1925), 161–88; Famiglietti, *Royal Intrigue*, pp. 1–22.

[28]   Guénée, *La folie de Charles VI*, pp. 116–19.

[29]   Ibid., pp. 123–6.

[30]   Ibid., p. 136 citing A. Brachet, *Pathologie mentale des rois de France* (Paris, 1903), pp. 593–606. Cf. Dodu, 'La Folie de Charles VI', who considers it to be an observation of his mother's thyroid condition.

[31]   Guénée, *La folie de Charles VI*, pp. 23–34, 136.

Harcigny's diagnosis of Charles's illness is based on ascribing to the king the bodily constitution of a youth who was not yet fully formed. Here, as in other accounts of the diagnosis of his illness, Charles VI's character and complexion are perceived in terms of certain commonplaces, topoi and systems of association connected with the moral and physical predispositions of young men.

To understand its full significance, Froissart's account of Harcigny's diagnosis needs to be read in the context of the Aristotelian and Hippocratic views of human development which dominated academic medicine and popular views of the body at this time.[32] In this system, the passage of life was imagined as the consumption of moisture by heat, as in an oil lamp. At the beginning of life there is too much moisture, and so the lamp does not burn vigorously. Thus childhood is characterised by coldness and wetness. In youth or adolescence, some of the moisture has burned off, and so the body functions more efficiently, reaching a state of hotness and wetness. Next, in the 'perfect age' of the body, enough moisture has been removed for the body to function most efficiently, and so a period of hotness and dryness is entered. Finally, in old age, the supply of moisture begins to run out, and a period of coldness and dryness sets in. The development of the body along these lines also had moral consequences. The excess of moisture in youth leads to 'inconstancy', which translates into both a lack of firmness of purpose and a tendency to fall into vice through the temptations of the body.[33] Thus, in late medieval sermons, didactic manuals and 'mirrors for princes' the youth is portrayed as susceptible to the delights of food, sex, alcohol, comfortable clothes and soft furnishings.[34]

Charles, as a young man, is characterised by an instability and moisture in his bodily make up which ultimately feminises him.[35] 'Mirrors for princes' followed Aristotle in portraying both youths and women as incomplete, unfinished men.[36] Even the youth's moist bodily constitution gave him something in common with women (held to be cold and wet) which distinguished him from fully formed adult males (held to be hot and dry).[37] Thus when Charles VI 'takes too much from the

---

[32] For what follows see J. A. Burrow, *The Ages of Man* (Oxford, 1986), pp. 12–35; E. Sears, *The Ages of Man* (Princeton, 1986), pp. 12–30; Fletcher, *Richard II*, pp. 60–73.

[33] Fletcher, 'Corruption at Court?'; Fletcher, 'Manhood and Politics', pp. 24–5; Fletcher, *Richard II*, pp. 66–7, 70–71.

[34] Works cited above, nn. 32, 33 and M. E. Goodich, *From Birth to Old Age: The Human Life-Cycle in Medieval Thought* (New York and London, 1989), pp. 90, 108, 121–32.

[35] Fletcher, 'Manhood and politics', pp. 23–4; Fletcher, *Richard II*, pp. 66–71.

[36] E.g. Giles of Rome, *Li Livres du Gouvernement des Rois* [*De Regimine Principum*], trans. Henri de Gand, ed. S. Molenaer (London, 1899), II.i.14, 20. Cf. D. Jacquart and C. Thomasset, 1988, *Sexuality and Medicine in the Middle Ages* (Oxford, 1988), pp. 17–18; T. Laqueur, *Making Sex: Body and Gender from the Greeks to Freud* (Cambridge, Mass. and London, 1990), pp. 25–62; V. L. Bullough, 'Medieval Medical and Scientific Views of Woman', *Viator*, 4 (1973), 485–501, p. 487.

[37] Giles of Rome, *De Regimine Principum*, I.iv.2, II.ii.15.

moisture of his mother', his complexion, the balance of humours and of the qualities of heat and moisture within him, exhibits both his immaturity, the fact that he has not yet reached the perfect, stable age, and links this to his feminine origins, and the cold and wet complexion characteristic of women. He is an 'inconstant youth' not just in personality but also in physical constitution.

It is this moisture, too, which explains why the illness from which Charles suffers is 'tourble', an upsetting into moist inconstancy of the fabric of his spirit, leading him into unpredictable, frenzied action, before he lapses into cold paralysis.[38] It also partly explains why the prognosis is generally optimistic, given a certain regime. If the king's unstable complexion is not disturbed by excessive stimulation, he will firm up with time, and the problem will cease to arise.

The logical consequences of this mixing of the physical with the psychological, and even the moral, are played out in Froissart's account of the reception of the news of the king's illness at the papal court at Avignon. The chronicler portrays Pope Clement VII and the cardinals at Avignon coming to a rather different, but at the same time remarkably similar diagnosis to that of de Harcigny, although one which is far less purely medical than the venerable doctor's. Hearing the news of the king's illness, the residents of the papal palace at Avignon put on a public appearance of shock, 'but they said amongst themselves that from a king who was young and full of his impressions and desires, one could not, and should not, expect anything else...'[39] It was the wilful characteristics of the king's youth that brought about Charles's bodily illness.

Froissart has those at the court of Avignon justify this remarkable opinion by arguing that the king's illness was a result of his bad upbringing. If Charles had had a 'reasonable rule' in his 'infancy and youth' and had been held to 'the counsel and ordinance of his uncles' this disaster would never have occurred.[40] On one level this seems to be a criticism of the king's insistence, against his uncles' will, on riding out to war on that hot day, which excessive behaviour brought on his attack of madness. But it is clear from the general cast of their alleged remarks that, for Froissart at least, it was also the failure to restrain the king's will in his youth which had produced not so much a bad character as a malfunctioning body.

An echo of this can even be heard in the well-informed but discreet account of Michel Pintoin, the monk of St Denis. According to this chronicler, the doctors concluded that the king's first illness had been provoked by the heating of his black bile, in turn caused by the king's anger at the late arrival of his uncles to go on campaign.[41] This initially seems like a strange diagnosis – black bile would nor-

---

[38] Described in *Froissart*, xv, pp. 48–9 and in the *Chronique du Religieux de Saint-Denys*, ed. L. Bellaguet (Paris, 1840) [hereafter *RSD*], vol. ii, p. 20.

[39] *Froissart*, xv, pp. 50–51.

[40] *Froissart*, xv, p. 51.

[41] *RSD*, ii, p. 20.

mally be cold and dry, not hot. Bernard Guénée suggests a likely explanation: the king's black bile had become heated and thus joined to his yellow bile – already hot and dry – to provoke a mad frenzy.[42] The king's complexion then cooled to such an extent that his heartbeat became difficult to discern. The doctors feared for his life, but Charles at length recovered.[43]

Once again, what at first seems to be a technical medical explanation is tied to a more general account of the king's illness which includes elements of both the psychological and the moral. The king's illness is provoked by an excess of heat, itself caused by his anger at his uncles. The reader would know that as a young, vigorous man, the king would already have a tendency to excessive heat. This could, as we shall see, find its expression in virtuous chivalric impulses. But in excess, particularly excess aimed against the uncles whose advice the king ought to have followed, it led the king into madness.

The reign of Charles VI was a particularly propitious time for the bringing together of medical knowledge and an ethical conception of politics. Authors of 'mirrors for princes' had long concerned themselves with the upbringing of future rulers, putting themselves in the role of the director of the conscience of the king's children.[44] With the minority and then madness of Charles VI this role had assumed a new importance, as the young king was succeeded by his sons as the object of the vital business of forming the morality of those who ruled. The work of Christine de Pizan stands as one example of the belief that the path for the regeneration of society lay in the proper education of the virtuous prince. Christine's concern with such matters was not just derived from the texts she followed, but also its resonance with the political circumstances of her day.[45] Tied up with this project was the need to take proper account of the particular tendencies of the youthful body, which finds an echo in the politics of Ricardian England.

At the beginning of her *Livre des Fais et Bonnes Meurs du Sage Roi Charles V* – begun in 1403 at the instance of the king's uncle, Philip of Burgundy – Christine details at length the dangers inherent in the upbringing of a youth.[46] On the one hand, the softness of children and youths makes them easily malleable. On the other, this malleability, coupled to lack of experience, made the youth subject to excessive appetites and bodily sin. She notes that both children and adolescents constitute a *tabula rasa* on which one could write or inscribe what one wanted.

[42] Guénée, *La folie de Charles VI*, pp. 133–4.
[43] *RSD*, ii, p. 20.
[44] J. Krynen, *Idéal du prince et pouvoir royal en France à la fin du Moyen Âge, 1380–1440* (Paris, 1981), pp. 75–6; Goodich, *From Birth to Old Age*, pp. 35–44, 111–14.
[45] Krynen, *Idéal du prince*, pp. 63–5, 75; A. L. Gabriel, 'The Educational Ideas of Christine de Pisan', *Journal of the History of Ideas*, 16 (1955), 3–21.
[46] Christine de Pizan, *Livre des fais et bonnes meurs du sage roi Charles Quint*, ed. S. Solente (Paris, 1936) [hereafter *LFBMC*], part I, chaps. ix–xiii.

With experience only of bodily delights, and none of speculative pleasures, it was no surprise that they were 'joyful, light and inconstant' (*joyeuses, légieres et de petite constance*). Youths changed quickly from joy to ire, from wanting to not wanting, and to other tender passions, as can be commonly seen in small children. She continued, significantly, that such tendencies were alleviated by growing into 'the perfect age of man', 'unless an obstacle obstructs the instrument, which is the body, by illness, or other accident'.[47] This, as Christine and her audience well knew, was precisely what had happened to Charles VI. Her description of the changeability and malleability of children echoes the description of the king's 'tourble'. For Christine, Jean Froissart, and even to an extent the monk of St Denis, Charles's illness was the endless continuation of the changeable temperament of youth. Like Oscar in Günther Grass's *The Tin Drum*, an accident had stunted his growth, indefinitely freezing him in a youthful state.

The bodily vices of youths are more immediately apparent in Christine de Pizan's general observations than her specific remarks about individuals. In her opening chapters, she warns of the dangers into which a youth risks falling, in particular an adolescent who has passed the first age of childhood and in whom 'heat and moisture are great'. In this period 'there is no one who could understand the diverse movements which are contained in this body, which by natural inclination, as if impassioned with appetite without order, do not yet know the line and correction of reason.'[48]

To read Christine de Pizan's work, one would have thought that Charles VI had escaped such snares. Telling of the stern morality of Charles V, she records how anyone who talked licentiously in the presence of the young dauphin would be banished from court.[49] She makes no mention of a tendency to bodily vice on Charles VI's part in her account of his mores.[50] Yet others were less reticent in ascribing to the young king a youthful susceptibility to bodily sin. Jean Froissart playfully alludes to these characteristics in portraying Charles' enthusiasm for marriage. Having seen Isabel of Bavaria at Amiens, the king is told that the marriage is to take place at Arras. But Charles wants to be married there and then. Only on Burgundy's avuncular insistence is he constrained to wait.[51] Elsewhere, Froissart reports that, visiting the papal court at Avignon, the king, the duke of Touraine and the count of Savoy 'who were young and of light spirit' spent the whole night in revelry with the local 'dames et dasmoiselles', even though they were lodged next door to the pope and cardinals.[52]

[47] *LFBMC*, I.xi.
[48] *LFBMC*, I.ix.
[49] *LFBMC*, I.xxix.
[50] *LFBMC*, II.xv.
[51] *Froissart*, x, pp. 351–2.
[52] *Froissart*, xiv, p. 37: 'qui estoient jeunes et de légier esprit'.

The St Denis chronicler is more censorious in his account of the king's mores. The monk asserts that Charles was not content to limit himself to marriage, although he concedes that he was never the object of scandal. Charles wore silk clothes which did not distinguish him from those of his court, we are told, sometimes dressing as a Bohemian or a German. The king was often involved in tournaments, which his predecessors had avoided after their anointment. Later in life, the chronicler sadly concludes, Charles suffered from loss of reason, but when he returned to himself, he did nothing with precipitation and always took counsel.[53]

Even this aspect of the king's unruly youth – the tendency to bodily sin – found its way into the simultaneously physical and moral explanation of his illness. In 1393, Froissart remarks that the first return of the king's madness was due to 'the great excess which in the past he had made in many ways in drinking and eating out of hours, and otherwise'.[54] In 1395, even the monk of St Denis intimates that doctors and theologians agreed that Charles illness came from 'the excesses of his youth'.[55] Again, in 1413, he repeats that a master of theology upbraided Louis, duke of Guyenne, the king's eldest son, warning him that it was 'as a result of the excesses of his youth that the king his father had fallen into an incurable illness'.[56] Bernard Guénée reads these judgements as references to the king's sexual misdemeanours.[57] Although there is something in this, these remarks clearly have a more general target than sexuality. It is the sins of eating, drinking and bodily excess that are here blamed for the king's illness. All the sins of *luxuria*, the absence of temperance, to which youth is prey are invoked, not just a failure of chastity.

It is telling to compare this portrayal of Charles VI in terms of the bodily constitution of youth with the use of similar topoi, but in very different ways, to criticize Richard II. Even when contemporaries attack the youthful excesses of the French king, and its woeful effect on his health, Charles himself is lightly treated. He is an object of pity, and occasionally of pathos, rather than of reproach. With the growing prominence of the king's eldest son, Louis, duke of Guyenne, the remarks of chroniclers and moralists increasingly took the form of warnings, with the king's young heir as the implied target, but even they are always careful, on the whole, to be respectful to the still-living king.[58]

---

[53]   *RSD*, i, p. 564.
[54]   *Froissart*, xv, p. 127.
[55]   *RSD*, ii, p. 406.
[56]   Guénée, *La folie de Charles VI*, p. 138.
[57]   Ibid.
[58]   Louis himself was accused of youthful carousing and keeping disreputable hours. See Krynen, *Idéal du prince*, pp. 65–8.

When the associations of youth were used to criticise Richard II it was not with such a light touch.[59] This has no doubt much to do with the fact that many of these critiques originate from just after Richard's deposition in 1399. Richard's moist, changeable constitution is just as physical as Charles VI's. This time, however, it is clear that this did indeed lead to sin, and to just retribution. One monastic chronicler reported that the king had a white, rounded and feminine face, which was occasionally corrupted with phlegmatic humour. The impression that this is an observation of Richard's changeable complexion is confirmed as the writer continues. He alleged that Richard's 'tongue was short and stuttering' (*lingua brevis et balbuciens*) and that the king was 'inconstant in his mores'. Spurning the counsel of old nobles, he adhered to the counsel of young men. Like Froissart on Charles VI, this chronicler alleges that Richard stayed up the whole night in drinking and other unmentionable things.[60] Less medical but equally hostile are the remarks made by John Gower in his *Vox Clamantis* in which he depicts a king spoilt by youthful company, following only his will, leading sin to spring up everywhere.[61] In a similar vein, the poet of *Richard the Redeless* paints a picture of a king who wilfully follows youthful advice dispensed by courtiers in attractive clothes, rather than the less attractively packaged advice of experienced knights.[62] Again bad life and bad government follow. Finally, Richard is condemned at his deposition in a sermon by Archbishop Thomas Arundel as a 'boy not a man', whose inconstancy in speech, wilfulness, and susceptibility to flattery tend to the kingdom's downfall, thankfully now averted by the usurpation of Henry Bolingbroke.[63]

No such weighty judgement fell on the shoulders of Charles VI. He was changeable, yes, he was childlike, certainly, and on occasion he gave evidence of excess. Yet all these things are met with relative indulgence. The same commonplace themes are used, but without the twist of the knife. But then, Charles VI was never deposed, or restrained against his will. His seizure of sole control of his own government at the age of 20 was only to last for four years.[64] With his madness, Charles could more easily be treated as an eternal youth in need of constant supervision by his benevolent uncles. When this benevolent rule broke down into factional strife and finally into civil war, the king's weaknesses served as a point of reflection on how the moral reformation of the kingdom could be achieved under

---

[59] See Fletcher, *Richard II*, esp. pp. 1–7, 14–22, 41–4, 56–8, 71–3 which discuss the texts cited below in greater depth.

[60] *Historia Vitae et Regni Ricardi Secundi*, ed. G.B. Stow (Philadelphia, 1977), pp. 166–7.

[61] John Gower, *Vox Clamantis* in *The Complete Works of John Gower*, iv, *Latin Works*, ed. G. C. Macaulay (Oxford, 1902), bk. 4, ll. 555–72.

[62] *Richard the Redeless* in *The Piers Plowman Tradition*, ed. H. Barr (London, 1993).

[63] *Rotuli Parliamentorum, 1278–1503*, ed. J. Strachey et al., 6 vols (London, 1767–77) [hereafter *RP*], vol. iii, p. 423.

[64] See works cited above, n. 14.

a new ruler who knew how to evade the snares of youth. Richard II, on the other hand, never went mad, but simply persevered with his attempts to gain full control of government, finally pulling the house down around his ears by his action against the Lancastrian inheritance in 1399.[65] Growing contestation of his rule and his eventual deposition set the scene for the most elaborated attacks against him.

Charles VI never had to be condemned. Indeed, his continuing presence on the throne meant he had to be treated with at least a measure of respect. For the most part, writers who deal with the character of the young French king spend less time stressing the temptations of bodily sin and the wilfulness which was held to characterise youth, and more underlining the young king's laudable, if as yet unmeasured, love of chivalry and warfare.

The St Denis chronicler, for example, tells a story of how Charles V early on discovered his son's martial desires. One day, they say, the elder Charles showed the young dauphin all the royal treasures and jewels and asked him to choose an object to his taste. To his father's surprise the future Charles VI disdained all the finery, and asked instead for a sword hung in the corner of the royal wardrobe. A few days later, the king decided to test his son further. He showed him a crown, richly encrusted with gold and precious stones, and a helmet, and asked him if he would rather be crowned or to expose himself to the dangers of war. The child, as we might have guessed, selected the helmet, and was rewarded with helmet and harness and arms made to fit his size.[66]

After Charles VI's coronation, writers continue to portray him as keen for military glory. Froissart shows Charles overflowing with enthusiasm for the proposal of the duke of Burgundy that he should intervene to suppress the rebellion of the Flemish towns. The duke of Berry's advice to take wider counsel, lest they later be accused of leading their charge into projects which were contrary to his interests, are swept aside by a king eager for combat.[67] When battle is joined at Roosebeke, the St Denis chronicler shows the king eager to take part. As Charles advances against the Flemings in the middle of the central guard, he hears for the first time the sound of arms, and prays to God for victory, invoking the saints, the Virgin Mary and St Denis. When the two sides clash, he has trouble restraining himself, not wishing to leave his own men in peril through shameful inaction, asking Philip the Bold, 'Why not aid our men, who face danger of death for us, and who prefer our glory to their own life?' The chronicler has the duke soberly reply that a king ought to aspire to win victory as much by his wisdom and prudence as by his sword.[68]

---

[65] C. Fletcher, 'Narrative and Political Strategies at the Deposition of Richard II', *Journal of Medieval History*, 30 (2004), 323–41; Fletcher, *Richard II*, pp. 249–74.

[66] *RSD*, i, pp. 22–4.

[67] *Froissart*, x, pp. 65–6.

[68] *RSD*, i, pp. 216–20.

In this episode, and others like it, Charles becomes another type of youth, still equally susceptible to outside impressions and sudden decisions, but this time led not by bodily impulses but by the desire for combat and glory. For whereas the youth was similar to women in terms of moisture and hence changeability, he differed from them in his strength, characterised by his superior heat.[69] In the unmeasured pursuit of war, this strength could come to be linked with excess and uncontrollability, qualities which in a different context could be used to explain the susceptibility of youth to bodily sin.[70] Christine de Pizan notes in one sentence the perils of 'insane loves' (*foles amours*) and the risk that 'by the heat of their blood', youths will provoke battles and riots.[71] Again, there is a humoral logic behind such assertions. Youth is characterised in complexion by an excess of 'blood', the hot and wet humour, leading to vigour, but also to a lack of controllability. It is from this that we get the idea of a 'sanguine' nature. For Christine, this leads youths to follow bad counsel, associate with their enemies and attack their friends, pursue their wills and not the pursuit of reason. The warlike tendencies of youths were by no means universally viewed with enthusiasm.[72] In the case of Charles VI, however, they do seem to be viewed, for the most part, in a positive light. If the king's chivalrous desires are excessive, his young age gives hope that they will be controlled in time.

Froissart's account of Charles's chivalric mores has been taken by a number of writers to be critical, the picture of a likeable but gullible clot easily manipulated by faction.[73] But all this has to be read into Froissart's account, since he nowhere adds an explicit or implicit critical commentary to this effect. The concern of the king's uncles not to be seen to influence him against his interests is portrayed as being as genuine as king's desire for battle.[74] In another episode, during the preparations for the invasion of England in 1386, the Constable, Olivier de Clisson, faced with bad weather at sea, only just makes it alive to the muster at Sluys. In the face of the conclusion that the sea is too dangerous to embark, Charles VI declares that he is a good sailor and will see for himself if the Channel is impassable.[75] In this passage, the reader is not clearly shown whether Froissart believes this to be proof of the king's idiocy, or of his frustrated (if naïve) enthusiasm for combat. Indeed, it seems likely that this is Froissart's dramatisation of an attempt by Charles and

---

[69] Fletcher, 'Manhood and Politics', p. 24; Fletcher, *Richard II*, pp. 63–5.

[70] Ainsworth, *Jean Froissart*, pp. 181–2.

[71] *LFBMC*, I.x.

[72] Consider, for example, the portrayal of youth in Chaucer's *Tale of Melibee*, on which see Fletcher, *Richard II*, pp. 160–61, 267, 273–4.

[73] Ainsworth, *Jean Froissart*, pp. 182–4; Sherborne, 'Charles VI and Richard II', pp. 161–2.

[74] *Froissart*, x, pp. 65–6.

[75] *Froissart*, xii, p. 20.

his uncles to leave harbour despite the bad weather, which is also reported by the monk of St Denis.[76]

More clearly apparent in Froissart's *Chroniques* and elsewhere is the sense of Charles VI, and his chivalrous enthusiasm, as the embodiment of the hopes of the French for deliverance from the English. Christine de Pizan's account of Charles's mores passes straight from his coronation at a young age to the hopes he embodied. Thus, she asserts, 'this young king began to reign, showing so well chivalric mores, nobility of heart (*courage*), largesse and concern to do honour to merit, that those who saw his childhood so inclined to arms and chivalry, and such a desire to go out and undertake great deeds, judged that the King Charles had been born, whom the prophecies had promised, who would perform great marvels.' She continues that all of this was confirmed by the marvellous victory which he achieved over the Flemings at the age of fourteen.[77]

The monk of St Denis, writing of the preparation for an expedition to counter an English incursion in Flanders in 1383 writes that 'From day to day the qualities of the king made hope grow'.[78] Charles, he asserts, 'believed that the moment had come when, with Mars as their arbiter, he would put an end to the discord between himself and the king his adversary.' The French king preferred to go before his enemies than suffer any longer the robbery and arson which his subjects had to bear. In an account of Charles VI's mores inserted after the king's dismissal of his uncles from their formal role as councillors, the chronicler notes that: 'All the good dispositions of youth were seen in him: capable with the bow and with the lance, prompt to arms, a good horseman, he displayed impatient ardour every time that enemies provoked him with their attacks.'[79]

No surviving text says such a thing of Richard II. Chroniclers and literary writers familiar with the Lancastrian accusation that the king raised taxes but waged no wars were not about to praise Richard's military vigour.[80] But they could have done. Richard took part in an expedition to Scotland which secured the retreat of an invading Franco-Scottish force in 1385, and an expedition to Ireland in 1394–5 which secured the submission of the Gaelic chiefs.[81] A further expedition in 1399 was only interrupted by Henry Bolingbroke's invasion.[82] From 1382 to 1386 the government pressed for money for a royal expedition to the continent with the king at its head and was frustrated only by socio-economic circumstances ill-

---

[76] *RSD*, i, p. 460.
[77] *LBFMC*, II.xv.
[78] *RSD*, i, p. 264.
[79] *RSD*, i, p. 564.
[80] *RP*, iii, p. 419.
[81] Fletcher, *Richard II*, pp. 127–43, 240–43.
[82] For the circumstances of Henry's invasion, see *Chronicles of the Revolution*, ed. and trans. C. Given-Wilson (Manchester, 1993), pp. 32–40, 107–61; Saul, *Richard II*, pp. 405–15; Fletcher, 'Narrative and Political Strategies'; Fletcher, *Richard II*, pp. 268–70.

adapted for the necessary expenditure.[83] Perhaps Richard II was not so different from Charles VI as all that. It now appears that the most famous chronicle passage describing how Richard lacked 'warlike spirit' is most likely a post-1399 interpolation.[84] One familiar Ricardian object, the Wilton Diptych, portrays the king accepting a military banner from the Christ child.[85] It shows the king as a surprisingly young man, with red cheeks indicating the hot and wet, sanguine temperament of youth. There was no more appropriate way to mark Richard's desire for chivalrous deeds, whether on Crusade, or some other expedition.

On the other hand, the expressions of enthusiasm and hope which accompany observations of Charles VI's martial enthusiasm are not quite as straightforward as they seem. Hindsight plays an important part even in accounts of Charles's qualities which were written whilst he was still alive. These writers made much of the hope which was supposedly provoked by the young king's chivalric tendencies in the full knowledge that this hope would be disappointed. The St Denis chronicler writes in the same passage of Charles's hope-giving martial ardour, and of his later madness. Christine de Pizan wrote eleven years after the king's first illness. It is tempting to speculate that our view of Charles VI would have been somewhat different if he had stayed sane, certainly when the English case is brought to mind. Whilst Charles's madness opened up a secure space for criticism of the government, Richard II himself became at length the only possible focus for criticism, as it became impossible to deny that the king fully knew his own mind.

In many ways Charles VI and Richard II were very similar in their character and preferences. They both shared the prejudices of their class. They were enchanted by chivalric enterprise, campaigned when they could, and risked splitting the political community by pushing military action when frugality in expenditure and tactful restraint would have done the job better. Both became attached to the men their fathers had trusted and vigorously resisted the agenda of their uncles. Significantly, both their reigns saw an efflorescence of vernacular literature which took up the moral systems presented in the 'mirrors for princes' and didactic manuals of the late thirteenth and early fourteenth century and applied them to contemporary events.[86] After his deposition, Richard II became a useful figure to invoke when discussing the virtues or faults of successive governments, by refer-

---

[83]   Fletcher, *Richard II*, pp. 97–150.

[84]   G. B. Stow, 'The Continuation of the *Eulogium Historiarum*: Some Revisionist Perspectives', *English Historical Review*, 119 (2004), 667–81.

[85]   For further discussion, see Fletcher, *Richard II*, pp. 16, 258–62; Fletcher, 'Manhood and politics', p. 28.

[86]   Krynen, *Idéal du prince*, pp. 39–71; *The Piers Plowman Tradition*, ed. H. Barr (London, 1993); J. Coleman, *English Literature in History: Medieval Readers and Writers 1350–1400* (New York, 1981); J. Mann, *Chaucer and the medieval estates satire* (Cambridge, 1973); A. Middleton, 'The Idea of Public Poetry in the Reign of Richard II', *Speculum*, 53 (1978), 94–114.

ence to the fatal vices or loathsome treasons which had supposedly led to this king's demise.[87] With Charles still alive, similar issues – taxation and its effect on the people, the need for moral and chivalric virtue on the part of the king and the control of royal finance – were dealt using the same moral tropes, but with a lighter touch. I would suggest that it is these circumstances which have lent such contrasting casts to their reputations as inconstant youths.

---

[87] Aston, 'Richard II and the Wars of the Roses'; S. Walker, 'Richard II's Reputation,' in *The Reign of Richard II*, ed. G. Dodd (Stroud, 2000), 119–28, 152–4; and now J. Nuttall, *The Creation of Lancastrian Kingship: Literature and Politics in Late Medieval England* (Oxford, 2007).

Latin Chronicles and Medieval Lives in the Middle English Prose Brut

WILLIAM MARX

The theme 'recording medieval lives' opens up a particularly interesting and useful perspective on a Middle English text that until recently has received little attention from medievalists, the Middle English Prose *Brut*.[1] Apart from the Wycliffite translation of the Bible, the *Brut* survives in more manuscripts than any other Middle English text.[2] This fact in itself is remarkable, and it is almost equally remarkable that the Middle English Prose *Brut* has been the object of so little interest among modern scholars. Why this is so is a question to which this paper will return, but first it will be useful to say something about the text itself. The *Brut* takes its name from the legend of the foundation of Britain by Brutus. This is the legendary history of Britain that is best known through Geoffrey of Monmouth. The narrative of the Middle English prose *Brut* begins with events leading up to the foundation of Britain and follows British history – in a number of versions – up to different dates in the Middle Ages. The Middle English Prose *Brut* began as an Anglo-Norman prose chronicle, and this Anglo-Norman text was compiled in England during the reign of Edward I (1272–1307). The original *Anglo-Norman Prose Brut* finished with the death of Henry III in 1272, but there were later continuations to 1307 (the death of Edward I) and to 1333.[3] What is referred to as the 'Common Version' of the Middle English prose *Brut* is basically a translation of the Anglo-Norman text. The Middle English narrative beyond 1333 is original composition in Middle English, and there are numerous versions, continuations, and revi-

---

[1]   *The Brut or Chronicles of England*, ed. by F. W. D. Brie, EETS OS 131, 136 (1906, 1908; reprinted as one volume 2000). Lister M. Matheson, *The Prose Brut: The Development of a Medieval English Chronicle*, Medieval and Renaissance Texts and Studies, 180 (Tempe, Arizona, 1998). R. E. Lewis, N. F. Blake, A. S. G. Edwards, *Index of Printed Middle English Prose* (New York and London, 1985), item 374. Afterwards *IPMEP*.

[2]   *IPMEP* 119.

[3]   Ruth Dean, with the collaboration of Maureen B. M. Boulton, *Anglo-Norman Literature: a Guide to Texts and Manuscripts* (London, 1999), items 42, 43, 44, 45, 46 (pp. 30–33). Julia Marvin's edition of the *Anglo-Norman Prose Brut to 1272* (item 42) is the first modern edition of any of the versions; see *The Oldest Anglo-Norman Prose 'Brut' Chronicle: an Edition and Translation*, ed. by Julia Marvin, Medieval Chronicles, 4 (Woodbridge, 2006).

sions of the narrative of the Middle English text into the fifteenth century, to the 1460s and the 1480s, and beyond.

The nature of the *Brut* may go some way to explaining why it has been neglected. The *Brut* falls somewhere between what has been traditionally thought of as historical writing or chronicle writing and 'literature', and neither historians nor researchers whose main interest is in literature have, in the past, been eager to claim the *Brut* as an area of responsibility or an area of research. The remark by the first and indeed only modern editor of the Middle English prose *Brut* serves to highlight the problem. Brie states in the preface to his edition for the Early English Text Society (1906):

> As literature, the Chronicle [i.e., the *Brut*] is as worthless – except for a few inserted poems – as a medieval Chronicle possibly can be.[4]

This is an aesthetic judgement, and it probably served to divert scholars of literature away from the *Brut* for many generations. Nevertheless, such a large body of Middle English writing, which was clearly of vital interest to fifteenth-century readers and compilers, as well as sixteenth-century readers, should not be ignored, and certainly the broadening of the parameters of scholarship and the growth of new historicism from the 1980s onwards have meant that vernacular historical narrative in general and the Middle English prose *Brut* in particular have begun to be seen as important areas for investigation.[5]

It might be assumed that the theme of 'recording medieval lives' would lead directly to chronicle writing or vernacular historical writing, for apart from recording the occasional natural phenomena such as earthquakes, the appearance of comets, floods, and generally inclement weather, chronicles record or, more precisely, give record to, events of human history. But it is the fact that chronicles or historical narratives are aiming to put into written record the events of history that makes them frustrating as sources for medieval lives in the broad sense of the term. It is a commonplace in discussions of vernacular historical writing that this type of narrative is effectively written backwards; that is, the construction of the narrative is dictated by outcomes, and the selection of details is therefore purposeful in that it reflects the design that governs the narrative itself.[6] This means that for the most part chronicles such as the *Brut* do not yield that kind of incidental detail that would provide insights into everyday medieval lives, that is, what individuals, especially ordinary individuals, did day-to-day, what they thought, what their frustrations and aspirations were. In a version of the *Brut* on which I

---

4   Brie (ed.), *The Brut*, 'Introduction', I: ix–x.
5   The first collection to bring together essays that reflect current trends in scholarship on the medieval prose *Brut* is *Readers and Writers of the Prose Brut*, ed. by William Marx and Raluca Radulescu, *Trivium*, 36 (2006).
6   See, for example, Paul Strohm, *England's Empty Throne: Usurpation and the Language of Legitimation 1399–1422* (New Haven and London, 1998), pp. 1–3.

worked for a number of years, I thought that I had come across examples of episodes built around incidental details that were in one sense inconsequential, that is, had no purpose in terms of the larger narrative strategy. Below is one of those passages, from the reign of Richard II:

> The xvj yere of Kynge Richard, Iohn Hende, beynge þat tyme maire off London, and Iohn Walworth and Henry Vanner shireves off London þat same tyme, a bakares mon of London bare a basket full of horsebreede into Fleete Streete towarde an hostre house. And their camme a yomon off the Bisshoppe of Sales-bury called Romayne, and toke an horseloofe oute off þe basket; and the baker asked hym why he didde soo, and this Romayne turned agayne and brake the bak-eres heede. And then camme peple oute and wolde haue arested þis Romayne, and he brakke fro ham and fledde into the bisshoppez place ...[7]

On the surface this seems like an episode that provides an insight into everyday life, in this case, street crime and intimidation in late fourteenth-century London. Indirectly, or inadvertently, this episode may give us this kind of insight, but that is not its purpose, for the narrative of which it is part is a chain of events that leads to Richard abandoning London and moving his court to York in 1392.[8] Generally, this type of narrative does not record much that is incidental; episodes are selected with a larger narrative purpose in mind.

What has come to be known as 'new historicism' or 'neo-historicism' has high-lighted important issues such as selectivity and purpose in historical narrative, and has gone a step further in raising questions about absences – what compilers leave out or suppress. It is argued that a major responsibility for the scholar or critic is to detect what is absent from a narrative, and this type of evidence provides clues for the concealed design, meaning, or purpose in a narrative or historical docu-ment. In the Preface to his book *England's Empty Throne* (1998) Paul Strohm sets out a central feature of a 'new historicist' approach or methodology, especially in relation to chronicle writing:

> Those texts which try hardest to ignore or exclude an event – to 'forget history' – tend to be the very places where the *absent event* stages its most interesting and complicated return. My own analysis thus continually relies on an enabling para-dox: that the places where a text has been most extensively rigged and reworked

---

[7]   The passage quoted is from *An English Chronicle 1377–1461: A New Edition*, ed. William Marx, Medieval Chronicles, 3 (Woodbridge, 2003), p. 14/9–17. The episode also appears in the continuation of the Common Version of the *Brut* (Brie II: 345/3–13), and appears in a briefer form in the *Chronicle of London, 1189–1483*, eds N. H. Nicolas and E. Tyrell (London, 1827; rpt., Felinfach, 1995), pp. 79–80.

[8]   *An English Chronicle*, 14/8–15/14; also Brie II: 345/3–348/5. See C. M. Barron, 'The Quarrel of Richard II with London, 1392–7', in *The Reign of Richard II: Essays in Hon-our of May McKisack*, eds F. R. H. Du Boulay and C. M. Barron (London, 1971), pp. 173–201; also Nigel Saul, *Richard II*, Yale English Monarchs (New Haven and London, 1997), pp. 258–9 and 343.

are the very places where the presence of an event-in-abeyance may be most cru-
cially felt or surmised.[9]

This kind of questioning is stimulating, but in the light of work on the *Brut*, I have
been provoked into taking a different approach to interpretation in the case of vernacular historical writing. What I am interested to explore is not what the new historicist critic perceives as absences or the missing parts of the narrative, but what
the medieval compiler perceived as absences or missing parts of the narrative. It
is possible to detect instances like this by examining the processes of compilation;
these provide an insight into the compiler at work, and our task is to interpret the
significance of this historic process of compilation itself. Constraints of space
mean that this paper will examine in detail only one instance where the medieval
compiler has detected an absence and has responded to the text, but it is intended
to serve as an outline for a method and approach to a specific type of vernacular
historical narrative.

The *Brut* is not a stable text but one that was subject to extensive revision and
adaptation, and this feature of the textual history of the *Brut* is what makes it an
important area for research. These revisions and adaptations come to light in what
Lister Matheson has identified as the 'peculiar versions' or recensions of the *Brut*.[10]
The term 'peculiar version' goes back to the early work on vernacular historical
writing by C. L. Kingsford in his book *English Historical Literature in the Fifteenth
Century*, first published in 1913.[11] Kingsford used the term 'peculiar' in its traditional sense of 'distinctive' or 'particular', although it is tempting to imagine that
the choice of term reflects Kingsford's puzzlement with the complexity of the
Brut's textual history. The 'distinctive version' of the *Brut* on which this paper
focuses is referred to by Matheson as 'The Peculiar Version to 1422: Group B' and
survives in two manuscripts: Aberystwyth, National Library of Wales MS Peniarth
397; and Oxford, Bodleian Library MS Bodley 754.[12]

The passage given below is the text of the latter part of the account of William
I or William the Conqueror in this 'peculiar version', here taken from Peniarth 397
(pp. 71–4). The portion of text set in standard type is from the Middle English
'Common Version' of the *Brut*, which is translated from the Anglo-Norman text,
and in Brie's edition is chapter 133.[13] The text set in italics is an addition to the
'Common Version':

---

[9]   Paul Strohm, *England's Empty Throne*, pp. xii–xiii. Emphasis is mine.
[10] *The Prose Brut*, pp. 256–334.
[11] Kingsford's book was first published in 1913 by Clarendon Press, Oxford, and reprinted
      in 1972 by Burt Franklin, New York.
[12] *The Prose Brut*, pp. 294–6.
[13] Brie I: 136/29–138/9.

[Peniarth 397, p. 71]

Off Kyng William Bastard and off the Kyng off Fraunce

Whenne William Conquerour, bastard Duke of Normondye, hade conquered alle Englond, vppon Cristesmasse Day tho next sewing [*following*], he lett crovne hym kyng at Westmynstre and was a worthy kyng and gaf to Englisshe men largely landes and to his knyghtis. And afturward he went ouer the see and come into Normandye and ther du[e]lled a whyle. And in the ij yere of his reigne he come agayn into Englond and brought with hym Maude, his wyff, and lett crovne hir Quene of Englond on Wittsonday.

And tho anon after the Kyng of Scotland that me [*men*] called Maucolum began to werre and to strif with the Duke William, and he ordeyned hym toward Scotland with his men bothe by lande and by watur forto distry the Kyng Maucolum, but they wer accordid. And tho the Kyng of Scotlond, Mancolum, become his man and helde alle his lande of hym, and Kyng William receyvid of hym his homage and come agayn into Englond.

And whenne Kyng William hade ben kyng xvij yere, Maude the quene died, on whom Kyng William hade geten mony fair childern. That is forto sayn Robart Corteyse, William Lerous, and Richard also that died, Henry Beauclerc, and Maude also that was the Erles wyff of Bleuys, and other iiij doughters. And aftur his wyfes deth, grete debate began betwex hym and the Kyng of France, [p. 72] Philippe, but att last they were accordid. And tho duelled the Kyng of Englond in Normaundy and no man with hym werred, neyther he with no man long tyme.

And the Kyng of Fraunce seide vppon a day in scorne of Kyng William that Kyng William hade long tyme leyen in chilbed and long tyme hade rested hym. And thus worde come to the Kyng of Englond therr that he lay in Normandy at Roen. And for this worde was he ylle payde and eke wondur wrothe toward the Kyng of Fraunce and swore by God whenne that he were areson of his geseyne [*childbed*] he wolde light a M^l candels to the Kyng off Fraunce. And anon he lette assemble a grete hoost of Normandy and of Englisshe men, and in the begynnyng of hervyst he come into Fraunce and brende alle the tovnes that he come by thorough alle the cuntre, and robbed and did alle the evel that he myht thoroghout Fraunce. And att last he brent the citee of Mande and comaunded alle his peple forto ber wodde and as moche as he myht brenne and hymself halpe thertoo alle that he myht with goode wille. And ther was grete heete what of fyre that was so grett and of the sonne that was wondur hoote that he stuffed hymself [*was stifled from heat*] and felle into a grete sekenesse. And whenne he saw that he was strong syke, he ordeyned and assygned alle Normandye vnto Robart Curthos, his sone, and alle Englond to William the Rous, and bequathe alle his tresour to Henry Beauclerc, his other sone.

And this was the cause why he was cald Bastard. For his fadur, Erl of Normandye, as he passed [p. 73] *thorough the cuntre he saw a wondur fayre woman that was gracioux, plesaunt and fayr, ledyng a daunce among other maydons. And anon he hade so grete desyr to haue this mayde that he wrought in suche maner that she lay by hym alle nyght and helde her long as she hade ben his wyff. And vppon hir he gate William, and his fadur called hym euermor William Bastard, and this name contynued vnto his lyfes ende.*

And anon aftir his fader Robart made a vow vnto Iherusalem, and or he went, he putte this William Bastard in the kepyng of the Erl Gilbart. And his fader

Robart as pilgryme dyed by the way homward. And anon this Erl Gilbart wolde haue made alle the lordes of the lande to don hym homage, and alle they hade grete endynacion, forasmoche that he was a basterd, to haue hym to hir lorde and souereyne. And afturward this Erl Gilbert was slayn and the Kyng of Fraunce toke this William Bastard vnto hym. And whenne he come to age he wox strong, hardy, and myhty, and avengid hym on alle his enmyes. And the Kyng of Fraunce made hym Erl of Normandye and wedded Maude, the Erlis doughter of Flaunders, and begate vppon her the sones above seid. And whenne he hade reigned xx yer and x monythes & xxviij dayes, of the v Ide of Steptembre vppon a Monday dyed this worthy conquerour and lithe in Cane in the chyrche of Seynt Steven, the yeer of Our Lord M^l iiij^{xx} and vij.

And this William Bastard was discried a man of right statur, full flesshly of body with a fers face and a playne forhedde, wel brawned [p. 74] *and myghtely that ther myht no man handel hit for harde, and he ioyed right moche of his strynkith* [strength]. *He was a grete plantere and setter of woodis insomoche that the tovnes that were distried he made to growe with woode. And in principaly festes he wolde be fedde wasfully* [extravagantly] *and louyd long to sitte theratte. And whenne he was in Englond he kepte his Cristemasse at Gloucestre, his Ester in Wynchestre, and his Witsontid at Westmenistre, and thus he devydid the yer in thre. He was also a right wyse man and a slye, ryche and right couetous, gloryouse of fame, a goode man to Holy Cherch, passyng sharpe and vengeable to hem that withstoode hym. In Hamptschyr xxx myle on lenkith he distroyed townes and chirches and made therof a forest and ordeyned these lawes, that whoso toke therin a best he shulde lese his eye and whosoo ravysshed a woman shulde forgone his stoones. He founded ij monasteries in Englond, oon at Bermondseye, another in Southsex wher he hadde his bataille.*[14]

This chapter begins with the coronation of William as king and his distribution of lands in England. After two years William has his wife Maude crowned as Queen of England on Whitsunday. The narrative includes an account of William's conflict with Malcolm, King of Scotland, and the eventual submission of Malcolm to William. Then, after William had been king for 17 years, Maude died, and at this point the text includes a list of their children, those who survived and those who had died. After some dispute with Philip, King of France, it is said that they reached an agreement and William lived peacefully in Normandy. Then comes a reference

[14] Aberystwyth, National Library of Wales MS Peniarth 397, pp. 71–4. The reading 'wel brawned and myghtely that ther myht no man handel hit for harde, and he ioyed right moche of his strynkith', which is common to the two manuscripts, goes back to a misunderstanding of the Latin source: William of Malmesbury, *'Gesta Regum Anglorum': The History of the English Kings*, ed. and trans. by R. A. B. Mynors, completed by R. M. Thomson and M. Winterbottom, 2 vols, Oxford Medieval Texts (Oxford, 1998, 1999), book III, chapter 279 (vol. I, pp. 508–9): *roboris ingentis in lacertis, ut magno sepe spectaculo fuerit quod nemo eius arcum tenderet, quem ipse admisso equo pedibus neruo extento sinuaret* (his arms extremely strong, so that it was often a remarkable sight to see no one able to draw his bow, which he himself, while spurring his horse to a gallop, could bend with taut bowstring). The translator has not understood that the reference is to William's bow.

to William's reaction to a perceived insult by the King of France, that William was slothful. This provokes William to violent attack against the King of France, which leads to William's death, and the division of his kingdom among his sons. At this point the Common Version of the *Brut* ends its account of the reign of William I.

Throughout, the narrative of the Common Version (in Anglo-Norman and Middle English) is highly political in nature with few details concerning William's personality or private life. The implication is that in this narrative, William's life is seen primarily in terms of its political and military significance. There is no need for sentiment or for anything of the private or personal. In the light of this approach to the life and career of a king – and this is typical of the Common Version of the *Brut* – we are seeing something of the function of the *Brut* in both its Anglo-Norman and Middle English versions. However, at this point, in this 'peculiar version', there is more. The text set in italics is material added to the Common Version. This is of a different kind from what appears in the Common Version of the *Brut*. It refers to aspects of William's life, even his conception and why he had the appellation 'bastard'. The text describes his early struggles and how in adulthood he overcame his difficulties and married well and reigned as king for over 20 years. And, in addition, there is a paragraph describing William's appearance, his preoccupations with destroying towns and planting forests, his character, namely his wisdom, courtesy, desire for fame, and the laws he put in place against criminal activity. Finally, there is a reference to his piety in founding two religious houses.

The additional material is not original to this 'peculiar version'. The first two paragraphs of the addition can be traced to the Latin text of the *Polychronicon* (book VI, chapter 19).[15] The third paragraph, the description of William I, is a synthesis of William of Malmesbury's *Gesta Regum Anglorum*, book III, chapter 279,[16] and Henry of Huntingdon's *Historia Anglorum*, book VI, chapter 39 which itself is based on the 'obituary' of William the Conqueror in the *Anglo-Saxon Chronicle*.[17]

What implications can be drawn from these additions to the Common Version of the *Brut*? These passages do not appear in the Anglo-Norman text; they are additions peculiar to the Middle English text, and they are drawn from Latin sources. The additions are remarkable for the way in which they expand for the vernacular text the picture of the life of William the Conqueror. We learn about William's bas-

---

[15]   Ralph Higden, *Polychronicon*, eds Churchill Babington and Joseph R. Lumby, 9 vols, Rolls Series (1865–86), vol. VII, pp. 118–29 (pp. 122–7).

[16]   Vol. I, pp. 508–09.

[17]   Henry, Archdeacon of Huntingdon, *Historia Anglorum: The History of the English People*, ed. and trans. by Diana Greenway, Oxford Medieval Texts (Oxford, 1996), book VI, chapter 39, pp. 404–407; *The Anglo-Saxon Chronicle: a Revised Translation*, ed. by Dorothy Whitelock with David C. Douglas and Susie I. Tucker (London, 1961), pp. 163–5.

tard origins, about his youth, about his appearance, and many other features of his character. Clearly the Latin tradition of chronicle writing with which the compiler of the peculiar version was familiar was interested in this kind of perspective on William the Conqueror. In other words, the compiler of the Middle English text – this peculiar version – has noticed and responded to the absence of this kind of material in the vernacular text, that is, the Common Version of the Middle English *Brut*.

It is possible that a 'new historicist' would have detected the absence from the Common Version of the *Brut* of the kind of material that appears in these additions. S/he might have asked the penetrating question: why does the *Brut* say nothing about William the man? And, conclusions or interpretations could be developed from that question. Nevertheless, it is equally intriguing, indeed, I would argue, more intriguing and also more revealing about the historical significance of this version or recension of the text, that the medieval compiler of this peculiar version of the Middle English prose *Brut* thought it important to ask this kind of question, and further made the decision to add this kind of material at this point to the account of the reign of William the Conqueror.

This peculiar version of the Middle English prose *Brut* is significant for the way it incorporates Latin materials, and there is a wealth of material of this kind to investigate. Another example is found in the treatment of Henry II. This is extensive, and again the compiler has incorporated into the Middle English text of the Common Version material drawn from Latin historical writing. For example, in chapter 140 the Common Version of the *Brut* refers to the conflict between Henry and King Stephen, the division of the kingdom, and Stephen's death.[18] At this point in this peculiar version the compiler introduces new material that refers, first, to Henry's accession to the throne. But, unlike the account of William the Conqueror, the compiler here also introduces material concerning the life of Henry at the beginning of the account of his reign. This is extensive; indeed, the new material for Henry II begins on page 113 of Peniarth 397 and runs to page 128, with a brief return to the Common Version of the *Brut* for the account of the murder of Thomas Becket. For this part of the narrative, the Common Version of the *Brut* is replaced almost entirely by material drawn from Latin chronicle writing.[19] The addition begins with a description of Henry:

> Whenne Stephene was deed come Henry, the emperesse son, nevew vnto the first Henry, of whom the manerys, vicis and dedes Gerard wrytith oponly in his distunctions. This Henry was a man of rody colour, a grete hede with a brode face and a brode breste havyng yeolo yen [*light coloured (? hazel) eyes*], with a love

---

[18] Brie I: 147/10–26.

[19] The compiler replaces *Brut* chapter 141–4 (Brie I: 147/27–151/20), apart from Brie I: 149/29–150/6. The compiler uses selectively the Latin text of the *Polychronicon*, book VII, chapters 21–4, vol. VIII, pp. 22–81.

[*low*] voice. Flesshely of body, a litle eter and drynker forto wast [*burn up*] his flesshenesse, vsyng for the same cause mekil hontyng, and otherwhile standyng and otherwhile goyng. A man of mene statur, wel letterd and wele langgaged, right myhty in dedis of armes, besy in his aray in werris, dredyng dovtable fortune, more mercifull to deede bodys thanne to lyfyng, mor mornyng for the ded thanne lovyng them that ben alyve. (Peniarth 397, p. 113)

This passage is part of a portrait of Henry, but much more extensive and detailed than that of William I. It includes Henry's virtues as well as his vices, and makes judgements about his actions: 'And he weddyd Elynor, that somtyme was the Kynges wyff of Fraunce, & from hym was departid ... wheche this Henry shulde not haue weddyd by ryght' (Peniarth 397, p. 114). Like the account of William I, that of Henry includes reference to his family origins, the taint of having been born out of an illicit relationship:

> Now lett vs speke of the moder of this seide Kyng Henry, for she was the wyff of the Emperour of Almaigne, whiche was called Henry, that was a goode man and an holy. For grete holynesse he went into feer cuntrees to mony an holy pelgremage. In whiche tyme alle agayne the law she toke another husbonde, the seide Geffrey Plantagenent, of whom come the foreseide Kyng Henry; and thus he was begeton and boron in avoutry [*adultery*]. And therfor, while this Hynry in his chilhode was noryshede in the Kyngis court of Fraunce, the holy abbot, Seynt Barnard, prophesyed of hym in the Kingis presence of Fraunce and seid, 'This chylde come fro the devil and to the devil he shalle'. (Peniarth 397, pp. 116–17)

In this 'peculiar version' the history of the reign is dominated by the personality of Henry II, as if the historical narrative were an extension of his life.

The reference to 'Gerard' and the account of the 'mannerys, vicis and dedes' of Henry II is to Gerald of Wales, but the compiler has taken this over from the *Polychronicon*, which he has translated from the Latin text.[20] The *Polychronicon* was translated into English on more than one occasion, but here we have an instance of the use of the *Polychronicon* for a very specific purpose; it is used to provide a perspective on Henry II, and replaces the much less nuanced account in the Common Version of the *Brut*. The compiler is giving, in the vernacular, a record of selected aspects of the life and character of Henry II.

This peculiar version of the *Brut* is of the fifteenth century, and the interest in the details of the personal life of important political figures may reflect a growing sense in fifteenth-century vernacular culture that the personal is political. But it is important to keep in mind that we can also trace this material in Latin writing back to an earlier period. There is much research to be done on the peculiar versions of the *Brut*, but on the basis of what is discussed here it is possible to argue three

[20] *Polychronicon*, book VII, chapter 21 (vol. VIII, p. 22). For Gerald of Wales on Henry II see *Giraldi Cambrensis Opera*, eds J. S. Brewer, J. F. Dimock, and G. F. Warner, 8 vols, Rolls Series (1861–91), V, pp. 302–6 and VIII, pp. 213–15.

points. First, the evidence of the introduction of this kind of material from Latin texts into the vernacular prose *Brut* argues for a movement towards the vernacularization of historical writing in the fifteenth century. Second, the different peculiar versions show that in the fifteenth century the vernacular *Brut* was being used as a vehicle or framework for the incorporation of material from Latin historical writing into a well established narrative framework in the vernacular. Third, as we see here, a special feature of the expansion of the narrative is that in many instances it is designed to record or give record to the lives of significant historical figures.

A final general point concerns method and approach to research in vernacular historical writing, a type of writing that is bound to be a focus for political and ideological questions. It is possible to interrogate texts for the significance of what is omitted or the 'events in abeyance', and much that is interesting emerges from this type of investigation. But in the peculiar versions of the Middle English prose *Brut* there are many instances where episodes and details are not omitted and held in abeyance, but are brought to the foreground. Of course the medieval reader of a peculiar version of the *Brut* is unlikely to be aware of what contributed to the narrative, but as researchers we are in a position to gain a special insight into those processes. The peculiar versions of the *Brut* provide a rich opportunity to investigate the processes of redefining the historical and political narrative in the vernacular. And, in this respect, it is significant that, in the examples discussed here, so much of the material that is added to the Common Version of the *Brut* records aspects of medieval lives.

John to John: the Manuale Sacerdotis and the Daily Life of a Parish Priest

SUSAN POWELL

Manuale Sacerdotis, the priest's handbook, is a five-part Latin text of between twelve and twenty chapters in each part, written probably at the end of the fourteenth or beginning of the fifteenth century by John Mirk, who was by then prior of the house of Austin canons at Lilleshall in Shropshire.[1]

Mirk's choice of Latin as the medium for the *Manuale* explains why it has been overshadowed by his two other works, the *Festial* and the *Instructions for Parish Priests*. Both these vernacular texts have been published,[2] but Mirk's third work, the *Manuale*, has not been printed, although it has been edited twice as doctoral theses.[3] The most detailed treatment in print is that of Alan Fletcher on the manuscripts and the *Manuale*'s place in the tradition of *pastoralia*.[4] The recognition that the *Manuale* has been previously accorded is not, however, commensurate with its interest, as it is hoped that this article will demonstrate, and an edition incorporating a translation with *en face* Latin text is currently in preparation by the present author in collaboration with James Girsch, on whose critical edition this article is dependent and to whose kindness and scholarship I am indebted.

[1] On Mirk, with particular reference to his *Festial*, see S. Powell, 'The *Festial*: The Priest and His Parish', in *The Parish in Late Medieval England*, eds Clive Burgess and Eamon Duffy, Harlaxton Medieval Studies XIV (Donington, 2006), pp. 160–76.

[2] *Mirk's Festial: A Collection of Homilies, by Johannes Mirkus (John Mirk)*, ed. Th. Erbe, Part I, EETS ES 96 (1905); *Instructions for Parish Priests by John Myrc*, ed. E. Peacock, EETS OS 31 (1868), rev. F. J. Furnivall (1902); *John Mirk's Instructions for Parish Priests*, ed. G. Kristensson, Lund Studies in English, 49 (Lund, 1974). S. Powell's edition of the *Festial* is to be published by the Early English Text Society.

[3] 'The *Manuale Sacerdotis* of John Myrc: An Edition', ed. M. W. Washburn (unpublished Ph.D. thesis, Chicago, 1974); 'An Edition with Commentary of John Mirk's *Manuale Sacerdotis*', ed. J. M. Girsch (unpublished Ph.D. thesis, Toronto, 1990).

[4] A. J. Fletcher, 'The Manuscripts of John Mirk's *Manuale Sacerdotis*', *Leeds Studies in English*, n.s. 19 (1988), 105–39. There are briefer studies in G. R. Owst, *Preaching in Medieval England: An Introduction to Sermon Manuscripts of the Period c.1350–1450* (Cambridge, 1926), pp. 47 (fn. 1), 245, 297, W. A. Pantin, *The English Church in the Fourteenth Century* (Cambridge, 1955), pp. 215–17, and P. Heath, *English Parish Clergy on the Eve of the Reformation* (London, 1969), pp. 1–4.

The base-text of the edition will be that of Oxford, Bodleian Library MS Bodley 632, from which all quotations in this article are taken. Thirteen *Manuale* manuscripts are extant, all of which date from the second half of the fifteenth century,[5] and all of which may have been in the hands of secular priests or regulars, judging by inscriptions and the other contents of the manuscripts.[6] Mirk himself was an Austin canon at Lilleshall abbey in Shropshire from at least the 1380s.[7] In the Preface to the *Manuale* Mirk calls himself prior,[8] whereas the colophon to the *Festial* text in London, British Library MS Cotton Claudius A.II. calls him canon,[9] which may suggest that the *Manuale* was a work of later life.[10]

Austin canons followed the rule of St Augustine but in comparison with monks they led active lives in the world, with an outreach duty and sometimes even serving as parish priest in churches attached to their abbey.[11] Mirk's three works are intensely practical and pedagogic. The *Festial* is a collection of ready-to-preach sermons, probably originally sixty-four in number, arranged (in Mirk's original format) from Advent Sunday to All Souls' Day, with a final sermon for the Dedication of a Church. Mirk explicitly stated in his Prologue that it was written for priests with little learning and few books who had to undertake the duty of preaching and teaching their parishioners all the principal feasts of the Church year.[12] The *Instructions* is similar in intention. Again, it is directed at the ill-equipped priest (specifically here, a curate). It is a 1,934-line pastoral manual in rhyming couplets (and so easily read and even perhaps in part memorised), which offers the priest guidance on his duties, particularly in relation to pastoral instruction (ll. 69–535),

---

[5]   They are listed by Fletcher, 'Manuscripts'. Cambridge, Trinity College Library MS B.ii.23 is precisely dated to 1474.

[6]   For example, Oxford, Bodleian Library MS Bodley 549 contains Carthusian tracts and was written in part by Stephen Doddesham of Sheen Charterhouse. Less certainly, Cistercians at Kirkstall abbey in Yorkshire may be linked with York, York Minster Library MS XVI.O.11 (Fletcher, 'Manuscripts', pp. 114–15, 122). For details of other manuscripts, see further in Fletcher, 'Manuscripts'.

[7]   For the dating, see S. Powell, 'A New Dating of John Mirk's *Festial*', *Notes and Queries*, n.s. 29 (1982), 487–89, and A. J. Fletcher, 'John Mirk and the Lollards', *Medium Aevum*, 56 (1987), 217–24.

[8]   For example, Oxford, Bodleian Library MS Bodley 632, f. 68 ('Iohannes, dictus prior de Lylleshull').

[9]   'Per fratrem Iohannem Mirkus compositus, canonicum regularem monasterii de Lulshull' (f. 125v).

[10]   Fletcher, 'Lollards', p. 222. This is not inherently unlikely, but, on the other hand, the references to him as canon are posthumous so cannot have the same status as the *Manuale* reference to his being prior, which is in Mirk's own dedication of the text.

[11]   For Mirk's associations with St Alkmund's, Shrewsbury, see Powell, '*Festial*', pp. 163–4.

[12]   For the Prologue (quoted from London, British Library MS Cotton Claudius A.II., f. 1v), see S. Powell, 'John Mirk's *Festial* and the Pastoral Programme, *Leeds Studies in English*, n.s. 22 (1991), 85–102, p. 86.

hearing confession (ll. 675–1698), the sacraments of baptism and confirmation (ll. 536–674), and the performance of the last rites (ll. 1699–1838). In the course of the work, Mirk deals with the Paternoster and Ave Maria (ll. 404–25), the Creed (ll. 426–53), the articles of the faith (ll. 454–525), the seven sacraments (ll. 526–35), the ten commandments (ll. 849–972), the seven deadly sins (ll. 973–1302), the seven deeds of mercy (ll. 1355–64), and the seven virtues as remedies for the seven deadly sins (ll. 1551–1624). The *Instructions* therefore covers material which it had been the duty of the priest to teach since the Fourth Lateran Council of 1215, but which had acquired greatest importance through the 1281 Lambeth Constitutions of Archbishop Pecham of Canterbury, and, more recently but for the other province, through the 1357 Injunctions of Archbishop Thoresby of York, the vernacular version of which is known today as *The Lay Folk's Catechism*.[13]

The *Manuale* is similarly a pastoral work, addressed to the priest, indeed, to a specific priest. It is however a different sort of work from the *Instructions*, and it does not provide the details of the tenets of the Church which the *Instructions* provides, although a little of its general advice is the same as that of the *Instructions*, such as what to do if an insect falls in the chalice.[14] It draws on the tripartite *Oculus Sacerdotis* (1320–8) of William of Pagula, particularly the *Sinistra Pars*, but to some extent also the *Pars Oculi* and the *Dextera Pars* which supplied Mirk's material for the *Instructions*.[15] The latter is in the vernacular, but Mirk wrote the *Manuale* in Latin for two reasons: firstly because he was writing a more academic work than the *Instructions*, one in which, for example, canon law is frequently quoted; and secondly because he had things he wanted to say to his addressee which were not appropriate for anything other than a clerical readership, indeed, which are dealt with, as Owst pointed out long ago, 'in remarkably outspoken fashion',[16] and which in another context would be called anti-clerical.

The addressee was one John (hence the first part of the title of this article, 'John to John'): 'To his dearest friend, 'dominus' J[ohn], vicar of A, John, entitled prior of Lilleshall: greetings in the name of the Author of salvation'.[17] Four of the

13   On *pastoralia* and preaching, see Pantin, *English Church*, pp. 189–219, L. E. Boyle, *Pastoral Care, Clerical Education and Canon Law* (London, 1981), H. Leith Spencer, *English Preaching in the Late Middle Ages* (Oxford, 1993), pp. 196–227, and, in relation to the *Festial*, Powell, 'Pastoral Programme'. For *The Lay Folk's Catechism*, see the edition by T. F. Simmons and H. E. Nolloth (EETS OS 118, 1901).

14   Cf. *Instructions*, ll. 1749–1838 *passim* (especially ll. 1825–34) and *Manuale* (MS Bodley 632, f. 87). If possible, the insect should be drunk, but, if not, it should be taken out and washed well over the chalice, after which the washing water should be drunk and the insect burnt.

15   L. E. Boyle, 'The *Oculus Sacerdotis* and Some Other Works of William of Pagula', *Transactions of the Royal Historical Society*, 5th series, 5 (1955), 81–110.

16   Owst, *Preaching*, p. 47 (fn. 1).

17   Of the ten manuscripts with this greeting, MS Bodley 632 is the only one to have 'B', not 'I' or 'Iohanni': 'Amico suo karissimo domino B., uicario de A., Iohannes, dictus

ten manuscripts with this epistolary address call him John 'de S.', and Alan Fletcher has argued that this might be John Sotton who was vicar of St Alkmund's Shrewsbury from January 1414.[18] Fletcher has demonstrated that 'vicar of A' (in eight manuscripts) for 'vicar of Alkmund's' is not impossible, although it is probably unusual (the date is also rather late), and the 'A' (which might be merely a token initial) is more likely to refer to a placename. If the addressee was a canon, like Mirk, with pastoral responsibility, 'A' could refer to a benefice owned by Lilleshall, such as Atcham in Shropshire or even Ashby de la Zouch in Leicestershire.[19] Whether or not a canon (and there is no evidence that he was), the relationship between the two men which prompted Mirk to write the *Manuale* may have been that of kinsmen – one of the chapter headings is: 'How the prior addresses his kinsman concerning the observance of the previous matters'.[20] Mirk himself, however, calls John only his 'dearest friend',[21] and, conventional amongst religous, 'dearest one'.[22]

Part 1 of the *Manuale* (eighteen chapters) focusses on the priest himself: what makes a good priest? and, rather more detailed, what makes a bad priest?[23] The distinction is, in fact, between good priests and 'modern priests', as in the heading to Chapter 7 of Part 1: 'That modern priests indulge more in worldly vanities than in divine exercises'.[24] The distinction between 'sacerdotes moderni', today's priests, and 'uita boni sacerdotis',[25] the life of the good priest, appears to strengthen the suggestion that Mirk is writing in older age from a position of wisdom and experience.[26] Good priests have due reverence for the priesthood and

---

[18] prior de Lylleshull: salutem in auctore salutis' (f. 68). Cambridge, Trinity College Library MS B.ii.23 has the initial 'N' (i.e. 'nomen', name). However, a later reference in the text makes plain that the recipient was indeed called John: 'Disce igitur et tu, Iohannes, Sanctum Iohannem diligere, et pro Deo et Sancti Iohannis amore elemosinas erogare' ('Learn therefore, you too, John, to love St John and to bestow alms in the name of God and for love of St John'), MS Bodley 632, f. 95v.

[18] Fletcher, 'Lollards', p. 222 and fn. 27.

[19] *Victoria History of the Counties of England*, ed. R. B. Pugh, *A History of Shropshire*, vol. 2 ed. A. T. Gaydon (London, 1973), 70–1, 78.

[20] 'Qualiter alloquitur prior cognatum suum de obseruancia premissorum' (MS Bodley 632, f. 97). However, the chapter headings are unlikely to be original, and it is perhaps conceivable that 'cognatum' renders 'fratrem', brother.

[21] See fn. 17 above.

[22] 'Karissime', e.g. MS Bodley 632, ff. 68, 69, etc. The *Instructions for Parish Priests* also address the reader specifically in terms such as 'þou preste curatoure' (l. 11), 'leue brother' (l. 1917), and 'dere prest' (l. 1913).

[23] See the Appendix for the parts and chapter headings in Girsch, 'Edition'.

[24] 'Quod moderni sacerdotes magis indulgent mundi uanitatibus quam diuinis exerciciis' (MS Bodley 632, f. 71).

[25] MS Bodley 632, f. 71v.

[26] That he is addressing someone of younger age and less experience is a corollary of this.

live unworldly lives – they avoid litigation, they despise the world, and they have not been promoted falsely. Bad priests prefer archery to contemplating the wounds of Christ and playing ball to using the quill;[27] they chant feebly in church but sing cheerfully enough in the pub; they are silent in the pulpit but noisy following the hounds; they chase after witticisms but are slow to look into manuscripts; they are illiterate, worldly, drunks and gluttons, gamblers, fornicators and (the final insult) businessmen.

The focus and aim of this first part of the *Manuale* is quite clear, but thereafter the structure of the book appears to have eluded most commentators (although Pantin seems to have discerned it). Fletcher thinks it 'new and idiosyncratic',[28] and even its editor, James Girsch, calls it 'a curious compound' and 'a derivative and discursive work' and feels that 'the principle of division between the Partes …is not always clear'.[29] Nor is its place in the pastoral tradition straightforward. Fletcher compares it with pastoral manuals of the thirteenth and fourteenth centuries, in comparison with which 'it might well appear eccentric; for example, it lacks the emphasis on confession and penance which is central to much of the thirteenth-century material, and the exposition of the six points of Pecham's programme which so frequently appears in fourteenth-century works'.[30]

However, these comments on structure and content are based on the assumption that Mirk was trying to do what others had done before him, that is, to produce a standard work of pastoral instruction in a standard format. Mirk is doing something different, reflective of his fresh and pragmatic approach to problems. He is indeed an intensely pragmatic man, and the *Manuale* is directed very closely at a specific problem (and, indeed, a specific person). The work is not intended to explain how to confess someone properly or how to baptise a child or what the seven deadly sins are (Mirk had already done that in the *Instructions*),[31] but to attempt to shock a young man (and hopefully other young men) into awareness of what being a priest actually means. The whole of the *Manuale* is imbued with the importance of the priesthood: 'the priesthood is indeed to be absolutely trembled at and greatly to be feared' (Part 1, Chapter 4).[32] It is imbued with the reverence with which the sacrament must be approached, the huge responsibility of the man who has been ordained to celebrate the Eucharist, and the duty of that

---

27   In the first clause, the association of a target with the wounded body of Christ is subtle, while the second clause depends on alliteration: 'Plus uero diligunt ad limites sagittare quam stigmata Christi mente tractare, palmare pilam quam occupare pennam' (MS Bodley 632, f. 71v).

28   Fletcher, '*Manuale*', p. 106.

29   Girsch, 'Edition', pp. XVII, XLII, XXXI.

30   Fletcher, '*Manuale*', p. 107.

31   This comment assumes (rightly, I think) that the *Instructions* was an earlier work.

32   'Tremendum est omnino et pertimescendum ualde sacerdotale officium' (MS Bodley 632, f. 70v).

man to live the life of a priest.[33] But above all, Mirk's concern is that one young man dear to him has taken the order of priesthood too frivolously and is not aware that 'the whole life of a good priest, if he lives rightly, ought to be a cross and a martyrdom' (Part 1, Chapter 7).[34]

We will return to that young man at the end of this article. If the contents of the *Manuale* are not those of a typical pastoral manual, nor is its structure typical of a pastoral manual. Girsch is right to say, as noted above, that 'the principle of division between the Partes ... is not always clear' . Mirk does not produce discrete Parts – he is happy to continue a previous topic in the first chapter of the next Part, a technique which intensifies the pace and flow of the work as a whole. He is discursive too, moving from one topic to another and then back again, but the topics are always related and the stream of consciousness flows as in thought or as in an actual letter (which we have no reason to believe this was not, at least in its first instance). With the ease of experience, he moves from the practical detail to the spiritual intention easily and properly. Mirk is equally relaxed about his structural divisions – there are no problems with minor internal divisions, for example, the three kinds of thoughts with which the devil tempts the priest (part 2, chapter 9),[35] or the three steps of the altar (part 4, chapters 7–9),[36] but the speed and energy of his writing sometimes tend to lead him away from his initial topic, so that, for example, the last four of the six special virtues needed by a priest remain elusive.[37] Nevertheless, none of these matters affects the real overall structure which is clearly discernible but has been largely overlooked by other commentators.

It is this structure which explains the rest of the title of this article: 'the *Manuale Sacerdotis* and the daily life of a parish priest'. As has been seen, Part 1 introduces the subject of the priest, what is a good and what is a bad priest. This is the real matter of the whole of the *Manuale*. It is not a pastoral manual as such. It certainly provides facts and details to do with the way in which a priest should comport himself in his parish, but these facts and details serve a specific purpose, less descriptive than didactic: to establish the authority and sanctity of the priesthood, not in the minds of the people (for whom Mirk obviously did not write), but in the minds of the priests themselves. Thus even a minor detail such as what to do if an

---

[33]   In Part 1, Chapter 5, Mirk derives 'sacerdos', priest, from 'sacra dans', offering sacred things, or otherwise 'satis dans', offering enough, that is, offering Christ who is enough for all (MS Bodley 632, f. 71).

[34]   'Tota itaque uita boni sacerdotis, si recte uiuat, crux debet esse et martirium' (MS Bodley 632, f. 71v).

[35]   MS Bodley 632, f. 80.

[36]   MS Bodley 632, ff. 89v–90.

[37]   The first is holiness (Part 2, chapter 3), the second innocence (Part 3, Chapter 1), the third perhaps cleanness (Part 3, Chapter 3), and it may be that the three steps of the altar (faith, hope, charity) are the final three (Part 4, chapters 7–9). Cf. MS Bodley 632, ff. 77v, 82v, 83v, 89v, passim.

insect falls in the chalice is less a rule to be learnt and remembered (though it is that) than an indication of how the priest's every action must affirm the sanctity of the sacrament and the reverence in which he holds it. The detail is not bureaucratic but essential.

To return to the structure: if Part 1 establishes the theme of the good and bad priest, Part 2 (fifteen chapters) appears at first not to offer a new topic but merely more of the same, that is, further advice on the proper behaviour of the good priest – how to comport himself amongst the undisciplined; always to keep in mind the sanctity of the priesthood; the six virtues specific to the priest, beginning with holiness. In fact, however, Part 2 begins a subtle journey through the daily life of the parish priest. This becomes apparent in Chapter 4,[38] which begins at the break of day, when the priest should follow the advice of St Hilary of Poitiers and repeat the Vulgate Psalm 53 three times, together with the Paternoster and the Ave, raising both his heart and his hands to God. He should then make the sign of the cross and humbly repeat a prayer (which Mirk sets out for him) of thanks for safe deliverance from the dangers of the night and for all God's benefits. In Chapters 5–6,[39] Mirk urges John not to love his bed too much. If Ambrose says that the sun should not rise on the bed of any Christian, how much more important it is that a priest should get up before sunrise. Anyway, the devil sends bad thoughts to the sleepy priest, which is why, when subdeacons are ordained, the bishop tells them to be wakeful, and why Peter Cantor quotes Cato's similar pronouncement. In these dangerous early hours of the morning, dreams and masturbation may preoccupy the young man, and Mirk offers advice on, and explanation of, both.

The priest has now started his day, and the rest of Part 2 takes him through the hours up to the end of the morning office. Mirk draws out the spiritual and doctrinal implications from the concrete details and backs up his words with scriptural, patristic, and legislative authorities, as well as with an occasional exemplary narrative.[40] First the priest gets dressed, modestly in mid-calf garments and certainly not in red, green or yellow (which, Mirk points out, are colours forbidden by the legate Ottobuono's 1268 constitutions). He should wear sheepskin or rabbitskin (no other sort of fur); he should not have a silver belt, dagger, sword, or knives, in short no worldly ornaments at all; and his tonsure should be correctly shaven. He should examine his conscience carefully at this point in the morning, before going to his church to say the office, proceeding at a decent pace, not too fast nor too slow; without sword or staff or bow and with no accompanying dogs

---

[38]   MS Bodley 632, ff. 78–78v.

[39]   MS Bodley 632, ff. 78v–79.

[40]   Although there are not as many as in the *Festial*, where Mirk's *narrationes* are an integral part of every sermon, the inclusion of these popular stories even in the *Manuale* with its clerical, not lay, audience demonstrates how integral they are to Mirk's teaching style.

or hawks, just with a book, reciting Psalms as he goes, and praying for the dead as he passes through the churchyard. Once in church, he should say the prayer 'Introibo ad altare Dei', that is, 'I shall go to the altar of God' (Vulgate Psalm 65: 13), take holy water, genuflect before the crucifix, and say a prayer in honour of Christ's wounds (Mirk suggests an appropriate one).[41] Then the priest should pause and cleanse his heart of all external thoughts and say the office carefully and solemnly – nor should he ever be late in doing so. Part 2 ends with advice on how important it is for a priest to confess even the smallest sins often (at least once a week according to Ottobuono), and to do the appropriate penance.[42]

At the end of Part 2 the priest has reached the conclusion of the morning office; Parts 3 and 4 will take him through the preparation, physical and mental, for mass and the celebration of the Eucharist; Part 5 will deal with his comportment during the rest of the day. The celebration of the Eucharist is the actual and metaphorical highpoint of the priest's day, hence its position here and the fact that it constitutes nearly half of the whole *Manuale*. It is not that the Eucharist is part of the daily service of the priest – he need not say or even hear mass every day, although he certainly should every Sunday (Part 4, Chapter 3).[43] The Eucharist is crucial to the daily life of the priest because it is the essence of the priest: his celebration of it is what sets him apart from other men, it is what brings him closest to Christ who first celebrated it and at the Last Supper instituted the sacrament of ordination. Every possible detail is given in Parts 3 and 4 (twelve and fourteen chapters respectively), all tending towards exactitude of ritual and proper recognition of the sanctity of the celebration.[44]

For example, in Part 4, Chapter 10, when the priest reaches 'Qui pridie' ('who, the day before ...'), he must remove all vain thoughts from his heart, and from there to 'Unde et memores' ('whence, mindful ...'), that is, throughout the consecration,[45] his attention should be directed to pronouncing all the words distinctly as in the canon of the mass. At 'Qui pridie', totally separated from the worldly and intent only on the spiritual, he should receive the Host humbly in his hands, raise his heart and eyes to God, believing that heaven is opened at that moment, and make the sign of the cross on the Host.[46] At the word 'fregit' ('he

---

[41] Mirk emphasises that divine office should only be said in church, not in a room or a garden, perhaps a reference to some of the unorthodox meetings held at the time.

[42] The illustrative *narratio* is one from the miracles of the local saint, Winifred, which Mirk also uses in the *Festial* (Erbe, *Festial*, pp. 100/14–101/2). See too fns 51 and 68.

[43] MS Bodley 632, f. 88.

[44] As an Arrouaisian house, Lilleshall placed great emphasis on the proper performance of the liturgy.

[45] *The Sarum Missal edited from Three Early Manuscripts*, ed. J. Wickham Legg (Oxford, 1916), p. 222/10–223/3.

[46] Almost as a footnote, Mirk adds that, although the priest makes the sign of the cross, the blessing comes from God. In all, the priest makes twenty-five signs of the cross in

broke ...'),[47] he must not break the bread but continue with the words of the consecration, 'Hoc est enim corpus meum' ('for this is my body') straight without a pause and then adore the body of Christ with head and body bowed and knees bent. He should not kiss the Host but raise it for the people to adore, but not too high and not touching it except with four specially consecrated fingers.[48]

With Part 4, the Eucharist is over, and Part 5 (twenty chapters) begins with the advice to engage in silent devotional reading after mass and points out that confessions are better heard after than before mass. (As usual, this is for an intensely pragmatic but also spiritual reason – that the priest may hear things during confession which would prey on his mind during mass.) He should not hurry to have lunch, and, when he does eat, he should behave decorously at the meal-table and leave as soon as he has finished. Unless he has a duty to perform, he should not go out after mass, and, if he does go out, it should be with a mature colleague. If he can, he should stay at home, do some manual labour or read or write or work in the garden. Later he will have dinner, although Mirk disapproves of dinner, saying that we eat dinner less for need than habit and greed, and commenting that he can be brief about the dinner of a good priest, because the dinner of a good priest ought to be brief (Part 5, Chapter 13).[49] After the meal, the priest should go to his room but not go straight to bed. Instead he should think through the day, ask pardon for anything blameworthy, and, if necessary, prepare for confession the following day. Then he may go to his bed and say a prayer of thanks for safe deliverance through the day, a prayer in which he includes his family and friends, benefactors, enemies, the Catholic Church, the souls for whom he is bound to pray, and the souls in purgatory. Finally he crosses himself and lies down for the night with another prayer on his lips. A subsidiary text in this final part weaves into the details of the end of the priest's day advice on other topics prompted by thoughts of closure – the appropriate behaviour of the sick priest and of the ageing priest, and the need to spurn the world and prepare for death.

The structure of the daily life of the priest is therefore apparent in the *Manuale*, and it is that on which this article focusses, not on the numerous related issues which arise out of the basic structure. One only should be mentioned here, as evidence of Mirk's orthodoxy (if such be needed) and his willingness to tackle (in a Latin work not for lay consumption) the most difficult problem of his day. His lengthy treatment of transubstantiation and the Lollard heresy arises naturally out of his description of the consecration of the elements and occupies the three fol-

---

the celebration of the mass, but each blessing comes from God.

[47]   *Sarum Missal*, p. 222/15.

[48]   As another quasi-footnote, Mirk cites Remigius and others as authorities for the fact that the canon of the mass should be said secretly and not loudly.

[49]   'De cena boni sacerdotis breuis sermo sufficit, quia ipsa cena breuis esse debet' (MS Bodley 632, f. 96v).

lowing chapters (Part 4, Chapters 11–13). He outlines the Lollard heresy and emphasises the crucial role of faith in the orthodox dogma and the irrelevance of human reason. In the sacred elements the body of Christ is fully present but hidden, 'like the sun behind a cloud, when only the cloud is seen, hiding the sun, but the hidden sun does not suffer any dimming of its brightness'.[50] Like the apostle Thomas, who saw Christ as man but believed in him as God, we see the accidents but believe the body and blood. This may be proved by the life of St Odo, Archbishop of Canterbury, whose clerks were converted from their lack of faith by the elements turning into the bleeding body of Christ.[51]

Mirk's way of working is to use the basic theme of priesthood, to interweave into it details of the daily life of the priest, and to produce a final work in which instruction and ideology are not separate matters but are dependent each on the other and explained each in relation to the other. The *Manuale* is by no means merely a technical guide, as the *Instructions* is. There are certainly rules to being a priest, and Mirk deals with them, but they are not by any means only rules to be observed externally – there are inner rules too. Indeed, Mirk has begun the *Manuale* with the statement that the good priest is one who follows a Rule. Adapting St Paul to the Romans so that 'regula' (rule) is substituted for 'lex' (law),[52] Mirk says: 'To be honest, living without a rule is nothing less than dying' (Part 1, Chapter 2).[53] Mirk himself followed the Rule of St Augustine, but the rule by which he says all priests should live is not a monastic rule but the rules of Christ's own life as they are revealed in the Gospels: love, obedience, poverty, preparedness,[54] contempt of the world, flight from worldly honours, not seeking after riches, carrying your own cross, and, last but not least, following Christ and sticking with him. Such observances are bitter at first but become over time sweeter than honey and the honeycomb to the servant of God.

Much can be learnt about Mirk from the *Manuale* – a moralist, disciplined, dedicated, pragmatic, a pedagogue, but also a very humane man. He clearly took deep offence at those priests who were happy to separate their lives from their vocation. Analogies with Chaucer's Parson are trite but pertinent: it would appear of Mirk that 'Cristes lore and his apostles twelve | He taughte but first he practised it hymselve'.[55] As he says to John: follow the rule of the Gospels 'so that you may live in a ruled and ordered way and offer the example of your good life to others'.[56]

---

50 MS Bodley 632, f. 91.
51 As at fns 42 and 68, the same *narratio* is used in the *Festial* (Erbe, *Festial*, pp. 170/29–171/11).
52 Romans 2: 12: 'Qui sine lege uiuunt, sine lege peribunt' ('For whosoever have sinned without the law, shall perish without the law'), MS Bodley 632, f. 70.
53 'Sane sine regula uiuere nichil aliud est quam perire' (MS Bodley 632, f. 70).
54 'Lumbos precinctos habere' ('having girt loins'), MS Bodley 632, f. 70.
55 Geoffrey Chaucer, *The Canterbury Tales*, General Prologue, ll. 527–8.
56 'Ut regulariter et ordinate uiuas et aliis bene uiuendi exemplum prebeas' (MS Bodley

This picture of Mirk corroborates the impression of the other works, but what we learn specifically from the *Manuale* is his solicitude for one individual, the John to whom John Mirk writes. He refers to this other John constantly in the *Manuale* – he makes a statement and adds: 'Ecce, karissime' ('see, dearest');[57] he gives a good example and adds: 'Tu igitur/ergo, karissime' ('therefore, you, dearest');[58] he gives a bad example and adds: 'Tu autem, karissime' ('but you, dearest').[59] He addresses him at greatest length in the Preface to the work and again in the last five chapters of the final Part. The *Manuale* itself is therefore enclosed (as it were) between the covers of John Mirk's letter to the other John. Unusually, this letter is found in nearly all the manuscripts.[60]

In the Preface Mirk presents himself as one who has taken on the task of drawing the draught of doctrine from the well of charity for the benefit of others, and as such he is confident that he in turn will taste the draught of eternal life from the springs of the Saviour. As the apostle James says, the man who turns the sinner back from his sin will save a soul from death and hide a multitude of sins.[61] This is an ominous start for John, the addressee, linking him to the Biblical sinner. At this stage it is at least allusive, but Mirk soon moves from the general to the specific to complain about those clergy who live undisciplined lives and for whom he has taken on himself to 'apply the medicine of correction to their wounds'.[62] This he will do with a strong will, with some learning, but mostly with the grace of God, and he will write to John for his benefit and that of others, as well as for his (Mirk's) own eternal merit. In doing so, he will write in a frank and direct manner – John should not be offended at his rustic style (of two evils, a holy rusticity is better than sinful eloquence).[63] Those who flatter John do not love him tenderly, and those

---

632, f. 70).

[57] MS Bodley 632, f. 71.

[58] MS Bodley 632, ff. 71, 72v.

[59] MS Bodley 632, f. 71v.

[60] The two abridged manuscripts, Oxford, Bodleian Library MS Hatton 97 and Cambridge, University Library MS Ff.i.14, omit the dedication, and Oxford, Bodleian Library MS Digby 75 is acephalous (Fletcher, 'Lollards', p. 224 (fn. 27) and, for a description of the manuscripts, '*Manuale*').

[61] James 5: 19–20: 'Si quis autem errauerit ex uobis a ueritate, et conuerterit quis eum, scire debet quoniam qui conuerti fecerit peccatorem ab errore uie sue, saluabit animam eius a morte et operit multitudinem peccatorem' ('My brethren, if any of you err from the truth, and one convert him: He must know that he who causeth a sinner to be converted from the error of his way, shall save his soul from death, and shall cover a multitude of sins').

[62] 'Medicinam correccionis eorum uulneribus apponere' (MS Bodley 632, f. 68).

[63] 'Melius est de duobus imperfectis rusticitatem habere sanctam quam eloquenciam peccatricem' (MS Bodley 632, f. 68). Pantin, *English Church*, comments on Mirk's 'elegant style' (p. 215), and Mirk's 'rustic' comment may be a reference to the informality and familiarity of his address to John.

who call him 'blessed' are in fact his seducers. Mirk will not be like them – indeed he will use the second person singular pronoun 'tu' throughout because the plural is a polite means of flattery and not appropriate to holy speech. Finally, at the end of the Preface, John is urged to read the book once and, then, not to throw it into a corner, but to keep on reading it, having it so often in his hands that he will think of it as '*Manuale Sacerdotis*', the handbook of the priest.

It is impossible to escape the conclusion from the Preface that Mirk sees John, vicar of A, as one of these derelict priests, whom he describes in the first Chapter of Part 1 as unsuited for their position, having been ordained or preferred for money or for frivolous reasons. He denies the thought – 'you have undertaken the priestly office lawfully' – but adds 'as I hope'.[64] He is perhaps the sort of man who might read the *Manuale* once and then throw it into a corner of the room, so that Mirk at the end of his Preface has to ask him not to do so but to keep it in his hands always.[65] There are other references in the work too which link John with poor scholarship (Part 1, Chapter 8, Part 5, Chapter 2)[66] and with the desire for worldly gain (Part 5, Chapter 16).[67]

Mirk's aim, he says, is to instil in John the fear of God, and the very first exemplary narrative in the *Manuale* is Bede's story (which Mirk also uses in the *Festial*) of the man from Cunningham in Northumberland who died and came back to life in order to tell his vision of hell, purgatory, and heaven (Part 1, Chapter 1).[68] Just as the *Manuale* begins with this warning of hell, so it ends much later with Mirk putting into John's own mouth an admission of his fear of hell. Mirk, as it were, fulfils his own wish to terrify John by having him enact his terror: 'I fear hell, I fear the face of the Judge, which is to be trembled at and feared by even the angelic powers. I begin to shake from the anger of the powerful one, from the face of his rage, from the crash of the falling world, from the conflagration of the elements, from the strong tempest, from the voice of the angel and from the harsh word ...' (Part 5, Chapter 19).[69] The young John is one whom Mirk cares for and thinks is worth

---

[64] 'Tu igitur, karissime, quia sacerdotale officium legitime, ut spero, suscepisti' (MS Bodley 632, f. 69).

[65] This is the origin of the title: 'ut, ex usuali in manibus deportacione, Manuale Sacerdotis nominare consuescas' ('so that, by its being usually carried in your hands, you may be accustomed to call it the priest's handbook'), MS Bodley 632, f. 68v.

[66] Mirk urges him, even if he cannot understand what he reads at the altar, nevertheless to read it out humbly, slowly and carefully, and, even if he can understand little of the scriptures, to increase his knowledge, as Mirk himself did, by assiduous reading (MS Bodley 632, ff. 72, 93).

[67] Mirk trusts that he may not lose the reward of heaven 'propter cupiditatem siue blandimenta mundi fallentis' ('on account of cupidity or the blandishments of the deceitful world'), MS Bodley 632, ff. 74, 97.

[68] MS Bodley 632, ff. 69–69v, cf. Erbe, *Festial*, p. 5/12–36. See too fns. 42 and 51.

[69] 'Paueo gehennam; paueo iudicis uultum, ipsis angelicis potestatibus tremendum et pertimescendum. Contremisco ab ira potentis, a facie furoris eius, a fragore ruentis

taking time over, but who, he fears, may in the end only be convinced by the horrors of hell. In these last several chapters (16–20), when the *Manuale* is effectively finished and Mirk focusses again solely on John (although he has not forgotten him for a moment throughout the work), he insists that he is writing only out of love and points out that he has only exposed the bad habits of others (not John's own bad behaviour, although it is implicit that he might have done so, had he so wished) and only wants him to live a perfect priesthood.

In the *Manuale* we find the recording of medieval lives on two levels: one general, a record of the daily timetable of the priest, a digest of the spiritual and moral attributes of the good priest, a resumé of the sins of the bad priest; the other particular: an exposé of two lives, one that of John, vicar of A, at the start of life – wayward, easy-going, a priest; the other that of John, prior of Lilleshall, at the end of life – disciplined, stern, a priest with a duty of care and a bond of love to that other priest. John might ask: 'You're the one criticising me – why aren't you the sort of person you want me to be?' (Part 5, Chapter 20),[70] and the older and wiser John would answer mildly that the weaker often encourages the stronger, like the trainer standing alongside the wrestler and encouraging him to manly deeds and the glory and honour that come with the promised reward.

---

mundi, a conflagracione elementorum, a tempestate ualida, a uoce angeli et a uerbo aspero.' (MS Bodley 632, f. 97v).

[70] 'Cur tu, monitor meus, talis non es, qualem me monendo esse desideras?' (MS Bodley 632, f. 98v).

APPENDIX

Contents of Oxford, Bodleian Library MS Bodley 632

Prefacio, Preface, f. 68

Capitula Prime Partis, Chapters of the First Part

14 *De sacerdote qui plus diligit tabernam quam ecclesiam*, Concerning the priest who loves the tavern more than the church, f. 74v

15 *De sacerdote aleatore*, Concerning the gambler-priest, f. 75

16 *De sacerdote fornicatore*, Concerning the fornicator-priest, f. 75v

17 *De sacerdote negociatore*, Concerning the businessman-priest, f. 75v

18 *Quare permittuntur sacerdotes fornicarii celebrare in ecclesia*, Why fornicating priests are allowed to celebrate in church, f. 76

Incipiunt Capitule Secunde Partis, Here begin the Chapters of the Second Part

1 *Quod sacerdos cautus esse debet inter indisciplinatos*, That the priest ought to be careful in the presence of those who are undisciplined, f. 76v

2 *Quod sacerdos sepe uocacionem suam debet reducere ad memoriam*, That the priest ought often to recall to mind his vocation, f. 77

3 *Quod sacerdos gradus uirtutum discere debet*, That the priest ought to learn the steps of virtues, f. 77v

4 *Quod bonus sacerdos primicias suas quotidie Deo offert*, That the good priest offers God his first fruits daily, f. 78

5 *Quod sacerdotem somnolentem terret diabolus dormientem*, That the devil terrifies the sleepy priest when he is asleep, f. 78v

6 *Quod talis esse debet sacerdos in occulto qualis est in publico*, That the priest ought to be the same in private as he is in public, f. 79

7 *De uestimentis sacerdotum*, Concerning priests' clothes, f. 79

8 *Quod sacerdos custodire debet cor suum a uanis cogitacionibus*, That the priest ought to guard his heart against vain thoughts, f. 79v

9 *Quod sacerdos cogitaciones suas debet discutere*, That the priest ought to examine his thoughts, f. 80

10 *Quod necessaria est sacerdoti consciencia bene regulata*, That a well-regulated conscience is necessary for the priest, f. 80

11 *De processu sacerdotis ad ecclesiam*, Concerning the progress of the priest to church, f. 80v

12 *Quomodo diuinum officium debet dicere sacerdos*, How the priest ought to say divine office, f. 81

13 *Quod in ecclesia et non alibi dicere debet sacerdos diuinum officium*, That the priest ought to say divine office in church and not elsewhere, f. 81

14 *Quod sacerdos sepe confiteri debet*, That the priest ought to confess often, f. 81v

15 *Quod non prodest sacerdoti confessio coacta sed spontanea*,That coerced confession does not benefit the priest, only spontaneous confession, f. 82

Incipiunt Capitula Tercie Patris Libelli, Here begin the Chapters of the Third Part of the Book

1 *Quod bonum signum est libenter audire uerbum Dei*, That it is a good sign to hear the word of God willingly, f. 82v

2 *Quod sacerdos innocenter debet uiuere*, That the priest ought to live innocently, f. 82v

3 *Quod sacerdos impollutus esse debet*, That the priest ought to be unpolluted, f.83v

4 *Quod sacerdos discernere debet inter carnalem et spiritualem pudiciciam*, That the priest ought to discern between carnal and spiritual chastity, f. 83v

5 *Quod sacerdos de membro muliebri legens non carnaliter sed spiritualiter debet intelligere*, That the priest reading about the female member ought to understand it not carnally but spiritually, f. 84

6 *Quod sacerdos Deum irritat qui cor suum libidinosis cogitacionibus occupat*, That the priest who busies his heart with lustful thoughts angers God, f. 84v

7 *Quod non debet sacerdos commorari cum mulieribus*, That the priest ought not to live with women, f. 84v

8 *Quod sacerdos segregari debet a peccatoribus*, That the priest ought to be segregated from sinners, f. 85v

9 *De casibus quibus sacerdos mortale peccatum incurrit*, Concerning situations in which the priest incurs mortal sin, f. 86

10 *De diuersis periculis contingentibus in missa*, Concerning various dangers occurring in the mass, f. 86

11 *De eodem*, Concerning the same, f. 86v

12 *Item de eodem*, Another chapter concerning the same, f. 87

Incipiunt Capitula Quarte Partis, Here begin the Chapters of the Fourth Part

1 *De eo quod sacerdos omni tempore mundus esse debet*, Concerning the fact that the priest ought to be clean at every time, f. 87v

2 *Quod sacerdos nullo modo presumat celebrare priusquam matutinas dixerat*, That the priest should in no way presume to celebrate before he has said matins, f. 88

3 *Quod sacerdos in uanum graciam Dei recipit qui corpus Christi nunquam conficit*, That the priest who never makes the body of Christ (i.e. celebrates mass) receives the grace of God in vain, f. 88

4 *De hoc quod, licet sacerdos debeat in omnibus diuinijs officijs esse deuotus, deuocior tamen debet esse in missa*, Concerning this, that, given that the priest ought to be devout in all divine services, yet he ought to be more devout in the mass, f. 89

Incipiunt Capitule Quinte Partis

9 *Quod sacerdos misericors et in elemosinis dandis hillaris esse debet*, That the priest ought to be sympathetic and cheerful in giving alms, f. 95

10 *De sacerdote sene et deuoto*, Concerning the devout old priest, f. 95v

11 *De sacerdote sene et discolo*, Concerning the bad old priest, f. 96

12 *Quod sacerdos senex et bonus totum se confert diuinis exercijs*, That the good old priest devotes himself wholly to divine exercises, f. 96

13 *Qualis debet esse cena sacerdotis*, What the dinner of the priest ought to be like, 96v

14 *Quomodo se habebit sacerdos bonus post cenam*, How the good priest will comport himself after dinner, f. 96v

15 *Oracio boni sacerdotis sedentis in lecto antequam cubat*, The prayer of the good priest sitting up in bed before he lies down, f. 97

16 *Qualiter alloquitur prior cognatum suum de obseruancia premissorum*, How the prior addresses his kinsman concerning the observance of the previous matters, f. 97

17 *Exemplum philomene et sagittarij*, The exemplary story of the nightingale and the archer, f. 97

18 *De proprietatibus philomene*, Concerning the properties of the nightingale, f. 97v

19 *De contemplacione penarum infernorum*, Concerning the contemplation of the pains of hell, f. 97v

20 *De contemplacione celestium gaudiorum*, Concerning the contemplation of the joys of heaven, f. 98

The Manuscript of The Book of Margery Kempe

PAMELA ROBINSON

Ever since the discovery of the unique manuscript of *The Book of Margery Kempe*, announced in 1934, Margery has provoked endless discussion. Her extreme emotionalism has offended many; she has been diagnosed with post-partum psychosis; she has been hailed as a feminist icon, who may or may not have been literate; she is viewed as a literary persona, a 'character called Margery', chosen by a 'self-conscious author, Kempe' whose *Book* is a work of fiction.[1] Whatever the work's popularity today, its survival in a single manuscript and the absence of any record of the existence of any other manuscript copy do not suggest that it immediately reached a wide audience. Extracts only, selected and re-arranged to form a sanitized abridgement that gives the reader no conception of the actual *Book*, were printed in the early sixteenth century by Wynkyn de Worde, 1501 (*RSTC* 14924) and again by Henry Pepwell, 1521 (*RSTC* 20972).[2] These editions could have consisted of between 400 and 600 copies, so at least the abridgement might have become a late medieval best-seller.[3]

However, only one copy of de Worde's edition, *A shorte treatyse of contemplacyon taught by our lorde Ihesu cryste or taken out of the boke of Margerie kempe of lynn*, survives[4] and it may be thought that, similarly, a fair number of

[1] Thus L. Staley in her edition of *The Book of Margery Kempe* (Kalamazoo, 1996), p. 8. The manuscript's discovery was announced by H. E. Allen in a letter to the (London) *Times*, 27 September 1934. The literature on Margery is vast, but for one diagnosis of her mental state see T. Drucker, 'The Malaise of Margery Kempe', *New York State Journal of Medicine*, 72 (1972), 2911–17.

[2] De Worde's edition consists of only seven pages as opposed to the manuscript's 123 folios of text. On the prints see S. E. Holbrook, 'Margery Kempe and Wynkyn de Worde', in *The Medieval Mystical Tradition in England*, ed. M. Glasscoe (Cambridge, 1987), pp. 27–46; J. Summit, *Lost Property: The Woman Writer and English Literary History, 1380–1589* (Chicago, 2000), pp. 126–38; A. Foster, 'A Short Treatyse of Contemplacyon: The Book of Margery Kempe in its Early Print Contexts', in *A Companion to the Book of Margery Kempe*, eds J. H. Arnold and K. J. Lewis (Cambridge, 2004), pp. 95–112.

[3] Cf. H. R. Plomer, 'Two Lawsuits of Richard Pynson', *The Library*, n.s. 10 (1909), 115–33, for the size of some Pynson editions.

[4] Holbrook, loc. cit., p. 43 n. 2 (following H. S. Bennett, *English Books and Readers 1475 to 1557* (Cambridge, 1952), p. 255) reports a second copy in the Huntington Library.

manuscripts could have been lost. The unique surviving manuscript (London, BL, Add. 61823) is clearly a copy of the version of the longer text and did not serve as de Worde's copy text. Whoever edited the text for printed publication had access to another manuscript.[5] Yet it is unlikely that many other copies were lost, for while codices containing essential texts for the friars, scholars or lawyers probably did suffer great losses such a situation is implausible for a vernacular work.[6]

The manuscript is small (205 × 140 mm), consisting of 124 paper leaves in eleven quires.[7] At the end of the ninth quire (f. 106v) the scribe leaves a blank space of six lines at the conclusion of Book I and begins Book II on the first leaf of a new gathering. Like many medieval manuscripts where separate groups of quires corresponding to major divisions in a text have been put together to form a single work, this volume has been produced in fascicules. Two different stocks of paper were used: a circle surmounted by a cross for quires 1–8 (ff. 1–96) and *tête de boeuf* for quires 9–11 (ff. 97–124). Although the scribe used different papers, they are well matched in quality. Folded in quarto the watermarks fall within the gutter of the manuscript and are difficult to see, but both were popular designs throughout the fifteenth century. Thus I cannot argue that it would only have been possible to find the combination of them at one particular period rather than another. The watermark evidence does not help in dating the manuscript.[8]

The text is written throughout by a single hand who finishes with the colophon (fol. 123) 'Jhesu me*r*cy quod Salthows'.[9] Salthouse probably came from the village of that name on the coast of Norfolk since he employs the distinctive orthography

---

This is a facsimile copy of the original in Cambridge University Library, Sel.5.27.

[5] The friendly priest who copied Margery's *Book* for her informs us in the proem to Book I that he had added a leaf to his copy on which to write the proem. In Add. 61823 this is not on an inserted leaf but an integral leaf of the first quire. Holbrook, loc. cit., p. 36, remarks on the different approaches to the text of the editor of *A shorte treatyse* and the reader who annotated the manuscript in red ink.

[6] On the loss rate of medieval manuscripts D. D'Avray, 'Printing, mass communication, and religious reformation: the Middle Ages and after', in *The Uses of Script and Print, 1300–1700*, eds J. Crick and A. Walsham (Cambridge, 2004), pp. 50–70, argues for a 'codicological haemorrhage' of mendicant collections of sermons.

[7] The collation is 1–8¹² (ff. 1–96), 9–10¹⁰ (ff. 97–116), 11⁸ (ff. 117–24). Ff. 1–80 have been damaged at the right hand edge so that it is only with f. 86, signed 'hij' that quire and leaf signatures become visible. Catchwords have frequently been cropped in binding.

[8] I have been unable to match them with any design in C. M. Briquet, *Les Filigranes*, ed. J. S. G. Simmons, 4 vols (Amsterdam, 1968). The nearest correspondence to the circle and cross appears to be Briquet no. 2985, but this is dated 1492 and is surely too late for the handwriting.

[9] Ff. 123v–124 are blank. A recipe has been added, f. 124v, by a late fifteenth-century hand. Salthouse's handwriting is illustrated by H. Kelliher and S. Brown, *English Literary Manuscripts* (London, 1986), pl. 7 (shows fol. 1); J. Roberts, *Guide to Scripts used in English Writings up to 1500* (London, 2005), p. 233 (shows fol. 123).

of that region, a spelling system so idiosyncratic that it is unlikely a copyist would have retained it if he wished to seek work beyond the boundaries of East Anglia. In the British Library's description of a Latin theological miscellany, Add. 62450, a manuscript like that of the *Book* formerly owned by the Charterhouse of Mount Grace, Yorkshire, an 'unusual pattern' of pricking is observed and said to be similar to that found in the *Book of Margery Kempe* MS.[10] Since Add. 62450 was copied at Mount Grace by one of the monks, John Awne (d. 1472–3), one might infer from this comment that a Yorkshire origin for Add. 61823 is suggested. However, both manuscripts have a frame ruling, that is, rather than ruling for every line, their ruling provides only for the margins which frame the text. Since such a frame ruling is commonly found in cheaply produced fifteenth-century manuscripts, the pricking only at the corners of the written space is not in fact unusual.

Salthouse wrote a mixed hand, employing both Anglicana and Secretary forms. Anglicana two-compartment **a** occurs alongside the Secretary single compartment **a**, Anglicana long **r** alongside Secretary short **r**, although the scribe does appear to use Anglicana two-compartment **g** consistently. His handwriting is small and cramped (33 long lines in a written space of 145 × 85 mm), with little space left between the lines. Descenders trail into the letter forms of the line below. Rubricated initials (for which Salthouse left guide letters in the margin) have been supplied in an amateur-looking way at the beginning of the text and of each chapter,[11] and punctuation and capitals at the beginning of sentences have often been emphasized with a touch of red ink. The book looks plain and unimpressive, and judging by its script I would date it to the mid fifteenth century.

The manuscript is bound in a typical fifteenth-century binding of sturdy wooden boards covered in tawed leather. Sewn onto five thongs, it has a rounded spine rather than the flat one of earlier medieval bindings. The covers have faded to a dirty brown colour, but they were originally (from the evidence of a turn-in) stained black. Two metal catches project from the board edge of the lower cover while two leather stubs, to which clasps would have been attached, remain on the board edge of the upper cover. The emergence of rounded spines can be tentatively dated to about 1450, while the method of fastening a volume by clasps from edge to edge seems to be associated with the latter part of the century.[12] The whole was originally kept in a chemise, now broken into three fragments and kept separately as Add. 61823*.

---

[10] *The British Library Catalogue of Additions to the Manuscripts: New Series 1981–1985*, 2 vols (London, 1994), p. 95; see also H. Kelliher, 'The Rediscovery of Margery Kempe: A Footnote', *British Library Journal*, 23 (1997), 259–63 at p. 259.

[11] The initial 'H' at the beginning of the text, 'Here begynnyth …', is 4-lines tall, while subsequent initials are 3-lines high.

[12] N. Hadgraft, 'English Fifteenth Century Book Structures', Unpublished Ph.D thesis, University of London, 1998, p. 261.

Although chemise bindings might appear to have had a particular association with manuscripts containing religious or devotional texts, it seems 'very likely' that most medieval bindings were once provided with a secondary covering of a protective chemise.[13] They are not often found, since chemises tended to be removed when books came to be stored upright, but they survive on such diverse volumes as copies of Statutes of the Realm, a copy of Roger Bacon's scientific works, and the cartulary of Godstow nunnery.[14]

The manuscript has been dated *circa* 1440 in some of the literature, but this date is based on that of a document found in the lower cover of the binding. Such a dating for the manuscript assumes that it and the document are exactly contemporary, but we do not know when these two first became associated. Moreover, because the binding has been repaired and the document is now attached to the stub of a modern pastedown its original function in the binding has been obscured.[15]

Dated London 1440, the document is issued in the name of Pietro del Monte (also known as Piero da Monte), protonotary and papal collector in England, Scotland and Ireland from 1435 to 1440.[16] His official remit was to collect taxes due to the papacy, but he also acted as the pope's eyes and ears (one of his letters to Eugenius IV gives the first account of the murder in 1437 of James I of Scotland, others are full of complaints about the weather and native customs).[17] A keen bibliophile, del Monte was an influential figure in the beginnings of English humanism.[18] However, the claim that he secured for Duke Humfrey of Gloucester (1390–1447) the services of Antonio Beccaria of Verona and Tito Livio Frulovisi of Ferrara as his secretaries has recently been questioned.[19]

---

[13] Ibid., p. 71.

[14] Cf. F. Bearman, 'The Origins and Significance of Two Late Medieval Textile Chemise Bookbindings in the Walters Art Gallery,' *Journal of the Walters Art Gallery,* 54 (1996), 163–87, Appx II.

[15] Cf. *The Book of Margery Kempe*, eds S. B. Meech and H. E. Allen, EETS OS 212 (1940), p. xxxiv, referring to a repair carried out c.1934.

[16] *Dizionario Biografico degli Italiani*, 38 (Rome, 1990), pp. 141–6; *Oxford Dictionary of National Biography*, 60 vols (Oxford, 2004), 38, pp. 783–84.

[17] R. Weiss, 'The Earliest Account of the Murder of James I of Scotland', *EHR*, 52 (1937), 479–91; for the duties of a papal collector, see M. Harvey, *England, Rome and the Papacy 1417–1464: the Study of a Relationship* (Manchester, 1993), pp. 74–6.

[18] D. Rundle, 'A Renaissance Bishop and his Books: a Preliminary Survey of the Manuscript Collection of Pietro del Monte (c.1440–57)', *Papers of the British School at Rome*, 69 (2001), 245–72; S. Saygin, *Humphrey, Duke of Gloucester (1390–1447) and the Italian Humanists*, Brill's Studies in Intellectual History, 105 (Leiden, 2002), pp. 172–93.

[19] D. Rundle, 'Two Unnoticed Manuscripts from the Collection of Humfrey, Duke of Gloucester, part I', *Bodleian Library Record*, 16 (1998), 211–24 at p. 212; Saygin, op. cit., p. 183 n. 2.

In 1438, and again in 1439, del Monte received a papal faculty permitting him to grant dispensation to a fixed number of clergy allowing each to be absent from his benefice for seven years yet still enjoy its fruits while studying at university.[20] This faculty is rehearsed in the document, written probably by one of del Monte's clerks. The hand is that of Cambridge University Library, MS Gg.i.34(i), one of two manuscripts of del Monte's own compositions that he presented to Duke Humfrey,[21] and is possibly that of his secretary Piero da Pesaro, of whom little is known.[22] Since the document has been mutilated the addressee's name is lost. However, he is described as vicar of 'Saham iuxta Ely'.[23] In 1440, when the document was written, the vicar of Soham, Cambridgeshire, six miles south west of Ely, was William Buggy, MA, BTh., Fellow of Corpus Christi College Cambridge.[24] He had been instituted vicar of St Andrew's, Soham, in 1427, and died sometime in Spring or Summer 1442, two years after the licence was issued. His will, dated 23 April 1442, does not mention any books.[25]

It has been surmised that Buggy heard of Margery when she visited the nuns of Denny Abbey, ten miles from Soham, and asked to have a copy of her autobiography made for him.[26] Assuming that this was the case, Buggy is then presumed to have tucked the document into the back of the manuscript and taken it with him when he left the town to go up to university. This seems unlikely, since the document has been cut down to fit into the binding with the resulting loss of his

[20] Cf. *Calendar of Entries in the Papal Registers relating to Great Britain and Ireland: Papal Letters,* VIII, ed. J. A. Twemlow (London, 1909), pp. 292–3 and 254–5.

[21] The MS contains a copy of Pietro's contribution to the Scipio/Caesar controversy: see Rundle, 'Two Unnoticed MSS'. Del Monte also presented the Duke with a copy of his *De virtutum et vitiorum inter se differentia* (the dedicatory preface is printed by A. Sammut, *Unfredo duca di Gloucester et gli umanisti italiani*, Medioevo e Umanismo, 40 (Padua, 1980), pp. 151–3), but the presentation copy no longer survives.

[22] Rundle, 'Two Unnoticed MSS', p. 218, suggests Pesaro copied Gg.i.34 (i); for references to him, see J. Haller, *Piero da Monte, ein Gelehrter und päpstlicher Beamter des 15. Jahrhunderts, seine Briefsammlung*, Bibliothek des Deutschen Historischen Instituts in Rom, 19 (1941), passim, and A. Zanelli, 'Pietro del Monte', *Archivio Storico Lombardo*, 4th ser., 8 (1908), 108–11. Pietro copied many of his own manuscripts; his handwriting is illustrated in D. Quaglioni, *Pietro del Monte a Roma: La tradizione del "Repertorium utriusque iuris" (c.1453)*, Studi e Fonti per la storia dell'Università di Roma, 3 (1984), pls I–IV.

[23] Printed *Book*, eds Meech and Allen, EETS OS 212, pp. 351–2.

[24] *BRUC* 104; Emden misidentifies him as vicar of Saham Toney, Norfolk.

[25] Proved in the Consistory Court of Norwich, see Norwich, Norfolk Record Office, Reg. Doke, f. 179v; and cf. J. R. Olerenshaw, 'Some Early Soham Wills', *Fenland Notes and Queries*, 4 (1898–1900), 249. The register is fragmentary and no note of probate survives, but surrounding wills were all proved in July 1442. Henry Faukes, Buggy's successor as vicar of Soham, was admitted 31 August 1442, see NNRO, DN/Reg. 5/10, f. 44.

[26] By C. S. Stokes, 'Margery Kempe: Her Life and the Early History of Her Book', *Mystics Quarterly*, 25 (1999), 47. For Margery's visit to Denny, see *Book*, eds Meech and Allen, pp. 202–03.

name. As it was a current licence to use the revenue of his benefice to finance his University career it is improbable that this mutilation would have occurred during Buggy's lifetime. I think rather that the document was found among his effects after his death and discarded, to be acquired by a local binder who used it as parchment waste in the binding.

It is unusual to find a document deliberately bound into a manuscript by its original owner. A letter of confraternity by William Wells II, Prior Provincial of the Austin Friars from 1433 to 1441, for John Morton and his wife, Juliana, dated York 1438, is carefully folded in two at the end of a copy of Nicholas Love's *Mirror of the Life of Christ* (Oxford, Bodleian Library, MS Bodley 131, ff. 148–49).[27] John himself copied the manuscript (f. 121v is signed 'Explicit vite christi quod Johannem Morton') and evidently wished to keep intact a letter of immediate relevance to him. Conversely, another letter, issued forty-two years earlier in 1396, by William, prior of the Carmelite convent at Scarborough, was cropped, turned sideways, and used as a pastedown in the lower cover of the binding of the same manuscript (now raised as f. 150).[28] This different treatment of the two letters graphically illustrates the contrast between a document intentionally preserved and a document regarded as waste and recycled in binding. In the case of the faculty to Buggy a strip of dirt down the face of what became the centre of the document after it was cropped, with the right hand part of it becoming more scuffed than the left, shows where it was once folded in two, and it probably served as a pastedown and endleaf before the binding was repaired.

We do not know how the manuscript of Margery Kempe's *Book* reached the Yorkshire Charterhouse of Mount Grace, where it was read and extensively annotated in red ink in the first half of the sixteenth century. Marginal annotations refer both to Richard Methley, 'R. Medlay was wont so to say' (f. 14v), and Prior John Norton, 'so dyd prior Norton in hys excesse' (f. 51v).[29] If we take the use of the past tense in the obvious sense to mean that both men had died (Methley by Spring 1528, Norton in 1522), this would mean that the annotations were made between 1528 and 1539 when the house was suppressed (although James Hogg has suggested that the wording may simply imply that their spiritual lives had entered a calmer phase, so that the annotations could be somewhat earlier).[30]

---

[27] For Wells, see F. Roth, *The English Austin Friars 1249–1538*, 2 vols, Cassiacum, Studies in St. Augustine and the Augustinian Order, 6–7 (New York, 1961–6), I, pp. 108–10 and II, pp. 322*–3*. The binding has the flat spine and evidence of a strap and pin fastening typical of the earlier fifteenth century.

[28] Rev. Prebendary Clark-Maxwell, 'Some Further Letters of Fraternity', *Archaeologia*, 79 (1929), 179–216 at p. 212.

[29] See Lincoln Cathedral MS 57, the unique manuscript of Norton's works, f. 57v, for a report of a vision Norton had in 1485; R. M. Thomson, *Catalogue of the Manuscripts of Lincoln Cathedral Chapter Library* (Cambridge, 1989), p. 40.

[30] J. Hogg, 'Richard Methley to Hew Heremyte A Pystyl of Solytary Lyfe Nowadayes',

Carthusian interest in devotional literature is well-documented.[31] Their custom of collecting, copying, and correcting books is exemplified by the activities of the scribe, Stephen Dodesham (d. 1482), and textual critic, James Grenehalgh (d. 1530).[32] Nevertheless, we know little of the collection in which the *Book of Margery Kempe* found a home.[33] There is no known extant library catalogue for any British Charterhouse, and of over 7,000 volumes recorded in Neil Ker's *Medieval Libraries of Great Britain* only 108 can be definitely assigned to any particular Carthusian house, although Ian Doyle has identified thirty-seven further volumes which are of English Carthusian origin.[34] None of Mount Grace's surviving books bears a shelfmark which would enable an assessment of the size of its library or the arrangement of its collections, such as survives from Hinton, Somerset.[35] A copy of the *Pupilla Oculi* was left to Mount Grace in 1433, while a copy of 'The Revelation of the Hundred Pater Nosters' was sent there from London.[36] In 1519 a collection of mainly liturgical books came that included a manuscript copy of the *Ars moriendi* and printed copies of the *Legenda Aurea*, Aesop's Fables and *The Shepherd's Calendar*.[37] An annotation by James Grenehalgh at the begin-

---

Analecta Cartusiana, 31 (1977), 91–119 at p. 91 n. 1.

[31]   M. G. Sargent, 'The Transmission by the English Carthusians of some Late Medieval Spiritual Writings', *Journal of Ecclesiastical History*, 27 (1976), 225–40; V. Gillespie, '*Cura Pastoralis in Deserto*' in *De Cella in Seculum. Religious and Secular Life and Devotion in Late Medieval England*, ed. M. G. Sargent (Cambridge, 1989), pp. 161–81.

[32]   A. I. Doyle, 'Stephen Dodesham of Witham and Sheen', in *Of the Making of Books: Medieval Manuscripts, their Scribes and Readers. Essays presented to M. B. Parkes*, ed. P. R. Robinson and R. Zim (Aldershot, 1997), pp. 94–115; M. G. Sargent, *James Grenehalgh as Textual Critic*, Analecta Cartusiana, 85 (1984). On Carthusian concern for correct texts, see M. G. Sargent, 'The Problem of Uniformity in Carthusian Book Production from the *Opus Pacis* to the *Tertia Compilatio Statutorum*', in *New Science out of Old Books: Studies in Manuscripts and Early Printed Books in Honour of A. I. Doyle*, eds R. Beadle and A. J. Piper (Aldershot, 1995), pp. 122–41.

[33]   J. Hogg, 'Mount Grace Charterhouse and English Spirituality', *Analecta Cartusiana*, 82/3 (1980), 1–43 at pp. 14–16.

[34]   N. R. Ker, *Medieval Libraries of Great Britain: A List of Surviving Books,* 2nd edn (London, 1964), p. 132. On English Carthusian libraries in general, see E. M. Thompson, *The Carthusian Order in England* (London, 1930), pp. 313–34; *Syon Abbey, with the Libraries of the Carthusians*, eds V. Gillespie and A. I. Doyle, Corpus of British Medieval Library Catalogues, 9 (London, 2001), pp. 609–10; and see also Dr Doyle's 'English Carthusian books not yet linked with a charterhouse', in '*A Miracle of Learning': Studies in Manuscripts and Irish Learning. Essays in Honour of William O'Sullivan*, eds T. Barnard, D. Ó Cróinín and K. Simms (Aldershot, 1998), pp. 122–36.

[35]   For books surviving from Hinton and their pressmarks, see *MLGB*, p. 101.

[36]   Thompson, *Carthusian Order*, p. 330; F. Wormald, 'The Revelation of the Hundred Pater Nosters. A Fifteenth-Century Meditation', *Laudate*, 14 (1936), 1–17.

[37]   Printed in H. V. Le Bas, W. Brown and W. H. St John Hope, 'Mount Grace Priory', *Yorkshire Archaeological Journal*, 18 (1905), 241–309 at p. 296; Thompson, *Carthusian Order*, p. 328; and J. Hogg, 'Life in an English Charterhouse in the Fifteenth Century',

ning of a lengthy digression peculiar to Mount Grace's copy of *The Book of Privy Counselling* (BL Harley 2373, f. 70v) refers to an old book, 'De quattuor gradibus humilitatis' (presumably St Bernard's *De gradibus humilitatis et superbiae*), in the house.[38]

Besides Harley 2373 (containing also *The Cloud of Unknowing*) and the manuscript of *Margery Kempe*, seven other manuscripts survive from Mount Grace: a patristic and theological collection dating from the first half of the fourteenth century (Trinity College Dublin MS 318),[39] and six fifteenth-century volumes. They contain copies of the *Meditationes vite Christi*, now assigned to Johannes de Caulibus, written and dated 1400 at Frieston, Lincolnshire (Ripon Cathedral MS 6),[40] Nicholas Love's *Mirror of the Life of Christ* (Cambridge University Library Add. MS 6578), Richard Methley's ecstatic spiritual meditations (Trinity College Cambridge, MS 0.2.56 [1160]),[41] the *Speculum spiritualium*, attributed to various authors (York Minster XVI.I.9),[42] and two theological miscellanies (BL, Harley 237 and Add. 62450). As well as the latter volume which was written by the monk John Awne, the copy of Methley's works and, probably, the *Speculum spiritualium* were written in the house.

In addition, three printed books are known: an edition of Anselm's works;[43] a Bible (Rouen: Pierre Olivier, 1512) given to Dom Robert Fletcher, who is reported to have had visions and who was one of twenty-seven inmates granted a pension at the Dissolution;[44] and a copy of Alphonso de Espina's *Fortalicium fidei* (Nurem-

---

Analecta Cartusiana, 233 (2004), 35–58 at p. 57.

[38] F.70v: 'In ueteri libro huius domus viz. de Montis gracie De quattuor gradibus humilitatis nulla fit mentio'; cf. *The Cloud of Unknowing and The Book of Privy Counselling*, ed. P. Hodgson, EETS OS 218 (1944), p. 153 n. 5. Doyle, *Syon Abbey*, pp. 651–2, suggests that a list of books in Lambeth Palace Library, MS 413, f. 59v, lent perhaps to a layman by a Northern charterhouse, c.1425, refers to Mount Grace.

[39] Cf. M. L. Colker, *Trinity College Library Dublin: Descriptive Catalogue of the Medieval and Renaissance Latin Manuscripts*, 2 vols (Aldershot, 1991), I, pp. 646–50 (I have not seen this manuscript).

[40] N. R. Ker, *Medieval Manuscripts in British Libraries*, 5 vols (Oxford, 1969–2002), IV, p. 211. The text ends, f. 121v 'Scripte in Freston circa Festum Annunciacionis beate Marie virginis Anno domini .1[...]4 Deo gracias'. For the author, see *Johannis de Caulibus Meditaciones vite Christi, olim S. Bonaventuro attributae*, ed. M. Stallings-Taney, Corpus Christianorum, continuatio medievalis, 153 (Turnhout, 1997), pp. ix–xi.

[41] M. R. James, *The Western Manuscripts in the Library of Trinity College Cambridge: A Descriptive Catalogue*, 4 vols (Cambridge, 1900–04), III, pp. 176–8; facsimile edn by J. Hogg, *Mount Grace Charterhouse and Late Medieval English Spirituality, The Trinity College Cambridge MS 0.2.56*, *Analecta Cartusiana*, 64/2 (1978). Hogg, 'Richard Methley', p. 96 n. 10, dismisses James's suggestion that the MS is autograph.

[42] *MMBL*, IV, pp. 717–18 (I have not seen this manuscript).

[43] Cambridge, Ridley Hall, R.H.L.E.2, printed at Strasbourg, after 1496? (I have not seen this book).

[44] Oxford, Bodleian Library, Antiq. d.F.1512/1; the ex libris on the title-page reads 'Liber

berg: Anton Koberger, 1494).[45] This polemic against heretics, Jews, Muslims and demons originally belonged to Thomas Scasby, one of the chantry priests of St William's College, York, who gave it to Mount Grace.[46] A further item, untraced, containing a work entitled the *Speculum discipulorum Christi* was sold at the last of Thomas Rawlinson's sales in 1733–4.[47]

The books that belonged to Mount Grace show every sign of being well read. Only the manuscript of Love's *Mirror* is handsomely produced with illuminated initials and border and, although Love was a house author, is likely to have been produced by a professional scribe and artist.[48] Otherwise the manuscripts are unremarkable productions. Frequent annotations provide evidence for the attentive reading of texts, among them the *Book of Margery Kempe*. This was extensively annotated by someone who used red ink. These annotations have been published by Kelly Parsons, who argues that the hand responsible for them was possibly that of John Wilson, prior from 1528 to 1539, who was preparing the text for the devotional use of an audience of lay women.[49] The manuscript's bilingual *ex libris* (f. iii 'Liber Montis Gracie. This boke is of Mouⁿtegrace') is cited as supporting evidence for this. While it is the only surviving volume to use the vernacular in such a context, it is worth noting that there is no standard wording found for ownership inscriptions at Mount Grace.

---

montis gracie ordinis cartusiensis qui datus fuit domino Roberto Fleycher a devoto ac venerabili Johanne Norton qui fuit xxiiij [ʒere] annis procurator et tresdecim prior montis gracie …'. For Fletcher, see Le Bas, Brown and St John Hope, 'Mount Grace Priory', pp. 261, 263; Hogg, 'Mount Grace Charterhouse', p. 8 n. 32.

[45]   Oxford, Bodleian Library, AA.61.Th.Seld. For Alphonso, see S. J. McMichael, *Was Jesus of Nazareth the Messiah? Alphonso de Espina's Argument against the Jews in the Fortalitium Fidei (c.1464)*, South Florida Studies in the History of Judaism, 96 (Atlanta GA, 1994), pp. 1–15; his Appx IV, pp. 513–603, prints a partial facsimile of the Koberger edition.

[46]   A faded note on the pastedown of the lower cover reads 'This is M. Thomas Scasby boke one of the <parsons> of the College of saynte Will*iam* w^tyn the <close> of yorke'. A later hand has added 'Ex dono thomas scasby domui montis gracie'.

[47]   B. J. Enright, 'The Later Auction Sales of Thomas Rawlinson's Library, 1727–34', *The Library*, 5th ser., 11 (1956), 23–40, 103–13.

[48]   Cf. A. I. Doyle, 'Some Reflections on Some Manuscripts of Nicholas Love's *Myrrour of the Blessed Lyf of Jesu Christ*', *Leeds Studies in English*, n.s. 14 (1983), 82–93, and see *Nicholas Love, The Mirror of the Blessed Life of Jesus Christ*, ed. M. G. Sargent (Exeter, 2004), pls 1–4 illus. ff. 2v–3, 114–114v. Nevertheless it is not so handsome as some copies, see K. L. Scott, 'The Illustration and Decoration of Manuscripts of Nicholas Love's *Mirror of the Blessed Life of Jesus Christ*', in *Nicholas Love at Wasada*, eds S. Oguro, R. Beadle and M. G. Sargent (Cambridge, 1997), pp. 61–86.

[49]   K. Parsons, 'The Red Ink Annotator of *The Book of Margery Kempe* and his Lay Audience', in *The Medieval Professional Reader at Work: Evidence from Manuscripts of Chaucer, Langland, Kempe and Gower*, eds K. Kerby-Fulton and M. Hilmo, English Literary Studies Monograph Series, 85 (University of Victoria, BC, 2001), pp. 143–216.

John Awne's compilation, containing works by or attributed by Awne to Gregory the Great, has been annotated in plummet (a piece of lead)[50] but the comments are so faint that it is difficult to read them. Passages of text that particularly interested this reader have frequently been marked by fleurons drawn in the margin or else a line drawn alongside them. In the second half of the century a reader of the early fifteenth-century copy of the *Meditationes vite Christi* (Ripon 6) used red ink to assign different chapters of that work to the days of the week; thus 'Die Martis' at the beginning of c. xiij (f. 19v), 'Die Marcurij' at the beginning of c. xix (f. 37), and so on. Someone else in the early sixteenth century appears to have been collating this copy against another one, for not only did he expand abbreviations he perceived to be difficult but he also made corrections to the text, at least for the first twenty-four leaves. Thus, for instance, the text's 'nut^i' is expanded to 'neutri' (f.5v), 'ordēs' to 'ordīēs' (for 'ordines' f.14), while he emended the text's reading of 'proferro' to 'profecto' (f. 3v), 'discipli^{le}' to 'displicibile' (f.16v), and supplied omissions. In c. v (*recte* c.iv, f. 9v) where, due to eyeskip caused by the frequent repetition of the word 'Hodie', the scribe had left out the sentence 'Hodie est solempnitas tocius celestis curie quia inchoatur eorum reparacio', our corrector supplied the missing text in the upper margin of the page. In light of Carthusian concern with and dedication to correct texts it is not surprising to find this scholarly approach to the manuscript's readings.[51]

Such an approach contrasts with the type of comment responding to the subject matter rather than to linguistic or textual concerns which is to be found in the margins of the manuscripts of the *Book of Margery Kempe* and the *Cloud of Unknowing*. Both volumes, which contain the only vernacular works surviving from Mount Grace, have been annotated in red ink by different hands. Both annotators have drawn attention to passages in these texts that they found interesting or relevant. Thus the annotator of *The Cloud* (Harley 2373) has frequently written 'nota', 'nota bene', or, occasionally, 'nota valde bene' in the margins. Whole chapters have been highlighted with the remark 'nota bene hoc capitulum' (chs 25, 26, 30, 31, 44, 46, 63, 68, 69, 75). In particular the annotator has given prominence to ch 55 (on the error of those who fervently and without discrimination condemn the sin of others) with the rubric 'Nota hoc capitulum et caue de suspeccione aliorum defectuum' (f. 51v); the following ch 56 (the error of those who rely on their own intellectual acumen and erudition rather than on the teaching of Holy

---

50   As illustrated by Christopher de Hamel, *Medieval Craftsmen: Scribes and Illuminators* (British Museum Press, 1992), pl. 16

51   See M. A. and R. H. Rouse, 'Correction and Emendation of Texts in the Fifteenth Century and the Autograph of the *Opus Pacis* by Oswaldus Anglicus', in *Scire litteras: Forschungen zum mittelalterlichen Geistesleben*, eds S. Krämer and M. Bernhard, Bayerische Akademie der Wissenschaften, Philosophisch-Historische Klasse Abhandlung, n.s. 99 (1988), pp. 333–46; also Sargent, 'The Problem of Uniformity in Carthusian Book Production', pp. 122–41.

Church) is marked 'Nota bene hoc capitulum et caue' (f. 52v). Whoever was responsible for these admonitions it was not James Grenehalgh who also saw this copy (see p. 137, above).

However, the *Cloud* annotator was restrained in his response to that text compared to the response of the so-called 'Red Ink Annotator' to the *Book*. The comments of the latter have been characterised as 'ecstatic' and 'highly personal',[52] and certainly reflect a deeper engagement with the text than my previous examples. The 'Red Ink Annotator' was not alone in annotating it, but his marginalia are much the most copious and testify to the emotional impact that the *Book* had upon him.[53] While he made some minor emendations to the text, supplying obvious omissions such as 'of' in 'a peyr \of/ spectacles' (f.3) or 'town \of/ lynn' (f.54), underlined lemmata ('Salue sancta parens', f.95v; 'ueni creator spiritus', f. 120v), and drew attention to specific passages with the word 'nota', these interventions are not as significant as his devout comments. Thus he responded to Christ's telling Margery that He has dearly bought her love with 'trew it is blyssyd lord' (c. 79, f. 92v). He jotted pious exclamations in the margins at the point where she is told of the grace Christ's servants can expect in heaven ('deo gracias in eternum', f.26, at the end of c. 22) or where we are told of the Carmelite Master Alan's recovery from illness and joyful reunion with Margery ('laudes deo in eternum Amen', f. 83, at the end of c. 70). His seemingly spontaneous and disparaging outburst, 'O ceci clerici' (c.52, f. 60), of the Archbishop of York's clergy who suspected Margery of heresy seems unlikely if he were preparing the text, as Parsons suggested, for local Yorkshire women.

A connection between this Carthusian annotator's reading, devotion and contemplative practice seems most evident in his reaction to descriptions of Margery's ecstasies and tears. Not only did he compare her comportment to that of his confreres, Prior Norton and Fr Methley ('so fa RM 7 f Norton of Wakenes of þe passyon', 'so dyd prior Norton in hys excess', 'father M was wont so to doo', ff. 33v, 51v, 85), but of Margery's fits of passionate weeping he commented 'Nota feruent loue' (c.17, f.20) and stressed such incidents by picking up words in the text and repeating them in the margins 'ters wᵗ loue', 'wel of ters', and 'nota feruor of loue' (cc. 19, 57, 82, ff. 20, 68v, 96v).

Such empathetic reactions to Margery's religious experience by a sixteenth-century monk, reading alone in his cell at Mount Grace, fittingly belong in a context where it is reported that three of the house's sixteenth-century brethren, Methley, Norton, and Fletcher, all had visionary experiences. There, if anywhere, the *Book* was destined to find an understanding reader.

---

[52]   Parsons, 'The Red Ink Annotator', p. 151.
[53]   Three other annotating hands can be identified.

The Will as Autobiography: the Case of Thomas Salter, Priest, Died November 1558

CAROLINE M. BARRON

The long will of Thomas Salter, drawn up when he was eighty years old, serves – as he surely intended – as his autobiography. From it we learn of his childhood in Norwich and of his apprenticeship later in the household of Henry Adams, a salter in London, and of his progress through the craft to become a liveryman of the company. It is clear also from his will that Thomas was a devout Catholic who, at some point, abandoned the salter's craft for the priesthood. He served as a chantry priest in the parish of St Nicholas Acon and at St Michael Cornhill and he directed that he should be buried in the church of St Magnus, which lay at the northern end of London bridge. Although a priest, Thomas Salter retained close links with the Salters' Company, and he was clearly a man of considerable wealth, with an extensive wardrobe and the resources to make charitable bequests amounting to some £300 in cash. Thomas Salter drew up his will in August 1558 confident that 'the most hollie Catholique Churche of Christe Jesus' was securely restored in England and that his body would lie in the lady chapel of St Magnus' church until the 'generall resurexcon day whiche I belyve faithfully shall come'.[1] But by the time Salter's will was proved on 19 December 1558, Queen Mary was dead, and the elaborate obits and masses and prayers which Salter had set out so carefully in his will were probably never carried out. Stow does not record his tomb in St Magnus church.

The will is remarkable for its length and for the detail and precision with which Salter recorded his wishes (see Plates 3–4). Indeed the will is so detailed that the scribe who copied it into the Register of the Prerogative Court of Canterbury was moved on two occasions to illustrate the will in the margins (see Plates 1–2). The over-riding impression is of a kindly, devout and meticulous man, proud of his Norfolk family and of his friends among the merchants of London, but also sensitive to the needs of those who were poor and ill. He was touchingly faithful to the friends of his youth. But behind the geniality and generosity there are hints of a

[1] For a transcript of Thomas Salter's will see the Appendix. The will has been divided into paragraphs and all references to the will in this article refer to these paragraph numbers. Will, paras 1 and 3. I am very grateful to Dr Matthew Groom who first brought Thomas Salter's will to my attention, and to Dr Martha Carlin for many helpful suggestions.

troubled past, perhaps a troubled conscience. Clearly Salter had fallen out with the parishioners of St Nicholas Acon where he found 'little kindness or frendeshippe';[2] he remembered Thomas Moone, a barber living in Smithfield, who had been a faithful friend when Salter was 'in great trouble' thirty years earlier,[3] and he left £5 to the Charterhouse at Sheen coupled with the request that they forgive him if he had offended them by word or deed long ago.[4] In an exceptionally long will occupying some ten pages, these are but the faintest whispers of unease.

* * *

Thomas Salter's childhood was spent in Norwich: perhaps he was born in the parish of St Paul there. Certainly by the time he was six years old he was going to school to be taught his letters by one of the sisters of Norman's Hospital, Dame Katherine Peckham.[5] The hospital had been founded in St Paul's parish in the twelfth century, but by the fifteenth century it was reserved for fourteen sisters (seven of whom lived in the house and another seven outside) who received small weekly pensions.[6] Presumably Dame Katherine Peckham was living in the house when she taught young Thomas, and he remembered her seventy-two years later as 'a verie good devoute sister'; and to all the sisters (he believed there were twenty-four of them) he left a weekly halfpenny wheaten loaf to be given to them every Sunday 'because I have greate truste that they will praie for me'.[7]

It is possible that young Thomas's surname was not Salter but that he acquired that name later when he came to London.[8] His will records nothing of his parents but, by the time he drew up his will, his closest relatives were the five children of Robert Symonds of Suffield (a village some ten miles north of Norwich), by his third wife Elizabeth, whom Salter claimed as his 'very near kinswoman'. Robert and Elizabeth were both dead by the time Thomas Salter was drawing up his will. The will of Robert Symonds had been drawn up two years before that of Thomas Salter; he refers to seven children. His eldest son John was already married to a wife Mary, and was to inherit Robert's copyhold lands and the

---

[2] Will, para 45.

[3] Will, para 34.

[4] Will, para 29.

[5] Will, para 20.

[6] For the hospital, see William Page (ed.), *Victoria County History: Norfolk*, 2 vols (London, 1906), ii, pp. 447–8; Carole Rawcliffe, *The Hospitals of Medieval Norwich* (Studies in East Anglian History, 2, 1995), pp. 61–89.

[7] See Carole Hill, 'Julian and Her Sisters: Female Piety in Late Medieval Norwich', in Linda Clark (ed.), *The Fifteenth Century*, 6 (2006), pp. 165–87, esp. pp. 185–6.

[8] In the will of Henry Adams, to whom Thomas had been apprenticed, drawn up in 1522 (by which time Thomas Salter had become a Carthusian monk), his old master left 20s. to his current apprentice on completion of his apprenticeship and 'to Thomas Adam 20s. to pray for me'. TNA PCC PROB/11/21, f.21 It is possible that this was a bequest to Thomas Salter, now in the Charterhouse, but at one time known, as was common, by his master's surname.

manor of Corlleys in Suffield. There were then three further sons by his third wife Elizabeth: Richard who was already married to a wife Elizabeth, John 'the younger' and Thomas who was not yet twenty-four. Three daughters are mentioned: Amy/Annys married to 'Bullocke', and then the two Elizabeths, the elder of whom was married to John Bozoun and the younger was not yet eighteen.[9] So Robert Symonds remembered two older children and all his five children born to his third wife Elizabeth. His eldest son John, who inherited the manor at Suffield, went on himself to have seven children (three sons and four daughters) and is commemorated by a remarkable tomb chest with a Latin inscription in the south aisle of Suffield church.[10] It is less easy to find out what happened to the five children of Robert Symonds by his third wife Elizabeth who were the beneficiaries under the will of their London kinsman.

Salter believed that his young relative John Symonds 'the younger' was living in the parish of St George Muspool (or Colgate) in Norwich, having completed an apprenticeship with the brother of Mr Leonard Sutterton, a Norwich alderman.[11] It seems likely that Thomas Salter knew young John (who had perhaps travelled to London before) because he designated him as the one to be informed when he died, and it is John who was to read out Salter's will to his brothers and sisters when they all came up to London to collect their money (and their wardrobes) in order that they 'shall perfectly see and knowe' that the executors 'be faithfull and true doers'. Salter is touchingly concerned about the difficulties and expenses that his five young relatives might face in travelling up to London, and he is anxious that they should not have to stay in the city for more than two days because of the expense: he specified that his executors were to spend forty shillings 'for their charges and expences' and to 'walcom them after a gentle facon'.[12] Whether the five country relatives ever received their £10 each and the items of Salter's clothing is not known.[13] The only one of them whose will survives is Thomas, who died in 1566, having been married to a wife, Dorothy, and leaving two daughters. He

[9]   Norwich Record Office, Consistory Court Will Register 265 Jagges, will drawn up 31 January 1556, proved 23 March 1556. Both Robert and John Symonds are listed as landholders in the manor of Suffield in a rental drawn up c. 1556, see British Library, Additional MS 36533, f. 18.

[10] Norwich Record Office, Consistory Court Will Register 514 Jarnigo, will drawn up 14 December 1584, proved 16 March 1586. The inscription on the tomb of John Symondes records that he died 14 December 1584.

[11] John Symondes, son of Robert Symondes of Suffield, 'yeoman' was apprenticed to Thomas Sutterton, grocer of Norwich, in 1549–50 for eight years, so he would have just completed his apprenticeship when Thomas Salter drew up his will, see Winifred R. Rising and Percy Milligan (eds), *An Index of Indentures of Norwich Apprentices Henry VIII – George II* (Norfolk Record Society, 1959), p. 159.

[12] Will, para. 25.

[13] Salter's original bequest to the five relatives was of twenty marks each (para. 23) but this was reduced in the codicil to ten pounds (para. 50).

had remained in Suffield and was buried in the church there.[14]

But Thomas Salter himself chose to leave Norwich and his Norfolk relatives and travel to London to seek his fortune there. It is quite possible that he was an orphan for he makes no provision in his will for prayers for his parents, which may be of significance in the will of a pious man who sought many prayers for himself. Salter probably came to London early in the sixteenth century because he refers to his time as a servant 'almoste fiftie yeres agone'[15]. His master was the salter Henry Adams who was not himself a Norfolk man, so that is not the connection that brought young Thomas into his service. While in the Adams household Salter made a number of friends whom he remembered fifty years later with small bequests: Robert Forest, a salter now living in Fenchurch parish, Joan Nayle, married to a joiner and living in St Olave's parish in Southwark, and Thomas Hollidaie, by the 1550s one of the Salters' almsmen and perhaps the source of Salter's charitable concern for this particular group of men.[16] It is remarkable, and a testimony to Salter's gift for friendship, that he not only remembered the young men and women with whom he had worked – and played perhaps – when he was an apprentice fresh to London from Norwich, but he had also kept in touch with these friends from his youth because, when drawing up his will, he knew where they were currently living in London: he had followed their fortunes, as perhaps they had followed his. It is clear that the young Thomas was carving out a successful career for himself, for within ten years of completing his apprenticeship he had entered the livery of the Salters' Company and, if his later will is anything to judge by, he was certainly prosperous. [17]

But when he was nearly forty, and clearly doing well in London, Thomas Salter decided to abandon the world of trade and to become a Carthusian monk at the London Charterhouse. Between September 1517 and March 1518 he passed rapidly through the various procedures and was ordained priest in St Paul's Cathedral on 20 March 1518.[18] The clever boy from Norwich who had become a successful London salter had turned away from the secular world to take up the most austere form of religious life then available to young men. The Carthusians combined

---

[14] Norwich Record Office, Archdeaconry Court Will Register Waterladde, f. 486, will drawn up 10 February 1566; proved 6 June 1566.

[15] Will, para. 35.

[16] Will paras 32, 33. and 35. Henry Adams drew up his will 6 March 1522, see TNA PROB/11/21, ff. 22v–23. From his will it seems clear that Henry Adams had come from Hertfordshire. Salter records that he and Joan Nayle were servants together in a house in Tower Street which may have been the home of Henry Adams early in the sixteenth century, but in 1522 he was living in the parish of St Botolph Bishopsgate.

[17] Will para. 13.

[18] See Virginia Davis, *Clergy in London in the Late Middle Ages: A Register of Clergy Ordained in the Diocese of London Based on Episcopal Ordination Lists 1361–1539* (London, 2000).

Benedictine monasticism with eremitical asceticism: the monks spent most of the day alone in their cells, studying, meditating or engaged in manual labour, and they emerged only to attend three daily services in the conventual church. A Carthusian monk lived his life in silence, broken only when he chanted in church and when he was allowed to walk outside the monastery once a week.[19] We know nothing of Salter's early career as a Carthusian, but he may not have been well suited to such a solitary life. His will suggests a man who had been friendly and gregarious in his youth, and the contrast with the large household of Henry Adams with its complement of young men and women, servants and apprentices, must have been sharp. But the decision to become a Carthusian monk had been Salter's own, adult, choice.

In the late 1520s, after ten years at the Charterhouse, Salter entered into the period which he refers to obliquely in his will as his 'great trouble'.[20] In 1529 William Tynbygh, who had been prior for nearly thirty years, resigned and was succeeded by John Batmanson who died two years later. John Houghton, who had been the prior at Beauvale, came to take over the leadership of the house during the years of extreme trial for the Carthusians of the London Charterhouse. Ten London Carthusians were executed in the following years for their hostility to the royal supremacy. Salter was not among them. Nor, on the other hand, was he among the rump of the remaining Carthusians who surrendered the house to the Crown in June 1538.[21] Thomas Salter's name was probably not remembered with honour among the members of the Carthusian brotherhood. As his will suggested, he had indeed offended the brethren in the Charterhouse, both in word and in deed.

At this distance it is hard to know what went wrong. It would appear that Thomas Salter did not get on well with the new prior, John Houghton. The cause of the trouble is not clear but one might guess that Houghton's austere, unbending lifestyle could not easily accommodate those who were less rigorous. For whatever reason, Salter attempted to run away and so was imprisoned in the conventual prison and while confined he suffered nightmares or delusions of some kind.[22] Some thought these were feigned in order to secure his release. But in June 1534 Salter emerged from prison to swear, together with all the other Char-

---

[19] For an account of the Carthusian rule, see Gerald S. Davies, *Charterhouse in London: Monastery, Mansion, Hospital, School* (London, 1921), pp. 41–5.

[20] Will, para 34.

[21] E. Margaret Thompson, *The Carthusian Order in England* (London, 1930), p. 387, n. 3. For accounts of the Charterhouse in this period see the updated account of the house by David Knowles in Caroline M. Barron and Matthew Davies (eds), *The Religious Houses of London and Middlesex* (London, 2007), pp. 247–60.

[22] Maurice Chauncy's account of the events in the London Charterhouse, which was originally published in Mainz in 1550, can be found in John H. P. Clark, *Dom Maurice Chauncy and the London Charterhouse* (Salzburg, 2006), ii, pp. 81–2.

terhouse monks, to the oath accepting the Act of Succession and thus the recognition of the validity of Henry VIII's second marriage to Anne Boleyn. But this submission did not secure for the monks the security and peace for which they hoped.[23] Two months later Thomas Cromwell visited the house, and while Cromwell was making a tour of inspection Salter seized the opportunity to talk with him and to rehearse his grievances against the Prior. He followed up this encounter with a letter to Cromwell written on 7 August 1534 in which he provided details of the harshness of Houghton's rule in the Charterhouse. Salter claimed that he could not go to confession because the brothers betrayed his confessions and so, un-confessed, he could not say mass nor receive the sacrament. He told Cromwell of a monk who had been so harshly treated by the brothers that he would have committed suicide had not the then prior, John Batmanson, sent him to a house of canons in the west country. But the current prior was much harsher than his predecessor and would not release Salter to go elsewhere.[24] Cromwell's response is not recorded, but he preserved Salter's autograph letter among his papers (see Plate 5).[25]

The protest to Cromwell did not secure instant release for Salter. He was still confined in the Charterhouse prison in 1535, but seems then to have been allowed out, at least as far as the cloister. Meanwhile Salter's adversary, Prior John Houghton, together with two other Carthusian priors who would not take the oath accepting the Act of Supremacy (November 1534) whereby the king became the supreme head on earth of the church in England, were executed at Tyburn in May 1535. Salter was clearly looking for a way to leave the house, for Jasper Fylioll reported to Cromwell in that year that two monks, Thomas Salter and John Darley 'would like to be out of the cloister' and that Darley had the prospect of a job in Salisbury.[26] It would seem that Salter (and Darley?) were successful for, by May 1537, when some of the monks finally agreed to swear the oath accepting the royal supremacy and ten others who were obdurate were sent to Newgate to die there of starvation, their names were not to be found in either group.[27]

Thomas Salter's evidence about the tensions within the Carthusian house, and the harshness of Houghton's regime there, may have been useful to Cromwell in

---

[23] Andrew Wines, 'The London Charterhouse in the later Middle Ages: An Institutional History', unpublished Cambridge PhD, 1998, pp. 206, 282–3.

[24] *Letter and Papers*, vol. 7, pt. 2 no. 1046, p. 408; printed in Thompson, *Carthusian Order*, pp. 387–90.

[25] TNA SP1/85.

[26] *Letters and Papers*, vol. 8, no. 601, p. 227, and vol. 9, no. 284, p. 95; printed in Thompson, *Carthusian Order*, pp 417–18; 427–8. John Darley was dispensed to hold any benefice with complete change of habit, i.e. to cease to be a religious and become a secular priest, 29 March 1536, D. S. Chambers (ed.), *Faculty Office Register 1534–1549* (Oxford, 1966), p. 49. There is no record of a similar dispensation for Salter, although he must have been dispensed in order to serve as a secular priest.

[27] Thompson, *Carthusian Order*, p. 387 n. 3.

breaking the unity and, ultimately, the will of the London Carthusians. In the words of Dom David Knowles, Salter 'spoke ill of his brethren and their superiors to their enemies'; and, in due course, the enemies rewarded the renegade monk.[28] From 1542 until his death sixteen years later Thomas Salter received a pension of £5 every year paid by the Court of Augmentations.[29] In these circumstances it is hardly surprising that when Maurice Chauncy returned to England in June 1555 to re-establish the Carthusian order in England at the Charterhouse at Sheen, Thomas Salter did not join him. Three years later the aged Thomas Salter left the modest bequest of £5 to the Sheen Charterhouse and asked the Prior and all his brethren to pray for him and to forgive him, 'if ever I have offended them longe before thies daies'. But the bitterness must have been deep. The calm and meticulous disposal of his accumulated personal possessions conceals the troubled conscience of Thomas Salter, a devout Catholic priest whose mid-life had, indeed, been a time of 'great trouble'.

When he left the Charterhouse Salter may have sought refuge in the house of Thomas Moone, a barber who lived in West Smithfield near to the sign of the Antelope, which would have been quite close to the Charterhouse. Thirty years later Salter remembered Moone as his 'faithfull frende' who had helped him in his time of great trouble.[30] It may be that the help which Moone gave Salter was medical. But Salter emerged from his trouble to find a job as a chantry priest serving a well-endowed chantry in the London parish of St Nicholas Acon. Here, by the time of the enquiry into chantries in 1548, Thomas was receiving a salary of £7 14s. and paid 6s. 8d. rent for 'a chamber in the churchyard'.[31] Although Salter claimed in his will that he had found 'little kindness or frendeshippe' in the parish yet he remembered several parishioners in his will. These were his neighbours Christopher Luter who had looked after him 'when anye sicknes was renynge' and Robert Henceball whom he declared to be 'verie friendfull unto me': each of them received five shillings, as did John Plomer, a hosier living in St Nicholas Lane who suffered from poverty and 'grevous dysease'.[32] Salter's charity to the parishioners did not stop there: he gave 12d. to each of the children of 'Goodman Browne' and 12d. to 'Goodman Jeremiar', a Dutchman and goldsmith, and a further 12d. to his 'honeste wiffe'.[33] And when it came to disposing of the furnishings of his chamber, his

---

[28]   Barron and Davies, *The Religious Houses of London*, p. 256.

[29]   *Letters and Papers*, vol. 17, no. 1258, p. 694; vol. 18, no. 436, p. 258; vol. 19, no. 368, p. 237; vol. 20, no. 557, p. 263; vol. 21, part 2, no. 775, p. 442; TNA, E 315/256.

[30]   Will, para. 34. In fact Thomas Mone, barber surgeon of St Sepulchre's parish, drew up his will in the same month as Thomas Salter and died before him since his will was proved 5 October 1558, Guildhall Library, Commissary Register 9171/14, f. 63.

[31]   C. J. Kitching (ed.), *London and Middlesex Chantry Certificate 1548* (London Record Society, 1980), p. 31. The certificate notes that Sir Thomas Sawter aged 68 received a pension of £5 p.a. in addition to his salary.

[32]   Will, paras 16 and 37.   [33]   Will, para. 16.

pots and brushes and little chests and leather bags and bottles and glasses and candlesticks, Salter divided these between Joan Standely 'the maid dwellinge in the parisshe' and John Busshope the parish clerk.[34] And in spite of the cool reception he had received, Salter provided £5 to pay for a new silver gilt pyx for the parish to be used on the feast of Corpus Christi and on Palm Sunday, to be made by a skilled goldsmith 'after a comly and decent facion' since it was to hold the sacrament of the altar. And around the foot of the pyx were to be engraved the words 'Pray for the sowle of Thomas Salter some tyme Chauntrie priest of this Churche'.[35]

Salter required his executors to organise three separate series of dole-giving. The first dole of halfpenny wheaten loaves were to be given to the poor people of the parish of St Magnus on the day when Salter was buried.[36] The second dole of 500 halfpenny wheaten loaves was to be distributed within three or four days of his burial in 'the parisshe where I was last in service'.[37] When he first drafted his will Salter intended to distribute a third dole of a penny to every poor person in the parish of St Nicholas Acon, but this clause has been crossed out in the original will and, instead, Salter chose to distribute larger sums to a small number of chosen people in the parish. The lack of friendship and kindness that Salter had found in St Nicholas Acon evidently led him to exercise more discriminating charity there.[38]

When the chantries were dissolved in the reign of Edward VI, Salter would have been unemployed and, perhaps, in personal danger because of his faith. It is possible that he went into hiding in the notoriously conservative parish of St Olave in Southwark, which may well have provided a 'safe home' for Catholics during the reign of Edward VI. When Mary came to the throne St Olave's parish was 'exceptionally prompt and thorough in restoring the usages and panoply of the pre-Reformation church'.[39] The Vestry decided to restore the church furnishings less than six weeks after Mary came to the throne, and on 5 December that same year they agreed to appoint 'Sir' Thomas Salter, clerk, as their morrow mass priest. In return for an annual salary of four marks 'towards the maintenance of his living' he was to celebrate an early mass every morning 'at such an house' as the church-

---

[34] Will, paras 42 and 43. Joan Standely (Stanley) died in 1569. There is no surviving will but probate was granted to her relative Alice Eccles, Guildhall Library, Commissary Register MS 9171/12, f. 195v.

[35] Will, para. 45.

[36] Will, para. 14.

[37] Will, para. 15. If the executors could not purchase enough bread then they were to distribute the 25 shillings in doles of 1*d.* for every two persons. 'or else' as Salter helpfully adds 'to every four persons one twopenny grote'. For Salter's last parish, see below, footnotes 49 and 50.

[38] Will, para. 16 and n. 8.

[39] Martha Carlin, *Medieval Southwark* (London, 1996), pp. 98–9. I am much indebted to Dr Carlin's account of the parish of St Olave in Southwark.

wardens should decide.[40] A new image of St Olave was made and 'a collection of lamps, banners, painted cloths, streamers and torches' was purchased to be used in the parish in the revived celebrations and processions at Palm Sunday, Easter, Whitsun, Corpus Christi, Ascension Day Christmas, and at the feast of St Olave. Vestments and Catholic service books were assembled with enthusiasm and in 1555 the performance of religious plays was revived when 'playing garments' were bought for the children who 'played the profyttes' on Palm Sunday. Moreover by May 1554, less than a year after Mary's accession, the pre-Reformation guild dedicated to the Name of Jesus had been revived in the church and it is likely that Thomas Salter, as the morrowmass priest, would have acted also as the fraternity priest.

It would not be surprising, therefore, if Thomas Salter, whose loyalty to the 'most hollie Catholique Churche of Christe Jesus' was never in doubt, even if he could not cope with the rigours of the Carthusian way of life, had found a haven in Edward's reign in St Olave's parish in Southwark, arguably the most fervently Catholic parish in sixteenth-century London. Salter was himself a 'pore' brother of the re-founded fraternity of Jesus, and he asked in his will that the masters and brothers of the fraternity should accompany his corpse from 'the howse where I die' to St Magnus Church and remain in the church until the mass and burial service were ended. And, as was his wont, Salter specified how they were to be dressed: 'in their clenely sadd (i.e. dark) coloured gownes and silke hodes and tippettes, and with the name of Jesus uppon their Brestes'.[41] In recompense for this display of brotherly solidarity Salter left them twenty shillings for a 'recreacon' and a further twenty shillings for the funds of the brotherhood in return for their prayers. Thomas Salter also knew, and remembered in his will, several parishioners of St Olave's. He left to Joan, the wife of Vincent Nayle, a joiner who lived 'next beyond' St Olave's church, six English crowns which, he carefully notes, is thirty shillings sterling, because 'she and I were servants togethir in one howse' in Tower Street fifty years earlier.[42] Salter also left a gold ring to 'goode mastyr' John Eston Esquire, a Justice of the Peace for Surrey and an MP for Southwark who lived in the parish. John Eston, in Edward's reign, had bought the silver gilt monstrance from the churchwardens of St Olave's for the considerable sum of £26 18s. 4d. (perhaps to hold it in safe-keeping) and then in Mary's reign he contributed 20s. towards 'the setting up of the altars'.[43] Thomas also requested that all the – very

---

[40] S[outhwark] L[ocal] H[istory] L[ibrary], MS 1622, St Olave's Vestry Book 1551–1604, ff.. 5, 5v. Payments of Salter's salary are recorded in the churchwardens' accounts for 1554–6 and 1556–8, MS 1635, St Olave's Churchwardens' Accounts, ff. 34, 53.

[41] Will, para. 12.

[42] Will, para. 33.

[43] S.L.H.L., MS 1635, ff. 14, 33. Will, para. 39. Salter appears to have thought better of this bequest since it is cancelled in the original will, perhaps because Eston seems later to have become a convinced Protestant. He died in 1565; see S. T. Bindoff, *The House of*

elaborate – wax tapers specified for his funeral were to be made by 'good Mr Day' the waxchandler of St Olave's parish provided that he would make them 'as good chepe as an other will do'.[44] Thomas Day not only supplied the parish church every year with wax tapers and candles, but served as a churchwarden and also, later, as an auditor of the accounts.[45] Salter was also befriended in St Olave's parish by the self-made entrepreneur, Henry Leeke, an alien brewer. Leeke had built up a considerable estate in the parish of St Olave and by 1554 he was one of the auditors of the churchwardens' accounts. He may well have had recusant sympathies and his sudden journey 'beyonde the sea to my frendys' in 1546, which led to his drawing up a brief will before his departure, may have been prompted by his catholic loyalties.[46] He had returned by 1554 and played a prominent role in his very catholic parish. The general pardon he obtained on the accession of Elizabeth may have been sought to cover some shady business dealings, but it may also have been connected with his known loyalty to the old religion.[47] In his will Thomas Salter gave Leeke a gold ring valued at four French crowns and also 'inumerable thanckes ... for the greate frendely love and favour that he bare unto me of long tyme, whiche was to the greate furthering of my welfare and honestie'.[48]

So when Mary came to the throne in 1553 and Catholicism was restored in England, Salter was once more able to work as a priest, although at first only as a morrowmass priest dependent upon the generosity of the churchwardens of St Olave's parish. Clearly he would have sought the security of an endowed chantry and the signs are that when he began to draw up his will he had not yet secured such employment: hence his frequent references to bequests to 'the parish where I was last in service' which clearly indicate that he did not know in which parish he would be serving when he died. But, in the course of drawing up his will, Salter appears to have secured employment in the parish of St Michael Cornhill. Several bequests of torches, originally destined for St Nicholas, have been altered in favour of the parish of St Michael and it is the curate of St Michael Cornhill who is asked to be present at Salter's burial service.[49] After the detailed description of the pyx to be given to St Nicholas parish, Salter notes, rather as an afterthought, 'And I give a lyke pixe to the said parishe of St Michaelles in Cornhill upon the like condicon'.[50]

Although Salter may have gone into hiding in St Olave's parish during Edward's reign, it would appear that he returned in Mary's reign to the rented

Commons 1509–1558, 3 vols (London, 1982), ii, pp. 108–09.

44   Will, para 7.

45   S.L.H.L., MS 1622, f. 2v; MS 1635, f.14, 76v

46   Ida Darlington (ed.), *London Consistory Court Wills 1492–1547* (London Record Society, 1967), no. 242.

47   For a rich biography of Henry Leeke, see Carlin, *Medieval Southwark*, pp. 165–7.

48   Will, para. 40.

49   Will, paras 4 and 6.

50   Will, para. 46.

chamber in the churchyard of St Nicholas Acon where he remained until his death: the distribution of his small personal possessions, including the 'vi glasses in my chamber windowe' to two parishioners suggests that he was still living in the parish of St Nicholas. But there is no doubt that he wished to be buried and commemorated in the church of St Magnus, lying at the northern end of London Bridge. Although St Magnus church was near to Southwark where Salter had served as a morrowmass priest and where he was a brother of the Fraternity dedicated to the Name of Jesus, yet his choice of a church where he was not a parishioner, and where he seems not to have had particular friends, is puzzling. It may be significant that the livings of both St Nicholas Acon and St Magnus were held at this time by Maurice ap Griffith, an Oxford graduate who began his life as a Dominican friar and was later consecrated as bishop of Rochester in April 1554. Griffith died at almost the same time as Salter and, like him, chose to be buried in St Magnus church.[51] Moreover St Magnus was a fine church, and Thomas Salter liked finery. Stow wrote that it was a 'fayre Parrish Church ... in which church have beene buried many men of good Worship.'[52] It may have been the fairness of the church and the quality of those buried there which attracted Salter. He asked to be buried in the Lady Chapel of the church in the vacant area near to the pew of the Alderman Master John Cooper.[53] Since Salter makes no other reference to Cooper in his will, his choice of burial near his pew does not suggest intimacy but, perhaps, social ambition. Salter, as one might expect, was clear about the exact way in which his burial and exequies were to be carried out. His funeral was to take place in the morning when the great bell of St Magnus church was to toll his knell from 6 am until noon. No sermon was to be preached either at the funeral or at the month's mind but, in the Lent following his burial, Salter provided six shillings for a sermon to be given by a 'sadde and discrete secular priest that is well learned and a good catholique in his lyvinge'.[54] Salter provided rewards for a number of curates, clerks and sextons whom he asks to be present at his burial service, but it was as a onetime member of the Salters' Company that Thomas particularly wished to be remembered. He asked the masters of the company to accompany his body to St Magnus church 'in their best lyvery' and to remain until the end of the burial service. Their attendance was to be rewarded with forty shillings to spend on a meal 'where it please them'.[55]

[51]   A. B. Emden, *Biographical Register of the University of Oxford 1501–1540* (Oxford, 1974), p. 248. John Stow, *A Survey of London*, ed. C. L. Kingsford, 2 vols (Oxford, 1908), i, p. 212. Stow does not mention Salter's monument.

[52]   Kingsford, Stow, *Survey of London,* i, p. 212.

[53]   Will, paras. 3 and 11. John Cooper, a fishmonger, had only recently (21 June 1558) been elected as the Alderman of Bridge Without. He had served as sheriff in 1551–2, but, according to Stow, 'was put by his turn of Maoraltie', and died in 1585, see A. B. Beaven, *The Aldermen of the City of London*, 2 vols (London, 1913), ii, 36.

[54]   Will, para. 4.   [55]   Will, para. 8.

Salter, as so often, specifies very carefully exactly what the torches and tapers burning at his funeral are to look like. In addition to four great tapers of yellow wax each weighing ten pounds, and twelve 'staffe torches' of yellow wax each weighing three pounds, Salter instructed his executors to pay fourteen or fifteen shillings for two 'cummely braunches of pure white waxe' (i.e. six-branch standing candlesticks) and between the branches there were to be five escutcheons: two depicting the five wounds of Christ, two with 'the letters of my name T and S knytte together' and one with the arms of the Salters' company.[56] During the funeral service the torches and tapers were to be held by the six almsmen of the Salters' company and a further ten poor freemen of the company. As we have come to expect, not only did Salter specify that all the poor men were to receive a sterling groat but also that they were to wear russet gowns costing twenty shillings each 'the saide gownes be wide and side downe to the ancle and wide poked sleves and narrowe at the hands after a palmers garment'.[57]

Between his burial service and his month's mind Salter asked that his grave be covered with a black woollen cloth embellished with a simple white cross, but during his burial service, and at his month's mind he asked the Salters for the use of their best hearse cloth.[58] At the month's mind service Salter wanted the same personnel to be present for the *Dirige*, and the mass, which was to be both read and sung. And the poor men of the craft were again to bear the torches and tapers wearing their russet palmers' gowns. After the service was over the contingent of salters was to return to Salters' Hall together with Salter's executor and the overseer of his will. Then, in due order, all the officers of the craft were to be lined up to receive the rewards that Salter had so carefully specified: aldermen and sheriffs of the company, 3s. 4d. each; wardens, 2s. 6d.; past wardens, 2s.; renter wardens, 1s. 8d.; past renter wardens, 1s. 4d.; liverymen of the company who came to his burial and month's mind, each 1s.; and the beadle who was responsible for ensuring that the members of the company were summoned to the funeral and month's mind was to receive a special reward of 40s. And in addition to these individual bequests Salter provided 40 shillings for 'a little recreacon' for all of them 'for I am not able to give them a great dynner'.[59]

Just as Thomas made detailed provision for his funeral, so he was very precise about his gravestone. He specified a grey marble slab on which there was to be an engraved brass made by a 'cunynge marbler' who lived on the south side of the parish church of St Dunstan in the West. The brass image was to depict a priest with his eyes 'cloosed togythir as all deademens eyes ought so to be', dressed in an alb and vestment and holding in both hands a chalice together with the conse-

56   Will, paras 5 and 6.
57   Will, para. 6.
58   Will, para. 8.
59   Will, para. 9.

crated host 'in a sunnie beame appearinge right above the chalice'. Above the head of the priest there was to be a scroll with the words *miserere mei deus: secundum magnam misericordiam tuam'*. At the foot of the image there was to be a tablet 'of Antick facon' which recorded that Thomas Salter, sometime priest of London, had departed from this transitory life in the year 1558 when he was eighty years old in the 'grace and greate mercye of god'. The exact date and month of Salter's departing are left as gaps in his text. And at the base of the brass there was to be an engraved escutcheon with the arms of the Salters' company 'bycause I was in my youth one of the said companye and lyverey'.[60]

Thomas Salter was, indeed, very attached to the company of the Salters and it is to them that he entrusted his major benefaction: his 'grett rewarde & gyfte' of 200 marks from which they were to buy lands and rents to produce an annual income. Needless to say, Salter was very precise as to how the income was to be spent. He had four objectives. His primary objective was to increase the stipend of the six almsmen of the Salters' company by two pence a week, and he carefully explained that this money was to be used to increase their salaries and not simply to replace other funding streams.[61] The second objective was to provide four sacks of coal once a year for the six almsmen.[62] In the third place the company was to oversee the keeping of his annual obit in St Magnus' church. Salter does not expect the master and wardens to attend the obit, but he hoped that the beadle and the six almsmen would do so and for this they were to be rewarded. In all, the costs of the annual obit were to amount to no more than 14s. 2d. And Salter's final stipulation was that 52s. was to be sent every year to the churchwardens of St Paul's parish in Norwich, who were to spend 12d. every week in buying halfpenny wheaten loaves for the twenty-four sisters in Norman's hospital or, failing them, for the poor of the parish. And, as if the wardens of the Salters were not given enough to do, Thomas even asks them to send an extra 12d. to the St Paul's churchwardens to buy a basket to be used for storing the bread. So in all, Salter calculated that the pensioners' salary increases would cost 52s. a year and the coal 16 shillings, the obit 14s. 2d., and the Norwich charity 52s. making a total of £6 14s. 2d. or just in excess of ten marks.[63] If the Company had invested the 200 marks in London property this might have been expected to produce annual returns of about 7%, or fourteen marks which would have covered the specified bequests and, perhaps, left enough for repairs to the properties.[64]

---

[60]   Will, para. 13. For a discussion of Salter's brass in the context of other London wills specifying particular engraved images, see Malcolm Norris, *Monumental Brasses: The Craft* (London, 1978), chapters 7 and 8.

[61]   Will, para 17.

[62]   Will, para 18.

[63]   Will, paras 19–22.

[64]   I am grateful to Professor Derek Keene for help on this point.

It seems evident that the Salters Company baulked a little at the responsibilities and tasks allocated to them under Salter's will. Although two of the witnesses to the original will were Edmund Keye and Robert Harding, both of whom were salters, it is not clear to what extent Thomas Salter may have discussed his plans and intentions with the Company itself before he drew up his will. The Company had been given a very substantial role to play in fulfilling Thomas's wishes: not only were the masters of the Company to accompany Thomas's funeral procession to St Magnus' church and stay until the end of the service in return for a forty shilling supper, but they were to oversee the administration, in perpetuity, of Salter's 'great rewarde' to the Company of two hundred marks. This money had to be invested in lands and rents and the income spent on a variety of charitable purposes, some of them at a considerable distance from London. City companies were increasingly burdened with such obligations and they were becoming rather more careful to ensure that the value of the bequest was sufficient to meet the obligations which were imposed.[65] In the course of drawing up his will, Thomas Salter may, perhaps, have had a stroke for the last few clauses are not written in his own hand, but by the notary, and at the end, although all the four witnesses signed their names, Thomas was able only to make a feeble, and smudged, mark (see Plate 4).[66] At some point after the completion of the will, Keye and Harding may have discussed the provisions of Salter's will with the Salters' Court of Assistants and it may have been decided to send a deputation to visit the dying Salter. The Court was clearly concerned that the sum which the company was being given was inadequate for the purposes Thomas had in mind. So on 8 October Thomas was persuaded to reduce the amount to be given to the poor of Norwich from 52 shillings to 26 shillings so that the other 26 shillings could be paid to the Salters 'in consideration of suche paymentes' as Salter had required to be made from the income of his gift. And in order to ensure that the Company received the full two hundred marks, Salter was persuaded to reduce the amounts to be paid to each of his five kinsfolk from twenty marks (£13 6s. 8d.) to ten pounds, since 'on better advisement' he realised that his money and goods 'woulde no further extend'. Moreover Salter's executors were to hand over one hundred marks by next Easter and the further hundred marks the following Christmas. It is clear that the Salters' Company intended to secure the 'great rewarde' that they had been bequeathed as quickly and as securely as possible. And, as some sort of payment, each of the three

---

[65]   Cf. John Tillotson, 'Early Tudor Executors in London and their work, with particular reference to the probate records of Sir John Rudston (d. 1551), mayor of London', paper read at the Institute of Historical Research, November 2007. I am grateful to Professor Tillotson for letting me see a copy of his paper in advance of publication..

[66]   The notary who completed the drafting of Thomas Salter's will, and witnessed the will and the codicil, was Thomas Bradforth who entered the Scriveners' Company in 1551. The last reference to him occurs in 1566, see Francis W. Steer (ed.), *Scriveners' Company Common Paper 1357–1628* (London Record Society, 1968), pp. 19 and 27.

members of the deputation from the Company was to receive twenty shillings from Salter's estate.[67]

Thomas Salter had a special affection for his Company because at its heart had been the fraternity dedicated to Corpus Christi in All Hallows church in Bread Street. The Salters had taken over the parish guild dedicated to Corpus Christi in the course of the fifteenth century and by 1483 this guild chapel in the church was known as Salters' chapel and the Salters maintained two priests in the church. Although in 1550 the Company had been forced to forfeit some of the rents that they had been given by the salter Thomas Beaumond in 1454, to fund a chantry priest and maintain his obit in the fraternity chapel in the church, yet it was still possible that the fraternity might be re-founded.[68] The unhappy impression remains that the Salters' Company in which Thomas had been proud to be of the livery when he was a young man, and for which he had a special affection because of the company's role as 'kepers of the seale of the fraternity of Corpus Christi in London', did not feel as warmly and generously towards their erstwhile liveryman as he felt towards them. Moreover their task in carrying out the provisions in Salter's will was made more difficult by the fact that between the drawing up of the codicil on 8 October and the proving of the will on 19 December, Queen Mary had died on 17 November: the very future of Catholic England was in doubt.

But if the Salters' Company was hesitant about the tasks allocated to them under the will of Thomas Salter, his executor faced an even more daunting task. Salter appointed only one executor, his 'trustie frend' Peter Honyborne, a draper; and his 'especiall frende and spiritual lover' Master Richard Kettil, the vicar of St Stephen's Coleman Street, was to act as the overseer. In recompense for this task Kettil was to receive a black gown and hood in addition to the other legacies he had already received under the will: Honyborne seems to have received no legacies and no reward for acting as Salter's executor.[69] There may have been some verbal arrangement between the two men. Honyborne (Honntingborne) appears to have been a parishioner in Thomas Salter's last parish, St Michael Cornhill, and when he drew up his own will in 1563 he ended it with words which were almost

---

[67] Will, para. 50. The three salters were Edmund Keye and Robert Harding who had both witnessed the original will on 31 August 1558, together with William Gonne. Keye died in 1567; Robert Harding was elected alderman of Broad Street ward in 1567 but died the following year, see Beaven, *Aldermen of the City of London*, ii, p. 38. The date of the death of William Gonne is not known.

[68] See J. Steven Watson, *A History of the Salters' Company* (London, 1963), pp. 6–9, 33; Caroline M. Barron, 'The Parish Fraternities of Medieval London', in *The Church in Pre-Reformation Society: Essays in Honour of F. R. H. DuBoulay*, eds Caroline M. Barron and Christopher Harper-Bill (Woodbridge, 1985), pp. 13–37, esp. pp. 14–15; Kitching, *Chantry Certificate*, no. 191; *Calendar of Patent Rolls 1549–51*, 6 vols (London, 1924–29), iii, p. 393.

[69] Will, para. 47.

identical to those used by Thomas Salter in closing his will five years earlier.[70]

It is difficult to know how well Honyborne and Kettil carried out their tasks in the changed religious climate of Elizabethan England. It is impossible to know whether Salter's funeral and month's mind were carried out as he had hoped. Stow, who lists the monuments in St Magnus' church in the 1590s, says nothing of Thomas Salter's tomb, although he does record the tomb of Maurice ap Griffith the catholic bishop of Rochester who died in the year after Salter.[71] Stow is notoriously selective and the fact that he does not choose to record Salter's tomb does not mean that it never existed.[72] On the other hand its blatant Catholic imagery, and emphasis on the chalice containing the body of Christ, might have made it a particular target for Protestant iconoclasts. But there is a legend in the Salters' Company that the almsmen of the craft were accustomed to visit Salter's monument once a year and knock on the tomb saying 'How do you do, brother Salter? I hope you are well'.[73] If there is any truth in the legend, then there must have been a tomb to be visited. The church was burnt in the Fire of 1666 and rebuilt.

The Salters Company received their bequest and observed the letter, if not the spirit, of Salter's will. By the nineteenth century they could refer to a copy of Salter's will in 'an old book of gifts' to the Company. The six Company almsmen received their extra two pence a week (as part of a weekly allowance of 10s. 6d.) and each almsman received from the Company a chaldron (1 cwt) of coals which, it was claimed, 'more than compensates for Thomas Salter's gift of four sacks of coal each'. The Company acknowledged that Salter had left money for the celebration of his annual obit each year in St Magnus' church 'with other payments for superstitious uses', and the Company paid their almsmen an extra fifteen shillings yearly in lieu of the three shillings which Salter had left them as a reward for going to St Magnus' church. The Company discharged its obligations for Salter's bequest to the poor sisters of Norman's Hospital in Norwich by paying £1 6s. each year to the churchwardens of the parish of St Paul 'for the use of the poor'. When enquiry was made of the churchwardens, they answered that the money was 'carried into

---

[70] Peter Honntingborne drew up his will 22 December 1563, TNA, PROB 11/46, ff. 316–17. Honntingborne translates Salter's final Latin peroration into English 'Into thy hands Lord I commend my spirit, thou hast redeemed me, Lord God of Truth'. Although this is a prayer in common use, it is not often found in wills. One of the witnesses to Honntingborne's own will was John Philpot, the rector of St Michael Cornhill.

[71] Stow, *Survey*, i, 212.

[72] On Stow's selectivity in recording monuments and tombs in London churches, see Christian Steer, 'Commemoration and Women in Medieval London', in Matthew Davies and Andrew Prescott (eds), *London and the Kingdom*, Harlaxton Medieval Studies, XVI (Donington, 2008), 230–45.

[73] Steven Watson, *History of the Salters' Company*, p. 33. I am very grateful to Katie George, the archivist of the Salters' Company, for searching the Company archives for information about the history of Salter's bequest.

the general charity account'.[74] It is noticeable that although the Salters Company had received 200 marks and invested it in lands and rents from which the income would have risen with inflation, yet in the three centuries since Salter's death, the amounts paid out in charitable payments had not increased at all. How was the increased income from Salter's bequest being spent?

Does his will bring us any closer to Thomas Salter himself? Is it reasonable to believe that the priorities and concerns apparent in the will reflect those of the man himself? We have seen that the will while revealing much about its author has also, probably deliberately. concealed a good deal. There is, for example, no reference to Salter's parentage or family as one might have expected: his origins remain deliberately obscured. We are not told in what way Elizabeth, his 'very nere kinswoman', is related to the testator. Likewise there is no reference to the twenty years he spent as a Carthusian monk in the London Charterhouse, and the reasons for his silence only become apparent through access to other sources. There is a further mystery which Salter does nothing to explain, and that is how he came to have so much money to dispose of at the end of his life. It is true that he appears not to have possessed any silver plate, which would normally have been mentioned in the wills of moderately prosperous secular men and women, but Salter was certainly 'cash rich'. In total his bequests amounted to nearly £300: his funeral expenses (£41 14s. 4d.); the bequests to fourteen named individuals (£24 6s. 4d.); the bequests to institutions (all prisons apart from the Charterhouse at Sheen) (£9 15s.); the bequests to his five relatives (£68 13s. 4d. reduced to £52); the two pyxes (£10), and the rewards to the three salters (£3). Then in addition there was the 'great rewarde' bequest of 200 marks (£133 13s. 4d.) given to the Salters' Company. This total of £291 2s. 4d. does not include the cost of his marble and brass tomb in St Magnus' church. Thomas Salter had probably been at one time a very successful salter who rose quickly to become a liveryman. But, surely, on entering the Charterhouse he would have surrendered all his personal wealth? It is true that individual Carthusians were allowed to own some personal possessions. When Thomas Golwyne, for instance, moved from the London Charterhouse to Mount Grace priory in 1519 he took with him a modest personal wardrobe, utensils of pewter and latten including items that had been given to him personally, and at least fourteen books.[75] It is possible that Salter left the London house with a comparable collection of personal items. But when he emerged again into the secular world he did so as a chantry priest earning £7 14s. p.a., augmented by his Charterhouse pension of £5 p.a. The wealth revealed in his will could not have been acquired by savings out of his salary. The source of this wealth remains a mystery.

---

[74] *Report of the Commissioners appointed by Parliament to enquire concerning Charities in England,* 32 vols (London, 1819–1840), vi, pp. 326–31; xxvii, p. 694.

[75] Davies, *Charterhouse in London,* pp. 323–5.

Some of Salter's priorities are apparent in his bequests: it is his relatives, and the Salters' Company who receive the bulk of his benefactions. The only institutions to benefit, apart from the Carthusian house at Sheen are the numerous London prisons: had Salter's sympathies for prisoners been aroused, perhaps, by his own experiences when confined in the conventual prison of the Charterhouse? And there is no doubting the importance which he attached to his funeral and his post mortem commemorations. But one of the most striking aspects of his will is the numerous bequests to individuals, each with a distinctive testimonial.

Another of Salter's priorities must surely have been his clothes. It is not simply that he seems to have quite a lot of them, but rather that he describes them with such meticulous attention to the details of their construction. It is true that Salter is meticulous about many aspects of his bequests but it may seem surprising that he, an ex-monk, is so fastidious about his clothing. In all he owned six gowns, two short gowns, four side gowns, one frock, one partlet (a ruff or collar) and three jackets. Although some of these were old, others were furred with cony and fittchewes (pole cat) or lined with fine worsted. In addition Salter had nine caps of satin, velvet and wool; ten pairs of ponyettes (cuffs); two pairs of new leather gloves which he kept under the mattress on his bed and an assortment of leather and velvet bags and pouches. None of this clothing seems to have been specifically the apparel of a priest, except for Salter's six tippets, the long black scarf which was worn by the clergy over their surplice. He left five of these tippets to his fellow priest Richard Kettil, but one of black sarsenet he gave to Elizabeth Symondes specifying that it was two ells long (but lacked two nayles, i.e. two inches) and suggesting that if she could not use it herself she might 'sell it to some honest priest that is well beneficed and have an honest pourcon of money for it'.[76] Salter also left two pairs of his best hose, two of his best shirts, two of his best towels and four of his best handkerchiefs to Richard Kettil, specifying 'that they be clene washed my said lynen before they be delyvered unto him'.[77]

It is clear that Richard Kettil was Salter's 'best friend'. In appointing him as the overseer of his will he calls him 'my especiall frende and spiritual lover', and elsewhere in the will he thanks him heartily 'for his great love and favour that he hath borne unto me of long tyme'.[78] Richard Kettil receives, in addition to the tippets and all the best linen, two gowns, a jacket and seven caps. He was also given the six books in Salter's chamber. These consisted of a great book containing sermons and the Gospels and another 'lesser book' of the Epistles. In addition Salter had a 'portuas', that is a portable breviary which brought together in a single volume, in

---

[76] Will, para. 23. For help in understanding the clothing of Thomas Salter I am grateful to Kay Staniland. See also: Janet Mayo, *A History of Ecclesiastical Dress* (London, 1984), p. 177.

[77] Will, para. 28,

[78] Will, paras 28 and 47.

abbreviated form, all the antiphons and lessons necessary for the celebration of the canonical office.[79] Salter's fourth book was a primer written, as was customary, in both English and Latin. The primer, or Book of Hours, was the devotional book of the laity and usually contained, among other devotional works, the office of the Virgin, the seven penitential psalms, a litany and the offices for the dead. Salter writes that his primer contained all the readings from the Epistles and Gospels in English for every Sunday and holiday (i.e. festival day) for the whole year. This would, indeed, be a very useful book for a priest to possess. The fifth book was called *Ortus Vocabulorum*, a Latin dictionary with English meanings which had been produced towards the end of the fifteenth century and was printed by de Worde in 1500.[80] And the final volume, described by Salter as 'a verie little boke', was a copy of *The Imitation of Christ* (*Imitatio Christi*) a famous manual of spiritual devotion, attributed to Thomas a Kempis (c.1380–1471), in which the Christian is instructed to seek perfection by following Christ as his model.[81] This is not a remarkable collection of books, but they would have provided Salter with the necessary tools for serving as a chantry priest. Only the *Imitation of Christ* suggests that he might have used books to deepen, or improve, his spiritual life. Moreover the listing of his books, in the middle of a catalogue of the different clothes to be given to Richard Kettil, suggests that Salter saw them as part of the furnishings of his chamber and that his eye fell upon them as he sat drawing up his will. The books are not described with the same intimacy and affection (or knowledge of their contents and defects) as are his clothes.

It might, perhaps, throw some light on Thomas Salter if we were able to find out more about his 'special friend and spiritual lover' Richard Kettil. Kettil had been vicar of St Stephen Coleman Street since 1530 and so, like Salter, he had lived through the upheavals of the religious changes of the mid-sixteenth century. Although Salter notes that Kettil was a Master of Arts, and in his own will Kettil describes himself as Bachelor of Law, yet there is no record of him to be found among the records of the alumni of Oxford and Cambridge universities.[82] The chantry certificate records that in 1548 he received a salary of £11 p.a. for serving

---

[79]   See Clive Burgess (ed.), *The Pre-Reformation Records of All Saints, Bristol*, Part 1 (Bristol Record Society, 1995), pp. xlv–xlvi.

[80]   See Nicholas Orme, 'Schools and School-books' in *The Cambridge History of the Book in Britain,* vol. 3, *1400–1557,* ed. by Lotte Hellinga and J. B. Trapp (Cambridge, 1999), pp. 449–69, esp. pp. 452, 460.

[81]   Will, para. 28. On the use of the *Imitatio Christi* within the London Charterhouse and its dissemination among the English Carthusians, see Wines, 'The London Charterhouse', pp. 252–4 and R. Lovatt, The *Imitation of Christ* in Late Medieval England', *Transactions of the Royal Historical Society*, fifth series, 18 (1968), pp. 97–122, esp. pp. 107–113.

[82]   George Hennessy, *Novum Repertorium Ecclesiasticum Parochiale Londinense* (London, 1898), p. 154; For Kettil's will see London Metropolitan Archives, DL/C/332, Vicar General's Book, f. 54v (or 56v) and DL/C/358/1, the Bishop of London's Book, f. 49.

a parish of some 800 people without any help except perhaps a single chantry priest.[83] In his will, drawn up 25 February 1561, Kettil betrays no signs of Catholic sympathies. He commends his soul to his Maker and Redeemer 'trusting only through his mercy to be saved'. He repented of his sins and affirmed that 'I steadfastly believe that Jesus Christ has suffered death upon the cross for me and shed his most precious blood for my redemption, earnestly remembering the great benefits that I have thereby, and I give hearty thanks therefore'. Kettil asked to be buried in the chancel of St Stephen's church near the place where he had been accustomed to sit. He left 6s. 8d. to be distributed to the poor of the parish on the day of his burial and 40d. for a sermon to be given by 'a well learned preacher'. The overseer of his will, as he had been of Thomas Salter's, was his 'gossip' Agnes Sturtell, now the wife of Richard Long, to whom he left a gold ring. Agnes had six children, three boys and three girls, and two of them, Richard and Margaret Sturtell, were Kettil's godchildren.[84] Whereas Salter had many good friends scattered around the City, Kettil found his good friends in the bosom of the Sturtell family. But although Kettil was a graduate he was clearly much less prosperous than his older friend: his bequests amounted in all to just over £4, which is indeed what one might expect of a man who lived on an annual salary of £11. So the nature of the relationship between Kettil and his older friend, Thomas Salter remains, like much else about Salter, elusive.

* * *

It may be time to draw the threads together. Young Thomas was born in Norwich in about 1480. He may well have been an orphan since he never refers to his parents or to his lineage. He was taught his letters by Dame Katherine Peckham, one of the sisters at Norman's Hospital in St Paul's parish in the city. By the first decade of the sixteenth century he was in London serving an apprenticeship with Master Henry Adams, a salter. At this time Thomas may have been known by the name of his master, namely as Thomas Adams. As a young man he made good friends among the other servants and apprentices living in the household of his master and elsewhere, and he kept in touch with his friends from those years throughout his life. Thomas did well: he entered the freedom of the City, became a member of the Salters' Company and prospered sufficiently to become a liveryman before the age of forty. By this time he had taken the name of his craft and was known as Thomas Salter. But suddenly his career veered off in a different direction and in

---

[83]   Kitching, *Chantry Certificate*, no. 103.

[84]   The Sturtell family appears to have lived in the parish of St Swithin. John Sturtell, presumably Agnes's first husband, had died in 1560, and five of the children, Richard, Christopher, Thomas, Martha and Margaret all appear to have died (of the plague?) in 1563. Only Mary, who had married and was perhaps living away from London, appears to have survived, see M. Fitch (ed)., *Index to the Testamentary Records in the Consistory Court of London*, vol. 2 (London, 1973), p. 257.

1517 he decided to become a Carthusian monk and to be ordained as a priest.

Thomas Salter was clearly a gregarious man who enjoyed the company of his friends and cared about them. He was doing very well as a rising young merchant in the Salters' Company and was likely to become a master or warden, or even an alderman of London. Perhaps it was some sort of trauma, or acute sense of sin, which led him to choose the austere and virtually solitary life of the Carthusian house. The call to become a secular priest would have been comprehensible, but the decision to become a Carthusian is hard to understand. As it was, it was clearly a mistake. Salter found the harsh and unsympathetic regime of the Carthusians unendurable: he may have been bullied. He sought to be transferred to a less severe monastic community and when this request was refused by prior John Houghton, Salter tried to run away but was brought back and confined in the conventual prison. Here he suffered nightmares and was, clearly, deeply unhappy.[85] So when Thomas Cromwell visited the house in 1534 Thomas, searching for a way out, told him of his troubles and followed up their meeting with a letter. At the root of his distress was the fact that he was unable to celebrate mass or to receive the sacrament because to do this he had to make confession, and yet, when he did confess the other brothers maliciously betrayed his confessions. Although Thomas did not secure his release immediately, by the time the remaining brothers had finally taken the oath accepting the Act of Royal Supremacy in May 1537, Salter's name was not to be found among them. The exact circumstances of Salter's departure from the monastery are unclear, but what is certain is that he managed to secure a £5 pension as other monks did. There is no record of his being granted a change of habit, but this must have happened because he became a chantry priest serving in the London parish of St Nicholas Acon, where he lived in a chamber in the churchyard with an income of nearly £13 p.a. Here in the parish he made some good friends, mainly among the humbler members of the community whom he remembered as his good and caring neighbours. He seems to have continued to live in his chamber in the churchyard and in his old age he was cared for by Joan Standely 'the maid' and the parish clerk John Bussshope, to both of whom he left all the furnishings in his chamber when he died. It is not clear what happened to Salter during the reign of Edward VI but he perhaps went into hiding in the sympathetic parish of St Olave in Southwark. He had good friends there including the influential Master Henry Leeke. When Mary came to the throne he became the parish morrowmass priest and joined the revived fraternity dedicated

---

[85] It is possible that at this time Salter consulted the anchorite monk at Westminster Abbey: in his will (para. 27) Salter left 40*d.* to 'my good and spirituall brother the anker at Westminster' and asked for his prayers. There is no record, however, of an anchorite at the restored Benedictine house at Westminster in Mary's reign, see C. S. Knighton, 'Westminster Abbey Restored' in Eamon Duffy and David Loades (eds), *The Church of Mary Tudor* (Aldershot, 2006), pp. 77–123. I am grateful to Dr Charles Knighton for his help in the search for an anchorite in Marian Westminster.

to the Name of Jesus and, at the age of nearly eighty, seems to have found employment once more as a chantry priest at the church of St Michael Cornhill. But he
clearly revived his links with the Salters' Company and it was to them, as to a family, that he entrusted his substantial trust fund to maintain his obit and his charitable concerns for the poor sisters of Norman's hospital in Norwich and the poor
almsmen of his own company. He wanted to be buried under a fine engraved brass
in the church of St Magnus.

Thomas Salter was not a martyr, nor was he an intellectual. He must have been
a good business man and a competent administrator, and no detail was too unim-
portant to be overlooked. He was observant, meticulous to the point of fussiness,
kind and charitable. He had a gift for loyal friendship and, perhaps, an inclination
to name-drop. There are signs of this in his will: his desire to be buried next to the
pew of Master John Cooper, the alderman; the importance he attaches to the fact
that his kinswoman Elizabeth had married a 'nere kinsman' to Mr Ralph Symonds
who had been a London Alderman and sheriff; young John Symonds was noted as
having served his apprenticeship with the brother of Mr Leonard Sutterton, a Norwich alderman and Salter's first personal bequest was a 'wreathed hope of fyne
golde' to Dame Katherine Dormer, the widow of the London alderman, Sir
Michael Dormer, sheriff and mayor of London who had died in 1545. Thomas
besought Lady Dormer to wear the ring every day in order to call the donor to
mind and pray for him, 'sometyme one of her little acquayntance'.[86] But Salter had
been able to seek help from a wide range of friends in his times of trouble. What
seems clear is that it was the decision to become a Carthusian monk, a spiritual
lifestyle for which he was completely unsuited, which was the great mistake of his
life. But he never turned back on his decision to become a priest: when the chance
came in Edward's reign, he did not, as many others did, abandon the priesthood,
nor did he get married. He remained faithful to that commitment, and for Thomas
Salter the mass remained at the heart of his faith. It was the body of Christ, mani-
fested in the bread and wine of the mass, that held his loyalty. To the two parishes
where he had served as a chantry priest he gave a pyx for holding 'the blessed
sacrament of the aulter in yt upon Corpus Christi day' and on his tomb he wished
to be portrayed as a priest holding in both his hands the precious chalice containing the consecrated host.[87] At the very beginning of his rehearsal of his 'grett
rewarde' to the Salters' Company he noted that they were the 'kepers of the seale
of the fraternity of Corpus Christi in London', and for Thomas Salter that was one
of the defining characteristics of 'the misterie and Crafte of the Salters companye'.
Salter clearly saw the Company as holding the seal in trust until the day came for

[86]   Will, paras 3, 23, 26, 30; for Ralph Symonds and Michael Dormer see Beaven, *Aldermen
       of London*, ii, pp. 26, 27; for John Cooper and Leonard Sutterton, see footnotes 11 and
       53.
[87]   Will, paras, 45 and 13.

the re-foundation of the fraternity.[88] And it was the Carthusians' refusal to allow him either to celebrate mass or to receive the sacrament which was the grievance he expressed most vehemently to Thomas Cromwell.

Thomas Salter knew that he had taken a wrong turning and that he had failed to live up to his monastic vows. He looked back wistfully at the days when he was a young man with many friends in the London and the prospect of a good career in the Salters' company. When he drew up his will he called to mind those who had helped and supported him in his long life with its great troubles and he turned confidently to Christ Jesus his merciful saviour. Salter knew that he needed the forgiveness of the brothers in the Charterhouse at Sheen, and he asked God in prayer perpetually on his tombstone, and at the hour of his death, to have mercy upon him 'a synnefull creature'.[89] The shields in the elaborate six-branch candlesticks expressed his loyalties: Thomas himself represented by an escutcheon bearing his initials of T and S, supported on the one hand by the arms of the Salters Company and on the other by a shield bearing the image of the five wounds of Christ.[90]

---

[88] Will, para. 17.
[89] Will, paras, 13 and 48.
[90] Will, para. 5.

APPENDIX

The Will of Thomas Salter dated 31 August 1558

This will was originally transcribed from the enrolled copy in the register of the Prerogative Court of Canterbury (TNA, PROB 11/42a, ff. 100v–105) and printed by Roger Greenwood in *Norfolk Archaeology,* vol. 38 (1983), pp. 280–95 and is reproduced by kind permission of the Norfolk and Norwich Archaeological Society. Greenwood's printed transcript has been checked against the enrolled copy and also against Salter's surviving original will which is almost entirely written in his own hand (TNA PROB 10/38).[1] Some minor corrections have been made to Greenwood's printed transcript and paragraph numbers have been inserted for ease of reference. The headings in bold were provided by Salter himself when he drew up his original will but they were not included in the registered copy.

Jesus aductor meus
1.   In the name of Almighty god Amen.The verie last daie of the moneth of August in the yere of our lorde god a thousand fyve hundred lviij [1558] and in the v th and vj th yeare of the Reignes of our most dread soveraigne lorde and most dreade soveraigne ladie Philippe and Marie by the grace of god kinge and Quene of England, Spayne, France, both the Cicilles, Jerusalem and Ireland Defendours of the faith Archduckes of Austria, Dukes of Burgundie, Millaine and brabant, Counties of haspurge Flanders and Tiroll. I Thomas salter of london Clerke, in my right mynde and good memorie then being, and also I truste in perfect love and Charitie with all my even Christen, and also in the verye true faith and belieffe of the most hollie Catholique Churche of Christe Jesus our most mercifull saviour and Redemer do make and ordeine this my present testament and last will in this due maner and fourme as it henceforth followeth and doth expiresse and shewe, that is to witte:

2.   First as it becomyth me a faithfull Christen man I do bequeath and give my sowle unto almightie god and to the glorious and most pur virgin marie mother of mercie & to all the hollie and blessed companye of heaven.

---

[1]   I am grateful to Professor Alan Nelson who alerted me to the existence of Salter's original will.

3.   Furthermor I will that my bodie be buried in our ladie Chappell within the parisshe Churche of St Magnus nexte unto london bridge in the voide paved grownde nexte unto the right wourshipfull Maister Cowpers pewe the Alderman, and there to lie and rest in the said hollie grownde till almightie god by his omnipotente power shall raise it up agayne out of the said grownde and erthe at the generall resurexcon day whiche I belyve faithfully shall come. And in the said Church of St Magnus I wilbe buried in the forenone, and have a fornones knyll rung frome vj of the Clocke till xij of the clocke at none with the greate bell in the saide churche, for the which saide knyll I do give to the said Churche x s. and for the pealles ringinge at my buriall Daye I do give them ijs. vj d. according to the use and custome of the said Churche.

4.   And at my said buriall neither at my monethes mynde I will have no sermon, but upon on Sondaie in the lente nexte after my buriall daye then to have a sermon either in the forenone in the saide churche by some sadde and discrete secular priest that is well learned and a good catholique in his lyvinge [fol. 101] and for his saide sermon making I do give him vj s. sterlinge. Also I will have iiij honest priestes to beare my bodie frome the howse where I die unto the saide Churche and there to be all the tyme of my buriall service and to laye me in my grave and for so doinge their saide service I do gyve to eche one of them xij d. Also to the Curate of St Magnus for doing his diligent service at my buriall I do give him xvj d. and to the other prestes and Clerkes of the saide Churche I do give everie one of them viij d. and to the sexten vj d. Also to the Curate of Sainte Mighell in Cornehill[2] if that he do goo with my deede bodie to St Magnus Churche and be at my buriall I do give him xij d. and to his parisshe Clerke viii d. if he be at my saide buriall. Also to the Curate of the parishe churche where my last service was if he do go with my deede bodie to the saide Churche and be at my buriall I do give him xii d. and to everie of the other priestes Clerkes or singingmen of the said parisshe Church I do give viij d. and to the Sexten vj d. if they be at my saide buriall and besides all these forsaid priests and Clerkes if there come anye more unbidden I then do give to everie priest a grote and to everie parisshe clerke iiij d. if there passe not x or xij of them.

5.   **The Wax chandler** Also I will have at my buriall ij cummely braunches of pure white waxe with sixe lightes & in the v paynes of eche of the saide braunches I will have theise v scutchons that is to witte one of the v wowndes another with the letters of my name T and S knytte together an other with the Salters Armes of London an other of the V wowndes and the last with the letters of my name againe the which ij saide braunches will cost xiiij or xv s.

---

²   In the original will changed from seynt Nycolas Acon by lomberd strete.

6. **The salters almesmen** Also I will have iiij great tapers of yallowe waxe at my buriall of the weight of x pounde. Apece and for the waste and makinge of them will coste vi or vii s. Also I will have xii staffe torches of yelowe waxe of the weight of iii li. apece whiche will coste xxiiij s. and I will that the salters vj almes men do beare vj of the saide torches and vj other pore men that be free of the said Salters company to beare the other vj torches and other vj torches and other iiij pore salters for to holde the iiij great tapers of waxe abowte my hearse in the dirige and masse tyme and for so doing their Dutie at my said buriall I do give to everie one of the said xvi pore Salters a Russet gowne of the price of xx s. and that the saide gownes be wide and side downe to the ancle and wide poked sleves and narrowe at the hands after a palmers garment and beside the saide gownes I do give to everie one of them a russet Boston Cappe of the price of xxii d. and also to everie one of them a sterling grote to paie for their dyners that daie. And I will that the sixtene pore men be at the dirige and masse of my monethes mynde in their saide garmentes to holde the saide torches as they did at my buriall without anye more rewarde then is above written saving onely I do give to everie one of them one grote sterling to paie for their dynner that daie after that my saide monethes mynde is past and gone. I do give to the saide Churche of St Magnus iiij of the saide staffe torches, and to the Churche where I was last in service other iiij staffe torches and to the church of Sainte Mighell in Cornehill[3] I do give the last iiii staffe torches.

7. Also frome the daie of my buriall till the daie of my monethes mynde be paste I will have a clothe of blacke wollen cotten with a white crosse of lynyng clothe sowed uppon it and layed uppon my grave & ij tapers of yellowe waxe one at the heade & an other at the feite of the full weight of ij li. a pece burning uppon my grave daie as longe as anye dyvine service is songe or saide in the fornone or afternone in the saide Churche of sainte Magnus & for the burning and waystyng of the saide ij tapers all the monethes space I do give to the waxe chawndler iiij s. sterling and I will that good Mr Day the waxechaundeler of St Olyves parisshe in southwerke have the ordeynyng and making of all the saide lightes, and to be well truely and honestlie paid for them, if that he will ordeine and make them as good chepe as an other will do.

8. **The Salters company** Furthermore I do hertely besiche all my goode masters of the wourshypful cumpany of the salters of london that I may have their best buriall clothe to be leyed uppon my Coffin at my buriall daie & my monethes mynde daie, bycause I was sometime one of their saide companye in my young daies as it is not unknowne unto them. And not only I have desired their saide buriall clothe for fortherining of myne honeste pore buriall, but for the moche more furthering of my said honeste buriall most humbly and lowly besichinge all my goode & worshipfull maisters of the salters company that they will followe me on

---

[3]   In the original will changed from seynt Nycolas Acon by lomberd stret.

my buriall daie to the saide churche of St magnus in their best lyvery and ther to tarie till the office of my whole buriall be ended and done and for their labour and paynes so taking for me I do give them by and by as sone as masse is done xl shillinges sterling for a recreacon for them to take it where it please them.

9. **The monthes mynde** And if it pleaseth my good maisters the salters to come againe to saincte magnus Churche in their said lyverye and to be at my monethes [fol. 101v.] mynde and to offer at my masse, then as sone as the saide masse is done to retorne to their hall againe and myne executor and overseer shall follow them by and by home to their haull to give them the rewarde that I have willed to be given unto them by this my present testament and last will that is to wytte as sone as the said companye is come upp in to their hall and do stand in ordre every man as they be in office and hath been in office or seniorite, if ther be anye alderman or Sherive of the said company and hathe been at my said buriall and monethes mynde with the said companye ther I give to the saide alderman iij s. iiij d. and to the shrive other iij s. iiij d. also, and to my good and worshipfull maisters the wardens of the saide companye then being I do give to eche one of them ij s. and vj d. sterling. And to all other that hath been wardens of the saide companye I do give ij s. sterling to everie one of them. And to eche one of the ij Renters xx d. sterling then being. and to everie one of these that hathe beene Renters of the Companye I do give iiij grotes sterling. And to all the residue of the saide companye that be in the lyverye and were at my buriall and monethes myde I do give to everie one of them xij d. sterling. But unto the bedell of the said companye then being, For the great labour and payne tayking in waring the saide companye to my said buriall and monethes mynd I do give him x s. sterling as sone as all the said rewardes be gyven to the said companye, I will that my executoure do give by and by to my good maisters the wardens of the saide companye xl shillings sterling of my good for a little recreacon for them & all the saide companye, for I am not able to give them a great dynner.

10. Ferthermore at and uppon the daie of my monethes mynde, I will have no more priestes and Clerkes at the Dirige & masse which I will have bothe redd and song in the forenone but the Curate of St Magnus and the other priestes and Clerkes of the said Churche and the foure honeste priestes that did beare me & leyde me in my grave on my burial daie. And to the Curate of St Magnus for doinge his duetie at my saide dirige and masse I do give him iiij grotes, and to the other said priestes viij d. apece and to everie one of the Clerkes of the saide Churche viij d. and to the sexten vj d.

11. **My buryall grownde** Furthermore for my buriall grounde in our ladie Chappell I do give to the Churche of sainct Magnus foure poundes sterling, and to be

paied well and truelie by myne Executour to the churche wardens of St Magnus uppon my saide buriall daie before v of the clock at night with great thanks.

12. **Jesus frateryte in Suthewerke** Moreover I do humbly besiche all my good maisters and bretherne of Jesus fraternytie holden and kepte in the parish of Olave in south werke, that they will come with all their hole companye in their clenely sadd coloured gownes and silke hodes and tippettes, and with the name of Jesus uppon their Brestes, and to follow my deade coorse frome the howse where I die unto St magnus Churche uppon my buriall daie as the worshipfull companye of the salters shall do the same, and to tarie in the saide Churche till my dirige masse and buriall shall be ended, and for thus doinge for me I give them xx s. for a recreacon and I do give them other xx s. to the maynteyninge of their saide godlie brotherode, for the whiche I trust that they will preye for me late one of their pore breathern.

13. **A marble stone for my grave** Moreover against my monethes mynde day I will have a fayre graye marble stone leyd upon my grave of the full length and bredth of my saide grave, and before the saide stone be leyed upon my grave I will that there be an Image of a preist with an albe and a vestment upon him graven in copper of a cunynge marbler that dwellithe in saincte dunstons parish in the West ageynste the sowth syde of the Churche, and that the saide Image be iij fote[4] in length, and that the saide Image do holde in bothe his handes the similitude [of a chalyce gravyn in copper & ye symylytude][5] of a consecrate ooste in a sunnie beame appearinge right above the Chalice that the saide Image holdeth in both his handes under the saide sunie beame and the eyes of the ymage to be graven cloosed togethir as all deademens eyes ought so to be and a lyttle above the saide ymages heade, I will have a rolle graven in copper and ther sett and these wordes next followinge to be graven in it thus saying *Miserere mei deus: secundum magnam misericordiam tuam* and right and just under the said ymages foote I will that ther be a large plate of copper laied and made lyke a tablett of Antick facon; And in the said tablet I will have theise wordes nexte following graven in it sayinge. In the grace and greate mercye of god here lyeth under this marble stone: the bodie of Thomas Salter priest sometyme of london whiche departed from this transytorie liff unto allmyghtie god upon the day of [fol. 102] the monethe and in the yere of our lord god M VC lviij he then being of the age iiij score yeres unto whose sowle: almyghtie god be mercifull. Amen. And right undre and next ioyned unto the saide copper plate I will have graven in a scutchin of copper the armes of the salteres companye bycause I was in my youth one of the said companye and lyverey.

4   In the original will 'and a halffe' is crossed out.
5   The words in brackets were added by Salter in the margin of his will but were omitted by the scribe who enrolled the will.

14. **Of the almes to be gyvyn at my buryall day owte of seynt magnus cloystour** Furthermore upon my buriall daie as sone as my deade bodie and the people that followeth it be come within St Magnus Churche dore I will that all such pore people as be within the saide Churche or nere abowte and without the saide Churche be sodenly and hastely called unto the Cloyster and while my dirgie masse and burial is a doinge to give to everie poore man woman and Childe a half penny lofe of newe baken wheaten breade and so lett hem departe out of the said Cloyster againe at the wicket that openeth into temes streate and if there be anye pore people in the saide parish that be so sicke lame or beddred that they can not come to receave the said almes then I will that myne Executour as sone as he hathe dyned the same daye do go home to their howses and to give to everie one of the said sicke lame or bedred one grote sterling in almes for to praye for my sowle and Christen sowles.[6]

15. **The ii d. dole** Also in the parisshe where I was last in service I will that their be given to the pore people of the saide parisshe within iij or iiij daies a halpeny wheaten lofe newe baked to the nomber of v hundred persons and vi skore to the hundred which saide breade will cost xxv s. and if the saide breade may not easely be provided, then let my Executour give my said almse in money that is to wytt to everie ij persons one peny or elles to everie fowre persons one two peny grote.

16. **The iii d. dole** Also in the parisshe of St. Nicolas Acon I do give theise rewardes and alms hereafter followinge, that is to witt to Christopher Luter bycause he was sometyme my nexte neybor and also redie to see unto me when anye sicknes was renynge I do give him v s. sterling, and to Robert henceball that was my late[7] nexte neybor and verie friendfull unto me to him I do give him other v s. and to John plumer bycause of his greate Disease and povertie I do give him other v s. and to everie one of the goodman browne smithes children I do give xij d. sterling and to the goodman Jeremiar ducheman and goldsmythe I do give xij d. and to his honeste wiffe other xij d. sterling.[8]

17. **The grett rewarde & gyfte to the salters cumpany** Moreover I do bequeath and give to the misterie and Crafte[9] of the Salters companye[10] kepers of

---

[6]   In the original will the words 'to pray for my soule and all xten soules' have been added above the line.

[7]   In the original will changed from 'is nowe'.

[8]   The following additional clause has been crossed out in the original will ' and to all other of ye seyd parische yt be pore and needy yf they wyll come in to ye seyd churche of seynt Nycols wt in iii or iiii days nexte aftur my buryall day by my executors assyngment I do geve to every pore man woman and chylde one sterlyng peny or els for lack of small money to geve to every ii persons two peny grote'.

[9]   The original will said simply 'the seyd salters'.

[10] The original will has inserted above the line 'kepers of the seale of the fraternyte of corpus christi in London'.

the seale of the fraternity of Corpus Christi in london with all my hole harte and mynde, besides the othir giftes and rewardes that be afore reehersed two hundredth markes of good and laufull moneye of england Upon this condition that they will faithfully and most truly performe and fulfill my godlie desir and charitable will, as it here playnely followeth and sheweth that is to witt: I will and desir that for this said ij hundred marks that I do give them that they will encrease ther vj almes mens lyvinges more than it is at this present daye that is to witt to give to everie one of the said vj almesmen two pence sterling everie weeke yerely and perpetually frome the recepte of the saide ij c. markes[11] more than they have hadd given them before these daies that is to witt where as before these daies they have given their said almes men but viij d. a week nowe to give them tenne pence a week and if they have before thies Daies given them ix d. a weeke then nowe to give them xi d a weeke and if before thes daies they have given them x d a weeke then nowe and from hensfourth to give them xij d. a weeke, and not in no wise to mynisshe nor decrease none of their charitable and great rewardes or giftes that they have given yerely before these daies to their saide almesmen not for this saide rewarde and almes that I do give them.

18. **Coolys for ye seyd poremen** Furthermore out of the said ij hundred markes I will that the said company shall give to the saide vj almesmen ones in the yere perpetually iiij sackes of great Coles to everie one of them suche as comyth dayly frome Croydon and bromeley and other places of leke Coles.[12]

19. **The dyrge & masse for myn obyte** Furthermore out of the said ij hundred markes I will the saide companye to keepe yerely and perpetually an obiit for me in the saide Churche of good St Magnus that is to witte to have a dirige and a masse redd & songe in the forenone by the priestes and Clerkes of the said Churche only and no more And I will that this moch money be spente at my Obite [fol. 102v.] and no more that is to Witte to the Curate of the saide Churche I do give xij d. if he do his Duetie and be at my obite and to the other priestes of the saide Churche if they be present at myne obite and do ther duetie at it I do give to ecche of them vj d. and to the other v singing men and ij sextens of the said Churche if they be present and do their duetie at my obite I do give to eche of them vj d. And for the Peales that be runge at my saide dirige and masse I do give them ij s. vj d. for so is the Duetie to the said Churche. And upon my saide obites day I will have a Coffin layde upon ij trestells over my grave and a Clenely hearse clothe layde upon it for all the dirige and masse tyme for the whiche I do give to the Churche vj d. And for the ij tapers of waxe of ij li. a pece that shall burne at the hearses endes till the

---

[11]   In the original will the words 'from the recept of the said ii c marks' have been added above the line.

[12]   In the original will the words 'of like coles' have been added by a different hand.

dirige and masse be ended and done and till he the Curate hathe sensed abowte the said hearse and hath saied Deprofundis. I do give to the wexchaundeler for the waiste and making of the saide ij Tapers xij d. And for as moche as I have humbly desired my saide good maisters the saltirs above written to be at my saide buriall & monethes mynde, therefor I will not be so bolde to desir or to loke that they shoulde come to my saide obite yerely and perpetually, But I do most hertlie desir them, that their bedill of their companye & their vj said almesmen may yerely and perpectually be at my said obyte and [the seyd bedyll][13] to offer the masse peny and for so doing and for his paynes taking att my said obite I do give him by this my last will xij d. sterling. And I will that the said almesmen do offer everie one of them an halpeny and for so doing I give to eche of them vj d. and so the whole expence of moneye at my said yerely obite is xiij s. vjd. and no more. But and if ther be iij or iiij singing Children that are belonging to the saide Churche and qwere then if they be at my saide dirige and masse I do give to eche one of them ij d. above the said some.

20. Off ye almes to be gyvyn at Norwyche Moreover out of the said ij hundred markes I will that the saide wardens and companye of the salters of london do delyver or cause to be delyvered yerely and perpetually upon newe yeres evins Eve to the Churche wardens of S. Paulis parishe within the Citie of norwiche in the counte of Norfolk two and fiftie shillinges of good and laufull money of england to be given in almes everie sondaie in the yere as it here followeth and sheweth that is to witte everie sondaie throughe the yere as sone as the highe masse is done in the saide parisshe churche of St Paule I will that the ij churche wardens of the said churche shall give xxiiij[or] halpeny wheaten bread loves that were newe baking on the satterday nexte before unto xxiiij pore sisters of Vincent Norman which builded an howse for sisters in the saide parisshe many yeres agoo. And if their be not xxiiij sisters in the said howse at this present daye to receave and have the said almes of breade everie sonday in the yere that is to witte everie one of them a halpeny wheaten lofe newe bake, then so manye good sisters as be or shalbe here-after I will that they be first served ever on the sonday of the said halpeny breade and the residue of the halpeny loves of breade that is lefte ungyven I will that it be given to the pore laye men and women in the said parishe of St paule. But in no wise to give my saide almes to suche laye people as be abhomynable swerers or advouterers or detractours or slanderers of their even Cristen for god hearithe not the prayour of no suche wicked people but he hearithe the prayer of all goode and faithfull cristen people and suche as fearith him lovith him & dreadeth him and kepeth his commandementes. our lord god give us all grace likewise to do the same. This foresaid perpetuall almes I have fownded and willed it to be given spe-

---

[13]   The words in brackets were inserted by Salter in the margin of his original will, but omitted by the scribe who copied it into the register.

cially to the said pore sisters bycause I have a greate truste that they will praie for me, and also bycause a verie good devoute sister of the saide howse of Vyncent Norman was the first creature that taught me to know the letters in my booke Dame katherine peckham[14] was her name, I was scoller iij score and xij yeres agoo with her in the saide parishe of St. paule. I besiche Jesu have mercie upon her sowle.

21. Nowe for as moche as the saide churche wardens doth take the labour and payne to Distribute and give the said xij penyworthe of bread everie sondaie all the yere therfor I do give to them the ij vantage halpeny wheaten bread loves that thei have brought them by the Baker everie satterday with the said xij peny woth of breades which said bread I would it shold be brought into sancte paules Churche either uppon the satterday before evensong or elles upon the sonday before mattens and to be put in a greate close basket that no myse not rattes do come to it and I desire my said good Maisters the salters that thei will give or send xij d. to the saide Churche wardens to prepare and to paie for suche a basket for the said breade, and if so be that the said Churche wardens will not take the labour and payne to distribute and give the said xxiiij loves [fol. 103] of wheaten bread to the saide sisters and poore laye people then let the parishe Clerke of the said St. Paules Church give the saide breade everie sondaie in the yere unto them and for so doing then I do give to the saide clerke the ij vantage halpeny wheaten loves everie sondaie throughe out the yere for his labour. And yet Furthermore if that my maisters the Wardens of the Salters company can here and perfectly knowe that the said almes is not given to the said sisters and pore laye people everye sondaie either in breade or ellis in money for scarseness of breade then I will that the said almes of breade be taken away frome them and to give it to their own almes men in london for ever.

22. **My mastyrs ye salters of london** Now I trust that my good maisters the salters of london doth right well perceave and knowe that the increasinge of ther said almes mens livings by me whiche is twelve pence sterlinge everie yere perpetually two and fiftie shillinges sterling and the xxiiij sackis of Colis that I have given to the said vj almesmen yerely and perpetually at the price of viij d. a sacke is iustly and yerely to be paid xvj shillinges sterling and the whole expence of money for all maner of charges at my saide obite and yeres mynde is xiiij s. ij d. And so then the said twise lij s. and the saide xvi s. for Coles and the said xiiij s. ij d. for my yerely obite the whole summe of the saide expences is no more but vj poundes xiiij s. ij d. sterling. And so then I trust that my good maisters the salters of london will purchase so moche with the said ij hundred markes in landes and rentes, that they shalbe able yerely and perpetually not to perfourme and bere onely the

14   Dame kateryn Peckam in the original will.

charges of the foresaid iiij expences accordinge to this my present testament and last will, but also with the overplus of the money that shall come of the landes and rentes they shalbe yerely upon my obites day to make for them selfes an honest recreacon in ther hall if it please them, and in so doinge I besiche god that moche goode may it do them, and besides all theis wordes I besiche them hertely that their poore almesmen may have that same day some parte of ther levinges.

Here foloweth the residue of this my present testament and last will

23. **Off ye gyftes & rewardes to ye v chyldren that Robert Symonds had by his last wyfe elizabeth** Furthermore I have dwellinge in the Countie of Norfolke v kynsfolkes that is to witt iij yongmen and ij yonge women and theis be their names Richarde Symondes John symondes and Thomas Symondes Elizabeth symondes and Elizabeth Symonds they were the Children of an honest yoman called Robert Symondes whiche was nere kinsman to Mr Raffe Symondes that was shriffe and alderman of london and the said iij yongmen and ij women were borne and Christened in the parishe of Suffeld x myle beyond Norwiche northwarde and the mother of them was ther fathers last wife, and she was my very nere kinswoman for the whiche I doo bequeath and give to her said V Children by this my present testament and last will as it here followeth and showeth that is to witt for as mooche as ther father and mother Robert and Elizabeth be bothe departed, I do give to ther said eldest sonne Richard Symondes twentie markes which is xiij poundd vj s. viij d. of good and laufull money of englonde and I give him my blacke gowne furred in the fore partes with black cony and lyned with black frese in the backe partes and I do give him also my night satten cappe and my shorte gowne of puke coloured wullen clothe without lyninge but lyned at the hande and about the necke with black woursted, and I do give him my lethir bagg with the latten ringes and the lether girdle with it And I do give to the second sonne John Symondes twentie markes of good and lawful money and I do give him my syde gowne of puke coloured wollen cloth furred in the fore partes with blacke budge and lyned in the the backe partes with black cotton and I do give him also my blacke chamlet frocke and my Jacket of black damaske and my partelet of tawney damaske. and I do give to their yongest sonne Thomas Symondes twentie markes sterling of good and laufull money of englonde And bycause his name is Thomas as myne is therfore I do give him my best side and goode gowne of puke colourde wullen clothe and faced in the fore partes and in the sleves with fyne tawny worsted and lyned in the backe partes with black Cotton, and I do give him also my black velvet powch and my blacke tuke bagge and my tawny chamlet Jacket and my blacke velvet night cappe newe made and my ij girdelles for my ij said powches one of black silke, an other of redd crule and my partlet of blacke satten and my partlet of tawney chamlett. Also I do bequeath and give to Elizabeth Symondes the eldes doughter of the saide Robert Symondes that he had by his last wiffe twen-

tie markes of good and laufull money of englond and I do give her also my side and longe gown of black worsted furred in the fore partes with fittchewes and lyned in the backe partes with blacke cotton, and I do give her my tippet of blacke sarsenet which is ij elles long lacking ij nayles and as she can not put the said gown and tippet to her owne use then [fol. 103v.] she may sell it to some honest priest that is well beneficed and have an honest pourcon of money for it, and I do give her also one paire of blacke ponyettes of damaske and an other payer of ponyettes of tawney damaske. Also I do bequeath and give to the said Robert Symondes yongest doughter called also Elizabeth Symons twentie markes of good and lau-full money of englond which is thirtene poundes vj s. viij d., and I do give hir my said tawney gowne of wollen clothe that is lyned in the fore partes with black cot-ton, and in the after partes with playne wollen cloth, and also I do give hir one paire of ponyettes of blacke damaske, an other paire of tawney chamblet, and an othir little paire of ponyettes of tawney damaske. and I do give her also my ij eldest and porest gownes one of marble color and an other of Russet and bothe of frese which will make her two good gownes or other garments for the wourkinge daye.

24. And besides all these foresaid giftes and rewards that I here gyve them the v saide children that Robert Symondes had by his last wife Elizabeth I commende me moste hertely unto them trusting that thei do nowe perfectly perceave and fynde that I have remembred them as ther lovinge frende and pore kinsman, for which I do most humbly beseche them so to praie dayly that after this transitorie life both I and they may come to the glorious life in heaven which is evermore last-ing amen.

25. Furthermore I hertely desir my executour & overseer to marke well my wordes that here nexte followeth which be these Certifyinge you of the trueth that the saide seconde sonne of the said Robert Symonds unto whome I have given xx ti. markes and part of myne apparell as it is above written whose name is John Symondes: he dwelleth in the citie of norwiche and in the parishe of St. George of muspole beyond the blacke fryers bridge, where for I besiche you that as sone as ye may conveniently after my monthes mynde is past, that you will sende your let-ter unto the saide John Symondes to give him knoweldge of my departing, and what I have given him and his said ij other breadern & ij sisters by this my present testament and last will and appoincte you them in your saide letter what tyme and daie they shall come to you, that they may be dispatched within ij daies next after ther comying upp, for it would be verie chargeable for them to lie longe here in the citie, and warne you them and charge them in your saide letter that thei bring no strangers with them, but to come themselves onelie and as secretelie as they can also and when they be come I praie you walcom them after a gentle facon, and make them honestie chere for the tyme they be here with you, for I truste I have

left enough with you for so to do and also I besiche you let the said John symondes see and reade to his ij breatherne and ij sisters what I have given them in this my present testament and last will by the whiche then they shall perfectly see and knowe that ye be faithfull and true doers of me, and besides the same somes of moneye that I have given them & my saide apprell, yet nevertheless at ther departing frome you I will that you do give them of my goodes fortie shillings more to paie for their charges and expences in commyng upp to london and going home againe into ther owne Countrie, and or ever they do departe frome you, see they do give you a verie sure acquittance of testymoniall, that ye have paied them and delyvered unto them that & all that I have given them by this my present testament and last will.

26. Moreover my welbeloved executour and overseer I desire you that ye do monishe and strately charge the said John Symondes in your said letter that he do bringe upp with him to london a sure and true testimoniall out of his contrie that he and his other ij breadren & sisters that comyth upp to london with him were there fathers V children that he had by his last wife Elizabeth which was my nere kinswoman and but excepte he bringeth suche a true testymoniall upp with him ye mowght be deceaved by him. For his father had two wifes before he marred my saide kinswoman, and by his ij other wifes he had many children. Moreover my well beloved executour and overseer in theis wordes nexte following, I do give you knowledge howe ye may have your said letter conveyed redily to the said John Symondes at Norwiche. At the taberd in graciouse streate lyeth many substanciall men of Norwiche and one in especial Mr. Leonarde Sutterton alderman of Norwiche and comyth verie often upp to london and he knoweth me and the said John Symondes verie well, and his howse where he dwellith, for the said John Symondes with the said aldermans brother was prentise & came out of his terme nowe of late yeres paste.

Here followeth my almes to all the prisons in london and nere abowte london.

27. **Ludgate preson Newgate preson** First unto the pore prisoners in ludgate I do bequeath and give tenne shillings of good and laufull money of England and to be bestowed uppon them in meate & drinke [fol. 104] when they have moste nede of relieffe and soccour and I hartely desir my good and trustie executour and overseer to see it delivered unto them that the Jaylours and kepir of the saide prisons do not beguile them of it, And unto the pore prisoners in Newgate I bequeath and give tenne shillings in meate and drinke when thei have most neide of relieffe and soccour. Also to eche of the ij Counters in london I give other tenne shillinges in meate and drinke to the porest prisoners of them. Also to the porest prisoners in the flete I give vj s. viij d. in meate and drinke when they have most nede of soc-

cour. Also to the pore prisoners in the marshalsey tenne shillings in meate and drink when they have most neide of soccour. Also to the pore prisoners in the kinges benche tenne shillinges in meate and drincke when they have most nede of it. Also to the pore prisoners in the counter in southwerke V shillings in meate and drincke when they have most nede of it. Also to the pore prisoners in the ij prisons at Westminster to eche of the ij saide presons I do give V s. in meate and drincke when they have most nede of it. Also to the pore creatures both men and women at bedlem that be madde and distracte of mynde I do give them tenne shillings in meate and drincke when they have most neide of it. Also unto my good and spirituall brother the anker at Westminster I do give him xl pence sterling for the whiche I desir him hertely to praie for me.

The rewards to be given to dyverse persons whose names and rewardes here followeth.

28. First to Mr Richarde ketill[15] vicar of St Stephen in Coleman Streate I give and bequeath my longe and side gowne of puke coloured wullen cloth which is faced in the fore partes with blacke woursted and lyned in the backe partes with other wollen course cloth and also I do give him my ij tippettes for a priestes wearing, one of them is of puke colourde wollen cloth and overlayde with black satten on the one side and the other tippett is also of fyne puke colourde wollen cloth and overlayd on the one side with fyne sarsnet and I do give him also my iij other tippettes of puke colourd wollen cloth and overlaide on the one side with woursted. And I do give him the vj bookes in my chamber that is to witte one great booke on sermons and gospelles and on other lesser book of Epistelles, the iij boke is my portuas, the iiij is a prymer bothe in englisshe and lattin, and all the pistells and gospelles in englisshe for everie sondaie and hollidaie that falled in the hole yere, the v booke is called *ortus vocabulorum* and the sixte is a verie little boke and it is called *Imitacio xpi* and I do give him my russett frese Jacket and ij paire of my best hoose and ij of my best shirtes, and ij of my best towelles, and iiij of my best handekerchers and that they be clene washed my said lynen before they be delyvered unto him. And also I do give him my V best cappes, and my ij night cappes of wollen, and my ij best paire of furred Cuffes, and ij payre of new gloves of leather which lieth under the mattresse within my bedsteede. And besides all theise said giftes that I have given him in this my present testament and last will I do most hertely commende me unto him, evermore thankinge him for his great love and favour that he hathe borne unto me of long tyme, besiching him of his charitie daily to pray for me.

29. **To the Charterhous** Also to the right worshipfull Father prior with all his bredren in the Charterhowse at Sheene, I do bequeath v pounde of good and laufull

15   Keetyll in the original will.

money of england that is to witt fowre pound towardes the edifyinge of ther said howse agayne, and the other xx s. to be spent upon a pyttance for the said prior & his bredren when it shall please them. And besides all this I do most hertely commend me unto them all and most humbly besichinge them to praie for me and also to forgive me if that ever I have offended them longe before thies daies, either by worde or deide.

30. **To my lady dormer** Also to the right worshipfull ladie Dame Katherine Dormer dwelling in the parishe of St. laurence Jurie in the Citie of london, I do bequeath and give my wreathed hope of fyne golde of the weight of vii angell nobles besiching her good Ladyshippe to weere it dayly upon her finger during her life, by the which doinge I truste her ladieshippe shall the better call me to mynde and to praie for me, sometyme one of her little acquayntance.

31. **Wyllyam Gyllott** Also I do bequeath and give V pound of good and laufull money of englond unto my great friende William Gillott of the Countie of Kent yoman and singleman and dwelling in the parishe of Westram vij myle beyond Croydon and besides this innumerable thanckes I do render and give unto him, for the great frendshipp and faithfulness that I have founde in him longe before this daie besisching him of his charitie to praie for me.

32. Also to the honest man Robert Forest[16] salter of london dwelling in fanechurch parishe I do bequeath and give him xl s. sterling for that he and I were servauntes together in one howse almost fiftie yeres agone besiching him of his charitie to pray for me.

33. Also to the good honest woman Jone Nayle the wiffe of Vincent Nayle the Joynour dwelling next beyond St Olavys Churche in [fol.104v.] Southwerke I do bequeath and give her vj englisse Crownes which is xxx s. sterling for that she and I were servants togethir in one howse in tower streate almost fiftie yere agone, besiching her of charitie to praie for me.

34. Also to the honest man Thomas Moone the barbour dwelling in Smythfelde nere to the signe of the Antlopp I bequeath and give xx s. sterling for that he was my faithfull frende when I was in great trouble about xxx yeres agone for the whiche I do hartely thancke him, besiching him of charitie to prey for me.

35. Also to Thomas hollidaie[17] one of the salters almes men I do bequeath & give him v s. sterling beside the other almes that I have given him for that he and I were servauntes both together with henrie Adams Salter of London almost fiftie yeres agone, and therfore I trust that he will prey for me.

16 Forreste in the original will.
17 Holyday in the original will.

36. Also to John Noble taylor dwelling in St. Swytunes lane I do bequeath and give him xl pence sterling trustinge that he will prey for me.

37. Also to John Plomer hooser dwellyng in seynt Nycolas lane bysydes Lumbard strete because of hys poverty & grevous dysease I do beqwethe & geve hym v schyllynges sterlynge besechynge hym of hys charyte to prey for me.[18]

38. **Edwarde barker** Also to my welbeloved good sonn Edward barker the sonne of Frauncis barker Citizen and merchaunt taylor of london, I do bequeath and give him tenne poundes of good and laufull money of englond and goddes blessing and myne with it for the whiche I trust he will prey hertely for me. But I will that the saide Francis Barker his father have the custodie and Use of the said tenne pound, till he the saide Edwarde be come to the full age of xxj yeres. And if so be that the saide Edwarde do die before that he be the full age of xxi yeres I do give then the saide tenne poundes to his father and mother Francis and Julian for the whiche I truste that they will prey for me.

39. Also to my goode mastyr m Eston esqwyer & justyce of peace dwellynge in ye parysche of seynte olave in suthewerke I do beqweth & geve hym a golde rynge of ye valoure of xx s. sterlynge besechynge hym of hys charyte to prey for me.[19]

40. Also to my singular and most intirly beloved good Master Mr. Henrie hooke otherwise called leeke, I do bequeath and give him a gold ring of the valour of iiij frenche Crownes besiching him of his charitee to prey for me, the said Mr. hooke dwellith in the saide parisshe of St. Olave in Southwerk and inumerable thanckes I do render and give unto him for the greate frendely love and favour that he bare unto me of long tyme, whiche was to the greate furthering of my welfare and honestie. I besiche allmyghtie god to rewarde him for it.

41. **Fraunces Barker** Also to the foresaid fraunis barker Citizen and merchant taylour of london dwelling in St. brides parishe in flete streate I do bequeath and give him three poundes vj s. viij d. of good and laufull money of englond and to his verie honest wiffe Julian, I do bequeath and give her xxxiij s. iiij d. I besiche them both to prey hertely for me.[20]

42. Also to Johan standely the maid dwellinge in the parisshe of St. Nicholas Acon by lombard strete, I give and bequeathe my pewter pynte pott and my ij brusshes

---

[18]   This bequest has been crossed out in the original will, presumably because it is repeated earlier (Item 16) and again later (Item. 44).

[19]   This bequest has been crossed out in the original will and does not appear in the enrolled copy.

[20]   At this point in the original will there is a change of ink/pen although the hand is the same.

one of ling and an other of hayre and my little Cheste without a keye and my best Russet felte hatt, and iij paire of ponyettes, one of woursted, an other of tawney Chamlet, an other of blacke Chamlet and my olde rounde Casket with a new covering and my lesser stole and xij d. sterling money.

43. And to John Busshope the parisshe Clerk of the said St. Nicholas I do bequeath and give him an olde gowne and a shorte that is in my Chamber of black wollen Clothe to make him a Cote or Jackett of yt if he will, and I do give him a pretie lether bagg of calves leathir and an erthen bottell with a tunell of white plate longing to yt and a lytle Drinking cruse of erthe and my vj glasses in my chamber windowe and myne Urinall glasse and the case with it, and my ij candlesticks of woode and my erthen potte of ij gallons and xij d. in money for the which I trust that he and his wiffe will praie for me.

44. Also to John plummer hosier dwelling in St. Nicholas lane beside Lombardestreate, bycause of his povertie and grevious disease I do bequeath and give him v s. sterling besiching him hertely to pray for me.

45. **To the churche of seynt Nycholas Acon** And albeit I found little kindness or frendeshippe in the said parisshe of St. Nicholas Acon, yet neverthelesse I will not withhold my good mynde frome the saide Churche but with all love and charitie I do bequeath and give to the said Churche of sancte Nicholas Acon towards the making of[21] a pixe of silver and gilte of the valour of V[22] pound sterling if my goodes will extend paying my other legaciis and bequests,[23] and that it be made by a cunnying goldsmyth after a comly and decent facion, for it shall serve to bere the blessed sacrament of the aulter in yt upon Corpus Christi day and palme sondaie, and other daies of solempnytie when it is commaunded, and I will that these wordes nexte following be written aboute the foote of the saide pixe thus saying, pray for the sowle of Thomas Salter some tyme Chauntrie priest of this Churche and I will that the pixe be made and given to the saide Churche of St. Nicholas within halfe a yere next after my departing daie if that all my debtes that is owinge me be gathered in by myne executour by the saide daie.

46. [24]And I give a lyke pixe to the said parishe of St. Michaelles in Cornhill [fol. 105] upon the like condicon.

---

21   In the original will the words 'towards the making of' have been inserted above the line.
22   In the original will 'tenne' has been crossed out and 'fyve' written above.
23   In the original will the words 'if my goodes will extend paying my other legaciis and bequests' have been inserted above the line.
24   At this point the writing of the original will is continued in a different hand which appears to be that of Thomas Bradforth the notary who is also the first witness.

47. The Residue of all and singular my goodes and Chattalles plate Redie moneye and debtes not given and nor bequeathed after my funerall expences done and my legacies perfourmed I give will and bequeath unto my most trustie frend Peter honyborne Citizen and Draper of london whome I do make ordyen and constitute my full sole executour of this my present testament and last will, and I desyre and praye my especiall frende and spiritual lover Mr. Richard kettell Master of Arte and vicar of St. Stephens in Colmanstrete aforesaid to be my overseer of this my present testament and last will unto whome for his good diligence and paynes herein to be taken, and to thentent he shall cause this my present testament and last will to be performed accordinge to my true intent and meanyng, I give and bequeath a blacke gowne and a hode over and besides the other legacies before appoincted him by this my present testament and last will provided allwaies and I will and my mynde is, that my said executour shall not be charged to paie thies my said legacies and bequests before the tyme he shall or may receave all my debtes where with to paie and discharge the same he doinge his good will and endevour in that behalf as he will answer before god anye charges compelling him to the contrarie not with standing.

48. And thus to conclude besiching most humbly and hertely the most high devine majestie of almyghtie god of his infinite grace and goodness to have mercie uppon me a synnefull creature and to forgive me all my synnes and also to give me that grace that in the houre of death when I shall departe from this transitore liffe I may in my right mind and memorie crie unto the with a lowde voice with theise wordes following, *In manus tuas domine commendo spiritum meum Redemisti me domine deus veritatis. Amen.*[25]

49. Thies being witnesses Thomas Bradforth notarie, Thomas Bayllis draper, per me Edmund Keye, per me Robert Harding.[26]

50. Memorandum[27] where the saide Thomas Salter by his testament and last will bering the date the last daie of Auguste anno 1558 hathe willed and appoincted that the wardens and companye of Salters in london in consideracon of the two hundred markes to them given by the saide testament shoulde delyver or cause to be delivered yerely and perpetually Upon newe yeres Evens Eve to the Church wardens of S. paules parishe in Norwich lij s. of good and laufull money of englond to be given in almes amongst other thinges as by the saide testament appereth, Notwithstanding after wardes the viij daie of Octobre in the yere abovesaid his will

[25] In the original will it appears that Thomas Salter may have made his mark, but the letters are smudged

[26] All four men have signed the original will

[27] In the original will the memorandum is written in a different hand.

and mynde was that there shulde be given and delivered but one half thereof that is to saie xxvj s. and no more and the other half to be to the saide companie of Salters in consideracons of suche paymentes as he appoincted them to paie by reason of the said ij hundred markes. And where also he had given and bequeathed to his fyve kinsfolke named in the same testament twentie markes a pece in money with other thinges he willed and his mynde was that they shoulde have but tenne poundes a pece if they were lyving bycause upon further respecte and better advisement he thought his money and goods woulde no further extend, and also he willed his executour named in the same testament to paie and deliver to the saide company of Salters the saide two hundred markes if he myght in maner and foorme followinge that is to saye the one half within a moneth after Easter nexte ensuying the said eight daie of Octobre, and the other half within a moneth nexte after Christmas then nexte following. And also he gave and bequeathed unto Robert Hardinge, Edmund Keye and William Gonne Citizens and salters of london three poundes of laufull money of England that is xx s. apeece. Witness hereunto, Thomas Balles, Thomas Bradforth notarie and Thomas Honnyborne.

51. Will, together with the codicil, proved in the Prerogative Court of Canterbury by Master Henry Cole, and execution of the will granted to the executor, Peter Honyngbourne, 19 December 1558.

Memorials of Ralph Woodford (d. 1498), Ashby Folville, Leicestershire: the Death of the Author?

PAMELA KING

The verbose but intriguing will of Ralph Woodford survives in the Prerogative Court of Canterbury.[1] He died in 1498 and was buried in the church of St Mary, Ashby Folville, in Leicestershire, where his monument, an incised slab showing a man in his winding sheet, also survives. His will and his tomb, together with other biographical information that can be retrieved, make Woodford an interesting case-study for his period and social class.[2] In particular, both the will and the monument appear to use orthodox formulations of piety as vehicles for deeply personal statements. This brief study, therefore, raises – without resolving – the perennial theoretical and methodological question of how far we can go with pre-modern biographical research in reconstructing the interiority of an individual life.

Ralph Woodford's tomb itself is not mentioned in his will, probably because it was already in place, although he does request that his funeral be conducted 'in reosonabull maner and formm as is nowe used'. The tomb conforms, up to a point, to an identifiable decorum. Its components are complicated. It consists of a stone slab, 220 cm by 110 cm, set into the pavement on the north side of the chancel of Ashby Folville church.[3] On the slab there is incised the shrouded effigy of a man in his winding sheet, measuring 132 cm long, standing on a greyhound couchant, and flanked by two crosses, each 141 cm long. Each cross rises from a pedestal, and across each stem is a scroll inscribed, *Disce mori*. Above the effigy's head is a large scroll inscribed:[4]

---

[1] PRO, PROB 11/11, ff. 183–4.

[2] The Woodford family have recently been the subject of study of 'gentle culture': J. Denton, 'Image, Identity and Gentility: the Woodford Experience', *The Fifteenth Century, V. Of Mice and Men: Image Belief and Regulation in Late Medieval England*, ed. L. Clark (Woodbridge, 2005), pp. 1–17. I am indebted to Nigel Saul for the reference to this article which was published between the initial delivery of this paper and its publication. Although this paper and Denton's arise from a common recognition that the primary sources surrounding Ralph Woodford make for useful case-history, our arguments are complementary, Denton arguing for the typicality of the case, while I am interested in its singularity.

[3] See Plate 6.

[4] See Plate 7.

Credo quod redemptor meus vivit et novissimo die de terra surrecturus sum. Et in carne mea videbo deum salvatorum (sic) meum.

There is also a marginal inscription which reads

Hic jacet Radulphius Wodford armiger consanguenius et heres Roberti Wodford militis videlicet filius Thome filii et heredis predicti Roberti Wodford Elizabeth una filiarum de Willielmi Villers armigeri uxor predicti Radulphi qui quidem Radulphius obiit iiii die marii anno domini MCCCClxxxxviii predicta Elizabeth obiit ix die augusti anno domini MCCCClxxi quorum animabus propicietur deus. Amen

and there is another inscription under the greyhound, this time in English, reading[5]

Of erthe I am formed and maked
To erthe I am turned all naked.

In the wall above the slab is another slab designed clearly as the location for an Easter Sepulchre surmounted by the Woodford crest held up by two wild men of the woods, a *rebus* clearly playing on the family name.[6] On either side are also angels holding up shields. The whole composition is thus a statement of social position and of significant piety, both elements being conventional in funerary monuments to members of the gentry of the period.

The form of the effigy combined with the inscriptions suggests that the tomb is designed to fulfill the function of a *memento mori,* reminding the viewer of the inevitability of the grave, the passing of earthly possessions, and the spiritual importance of making a good death. The iconography of the cadaver monument, which found vogue in England from the second quarter of the fifteenth-century, has often being associated with these commonplaces. However, the compositional association of a shrouded effigy with an Easter Sepulchre suggests a more optimistic reading of the iconography. The structure that evolved to accommodate the liturgical rites of Good Friday and Easter Sunday was first described in an English context in the *Regularis Concordia*, and was used on Good Friday for a simulated burial of Christ in the form of either a cross or the Host, and its subsequent resurrection on Easter Day.[7] Most Easter Sepulchres were temporary structures made of wood and embroidered cloths, always in the north aisle, but permanent Easter Sepulchres where they existed were constructed on the north chancel wall and could take the form of a niche, a table tomb with or without a canopy, a stone chest, or a separate chapel. In terms of its form, the Easter Sepulchre, therefore, had funerary associations - which explains its combination in cases such as Ralph Woodford's with an individual memorial and chantry foundation – but was also directly linked with the promise of the Resurrection.

[5] See Plate 8.

[6] See Plate 9.

[7] See P. Sheingorn, *The Easter Sepulchre in England*, Early Drama, Art and Music Reference Series 5 (Kalamazoo: Medieval Institute Publications, 1987).

The iconography of Easter Sepulchres in fact almost always focuses on Resurrection imagery, frequently incorporating the sleeping soldiers, the angel guarding the tomb, and the visit of the three Maries to the empty tomb. Where it forms part of a funerary monument and effigies supplant the Resurrection imagery, these correspondingly look forward to the General Resurrection and show the shrouded figures not as images of bodily decay but as figures rising from their graves on the last day. Examples of shrouded effigies conforming to this iconography are relatively common and can be seen in the brass commemorating Agnes Bulstrode, in the church of St Laurence, Upton, Bucks (1472); that of the entire family of Thomas Spryng, St Peter and St Paul, Lavenham, Suffolk (1486), and in a clear Easter Sepulchre setting, that of William Feteplace and his wife (1516) in the church of St Mary, Childrey, Berks.[8] The focus of these compositions is obviously different to the *memento mori* purposes of the rotting or skeletal figures in their shrouds shown in the memorials to, for example, Richard Aylesham and his wife, in St Michael's, Aylsham, Norfolk, or to the now anonymous husband and wife commemorated in Sedgefield, Co. Durham.

All the possible nuances in iconography of the shrouded effigy, in brass and in stone, cannot be adequately rehearsed here. Suffice to say that Ralph Woodford's memorial falls within a recognizable iconographic range, and although *disce mori* and the English inscription are both *memento mori*, the Latin inscription links it with the Resurrection imagery of the Easter Sepulchre which forms part of the total composition. The composition in which Woodford is commemorated, however, does not incorporate the double or single carved stone effigy favoured by the lay and clerical elite of his day, and neither did he choose a brass, as was conventional amongst men of his rank. The tomb is an incised slab, and the earliest in the British Isles to show the deceased in his shroud. Such slabs are relatively common in the fifteenth century in the Low Countries in particular, but there the body is usually – and often luridly – dead.[9] Moreover the workmanship and composition of the Woodford tomb is outstandingly impressive for a rural parish church, such that Greenhill considered it to be the finest figure on an incised slab in England.[10] It is possible to trace the networks through which the fashion for shrouded effi-

---

[8] For an analysis of the different ways in which the iconography of the cadaver effigy may be understood see, P. M. King, 'The Cadaver Tomb in England: Novel Manifestations of an Old Idea', *Church Monuments*, 5 (1990), 26–38. This article draws on my unpublished DPhil thesis, 'Contexts of the Cadaver Tomb in Fifteenth-century England', University of York (1987) which contains a descriptive catalogue of shrouded effigies in the British Isles to 1558.

[9] See K. R. Cohen, *Metamorphosis of a Death Symbol* (Berkeley, 1969) for a range of continental examples.

[10] F. A. Greenhill, *The Incised Slabs of Leicestershire and Rutland* (Leicester, 1958), 27–9; *Incised Effigial Slabs: a Study of Engraved Stone Memorials in Latin Christendom, c.1100 to c. 1700*, 2 vols (London, 1976), I, p. 287; II, p. 26 and pl. 151a.

gies passed in fifteenth-century England, but Woodford did not belong to any of the wider political and social networks concerned. This tomb is a one-off, and the inspiration for its medium and composition quite unrecoverable. Additionally Nichols observed that the figure on the tomb had no head, which seems odd for such a fine, individual and expensive piece of work commissioned in the lifetime of the man to be commemorated.[11] Greenhill pointed out that the cartoon was drawn on the slab in pitch and the face was perhaps never incised, a deficiency picked up only when the pitch wore off.[12] Did Ralph Woodford's ambition exceed his wallet, or did the sculptor die or simply forget? The head was incised in the nineteenth century.

Like the tomb's overall composition, the will's structure and procedure is superficially orthodox, beginning with a preamble concerning the fate of the soul and making provision for the burial of the body, moving on to make bequests to parish churches and religious houses, and making chantry provisions, before finally attending to family matters. The long preamble has, however, its unusual features:[13]

> I Raife Woodforde of Ashby Folville considering how I shall as others have done before me *depar*te from this wreched worlde when it pleases oure Lord Jhesu to call me. And be cause I se daily in experience as yet that grete diseveraunce and variaunces oft tymes ben moved and fallen after the deth of man, insoas by cause of negligence and ignoraunce of theme that shulde dispose theme selfe to doe wilmor especially ordeyn them when they haue tym and power or elles ther tresor in longe liffe and soo abide to In reson come and thann they may not & tharnot but god knowith. And therefore be leve and trust of *Our* Lorde Jhesu In eschewing of all suche doubt and *per*elles whiles our Lorde hath given me space and tyme I being in good and hole mynde and also disposition of my *per*son, thanked be Jhesu, the xv day of Aprill in the yer of our Lorde m'ccccclxxxxv and in the yer of the Reigne of King Henry the vii[th] xi[th.] At asheby Folevyll afore saide in the countie of Leicester, be firm advice and good deliberacon make, renewe and declare this my wit, testament, Last Will and Intent of all my Fesimpull Landes and tenements, And of my moveable goodes and vnmoveable to be trewly done and *per*formed in the mann*er* and fourme as folowith. That is to sey I be sette and bequeith my soul to our Lord Jhesu crist and to his mod*er* our Lady saint mary and to all the hole Felowship of heuen, and my body to be buried and to haue resting place w*ith*in the chauncelle of the parishe churche of Asheby Folevylle aforesaide before the Image of oure Lady where my wif ligges, to making of the which chauncell I haue paide v m*ar*cs and more.

[11] J. Nichols, *The History and Antiquities of the County of Leicester ... Including also Mr Burton's Description of the County, Published in 1622, and the Later Collections of Mr Staveley, Mr Carte, Mr Peck and Sir T. Cave*, 4 vols (London, 1795, 1815, 1795–1811), III, p. 26.

[12] Greenhill, *The Incised Slabs of Leicestershire and Rutland*, p. 29.

[13] Extracts from the will are transcribed preserving the orthography of the original, with added light punctuation. Abbreviations are expanded in italics. Line breaks are not original.

Much of this is the formulaic material which had become standard in the more expansive wills in English throughout the fifteenth century, but the reference to the 'diseveraunce and variances oft tymes ben moved and fallen after the deth of man' and the desire to 'eschew' 'all such doubts and perils' are singular, and seem redolent with particular anxiety.

The following bequests to the Church are equally detailed and specific:

> Also to the prior of kirkeby bellare vj s viij d And to the hole couent of the same place xs. Also I bequeith to eche of the houses of the thre ordres of the fraires in Leicester x s, And to the house of freres of our Lady of Stamford x s, to pray for my soule the soule of Elizabeth my wif the soules of my fader and moder may soone be redemed to hevenly Joes,[14] and the soules of all mynne awncestors and all xpian soules, that be holy memoriall prayere my soule my wif soule and the soules of my Fader and my moder may be redemed to heuenly Joyes. Also I beseck all suche parsons as shall minister for me at the day of my buriall or any othyr tyme that they will geve and distribute to euery preist that comme to my buriall iiij d, And to euery clerke with surples ij d, And to euery clerk without surples j d, And to distribute and geue xl s in money amonges other pover mene & womene. Also I will that my rest and the day of my buriall be made in reasonabull maner and formm as is nowe vsed. Also I Will that v pover men there shall holde v torches a bout my herse the saide day of my buriall eche of theme to haue a blake gown with an hode of the samme and iiijd in money. Also I haue given to the clerkes of Assheby Foleuyll my messe book, my portewes with a newe cowpe, and xl s to making of the stepill. Also to the church of Knapton [Knipton] xl s with xxx s paid. Also to the churche of Sproxton xx l to making of a newe tabull of saint John Baptiste within my chapell in Sproxton Churche, which saide Church xx s was geven by John Loritte to be prayed fore in the same church. Also I bequeith to the churche of Skillington in Lincolnshire which I was born in to the chapell of our Lady xiij s iiij d. Also to the church of Wybirby [Wyfordby] x s, To the Chapell of Saint John Baptiste in Brantyngby.

All the places mentioned in this section can be located in an area closely surrounding the town of Melton Mowbray.[15]

After this the testator moves on to make bequests to family and servants and a large number of cattle and sheep are distributed around the Leicestershire-Lincolnshire border. The attention to detail, bounding on pedantry, reaches its climax when he stipulates that all the details concerned with his chantry be 'put in writing in a bill and delivered to the abbeys and priories and to the four orders of friars' who are his beneficiaries. He then returns to the details of the chantry, particularly the provision for wax candles until the end of the world, and a few overlooked details such as bequests for a servant girl and a little maid his daughter keeps for alms. There is also the slightly surprising first reference to a second wife, Margett, and a request for prayers for a namesake uncle Raife who was killed at Leicester, possibly at Bosworth.

[14] 'hevenly Joes' – presumably 'heavenly joys'.
[15] See map.

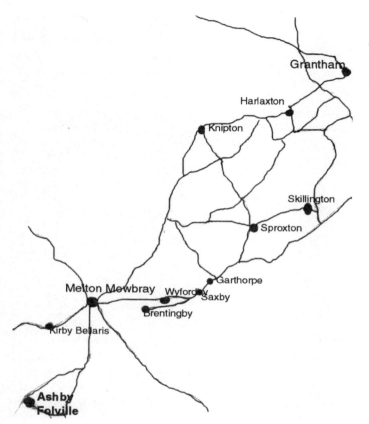

Map: villages mentioned in the will of Ralph Woodford (copyright: Pamela King).

Wills are, eponymously, intentionalist documents, dead authors ironically giving the lie to the Barthesian, 'death of the author', the theoretical assertion that the author's intention cannot be reconstructed. Medieval wills were also, however, written within a particular textual decorum which dictated hierarchy, sequence and priority, as well as supplying a number of standard formulae for expressing the author's intentions. In the case of Ralph Woodford, the formulaic nature of the will is apparently stretched and fissured in ways which reveal not only what he wanted to have done with his property after his death, but which, combined with a relatively full range of substantiating detail from other record sources, invites the reader to speculate why.

Ralph Woodford was one of only two who headed what Denton defines as 'a substantial gentry family' throughout the fifteenth century.[16] He was named as sole heir of his grandfather, Robert Woodford, knight, in a writ of 1456, his father, Thomas being already dead.[17] However Ralph's grandfather had set about systematically disinheriting him and had had a cartulary drawn up around the same

16   Denton, 'Image, Identity and Gentility', pp. 1–2.
17   *CFR, 1452–61,* 136, 160.

time, possibly for the purpose of recording the heritage of the family because its future was uncertain.[18] Ralph's son Robert, presumably as part of the process of executing his entitlements within the will, testifies in a memorandum recorded by Nichols, the Leicestershire antiquarian, as follows:[19]

> Memorandum, that Syr Robert Wodford gauffe by fyne to hys younger sones the manours of Wyssurby, Brentyngby, Sproxton, Thorp Arnold, Burton S. Lazarus, and Knypeton, to diserytt Raufe hys eldysde [son's] sone, bycause of a grouge that he had agenste the said Rauffe, and that was by cause the Villars had marryd hym agenste the said Robert's mynde; and be counsell of hys younger sones, he dyd burne two quarters of evidences yn Ascheby haule, as oulde men could testyfye; and then the said Raufe, after hys dyssese, enteryd yn the manour of Asscheby; and founde a dede, by the which the vycar of Asscheby was ynfeffeed; and he over-lyffed the other fiffes; and gave a state of hys … and fyne. And I Robert Wodford say, of my fydelyte and truthe, that my fader Rauff Wodford, shewed me the dede yn hys clousett by the grette chamber, and said that by that dede he held all hys lands, The whyche dede is yn the possessyon of my brodyr Matthew Wodfcrd, or else in my brodyr John's, Robert Wodford.

This memorandum brings many of the slightly eccentric details of the will into sharp focus: that cluster of villages,[20] the desire to have everything written down in quintuplicate, and the windy preamble worrying on about 'disseveraunce' and 'variance'; even the repetitive references to the unfortunately twenty-six-year-dead Elizabeth (née Villers) to the near exclusion of her presumed successor Margaret.

In the case of Ralph Woodford, one is left with imponderables. In particular, given the context and sentiments of the will, does the tomb too represent the exercise of individual expression within the range of orthodox decorum? In the realms of what may loosely be called 'imaginative literature' we can accept the evidence of a Thomas Hoccleve or a Margery Kempe that persons living in the Middle Ages were not exempt from being psychologically shaped by individual life-experience and capable of articulating that experience. The question, then, becomes one of the nature of evidence. The will and tomb of Ralph Woodford certainly suggest at least the imprint of an anxious individual shaped by family betrayal, political manipulation and, who knows, the experience of civil war.

[18]   Denton, 'Image and Identity'. pp. 8–9.
[19]   Nichols, *The History and Antiquiies of the County of Leicester,* III, p. 26.
[20]   Denton, pp. 10–11, sees in the cartulary a desire in the family to define its status through royal service and the possession of manorial lordship, as 'possession of the manor of Brentingby and the associated coat of arms provided them with a sound basis for gentility within Leicestershire', as incomers of status to the locality.

The World and the Soul: the Will of
Lady Isabel Morley (d. 1467)

CAROL M. MEALE

In the autumn of 1463 and again at Easter in 1464, a Cambridge graduate and doctor made the lengthy and difficult journey from the University town to south-west
Norfolk to attend to a dowager in her sickness. The woman was Isabel, Lady Morley, a widow of some twenty-eight years,[1] and the doctor, Master Thomas Reed.[2]
It was on 3 May 1464 that Lady Isabel made her will, perhaps in some haste, but
the doctor's ministrations were evidently successful in enabling her recovery, to
the extent that she added a codicil on 1 September later in the year, listing legatees 'not remembrid nor namyd' originally, and she did not actually die until 8 February 1466/7, the will being proved on the 27 February.[3] As a member of the
powerful dynasty of de la Pole – Isabel was the daughter of Michael, 2nd earl of
Suffolk, who died at Harfleur in 1415, and sister of William, 1st duke of Suffolk –
her lengthy testament, covering seven folios, offers the opportunity to examine
not simply the details of the worldly wealth and accoutrements of a fifteenth-century noblewoman but also her spiritual life and values. It is this apparent duality of
interest which provided the impetus behind this essay, which will explore how,
and if, it was possible to reconcile the opposing demands of the world and soul.

The luxurious nature of Isabel's material existence is indicated by some of her
specific bequests. To Sir William Stather, her household chaplain and steward,
described as 'clericus denariis [sic] domine' in her household accounts of 1463–
64, aside fom her 'litill missale', 'his hole wage for the yer that I decesse, in a boole

---

[1] Thomas, Lord Morley died 6 December 1435: *Complete Peerage*, 9 (London, 1936), p.
   218. Lady Isabel's household account roll for this time is London, BL, Additional MS
   34122A, cited in C. Richmond, 'Thomas Morley (d. 1416) and the Morleys of Hingham',
   Norfolk Archaeology, 39 (1984), 1–12 and *The Paston Family in the Fifteenth Century:
   The First Phase* (Cambridge, 1990), p. 122, n. 26.

[2] On Reed see A. B. Emden, *A Biographical Register of the University of Cambridge to
   1500* (London, 1963), p. 475 and C. Rawcliffe, 'Sickness and Health', in *Medieval Norwich*, eds C. Rawcliffe and R. Wilson (New York and London, 2004), p. 91.

[3] *Complete Peerage*, 9, p. 219. Her will, NRO, NCC Reg. Jekkys, ff. 50–53, is transcribed
   at the end of this article and is also partially excerpted in F. Blomefield, *An Essay
   towards a Topographical History of the County of Norfolk*, 2nd edn, 11 vols (London,
   1805–10), 2, pp. 430–31.

of siluer playn', and her 'best chales', she left'a manuelle chaundelere with an handell of cypresse and a plate of siluere at the bak'. This last is an extraordinary detail:
the 'chaundelere' was perhaps most likely a portable candlestick, or sconce, with
a reflective backing to enhance the light it shed.[4] In the later codicil she specifies
that a 'litill white carpite with birdis blew, red and grene and my tostyng iren of
siluere' were to go to Godefrey Joye, alderman of Norwich and one of her executors. These references to the practical, but expensive, utilities of daily life spring
to the eye: she evidently enjoyed these objects and treasured them. Other material bequests are equally precisely described and enumerated. Her daughter, Anne
Hastings, with whom she was staying whilst she was ill, was to receive tablecloths
'of diaper marked with lyones', 'sex seruitoris (napkins) of the best diaper', other
tableware, towels, bedlinen and items of silver, in addition to Isabel's 'pruce cofir
with lok and key of siluer' – the term 'pruce' meaning either that it came from Prus-
sia, or was made of spruce fir wood.[5] Once more, there is delight in itemising, also
for Anne, her 'ij pouderboxes' (probably spice-boxes) 'and a flagon gilte, the
qwyche all iij arne spered in a cas of ledir'. Aside from these bequests, in others are
listed all the elaborate silver and silver-gilt cups, bowls, basins and the chafing dish
which would have shone on her dresser or cupboard at times of feasting or celebration,[6] each described so that there could be no mistaking which item was to go
to whom.[7] This, after all, is the noblewoman whose advice on procedure and eti-
quette was highly regarded and whose advice, following the death of Sir John Fastolf in 1459, Margaret Paston sent her eldest son to procure on the public and
private decorum the Paston family should display during the normally festive season of Christmas: Isabel's cousin replied that at the time of her husband's death,
in her household 'þere were non dysgysynggys nere harping nere lvtyng nere syn-
gyn, nere non lowed dysportys, but pleyng at the tabyllys and schesse and cardys'.[8]

---

[4]   I am indebted to Jenny Stratford for informing me that amongst the many candlesticks
      owned by Richard II only one of gold, the smallest, weighing 3 ozs, was designed to be
      held in the hand. Another, heavier, silver-gilt item for 'holding the candle at the Feast
      of the Purification' may have come from the chapel of Thomas duke of Gloucester.
      These details are taken from her work on the ARHB funded project, 'Richard II and the
      English Royal Treasure'.

[5]   The scribe who made this copy of her will was evidently unfamiliar with the term
      'pruce': he initially copied it wrongly.

[6]   See J. Stratford, *The Bedford Inventories* (London, 1993), passim, for the importance
      of sumptuous display amongst the nobility.

[7]   To dame Eleanor Morley, the daughter of Isabel's only son, Robert, who died in 1442,
      prior to the birth of his only child, 'a cuppe standyng' is identified as having 'a serpen-
      tine in the boton': serpentine was a distinctly veined light green or yellowish-green
      rock mined in the Tuscan Apennines and other areas of Italy.

[8]   *Paston Letters and Papers of the Fifteenth Century*, ed. N. Davis, 2 vols (Oxford, 1970,
      1976) 1, no. 153. 'My Lady Morley' was sometime a dining companion of Agnes and
      John Paston: see Davis, 1, no. 35.

This pleasure in the material was not, however, confined to the realm of the secular. Take the chapel fittings left to her son-in-law, John Hastings, esquire, of Elsing and Gressenhall: 'a litell chales; ij cruettes gilte; a paxbrede gilte; a pixt of siluer for the sacrament; the reed vestment of cloth of gold and the white awtere clothis of silk'. Her gifts to the parish church of Hingham, a village some seventeen miles to the west of Norwich, where she was to be buried next to her husband before the image of the patronal saint, Andrew, were equally lavish. Her 'longest carpett with whyte floures' was to lie before the high altar there, and unspecified relics were to go to the church, contained within 'a tablet of gold garneyshed with perle ... a berall in the same tablet, with ij ymages: one of the Rusurreccion and another of Our Lady'. And the final words of her codicil – 'I bequeth to the parych chirch of Swanton Morley an hole westement of blak velvet with the orfreys that I made therto' – indicate that her gentlewomanly skills of embroidery decorating what was either a chasuble or a cope, were used to the service of God.[9]

Indeed, her spirituality is evident from the opening of the testament. She requests that, were she to die in her 'place' in Norwich, her body should be borne 'in hasty wyse as itt can goodly to be don' to the Chapel in the Fields for a funeral mass to be said prior to her final journey to Hingham. Her choice of this chapel – the college of secular priests in the south-west of Norwich, otherwise known as St Mary in the Fields – is interesting, in that it had particularly close ties with St Peter Mancroft, in which parish Isabel lived as a widow (it was only to this Norwich church that she left any money).[10] In the words of Christopher Harper-Bill and Carole Rawcliffe, 'the college [of St Mary] expressed the religious spirit of the city far more than did the cathedral'.[11] It was a prestigious foundation. In the event of death in Norwich, Isabel's body was to be accompanied to Hingham by fifteen torches, and once there, fifteen poor men from amongst her tenants were to hold the torches and five poor women, all dressed in black, were to hold tapers of two

[9] Swanton Morley may have held a special place in her affections, as it was her jointure: Richmond, 'Thomas Lord Morley', p. 4. The gift of advowson was held by the Morleys and in 1453 Isabel presented William Stather (mistranscribed as Strather) to the rectorship: Blomefield, *Essay towards a Topographical History of the County of Norfolk*, 10, p. 57. Stather was also master of the chapel of St Nicholas at Rougham, Gressenhall (Blomefield, 9, pp. 515–16), a preferment which must have come about due to his mistress's influence with her daughter and son-in-law.

[10] Her devotion to the 'holy masse of Ihesu' there is attested to by her contribution to the window of the north chancel chapel, so dedicated; see BL MS Harley 901, fol. 28v. I am grateful to Dr David King for this information. In this charitable act she was joined by Dame Katherine Felbrigg, who was evidently a friend: Katherine left Isabel a cross of gold in her will of 14 February 1457: Blomefield, *Essay towards a Topographical History of the County of Norwich*, 8, p. 110.

[11] C. Harper-Bill and C. Rawcliffe, 'Religious Houses', in *Medieval Norwich*, eds Rawcliffe and Wilson, 115–18 (p. 118); N. P. Tanner, *The Church in Late Medieval Norwich 1370–1532* (Toronto, 1984), *passim*.

pounds in weight during her requiem mass. Yet this was no empty display of power and status, even after death. The second greatest sum which she left was of twenty pounds, to be distributed by her executors amongst poor people 'that askin for goddis love fro my departing owte of this present lyffe onto the tyme that I be beridd, as wele in Norwich as in the wey to Hengham and also at Hengham the day of my sepultre'. John and Anne Hastings, with eight members of their household, similarly were to be dressed in black at Isabel's expense, if it were possible for them to be present. Despite the seeming ostentation of this display, it is also surely an exemplary demonstration of the reconciliation between the flesh – the honour which was due to her as Lady Morley – and the spirit – the charitable impulse. A similar concern for the well-being of the poor is evident in her numerous bequests to her tenants past and present which, for all nine of the manors, or towns, came to four pounds eleven shillings and eight pence (it is important to note that only five properties were held in dower).[12] It is also evident in her legacies to the lepers at the gates of Norwich and Beccles[13] and the payment of overdue debts of prisoners held at the Castle and Guildhall in Norwich, and even to her request that all her 'dayly seruants' should be rewarded according to their due and kept together for the space of forty days after her death, thus allowing them greater security than they might otherwise have had. Loyalty was evidently two-way in Isabel's household: named servants receive legacies in her codicil, notably her most intimate female companion, Johane Multon, her 'chamberere' who was left a 'litill federbed; a peyr shetts; my mantill furred with blak and x marcs [six pounds thirteen shillings and four pence] of money'.[14]

It is notable as well, with regard to how she expressed her piety, that of the bequests to the churches held both by her in dower, and by her heir, the greatest sums, with one exception, were to their repair. Nowhere does she ask for a public commemoration of her gifts, by way of specially commissioned windows, fonts or other architectural features: the money was apparently to be spent anonymously, for general upkeep. The one exception to the rule for money for fabric repair was at Buxton; here the greatest sum was left to the Guild of St Andrew, of which she was a sister.[15] Each bequest to a monastic foundation, as listed in the

---

12   Richmond, 'Thomas Lord Morley', p. 4; the dower lands were held at Aldeby, Hockering, Swanton Morley, Foulsham and the hundred of Eynesford: *Complete Peerage*, 9, p. 218; BL, Add. MS 34122A.

13   There was only one leper-house at Beccles, dedicated to SS. Mary Magdalene and Andrew. I am indebted to Mr James Woodrow, Honorary Curator of the Beccles and District Museum for this information, which is used in the calculations in the Table of bequests.

14   Other servants named are John Dyton and Master John Norwich: BL, Add. MS 34122A. Of others mentioned in the will, Thomas Wase, or Wace, was a 'gentleman' of Norwich and Ivetta Bumpstede 'widow' of the same city: see R. Virgoe, 'A Norwich Taxation List of 1451', *Norfolk Archaeology*, 40 (1988), 145–54, p. 149.

Table, was for prayers for her soul, the monies to be divided equally amongst those who so prayed. The choice of institutions is conventional enough for a Norfolk woman, even down to the bequest to the Franciscan nuns of Bruisyard in Suffolk; her sister-in-law, Elizabeth de la Pole, was recorded as prioress at Bruisyard in 1436 and Elizabeth's daughter, Katherine, Isabel's niece, was professed as a nun there in 1423, but the lack of mention of either of them indicates that they may have been dead by the time Isabel drew up her will.[16] The bequest to the little-known Austin Canons of Beeston Regis, whose institution lay on the north coast of Norfolk, between Sheringham and Cromer, is explained by the Morleys' holding of the patronage there.[17] In remembering two of the anchoresses of Norwich, Dame Julian Lampett at Carrow and Dame Anneys, or Agnes at the church of St Julian's, Conisford (Julian of Norwich's possible successor) Isabel was like many of her fellow town-dwellers.[18] In monetary terms alone, the most outstanding feature of the testament is the request for fifty-three pounds six shillings and eight pence to be 'disposyd and payed by myn executors', either at Hingham (or, more mysteriously, at Cambridge), 'to an honest prest praying for my lordes soule and our faders, moderes, auncestres, good doers and for all cristen soules', for as long as the money will last. Clearly, given this last clause, this cannot be a request for the establishment of a perpetual chantry, but rather for the employment of a chantry priest. In terms of money expended, sending a priest to Rome cannot be precisely accounted for, but it once more illustrates the extent of Isabel's pious intention.

In terms of her private devotional life and practice, her will gives some few clues. At the time of her death she had three priests in her household: Sir William Stather, who evidently had many other duties to occupy him, and Masters John Wergeant and John Norwich, the latter of whom had been with her for some years.[19] Whilst her literacy, in the modern sense of being able to write as well as to read, is in doubt (she set her 'sele of … armes' on the first part of the document, rather than her signature) she did leave books – five of them, all service books. The gift of her 'litill missale' to William Stather has already been noted; her 'principall massebook' was to go to her son-in-law, John Hastings, along with her chapel furnishings; Edmond Bokenham, esquire, councillor, retainer and executor, was to receive her 'best sawter', along with money, a gilt cup and six goblets; Alys Wryght her 'sawter with claspis of siluer'; and, lastly, Anne Hastings was to have

---

15   This guild is not recorded in H. F. Westlake, *The Parish Gilds of Medieval England* (London and New York, 1919), p. 190, but see Blomefield, *Essay towards a Topographical History of the County of Norfolk*, 6, p. 442, n. 5.

16   On these two women see R. E. Archer, 'Jane with the Blemyssh: A Skeleton in the de la Pole Closet?', *The Ricardian*, 13 (2003), 12–26, pp. 16–18.

17   Blomefield, *Essay towards a Topographical History of the County of Norfolk*, 8, pp. 91–2.

18   Tanner, *The Church in Late Medieval Norwich*, pp. 199, 200.

19   See n. 14, above.

her 'litill primere that I occupie daily'. This last legacy is perhaps the most revealing, in that it shows the extent of Isabel's personal piety and private rituals, and it
also stresses the female line of this piety: it is the most personal of the books and
thus acquires an almost talismanic quality as it is passed from mother to daughter.
None of these books, to my knowledge, has been identified, or survives, but they
are likely to have been, in the main, *de luxe* productions.

Thus far, I have concentrated on Isabel's loyalty and sense of responsibility and
obligation to her household and her tenants. Her closeness to her daughter Anne
and her husband has been observed, but she remembered others with similar
punctiliousness. Anne's two daughters, for instance, are named immediately after
their mother, Isabel Boswell, receiving bedlinen and 'ij pelowes of the best' and
her sister, Elizabeth, 'a girdill of gold eneyled (enamelled) with blak'. Their
brother, Sir Hugh Hastings, only remembered in the codicil, was to have her 'pleyn
standing cuppe gilte'. To her granddaughter, 'dame Elianor ... the lady Morley' she
left a valuable cup, and to Elianor's mother, Elizabeth, widow of Isabel's son, 'a
cuppe of siluer chasid with a couyre therto'.[20] Goddaughters, too, were rembered.
Dame Isabel Bolton, nun of Barking, had a legacy of one pound, whereas Isabel
Wryght received a newly-covered featherbed complete with linens and hangings,
Isabel's 'trussing cofer' (for travelling) and ten pounds in money. Important
though her children, their children and her godchildren obviously were to her,
Isabel was a de la Pole, and members of her birth family figure largely. The first person to be named in the will is her sister, Katherine, abbess of Barking from 1433
until her death forty years later.[21] If Katherine outlived Isabel she was to receive
ten marks. Next to be mentioned is Dame Katherine Stapleton, Isabel's cousin,
daughter of Thomas de la Pole and wife, firstly, of Sir Miles Stapleton of Ingham in
Norfolk, and patroness of the poet John Metham. Her legacy was Isabel's 'best
mantill furred with grey'.[22] Finally, as overseer of her testament, she appointed her
nephew, John, duke of Suffolk, son of William de la Pole and Alice Chaucer, to
whom she bequeathed, 'for his labor and supportacion', her 'salte gilte with on
couyre'. Whatever posterity may make of John de la Pole, he was evidently valued
by his aunt.[23] Equally, the lawyer John Heydon of Baconsthorpe's modern reputa-

---

[20] For the cup given to Eleanor, called by Isabel 'my doughter', rather than granddaughter, see n. 7 above. There is some confusion over the naming of Robert's widow: the
Complete Peerage gives her name as Elizabeth, 9, p. 219, but both Eleanor and Elizabeth are given by W. Rye, *Norfolk Families*, 2 vols (Norwich, 1913), 1, p. 568. It was,
however, through Isabel's granddaughter Eleanor's marriage that the lordship of Morley passed to the Lovel family.

[21] *Victoria County History: Essex*, 2 (London, 1907), p. 121, although it is wrongly stated
here that she was one of the three daughters of Michael, 3rd earl of Suffolk.

[22] Katherine de la Pole/Stapleton/Harcourt is the subject of an ongoing study by the present author.

[23] See, e.g., J. A. F. Thomson, 'John de la Pole, Duke of Suffolk', *Speculum*, 54 (1979),

tion has fared as badly as the Paston family would probably have welcomed[24] but, as a trusted and long-serving adviser to Isabel, he was left ten pounds, only half of which was to cover his role as executor.

There is one last characteristic of this testament which should be mentioned, and this is Isabel's concern for legal niceties, which may well have been generated by her many years as a widow. She gave detailed instructions as to the execution of her testament. She begins by stating that all goods not assigned should be gathered together and valued by impartial men and that if John Hastings, or any of her executors wished to buy any of these objects, they should pay the market value for them. She then calls for all four of her executors to stand together should any legal matter arise from the will, and proceedings be taken against only one of the four. This was to apply to any appeal to 'the lawe temperall or spirituall'. She requests that probate should be carried out with all possible haste, which it evidently was, and then, allowing for the possibility that any one of her executors should prove himself unwilling to act on her behalf, she enjoins that he should 'be sworn and charged afore the Busshopp or his ordinarie' and be excluded from all administration and 'occupacion of all my goodes legat and not legat'. Her final injunction is that one of the four should be chosen by his fellows to receive 'all the areages and dutes of all my seid livelod after my deces immediately', in order that her wishes should be despatched. The constant refrain of this passage is that all four men should act in unison, and this is where John Heydon's role is crucial, for she stipulates that he should give assistance and counsel so that the executors 'be not wrongfully vexed'. This covering of all legal angles must have been necessitated in large part because of the complexity of the financial arrangements to be made. The actual sum of money involved, leaving aside the expenditures not precisely accounted, was one-hundred-and-eighty-six pounds and a shilling. Given that Colin Richmond has estimated Isabel's annual income from her dower lands (which, aside from Aldeby, near Beccles on the Norfolk–Suffolk border, lay in a rough quadrant from the west to the north of Norwich) as 'about £170',[25] it would seem that she had made her calculations diligently, with any shortfall to be made up by the sale of the residue of her goods.

Time, if not record, has dissipated those qualities of Isabel Morley such as loyalty, charity and her role within the local community so eloquently displayed in her testament, but there is one survival which ties together the threads of her

---

528–42. Another instance of the ties between Isabel and the de la Poles is the presentation of Simon Brailis as rector of Swanton Morley in 1437 by her: Brailis, who in 1456 was chaplain and Household Treasurer to Alice de la Pole (London, BL Egerton Roll 8779), preceded William Stather in this role; cf. n. 9 above.

[24] E.g. in his role in the disputes over Gresham and East Beckham: see Richmond, *The Paston Family: The First Phase*, pp. 57, 60, 155; 111, 114, n. 216 and cf. p. 171, n. 17.

[25] Richmond, 'Thomas Lord Morley' p. 4. In 1451 Isabel's landed income was assessed at £82, which seems low: see Virgoe, 'A Norwich Taxation List of 1451', pp. 149–51.

devotion, both to religion and to her only husband, and to her attachment to worldly display. This is the tomb at Hingham, where she is buried with Thomas (Plate 10). It is a magnificent red stone structure which was constructed in part by a mason who worked on the Erpingham Gate of Norwich Cathedral, in addition to other local ecclesiastical buildings.[26] Situated in the north chancel of St Andrew, it reaches to the top of the chancel wall and contains a riot of sculptural detail, including coats of arms; weepers, both male and female; the figure of Christ in majesty and a depiction of the Annunciation (Plate 11). Of particular interest are the badly defaced figures of saints which line the arch rising from the tomb chest, which once held a double brass of the couple and which perhaps was used as an Easter sepulchre.[27] From west to east, these have tentatively been identified as SS Catherine; John the Evangelist; Margaret; Mary Magdalene; John the Baptist; Michael (Plate 12); an unidentified bishop and George. Does this choice speak to us of especial devotion to these saints and martyrs? The style of the architecture and some of the heraldry indicates that the tomb was begun after the death of Thomas Lord Morley, although this does not necessarily mean that orders for its construction may be accredited to Isabel herself. Work certainly continued upon it for many years, though: as late as 1463–4, a payment of sixty shillings was made 'pro pictura tumbe domine apud Hingham'.[28] Whilst there is no sense in which the church of St Andrew is a shrine to the Morley family, and in particular to Isabel, unlike Ewelme church, where her sister-in-law, Alice Chaucer, lies in state,[29] Isabel and Thomas's tomb is the focal point, a fitting intersection between the world and the soul.

[26] R. Fawcett, 'The Master Masons of Later Medieval Norfolk', in *A Festival of Norfolk Archaeology*, eds S. Margeson, B. Ayers and S. Heywood (Hunstanton: Norfolk and Norwich Archaeological Society, 1996), 101–26, pp. 121–4. See also N. Pevsner, *North-West and South Suffolk* (Harmondsworth, 1962), pp. 51, 197 and pls 42, 43.

[27] R. Fawcett, *The Architecture and Furnishings of Norfolk Churches: A Guide* (Norwich, 1974), p. 10; P. Sheingorn, *The Easter Sepulchre in England* (Kalamazoo, Michigan, 1987), p. 246. It should be stressed that there is no firm evidence for its use in this way.

[28] BL, Additional 34122A; *Complete Peerage*, 9, p. 219, n.c.

[29] See, e.g., J. A. A. Goodall, *God's House at Ewelme: Life, Devotion and Architecture in a Fifteenth-Century Almshouse* (Aldershot, 2001).

APPENDIX 1

Lady Isabel Morley: Monetary Bequests: NRO NCC Reg Jekkys, fols 50–53

Churches	£	s	d			
Seint Petir of Mancroft		6	8			
[St Peter Mancroft]	2	0	0			
		14	4			
Chapell in the Feldes	1	0	0			
[Chapel of St Mary's in the Fields]	1	0	0			
Hengham		6	8			
[Hingham]	3	6	8			
Aldeby	1	6	8			
Buxton		6	8			
		13	4			
		13	4			
Swanton [Morley]		6	8			
Wurthyng [Worthing]		3	0			
	1	10	0			
Byntre [Bintree]		6	8			
Fulsham [Foulsham]	2	0	0			
Hockering		3	4			
	1	10	0			
Sub-total				£17	14s	0d

Monastic Foundations						
Monks of Norfolk in Norwich	2	0	0			
Beston [Beeston Regis] (Austin Canons)	2	0	0			
Austin Friars	2	0	0			
Dominican Friars	1	6	8			
Franciscan Friars	1	6	8			
Carmelite Friars	1	6	8			
Carhow [Carrow] (Benedictine)	1	0	0			
Bresyard [Bruisyard] (Franciscan)	1	6	8			
Sub-total				£12	6s	8d

Anchoresses						
Dame Julyan of Carhowe		6	8			
Dame Anneys of St Julyannes		10	0			
Sub-total					16s	8d

Tenants	£	s	d			
Aldeby		10	0			
Buxton		5	0			
Swanton/Wurthing	1	6	8			
Fulsham		13	4			
Byntre		3	4			
Hockering		5	0			
Mateshale & Mateshale Bergh [Mattishall & Mattishall Burgh]		5	0			
Tuddenham [North]		3	4			
Hengham	1	0	0			
Sub-total				£4	11s	8d

Individuals	£	s	d			
Katerine de la Pole, abbess	6	13	4			
Isabell Bolton, nun	1	0	0			
Thomas Wase	2	0	0			
Edmond Bokenham, esquire	6	13	4			
Sir William Stather	6	13	4			
Edmund Harsik, gentleman	4	0	0			
John Heydon	5	0	0			
John Heydon	5	0	0			
Edmond Bokenham	5	0	0			
Sire William Stather	5	0	0			
Godefrey Joye, alderman	5	0	0			
Isabell Wryght	10	0	0			
Johane Multon	6	13	4			
John Dyghton	2	0	0			
John Herman	2	0	0			
John Boteler	2	0	0			
Maister John Wergeant	1	0	0			
Maister John Norwich	1	0	0			
Sub-total				£76	13s	4d

Sundries	£	s	d			
Poor mourners	20	0	0			
Priest to say masses	53	6	8			
Lepers at Norwich		10	0			
Lepers at Beccles		2	0			
Sub-total				£73	18s	8d

Expenditure not accounted
Prisoners in Norwich Castle & Guildhall
A Priest to go to Rome
Black clothing for immediate Mourners
Black clothing for tenants of Hingham
Money to keep daily servants

Grand Total				**£186**	**1s**	**0d**

APPENDIX 2

Will of Isabel, Lady Morley (d. 1466/7)

NRO, NCC Reg. Jekkys, fols 50 – 53

[fol. 50] In the name of God, Amen. The thredde day of the moneth of Maij, the yere of Oure Lordys incarnacyon ml cccc lxiiij, I, Dame Isabell, lady of Morley, being in my hoole wyt and mynde, in my place within the citee of Norwich make my testement in this manere. First I comend my soule to Goddes mercy, to Oure Lady and to all the company of heven, and my body to be beryed in the chauncell of the parysche chirch of Hengham, before the ymage of Seint Andrew, by the body of my lord my husbond, on qwose soule God haue mercy. Also if it fortune me to decesse within the cite of Norwych I will that my body be born to the chirch of the Chapell in the Feldes, ther to be seid a masse for my soule in hasty wyse as itt can goodly to be don, and aftir that masse my body to be caryed to Hengham with xv torches, ther to be beried as itt is before said. Also I will that xv pore men of my tenauntes shall holdyn the seid xv torches at my derige[1] and masse of requiem, and they to haue xv gownes of blak with as many hodys. Also I will that v pore women, the which shull holdes v taperys of wax att my derige & masse, euery tapere the wyght of ij pownde wax haue […] v gownes of blankett & v kerches of threed. [fol. 50v] And the seid taperes to be brent afore the sacrament nere the place of my sepulture so that they successeuely bene spent. And I will ffirst that my dettys be payed withowtyn any abatyment. Also I will that euery preest being att my dirige and att the masse of requiem at Hengham haue iiijd, and euery clerk ijd. Also I will that in all hast possibill aftere my decesse xv xx masses with as many placebo[2] and diriges be said for my soule, for euery masse, placebo and dirige to be rewardid iiijd. Also I bequeth to the heigh auter of Seint Petir of Mancroft, vjs viiijd. Also I bequeth to the reparacion of the same chirch of Seint Petir, xls. Also I bequeth to the sustentacion of the holy masse of Ihesu in the same chirch, xiijs iiijd. Also I bequeth to the heigh autere of the Chapell in the Feldes, xxs. Also I bequeth to the prestes and clerkes of the seid Chapell, to be devided among them in equale porcions, and ther to do a soleme dirige and masse for my soule, xxs. Also I bequethe to the monkes of the counte in Norwich among them to be diuided in equale porcyons and ther to do a soleme dirige and a masse for my soule, xls. Also I bequeth to the prior of Beston and to his brethren, to sey a

---

[1]   Matins of the Office of the Dead.   [2]   Vespers of the Office of the Dead.

solemne dirige and a masse for my soule, to be deliuered among hem and to other men of the same place, xls. Also I bequeth to the heigh autere of the chirch of Hengham, vjs viiijd. Also I bequeth to the reparacion of the same chirch, v marcs. Also to the seid same chirch a tablett of gold garneshyd with perle, conteynyng certeyn relikes within, a berall in the same tablet, with ij ymages: one of the Rusurreccion and anothir of Oure Lady. Item I bequeth to the same chirch my longest carpett with whyte floures to lye before the heigh auter. Item I bequeth to my suster, Dam Katerine, the Abbas of Berkyng, yif she liff lenger than I, x marcs. Also I bequeth to Dame Isabell Bolton, nunne of Barkyng, my god doughter, xxs. Also I bequeth to the Frere Austeneres in Norwich to pray for my soule, xls. Also I bequeth to the couentes of the Frere Prechours, Frere Menours and Frere Carmins in Norwich, to iche couent to pray for my soule, xxvjs viiijd. Item I bequeth to the reparacion of the parich chirche of Aldeby, xxvjs viiijd. Also I bequeth to my pore tenauntes of the same town to be devided among hem, xs. Also I bequeth to the heigh awtere of Buxton church, vjs viijd. Item to the reparacion of the same chirch, xiijs iiijd. Also to the [fol. 51] Gilde of Seint Andrewe in the same town, qwereof I am a sustere, xiijs iiijd. Also I bequeth to my pore tenauntes of the same town, vs. Also I bequeth to the heigh awtere of Swanton vjs viijd. Item I yeve to the heigh autere of Wurthyng, iijs iiijd. Item to the reparacion of the same chirch, xxs. Also I bequeth to my pore tenauntes of Swanton and Wurthing, to be devided amonges hem, xxvjs viijd. Also I bequeth to the reparacion of the chirch of Folsham, xls. Also I yeve to my pore tenauntes of the same town, xiijs iiijd. Also I bequeth to the parych chirch of Byntre, vjs viijd. Item to my pore tenauntes of the same toun, iijs iiijd. Item I bequeth to the heigh awtere of the parich chirch of Hokering, iijs iiijd. Item to the reparacion of the same chirch, xxxs. Item to my pore tenauntes of the same toun, vs. Item I bequeth to my pore tenauntes of Mateshale and Mateshale Bergh, vs. Also I bequeth to my pore tenauntes of Tuddenham, iijs iiijd. Also I bequeth to my pore tenauntes of Hengham, to be disposed among them after my decesse, xxs. Also I will that myn executors dispose for me to the pore people that askyn for goddis love fro my departyng owte of this present lyffe onto the tyme that I be beridd, as wele in Norwich as in the wey to Hengham and also at Hengham the day of my sepulture, xxli, yif it need, after the discrecion of myn executores. Also I bequeth to my sone John Hastings my principall massebook; a litell chales; ij cruettes[3] gilte; a paxbrede[4] gilt; a pixt[5] of siluere for the sacrament; the reed vestment of cloth of gold and the white awtere clothis of silk. Also I bequeth to my doughter Anne, the wife of the seid John Hastings, yf that she liffe lengere

[3]   Small vessels for holding the wine and water during Mass.
[4]   A tablet of wood, precious metal or ivory imprinted with a sacred image, such as the Crucifixion, which stood on the altar during Mass and was used for the priest and congregation to share the kiss of Peace.
[5]   A vessel in which the consecrated host was kept.

than I, my best bord clothis of diaper[6] marked with lyones. Item a sornappe[7] of the same werk diaper; a long towale of diaper for the same clothes conteynyng in length xviij yardes; ij couerpaynes and sex seruitoris[8] of the best diaper; a cupbordcloth & ij short tuales of warke for wasshyng; my litill primere that I [...] occupie daily; my [...] pruce cofir with lok and key of siluer; ij pouderboxes and a flagon gilte, [fol. 51v] the qwyche all iiij arne spered[9] in a cas of ledir; 1 peir of shetis of lawne; a peire shetis of reynes[10] with an hede shete; v seruyng bolles of siluere gilte; my litill great pott of siluer; an holle basyn of siluere. Also I bequeth to Isabell Boswell, doughter to the seid Anne, a peire sheets of iij elne[11] brede with an hed shete; another peyre of shetis; ij pelowes of the best. Also I bequeth to Elizabet, suster to the seid Isabell Boswell, a girdill of gold enelyd[12] with blak. Also I bequeth to Dame Elianor my doughtere, the lady Morley, a cuppe standing with a serpentine in the boton. Item I bequeth to Dame Katerine Stapilton my best mantill furred with grey. Also I bequeth to Elizabet Morley a cuppe of syluer chasid with a couyre therto. Also I bequeth to Thomas Wase, xls. Also I bequeth to Edmond Bokenham, sqwyere, a gilt cuppe standing cuvid, with a lebbardes hed in the bottom; x marcs in money; my best sawter; a layer of siluer cuvid, with vj goblettes closed therin and hert of gold with an holy lombe. Also I bequeth to Sire William Stather my litill missale; a manuelle chaundelere with an handell of cypresse and a plate of siluere at the bak; x marcs of mony; his hole wage for all that yer that I decesse, in a bolle of siluer playn, and my best chales. Also I bequeth to Edmond Harsik gentilman for to prey for my soule vj marcs in mony. Also I bequeth to Alys Wright my sawtere with claspis of siluere. Also I will if it fortune any presoners the day of my deces to abide in the castell or in the Gilde Halle of Norwich because of one poure of payment for his fees, I will the fees of all suche be payid of my goodes and they to be deliuered. Also I bequeth to Dame Julyan, anchoresse at Carhowe, vjs viijd. Also I bequeth to Dame Anneys, anchoresse of Sent Julyannes in Cunfford, xs. Also I bequeth to the prioresse of the nunnes of Carhow, to be devyded among hem, and ther to say a solempne dirige and a masse of requiem for my soule, xxs. Also I bequeth to the Abbas, and [...] to the nunnes of Bresyard on the like wise to be devided among hem, and therto sey a solempne dirige and a masse of requiem for my soule, xxvjs viijd. Also I will that all my siluere vessels and plate that remayneth over my testement be sold incontinent att my deces, to performe and discharge my bequest in my testement, and the cost that sufficiently shall perteyn to my sepulture. [fol. 52] Also I will that all my othir goodes not legat nor

6   Geometrically-patterned cloth.
7   Latin: over-tablecloth.
8   Not in MED. Most probably of Latin derivation, meaning napkins.
9   Fastened.
10   Fine linen cloth from Rennes in France.
11   One ell equalled forty-five inches.
12   Enamelled.

assigned incontinent after my deces gadered togidder into place close and sekir in all hast possibill to be prised by indifferent men. And than I will that my sone John Hastings and all my executors, if they will bye any of the goodes, haue ther desire, iche man part conuement for hym paying therfor incontinent the price as anothir man shuld. Also I will that if any action or querell be takyn in the lawe temperall or spirituall for any matere growing by me or for me ayens ony of myn execyutors sin-glerly, that than suche accions or querell be answered and satisfied by all myn executors of my propir goodes and catall. Also I will that liij li vi s viij d be disposyed and payed by myn executors to an honest prest praying for my lordes soule and our faderers, moderes, auncestres, good doers and for all cristen soules in the parich chirch of Hengham, or elles at Cambrigg, with the avyse of myn executors as long as the sum of liii li vj s viij d will indur to his resonabill stipend and vages. Also I will haue a prest to Rome. Also I will that this testament be aprobat in alle hast possibill after my deces, and if so be that ony of myn executors vnderneth in this testement namyd refuse to take charge of performyng and executyng of this my seid testement, than I will that he or they so refusyng or themself absentyng, to be sworn and charged afore the Busshopp or his ordenarie[13] be plenely excluded and sequestred from all administracion & occupacion of all my goodes legat and not legat. Also I will that my sone John Hastings with vj of his men, my doughter, his wife, & her ij women haue gownes of blak to bring me to my sepul-ture if they be ther present. Also I will that my executors, my daily seruantes and also my officers that will attendid to do my body seruice & wurshipp att my decesse and sepulture haue also gownes of blak of my cost and charge. Also I will that one of myn executors be the avyse of all his coexecutors only shall haue the receyvyng of all the arerages[14] and dutes of all my seid livelod after my deces immediatly, and he to do his trowe [fol. 52v] diligens in receyvyng of them and my seid arrerages so receyuid, he to make a write to his felawis executors, and so my goodes to be disposed acording to my testement and last will be the assent of hem alle. And that noon of myne executors receyve nor take noon of the seid arrerages nor dutes but be the assent of the forseid executors assigned. Also I will that none of these execu-tors make none relese nor acquietaunce of the seid arreges and dutes but be the assent of all my executors. Also I bequeth to John Heydon, if he will yeve assistens and good counsel that myn executors be not wrongfully vexed, cs. The residewe of all my goodes wheresoeuer thei be or may be founden I yeve and bequeth to myn executors for to pay my dettes and to performe my last wille and the ovir-pluce[15] to be disposed for my soule. And as for survisor of this my present teste-ment I assigne and ordeyn my lord and nevew, John the Duke of Suffolk, to qwome I yeve and bequeth for his labor and supportacion myn salte gilte with on couyre. And as for myn executors I assigne ordeyn and make my sone John Hastings,

---

13   Deputy.
14   Debts.   15   Surplus.

Edmund Bokenham, Sire William Stather, prest, and Godfrey Ioye of Norwich, alderman. And I will that myn seid son John Hastings haue for his labor, if he take charge, my best gilt cuppe chased, with the couyre, and my siluer pot pleyn with the blak lyon. Also I wille that eche [...] othir of myn executors haue for her labor an cs. In wittenesse herof to this writyng I haue set therto my seale of myn armes, yeven the yere & the day aboue written.

In the name of God, Amen. I, Dame Isabell lady Morley, being in good and hoole mynde the ffirst day of the moneth of Septembre the yere of Oure Lord ml cccc lxiij make this sedule in fulfillyng of my testement and last will of diuers persones and parcels in my testement not remembrid nor namyd. First I bequeth to Anne, the doughter of John Arundell, a basyn and 1 ewyre; ij saltes wherof one is gilt with the cowire; 1 cuppe gilt with the covyre; ij cuppes sengill, acordyng therto; a cuppe of siluere with the covyr and ij cuppes sengill acordyng therto; a chasyng chau-fyre[16] of siluere; ij spones gilte and xij spones of siluere. Item I bequeth to Sere Hewe Hastinggs my pleyn standing cuppe gilt. Item I bequeth to Godefrey [fol. 53] Ioye, alderman, my litill qwhite carpite with birdis blew, red and grene and my tostyng iren of siluere. Item I bequeth to Dionyse Bokenham a playne cuppe of siluere. Item I will that Iuetta Bompsted haue one of my gownes. Item I bequeth to Isabell Wryght, my goddoughter, a fedderbed with the newe tyke;[17] a trawn-som;[18] ij pillowis; ij blankettes; ij peyr shetys; a couerlyght of white wursted; a selor[19] and a testor[20] within; curteynes of lynen cloth; my trussing cofer and xli of mony. Item I bequeth to Johane Multon, my chamberere, my litill federbed; a peyr sheets; my mantill furred with blak and x marcs of money. Item I bequeth to John Dyghton xls. Item I bequeth to John Herman xls. Item I bequeth to John Boteler xls. Item I will that all my dayly seruants be rewardid after ther abydyng hath be with me afore my decesse, and as ther seruice and diligence may be vndirstond by myn executors. Item I will that all my dayly seruants be kepte togedir att my costis and charges by the space of xl dayes after my deces. Item I bequeth to Maister John Wergeaunt xxs. Item I bequeth to Maister John Norwich xxs. Item I bequeth to euery howse of leperis at the gates of Norwich, and also at Beccles, ijs. Item I bequeth to the parych chirch of Swanton Morley an hole westement of blak vel-wet with the orfreys[21] that I made therto.

Probate granted penultimate day of February, 1466/7.

---

16   Chafing dish.
17   Ticking, or covering.
18   Bolster.
19   A canopy for a bed.
20   Given the phrasing, probably the wooden framework for the canopy.
21   Embroidered bands or borders for ecclesiastical vestments, such as a cope or chasu-ble.

Anne Harling Reconsidered

DAVID J. KING

'Both indomitable and sentimental, intensely religious and rigorously practical'. Thus has Gail McMurray Gibson characterised Anne Harling, the thrice-married childless wealthy heiress from fifteenth-century Norfolk who is the subject of this paper.[1] Gibson is one of a number of scholars who have written about Anne and more recent contributions include those by Anne Dutton and Jacqueline Jenkins.[2] Gibson's summary view of Anne is perceptive, but there is more to be said about this important intriguing figure than has appeared thus far. This paper will gloss and extend aspects of her life already discussed and will add fresh perspectives based on a study of the church at East Harling of which she was a generous patron.

A brief account of her life will establish a context.[3] Anne was the only child of Sir Robert Harling of East Harling and Jane Gonville, herself sole heiress of the family who had founded Gonville Hall in Cambridge and Rushworth College near East Harling. Born in about 1426, she lost her father in battle in France in 1435; it is not known when her mother died. Two years later her wardship was sold to another warrior, Sir John Fastolf, her father's uncle by marriage, who married her off in 1438 to a third soldier, Sir William Chamberlain, at least fifteen years her senior. Anne was already a considerable heiress, having inherited at least fifteen manors and ten advowsons in Norfolk, and four manors and one advowson in Suffolk, and the marriage settlement negotiated by Fastolf reflects this. In the agreement dated

[1] G. M. Gibson, *The Theatre of Devotion. East Anglian Drama and Society in the Late Middle Ages* (Chicago and London, 1989), p. 97.

[2] A. Dutton, 'Piety, Politics and Persona: MS Harley 4012 and Anne Harling', *Prestige, Authority and Power in Late Medieval Manuscripts and Texts*, ed. F. Riddy (Woodbridge, 2000), 133–46; J. Jenkins, 'St Katherine and Laywomen's Piety: The Middle English Prose Life in London, BL, Harley MS 4012', in *St Katherine of Alexandria. Texts and Contexts in Western Medieval Europe*, eds J. Jenkins and K. J. Lewis (Turnhout, 2003), 153–70.

[3] The biographical details given here mainly follow F. Blomefield, *An Essay towards a Topographical History of the County of Norfolk*, vol. 1 (London, 1805), pp. 319–22, 326–28; [E. K.] Bennett, 'The College of S. John Evangelist of Rushworth', *Norfolk Archaeology*, 10 (1888), 276–380; Dutton, 'Piety, Politics and Persona', pp. 133–5 and Jenkins, 'St Katherine and Laywomen's Piety', p. 158. Deviations from and additions to these sources are footnoted separately.

2 August 1438 Sir William was to pay her guardian 1000 gold nobles before the marriage and 1500 marks of gold within twelve months of it. Sir William Chamberlain came from Gedding in Suffolk and had lands in Weston Favell in Northamptonshire. Having married well, it appears that he settled at East Harling, although his military duties in Normandy kept him away from home and his young wife for long periods. In July 1439 he sailed for Honfleur and took charge of the town of Meaux.[4] Probably under orders, he surrendered the town to the French in August of that year and was imprisoned for a time in Rouen. He was again captured in 1446 and had to pay a ransom for his release, causing him considerable financial loss.[5] Between these two periods of captivity he spent some time in England, being occupied with his manors in Rushworth in 1441 and serving two years later on a commission of array in Kent.[6]

Following his release in 1446, Sir William returned to England and in the next year was granted a royal licence to found the Harling Chantry in East Harling church.[7] This was allowed without the usual fee or fine as a reward for good service in France and on account of the poverty he incurred when he had to pay his own ransom. The founding of the chantry was to be in fulfilment of the terms of the will of Sir Robert Harling, Anne's father, who had died in 1435. Anne was then about twenty-one and it appears that from this time onward until about 1467 she devoted much of her energy to organising the rebuilding and decoration of East Harling church.

Chamberlain was made a Knight of the Order of the Garter in 1461 by Edward IV to reward his bravery in the French wars, but died the following year, leaving Anne a childless widow. By and probably in 1467 she had married her second husband, Sir Robert Wingfield, the second son of Sir Robert Wingfield of Letheringham, and had adopted Robert Wingfield, her new husband's nephew.[8] The Wingfields had political ambitions, and Sir Robert the younger, who had previously been in service with the Duke of Norfolk, went into exile with Edward IV in 1470. His loyalty was rewarded by his appointment to the office of Controller to

[4]   R. A. Griffiths, *The Reign of King Henry VI* (Stroud, 1998), p. 458; G. L. Harris, *Cardinal Beaufort, a Study of Lancastrain Ascendency and Decline* (Oxford, 1988), p. 283.
[5]   K. Mourin, http://www.norfolkheraldry.co.uk (21/02/06).
[6]   Bennett, 'Rushworth College', p. 362; *Calendar of Patent Rolls, 1441–46*, pp. 199–200.
[7]   *Calendar of Patent Rolls, 1429–36*, p. 65.
[8]   In Norfolk Record Office, MSS KIM 2L/8, 2L/9, 2Q/18, all dated April 9th 1467, they are named as man and wife. Sir Robert Wingfield's nephew Robert was almost certainly the seventh son of Sir John Wingfield of Letheringham and was born in or before 1464; see *Oxford Dictionary of National Biography* (Oxford, 2004), vol. 59, p. 736. Anne says in her will of 1498 that she brought him up from the age of three, which would place the adoption in or before 1467, very probably around the time of the marriage; see PRO, PROB 11/11. For further details of her second husband's political career, see Dutton, 'Piety, Politics and Persona,' p. 134, n. 9.

the King's Household from 1474 to 1481, in which latter year he died. Anne remained a widow for some ten years, but in 1491 married for the third time, her husband being John, fifth Lord Scrope of Bolton. He died in 1498, a few weeks before Anne. She was 72 or 73 and had no children. Her very long and detailed will has attracted attention, as it provides for bequests to 58 religious institutions and 133 individual people, ranging from generous bequests of money, vestments and liturgical furnishings for East Harling church, to 20*d*. to Riddlesworth church.[9] Gibson discusses it in some detail, stressing the strength and clarity of the voice heard in it, the care and tact of the bequests, but also the implicit contractual nature of the gifts to institutions and individuals, with prayers for her soul and those of her ancestors being the required recompense.[10]

Gibson's main interest was the evidence for medieval theatre in East Anglia, and she provides evidence from some now-lost churchwardens' accounts for dramatic interludes held at the church gate in the 1450s and 1460s at East Harling, which she thinks Anne probably saw, although there is no direct evidence for this.[11] She also looks at the surviving visual evidence of the stained glass in East Harling church given by Anne, seeing it as reflecting Anne's preoccupations with her childlessness, but discussing also in this context Anne's foundation of a chapel in her church dedicated to St Anne in the 1460s, and her later endowment in 1490 of Rushworth College with additional resources to provide a free grammar school for thirteen children, five of whom shall be raised in the college and known as 'Dame Annys Childeryn'.[12] Dutton's article concentrates on Anne's ownership of a collection of religious treatises and other writings, now Harley MS 4012. She dates its production to the 1460s and stresses the strong penitential aspects of its contents, and while seeing Anne's possession of the book as evidence of a genuine piety, suggests that it may also have played a part as a social construct, helping to establish her reputation as a respectable and pious lady, useful attributes which could have been used by Anne if she had served in the court of Edward IV, which had a reputation for licentiousness and immorality, although she provides no concrete evidence of Anne's presence there.[13] Jenkins focuses on the prose Life of St Katherine in Harley 4012, linking its Prohemium with other items in the miscellany, which together formed a group not seen elsewhere and which were probably chosen specifically by Anne. They share a common theme stressing devotion to the Passion of Christ.[14]

---

9   The transcription in *Testamenta Eboracensia*, vol. 2, p. 151 is not quite complete.
10   Gibson, *The Theatre of Devotion*, pp. 97–9.
11   Gibson, *The Theatre of Devotion* p. 101.
12   Gibson, *The Theatre of Devotion*, pp. 101–06.
13   Dutton, 'Piety, Politics and Persona', pp. 135–6, 140–43.
14   Jenkins, 'St Katherine and Laywomen's Piety', passim.

Harley 4012 has, however, further light to shed on Anne's emotional and reli-gious life. Jenkins has looked at the way in which the manuscript was compiled. The first eight items had appeared in another manuscript, and Jenkins suggests that this provides evidence that such manuscripts were copied from a 'standard volume', with the addition of special items chosen by the owner.[15] The extra items selected by Anne included a unique Prohemium to the Life of St Katherine replac-ing the account of her childhood, conversion and mystical marriage included in other copies of the Prose Life.[16] This Prohemium emphasises how St Katherine constantly remembered the Virgin Mary's 'mekenes and compassion with the lam-entable teris of pite' which she displayed as she contemplated her son's Passion.[17] Jenkins adds to the Prohemium a poem on the Passion in the manuscript and a second poem described as a prayer evoking the Passion that follows it. All three are examples of affective piety, enabling the reader to visualize and identify with Christ's agony and Mary's suffering as she watched.[18] It is of interest to compare this with the iconography of the glass which Anne commissioned for the east win-dow of the Harling chapel, probably also in the 1460s, which would have been a more public act of piety.[19] There were fourteen main-light narrative scenes depict-ing incidents in the life of the Virgin from the Annunciation to Pentecost (see Plates 13–17).[20] It is noticeable that only three are devoted to the Passion: the Betrayal, Crucifixion and Pietà, while the two preceding scenes, those of the Twelve-Year-Old Jesus in the Temple and the Wedding Feast at Cana are less often selected in such cycles and could have been replaced by Passion incidents such as the Flagel-lation and Crowning with Thorns, as at St Peter Mancroft in Norwich. The proba-ble reason for this is that the window was intended to focus on the Virgin, being in the Lady Chapel, and scenes depicting her were given preference.

Two other items in the manuscript that can be linked personally to her are *the Pardon of the Monastery of Shene which is Sion*, listing the indulgences available to those who visited Syon Abbey, and *The Lif of Sent Anne*.[21] Anne's connection with Bridgettine piety at Syon, where she was a lay sister, may be reflected in the iconography of the Nativity panel in her window, which is based on the vision of St Bridget of Sweden in which Mary kneels with hands raised in adoration before

[15] Jenkins, 'St Katherine and Laywomen's Piety', p. 165.
[16] The Prohemium is on f. 115r–v of BL, Harley MS 4012; it is transcribed in Jenkins, 'St Katherine and Laywomen's Piety', p. 168.
[17] Jenkins, 'St Katherine and Laywomen's Piety', p. 161.
[18] Jenkins, 'St Katherine and Laywomen's Piety', pp. 162–4.
[19] See below for the dating of the window.
[20] The iconography of the main lights can be reconstructed using the extant fourteen pan-els now in the east chancel window and the description in BL, MS Lansdowne 260, f. 184v. See the Appendix for the reconstruction.
[21] BL, MS Harley 4012, ff. 110–113 and 130v–139v.

the Infant Jesus, who emits rays of light (see Plate 16).[22] The related Mancroft window has a Nativity panel with the traditional iconography.[23] Hill has highlighted the importance of the cult of St Anne in Norfolk, and Anne Harling founded a chapel dedicated to her name saint at East Harling.[24] Thirteen of the female recipients of legacies in Anne's will of 1498 bore her name, three of them goddaughters, some of them no doubt named after their influential benefactor, who had particular reason to be devoted to St Anne because of her connections with late childbirth.[25] Her miraculous conception of the Virgin in old age would have been an obvious source of comfort and hope to Anne as the years passed without she herself conceiving. When Sir William Chamberlain died in 1462 she was 36 and it would have been in the 1460s that her concern and hopes would have been at their keenest, and the inclusion of a life of St Anne in the manuscript made for her at this time is not surprising.

Among the issues arising when assessing the ways in which such manuscripts were used are those of female literacy and frequency of use. Both can be addressed in this case by a close examination of the manuscript as a material object. Much of this manuscript is in fairly pristine condition, notably the first and longest item, *The clensing of man's soule*, but a few sections show signs of heavier use, the parchment having a softer feel, the pages being rather dirty and in some places the ink being worn and faded, presumably as a result of a finger being run repeatedly along the lines of text to follow it. These worn sections enable us to look over Anne's shoulder as she reads her favourite sections and give us valuable insights into her thoughts and feelings. We cannot know when this intensive use took place, but the indications are that it was by Anne herself and that at least the first of the passages I shall quote related to the period we have been discussing.

The most noticeable of these worn sections is in the Life of St Anne where Joachim, St Anne's husband, is told:

> For þey þat be wedded in true wedlok
> And solonge tyme and no child haue
> Þer shalbe a good child withouten lacke
> As many men be oþer childe or knaue.
> Þerfore Joachym I do þe to weten

---

[22]   This is not an exclusively Bridgettine depiction, however, as the Christ child still lies in a manger, and the midwives and Joseph are present. For the vision, see *The Liber Celestis of St Bridget of Sweden*, ed. R. Ellis, Early English Text Society, OS 291 (Oxford, 1987), pp. 485–7.

[23]   D. King, *The Medieval Stained Glass of St Peter Mancroft, Norwich*, Corpus Vitrearum Medii Aevi, Great Britain, vol. 5 (Oxford, 2006), p. 31.

[24]   C. Hill, *Incarnational Piety: Women and Religion in Late Medieval Norwich and its Hinterlands*, unpublished PhD thesis, University of East Anglia (2004), pp. 164–233; for the chapel of St Anne, see below.

[25]   See n. 9.

Þat þu shalle haue a childe within few dayes.
Trust my tale true þogh hit be not writen
For god þat is almyghte on þis wise saes.[26]

This removes, I think, any doubt that Anne could read. The book has her name in it and the finger following the text was surely hers.

Anne's forlorn identification with the promise to Joachim that 'Þere shalbe a good child withouten lacke' came to nothing, and three folios further on in the Life of St Anne another rubbed passage may point to the source of Anne Harling's later compensatory endowment of places for five children to attend services at Rushworth College, receive an education and be known as 'Dame Anny's childeryn'.[27] It comes at the point where Joachim and Anne have taken the Virgin to serve in the temple:

And faire of fface and fetowrs of goddes grace
Joachym and Anne left hir þer behinde
In þe forsaide tempill as þei made there awy
Þat she shulde serve god þat what tyme were
And so did she devotely and I shall tell you how
She and oþer childer that maide childrenne were
Were take to þe tempill unto a sertayne age
In þat place to abide and þere lawes to lere
And so be kepte in clennes from synne and outerache
Þer was þe right rule þat owre lady kepte
Ffor as a wise woman hir will was to wirke.[28]

It is easy to see how her thoughts might have moved from a contemplation of Anne and Joachim leaving Mary in the temple to be kept in cleanness from sin and outrage to her own endowment of Rushworth to send the five boys there to be educated in the ways of the Lord.

Dutton characterizes the overall nature of the texts in Harley 4012 as 'penitential', but they are not all purely of this kind, and some which are not are those which show signs of most use, which may have something to say about the nature of Anne's piety.[29] Apart from the Life of St Anne mentioned above, a text on the Creed is well-thumbed, the most worn section being the line of the Creed which reads: *Et in Ihesum Cristum filium eius unicum dominum nostrum.*[30] This

26   BL, Harley MS 4012, f. 133v. This passage is much less specific and therefore much more readily applicable in Anne's mind to herself than the equivalent passage in the Joachim and Anna episode in the N-Town Play; see *The N-Town Play*, Early English Text Society, SS 11, ed. S. Spector (Oxford, 1991), pp. 78–9). In this and the following extracts abbreviations have been silently expanded and upper case given to the initial letters of each line of verse.
27   Bennett, 'Rushworth College', p. 369.
28   BL, Harley MS 4012, f. 135.
29   Dutton, 'Piety, Politics and Persona', p. 137.
30   BL, Harley MS 4012, f. 84v.

underlines Anne's devotion to Jesus as son of God, resonating with her own wish to be a mother.

Another much read section contains the poem and prayer on the Passion, the latter accompanied by an indulgence, and therefore presumably copied. The first is known only in this manuscript.[31] Here is the stanza on the Crucifixion:

> The blod from thy hert fast gan ran downe
> Þi side was launsid with longis spere
> On þi hed an vnniytly crowne
> For suche a kyng right semple to were
> Many of thy foes forsothe were ther
> And kried full faste crucifige
> All was in þe disspite of the[32]

This poem is markedly inferior to that which follows. It starts with a prayer to Jesus, moves on to invoke and describe the Crucifixion, then suddenly changes to a more chronological account of the Passion, beginning with the judgement of Pilate followed by the scourging and then a non-canonical episode in which Jesus is kept overnight in a 'vaute of stone' where he suffered from the cold and which caused great sorrow to the Virgin and St John.[33] This would seem to be inspired by the image of Christ on the cold stone, an invention of North European medieval piety. Dürer's later version of this image has Christ sitting in a space which could be termed a 'vault', but normally this image occurs outside, and does not suggest that Christ was kept overnight in prison. It is, however, the kind of imaginative extension to the Passion story which resulted from empathic meditation on Christ's sufferings.[34] The poem is written in seven-line stanzas of rime royal, but with no attempt at pentameters or any kind of metrical regularity. The stanza immediately after this incident begins with an extra-metrical additional line and describes Jesus being brought out into the street and being bound hand and foot.[35] The non-biblical prophesy of the Sybil comes next, followed by Jesus being brought out of prison and set on the road to Calvary, where he meets Veronica, another legendary

---

[31] BL, Harley MS 4012, ff. 106–9.

[32] BL, Harley MS 4012, f. 106.

[33] 'Then broughte thei þe in to a vaute of stone | And ther all nyght þu didist suffer colde | Þi moder and Iohn for þe made gret mone | Which sorrow of no tong kanne be tolde.' BL, Harley MS 4012, f. 106v. See C. Brown and R. H. Robbins, *The Index of Middle English Verse* (New York, 1943), 1779; for an edition, see E. Wilson, *Notes and Queries*, 202 (1977), pp. 485–7. Wilson agrees this poem is inferior to the second one, but sees it as 'not without literary merit'.

[34] For the image of Christ on the cold stone, see G. Finaldi's catalogue entry in G. Finaldi et al., The *Image of Christ* (London, 2000), pp. 120–21. I am grateful to Carole Rawcliffe for help with this point. For the Dürer, see A. Smith and A. O. della Chiesa, *The Complete Paintings of Dürer* (London, 1971), p. 95. Here it is confusingly called 'Christ in the Sepulchre with the Symbols of His Passion'.

[35] BL Harley MS 4012, the last line of f. 105v.

incident. The lack of faith of St Peter and the other apostles is contrasted with Mary's steadfastness and the Crucifixion ensues, the poem finishing with a prayer for a good death. The whole is addressed to Jesus in the second person. It was clearly not written by an ecclesiastic or scholar, but by a lay person with a rather muddled recall of the Passion narrative and a less than perfect grasp of Middle English metrics and Latin.[36] This suggests the possibility at least that Anne Harling, or perhaps one of her friends, was the author, an idea consistent with the fact that the poem appears in this manuscript only.[37]

Whereas the first poem was addressed by the poet on behalf of 'us sinners' to Jesus, the second one is in the voice of Jesus speaking to a brother.[38] The poem again invites empathic identification with the suffering Christ:

> Of sharpe thorne I haue worne a crowne on my head
> So rubbid so bobbid so rufulle sored
> Sore payned sore strayned and for þi loue ded
> Unfayned not demed my blod for þe shed
> My fete and handis sore
> with sturde naylis bore
> What myght I suffer more
> Þen I haue sufferde man for þe
> Com when þu wilt and welcome to me[39]

Both of these well-fingered texts are examples of the kind of aids to affective piety involving a projection of feelings onto the person of the Christ of the Passion which are a feature of late medieval popular religion.

A final quotation from Anne's favourite reading as evinced by the condition of her manuscript comes from near the beginning of the prose Life of St Katherine:

> This quene Kateren was then of the age of XVIIJ yere abiding in here pales whiche was was [sic] well emparelid with riches and enhabite with seruantis and as she sate musing in hir stode and contemplacion of hir moste dere lorde and truee spouse she harde an huge noise of instrumentis and song and kryng of bestis. Wondering gretly what hit myght be and callid a messauntger unto hir commaunding hym toe bringe the sartaynete what hit ment or shulde mene. Hoo in haste kamme agayne and sartefide the trauthe and deuysid & informed hir of the truthe and all the maner of giding. And when she understode the informacon of the truthe she pensiued and sorowid gretly for the dishower donne to or saueower and very spouse who was supplanted be idolatrye which she myght not endure to suffer.[40]

---

36 Christ's word on the cross 'sitio' is spelled 'cicio' in verse 2, which suggests an aural comprehension of the word. I am grateful to Carole Rawcliffe for help with this point. The word 'crucifige' in verses 3 and 5 is correctly spelled.

37 *IMEV* 1779. More work needs to be done on the language of this poem to attempt to ascertain its dialectal location.

38 BL, Harley MS 4012, ff. 109–109v.

39 BL, Harley MS 4012, f. 109v.

40 BL, Harley MS 4012, f. 116.

Why this passage should have been much read by Anne is harder to say. One possible reading is that it resonates with a period or periods in her life when her desire for quiet 'contemplacion of hir moste dere lorde' was disturbed by the noise and clamour of daily life. She may have been thinking of life at East Harling. Perhaps more probable is that Anne's concentration on this passage dates from a later time in the 1470s when, as seems likely, she was at court with her husband. Life in the entourage of Edward IV would have provided fewer opportunities for private piety and prayer than when she was at home.

If the Harley manuscript reveals Anne to us in her most intimate and personal moments, her church reveals a more public face, but still one in which her own preoccupations are still visible. Today this is most clearly seen in the window made for the Harling chantry, reconstructed from glass now in the east chancel window and an antiquarian source and made almost certainly in the 1460s.[41] The bottom row depicted in the two centre lights the Annunciation and Visitation (Plates 14–15), including the clearly pregnant St Elizabeth in her maternity gown (depicted a second time at East Harling in a fragment from another window). These scenes were placed between donor panels with Anne and Sir William on the left and her parents on the right.[42] Thus each time she raised her eyes at mass in the family chantry chapel she would have seen images of pregnancy, of herself, and of her family, and in the second row, scenes from the Infancy of Christ (Plates 16–17). The Passion scenes above that we have discussed may have formed part of the same private devotional practice. There was a belief that the Virgin Mary did not experience the pangs of childbirth until she witnessed her son's death on the cross, and it may be that Anne's identification with Mary's painful contemplation of the Passion was linked in her mind with a desire to feel the pains of childbirth.[43]

---

[41] C. Woodforde, *The Norwich School of Glass-Painting in the Fifteenth Century* (London, 1950), pp. 42–55 described the panels in their present position in the east chancel window. The glass was removed from the church almost certainly by the recusant Lovell family, who bought the manor and advowson in the early sixteenth century. It was found in the eighteenth century in the hall and restored to the church, being placed in the east window. For the Lovells, see G. L. Harrison, 'A Few Notes on the Lovells of East Harling', *Norfolk Archaeology*, 18 (1914), 46–77, and D. J. King, 'Who was Holbein's Lady with a Squirrel and a Starling?', *Apollo*, 159, new series (May 2004), pp. 42–9. For the glass at East Harling, see also D. J. King, *The Medieval Stained Glass of St Peter Mancroft, Norwich*, Corpus Vitrearum Medii Aevi Great Britain, vol. 55 (Oxford, 2006), pp. cxlviii–cli; CVMA catalogue entry for East Harling at www.cvma.ac.uk (Publications/Digital Publications).

[42] The donor panels were recorded in this window in an antiquarian manuscript of c. 1575 (BL, Lansdowne MS 260, f. 184v). Another antiquarian drew a sketch of the figures of Sir Robert Harling and Joan Gonville, Anne's parents, kneeling facing to the left (Norfolk Record Office, MS DS. 594 [352 x 3]).

[43] C. Hill, *Incarnational Piety*, p. 197.

The design of the Harling chantry chapel window also contains elements that work together to add an entirely different dimension to the discussion of Anne Harling's life. To make this clear we first need to recall an historical event. On February 2nd 1461, Candlemas, or the Feast of the Purification of the Virgin Mary, Edward, Earl of March, soon to be Edward IV, was with his army drawn up on the plain of Wigmore, west of Mortimer's Cross in Herefordshire. About ten o'clock on a cold and frosty morning, there appeared to Edward and his men a meteorological phenomenon called parhelia, whereby three suns, low in the sky, are seen. Edward seized the moment and exhorted his men to victory in honour of the Trinity, and on that day or the next defeated the Lancastrian forces in the battle of Mortimer's Cross.[44]

In the reconstructed East Harling window, each of the first three scenes of the second row has in the same position at the top centre of the panel the star of Bethlehem (Plate 15). This triple star/sun arrangement is suggestive, but on its own not sufficient to indicate a hidden reference in the glass to the Yorkist victory. However, the next panel depicts the Presentation of Christ, celebrated at Candlemas on 2 February, the date of the parhelia sighting, and as a clinching detail, Simeon has on his cope a Yorkist rose (Plate 17). As with other cases of hidden propaganda there is some disguise, as the star of Bethlehem is not the sun and the rose is painted with yellow stain, but the combination is unmistakeable. Hughes has demonstrated adequately, if rather over-enthusiastically, the lasting use made by Edward and his followers of the symbolism of the suns.[45]

In hindsight, it is not surprising that such an allusion should be present in Anne's window. The recent granting of the Order of the Garter to Sir William Chamberlain by Edward is but one indication of where the family's sympathies lay at this time.[46] The entourage of the recently deceased Sir John Fastolf, which continued to have dealings with Anne long after she ceased being his ward, was closely associated with that group of intellectuals including astrologers, alchemists and antiquarians which, as Hughes has shown, played a crucial role in promoting Edward IV as the chosen answer to the country's problems, and William Worcester was prominent in this.[47] He visited East Harling to help with Sir Robert Har-

---

[44] C. Ross, *Edward IV* (London, 1983), pp. 31–2; J. Hughes, *Arthurian Myths and Alchemy: The Kingship of Edward IV* (Thrupp, 2002), pp. 81–3.

[45] Hughes, *Arthurian Myths and Alchemy*, pp. 81–5, 88–95. For similar instances of political propaganda in Norfolk glass, see D. King, 'Reading the Material Cultures: Stained Glass and Politics in Late Medieval Norfolk', *The Fifteenth Century, VIII: Rule, Redemption and Representations in Late Medieval England and France*, ed. L. Clark (Woodbridge, 2008), 105–34.

[46] Dutton, *Piety, Politics and Persona*, p. 134.

[47] Hughes, *Arthurian Myths and Alchemy*, pp. 33–46, 238–63. Hughes mentions Worcester in connection with the attempts during the latter part of Henry VI's reign to persuade the king to adopt a more aggressive policy in France, and with the promotion of

ling's tomb in 1460 and might easily have extended his interest in Harling chapel for a few years and been involved in the devising of the window next to it.[48] It may be of significance here that the scribe who wrote Anne's manuscript appears to have worked on others for Sir John Fastolf.[49] She owned a copy of Christine de Pisan's *Epistre D'Othea*, which although described as a French book in her will could have been the translation made by Stephen Scrope, Fastolf's stepson, in 1440.[50] Anne's grandmother was a Mortimer, linked not by blood to the Mortimer's of Wigmore Castle, but by a common manorial allegiance to the earls Warenne.[51] Edward put great emphasis on his royal descent through the female line via Anne Mortimer, and is said, like Anne Harling, to have had a devotion to St Anne.[52] Moreover, her relative Sir John Ratcliff was killed at the battle of Towton.[53]

If her window establishes a Yorkist proclivity at a time probably preceding her marriage to Sir Robert Wingfield, a document produced during this marriage suggests that this continued for many years. This is hardly surprising in view of Sir Robert's royal service, but may also serve to support Dutton's surmise that she perhaps served at court. Part of a will made by her was enrolled in the online CR. It

---

Roman imperial ideals which characterised the second part of Edward IV's reign, but he would undoubtedly have been in sympathy with the successful and vigorous efforts of Edward in the early 1460s to establish his kingship.

[48] C. Richmond, *The Paston Family in the Fifteenth Century; Fastolf's Will* (Cambridge, 1996), p. 74. Worcester had already acted in connection with Sir Robert Harling, when he went to Normandy c. 1440 to gather evidence for a lawsuit arising from the death of Sir Robert at the siege of St Denis in 1435. K. B. McFarlane, *England in the Fifteenth Century* (London, 1981), p. 203.

[49] Dutton, *Piety, Politics and Persona*, pp. 135–6; O. Pächt and J. J. G. Alexander, *Illuminated Manuscripts in the Bodleian Library*, I (Oxford, 1966), pp. 53–5, 57; E. Wilson, 'A Middle English Manuscript at Coughton Court, Warwickshire, and British Library MS Harley 4012', *Notes and Queries*, 202 (1977), pp. 295–303. Dutton cites Pächt and Alexander's attributions of manuscripts, but confuses the illuminator called 'the Master of Sir John Fastolf' with the unknown scribe who wrote some, but not all of the texts referred to. The manuscripts written by a hand similar to that of Harley 4012 and mentioned by Dutton should be limited to Oxford, Bodleian Library, Laud Misc. 570 (Christine de Pisan, *Livre des quatre vertus* and *Epître d'Othéa*), Ashmole 764 (heraldic manuscript) and Oxford, University College, MS 85. To these Wilson adds the Grant of Arms to the Company of Tallow Chandlers in London, 24 September, 1456, and three of the Paston Letters, written by a scribe of Sir John Fastolf at Caister in 1455–6.

[50] PRO, PROB 11/11. For Scrope's translation, see *The Epistle of Othea, Translated from the French Text of Christine de Pisan by Stephen Scrope*, C. F. Bühler, EETS o.s. (Oxford, 1970).

[51] *Complete peerage of England, Scotland, Ireland, Great Britain and the United Kingdom, extant, extinct or dormant*, ed. G. E. Cokayne, H. Doubleday and H. de Walden, vol. 9 (London, 1936), p. 243.

[52] Hughes, *Arthurian Myths and Alchemy*, pp. 118, 122–3, 137.

[53] Ross, *Edward IV*, pp. 36–7.

concerns her wish that her husband Robert should have some of her property, with power to sell the reversion to perform her will and carry out deeds of alms for her soul and those of their parents and her first husband, by the assent of nineteen friends, which are listed.[54] An analysis of these 'friends' gives an invaluable insight into her social status and connections at this time. There is not space to deal with them all. They consist of relatives, churchmen, lawyers and landowners, typical of the type of advisors a wealthy lady might use for her business affairs, but some of them may throw light on whether Anne attended the Yorkist court. The first mentioned was William Dudley, bishop of Durham.[55] He had earlier held various royal appointments, including Dean of the Chapel Royal from 1470 to 1476, Chancellor to Queen Elizabeth from 1471 to 1474 and Dean of St George's, Windsor in 1473. Another prominent churchman on the list was John Morton, the future cardinal and archbishop, and at that time Master of the Rolls and Archdeacon of Norfolk.[56] The Archdeacon of Suffolk, William Pikenham, also appeared. He was later to become the Master of the college at Stoke-by-Clare, which had strong Yorkist links.[57] Another friend, William Felde, is designated as 'chantour' of Fotheringhay, the Yorkist college of priests in Northamptonshire where Edward IV's mother, Cecily, Duchess of York, had lived for several years. In 1495 he became master there, and was given a bequest in Anne's final will in 1498.[58] In Cecily's will of 1495, she leaves bequests for Fotheringhay and Stoke-by-Clare colleges, and her executors include William Pikenham, William Field and Thomas Lovell, Esq.[59] The Lovells of Barton Bendish in Norfolk were connected to Anne Harling, appeared in her will and eventually acquired the manor and advowson of East Harling after her death.[60]

[54] *Calendar of Close Rolls, Edward IV, Edward V, Richard III, 1476–1485*, pp. 137–9. Those listed are: William Dudley, bishop of Durham; John Wyngefeld, knight; John Henyngham (Heveningham), knight; Henry Grey, knight; John Morton, Master of the Rolls, archdeacon of Norfolk; William Pikenham, archdeacon of Suffolk; Ralph, prior of Penteney; John Heydon; Edmund Bokenham; Henry Spelman; Roger Tounesende; William Bardewelle; James Hoberd; Henry Costesey, master of Russheworth; William Felde, chantour of Fodrynghey; John Bulman; Thomas Chamberlayne; Simon Blake; John Aylward, parson of Estharlyng.

[55] *Oxford DNB*, vol. 17 (Oxford, 2004), pp. 118–19.

[56] *Oxford DNB*, vol. 39 (Oxford, 2004), pp. 421–5.

[57] A. B. Emden, *A Biographical Register of the University of Cambridge to 1500* (Cambridge, 1963), pp. 464–65.

[58] Emden, *Biographical Register*, p. 223. In her will she says: 'Item I wyll and bequeath to William Feld maister of Fotheringay for a Remembrance my little Candilstik of silver with a steele to pray for my husbands and me. And to kepe a solempne dirige & a masse for them & me and xxs to sett up my husbands armys & myn departed in a wyndowe', PRO, PROB 11/11.   [59] PRO, PROB 11/10.

[60] G. L. Harrison, 'A Few Notes on the Lovells of East Harling', *Norfolk Archaeology*, 18 (1914), pp. 46–77; D. J. King, 'Who was Holbein's Lady with a Squirrel and a Starling?', *Apollo*, 159 (May 2004), pp. 42–9.

Anne's participation in court life remains probable but unproven. Her contributions as patron of East Harling church, however, are much more firmly established and have already been alluded to. Some of them can be discerned from the present fabric of the building and others are recoverable from antiquarian sources, most notably from a seventeenth-century copy of a damaged medieval bede roll which records albeit imperfectly what she had done. There are some later additions to the roll, but the part relating to her can be dated to between her death in 1498 and that of Sir Thomas Lovell in 1524. After an introduction there follows a request for prayers for John, Lord Scrope (her third husband) and Lady Anne, Lady Scrope, 'which good Lady did edify the body of this new church … from the first foundation in the earth … and bore at her own charge all manner of costs for stuff, masonry … and workmanship'. She also rebuilt the walls of both aisles and made a new r… [perhaps the roof of the Harling Chapel], 'right substantially and well, costeously framed and embowed'. She provided the masonry and glazing for the windows on the south side and built the battlements on the steeple and the lantern. Next, the provision of various vestments is recorded, including two sets of blue velvet with images and one of white chamelet, and others of crimson and black velvet. Finally, mention is made of her edifying the Chapel of St Anne, 'where her body is interred'.[61]

The bede roll indicates a fairly thorough rebuilding of the church by her, involving the completion of the tower, finished in 1449, according to Blomefield, and the reconstruction of the nave and aisles with the addition of the Chapel of St Anne on the north side of the chancel.[62] As the text is defective, it is possible that other parts of the building were involved, including the clerestory (already implied), and the east chancel window, both of which can be shown to have been glazed by her. The south-east chancel window was also made in the fifteenth century and was almost certainly provided by her as patron. The rood screen to the chancel was her gift, as the heraldry on the surviving panels demonstrates. The only evidence we have for the south porch, which was built in a later campaign from that of the south aisle, is the statement in the bede roll that it was finished by Sir Thomas Lovell, who died in 1524, thus leaving open the possibility that it was started by Anne. Some of these works would have been done in the name of one of her three husbands, but the facts that the patronage of the church and the ownership of the many manors which provided the wealth for the rebuilding came from her inheritance and that East Harling was her home town makes it reasonable to attribute the patronage to her, and this is the import of the bede roll.

Reference has already been made to the Harling Chapel and its east window. It is evident from the fabric of the south aisle that the whole aisle was conceived

---

[61]   Norfolk Record Office, MS D.S. 594 (352 x 3). The copy of the bede roll accompanies some notes on the church dated 1667 and in the same hand.

[62]   Blomefield, *History*, vol. 1, p. 326.

as part of the chapel, which was also the Lady Chapel, with the first two bays seen as the 'chancel' enclosed by the screen and the three western bays acting as the 'nave' (Plate 18). This unity is indicated by a hitherto little considered part, the roof. This has in its spandrels a series of carved badges and heraldic shields, some removed, of outstanding quality which are all connected with the families of Anne Harling and her first husband. and which may provide some indication of the time-scale involved in the rebuilding of the aisle. A Mortimer fleurs-de-lys is seen; unicorns, baskets and an apron can be linked to the arms and badges of the Harlings, and a quiver with feathers and shield in a garter to Sir William Chamberlain, giving a broad date range of 1438 to 1462, during which time Anne was married to him.[63] This may be refined by the carved bulls in bays one and three (Plate 19), which may refer to Walter Lyhert, bishop of Norwich from 1446 to 1472, whose arms were *argent a bull passant sable within a bordure of the second bezanty*, and the garbs placed in front of the bulls, which could be for Cardinal John Kempe, in his capacity as archbishop of Canterbury, which position he held from 1452 until his death in 1454, thus possibly indicating that the roof of the aisle was being constructed at this time.[64] Kempe's arms were *gules three garbs within a border engrailed or*.[65] On June 29th 1457 a grant was made, with the permission of Bishop Lyhert, by Sir William Chamberlain and his wife Anne, appointing John Cavendyssh to serve as the first chantry priest and endowing a salary for him.[66] Presumably this meant that the building was roofed and sufficiently complete for masses to begin in the chantry.

By 1460, the construction was probably finished and its furnishing underway, as is shown by a reference in that year to William Worcester riding to East Harling with a Norwich marbeler 'to see about the making of the tomb for Sir Robert Harling'.[67] Sir Robert was related to Sir John Fastolf, William Worcester's late employer. Worcester had travelled to France after the death of Sir Robert Harling to help with a legal suit in connection with his death.[68] The tomb is still to be seen at the east end of the south aisle (Plate 20), and presents particular problems of interpretation in its present state. It takes the form of a tomb chest set in a canopied niche. A brass inscription on a fillet round the top edge of the chest

---

[63] Woodforde briefly mentions the baskets and quivers of feathers carved on the roof, but not the other motifs. Woodforde, *The Norwich School*, p. 54. For the marriage dates, see Dutton, 'Piety, Politics and Persona', p. 134.

[64] For Lyhert's arms see *Dictionary of British Arms: Medieval Ordinary*, vol. 1, eds H. Chesshyre and T. Woodcock (London, 1992), p. 247.

[65] For Kempe's arms, see J. W. Papworth and A. W. Morant, *An Alphabetical Dictionary of Coats of Arms* (London, 1874), p. 897.

[66] Norfolk Record Office, MS 20101 (38C3).

[67] See note 45. For Norwich marbelers at this time, see R. Greenwood and M. Norris, *The Brasses of Norfolk Churches* (Woodbridge, 1976), pp. 22–4.

[68] See n. 44.

informs us of Sir Robert's death in Paris and his burial in the tomb.[69] Two alabaster effigies of a man in armour and a lady are now placed on the tomb, and have been there since at least sometime between 1570 and 1580, but they lie awkwardly together and do not belong on the chest, the man's armour and the lady's dress dating them to the late fourteenth century.[70] The male figure can be identified as Sir John Harling, father of Sir Robert, buried here c. 1392.[71] The tomb canopy was probably made originally for him and the effigy moved elsewhere c. 1460 when Sir Robert's tomb was placed there. It may have been placed in the chancel, perhaps next to the east wall to the right or left, and then moved back to the Harling chapel when these positions were used for the Lovell tombs now seen there in the 1560s.[72]

The east window of the Harling Chantry can be dated to after 2 February, 1461, as discussed above. The two donor panels recorded in the window depicted Sir Robert Harling and Joan Gonville, Anne's parents, and Sir William Chamberlain and Anne herself.[73] As Sir William died in 1462, it is probable that the window commemorated him as well as Anne's parents. The glass was painted by the John Wighton workshop which also made several windows for the church of St Peter Mancroft in Norwich. This was the leading parish church in Norwich and the donors of its windows were of high status, including Robert Toppes, the richest merchant in the city. John Wighton was one of two Norwich glaziers who became an alderman and the work of his atelier can be seen in many Norfolk churches. He was dead when the East Harling window was made and one of his former apprentices, John Mundeford, appears to have taken over the business and may have painted this window.[74] That Anne should have chosen the leading Norwich workshop to paint her window is not surprising in view of her own status as a wealthy heiress and wife of a Knight of the Garter.

Sir William Chamberlain lies buried with Anne in the tomb which separates the chapel built by Anne dedicated to her name saint and the chancel (Plate 21). In her

---

[69] BL, MS Lansdowne 260, f. 184v; N. Pevsner and B. Wilson, *The Buildings of England. Norfolk 2: North-West and South* (London, 1999), p. 320.

[70] BL, MS Lansdowne 260, f. 184v.

[71] He has the Harling unicorn on his breast, and the date of the armour is compatible.

[72] The date of the tomb canopy needs further consideration. It has an ogee arch at the top and sub-cusping within the arch, both compatible with a date in the second half of the fourteenth century. The parclose screen in the eastern bay of the chapel is earlier than the main screen facing west and appears to be of late-fourteenth-century date, judging by the tracery pattern. For the Lovell tombs, see BL, MS Lansdowne 260, f. 184; Pevsner and Wilson (1999), p. 320 and King, 'Who was Holbein's Lady with a Squirrel and a Starling?', p. 45.

[73] They are both described in BL, MS Lansdowne 260, f. 184v and there is a pen and ink drawing of Sir Robert and Joan in an unfoliated manuscript dated 1667, Norfolk Record Office, MS DS. 594 (352 x 3).

[74] For the Mancroft glass, donors and glaziers, see King, *St Peter Mancroft,* especially the Introduction to the Toppes Window and Appendix I, pp. clxix–cxcvii, 137–9.

will of 1498, Anne asks to be buried there according to the promise which she had made to Sir William.[75] The brasses of Anne and William which were originally fastened to the upper surface of the altar tomb have been lost, but the indents of their figures, mottoes, badges and shields are visible.[76] At the top of the canopy on the chancel side is the heraldic achievement of Sir William; that of Anne is in the same position within the chapel, where on the east side of the altar (liturgically, the north) there is a niche which would have held the dedicatory statue of St Anne. A north window of four lights illuminates the chapel, and this was glazed with donor figures of herself, twice, with each of her first two husbands, dating the glass and perhaps the completion of the chapel to after her marriage to Sir Robert Wingfield in 1467 or thereabouts. Three of the figures, of which those of the two husbands are extant in the east chancel window, bore invocations to the persons of the Holy Trinity, and the fourth to the Trinity as a whole.[77] Such tombs were rare in Norfolk in the fifteenth-century, and Anne may have been inspired by the most grandiose example, the Morley tomb at Hingham, completed in 1462, the year Sir William died. There, figures kneel in blank arcading resembling a window at the back of the altar tomb.[78] At Harling, the kneeling figures beyond the tomb, as viewed from the chancel, are placed in an actual window as stained glass. Opposite the chapel, on the south side of the chancel, is the only fourteenth-century window to survive the rebuilding. One possible reason for this is that Anne's original plan was to rebuild and glaze it with a Life of St Anne to complement her chapel on the north

[75]   '… and my body to be buryed in the Chapell of seint Anne joined to the Channcell of the Churche of the holy appostellys of seint Peter and Paule in Estharlyng in the tombe w(i)t(h) my late worshypfull husband Sir Will(ia)m Chamberleyn according to my promise made unto hym afore this tyme.' PRO, PROB 11/11.

[76]   For the tomb, see W. B. Slegg, 'The Chamberlain Tomb at East Harling, Norfolk,' *Transactions of the Monumental Brass Society*, vii (1934–42), pp. 126–9.

[77]   The window can be located in the St Anne Chapel and reconstructed from the evidence of the two extant panels and of the antiquarian record. In the first light was a kneeling figure of Anne facing to the right with 'Orate pro bono statu et vita Anne uxoris' beneath, and 'Pater de celis deus Miserere nobis' on a scroll over her head; in the second, Sir Robert Wingfield facing to the right, with 'Roberti Wingefeld militis ac' below, and 'fili redemptor mundi deus Miserere nobis' above; in the third, Sir William Chamberlain, facing left, with 'Willielmi Chamberleyn militis' below, and ' Spiritus sancta dei miserere nobis' above, and in the fourth light, Anne, facing left, with 'Sancta Trinitas unus deus Miserere nobis' above. See BL, Lansdowne MS 260, f. 184v, Blomefield, *History*, vol. 1, engraving between pp. 326 and 327, and BL, Additional MS 17462, *Powell's Topographical Collections*, f. 215. Anne's Yorkist sympathies (and those of her husband) may be reflected in the choice of the Trinity texts for this window. After the battle of Mortimer's Cross and the triple-sun parhelia sighting, Edward IV often invoked the Trinity in support of his campaigns. See Hughes, *Arthurian Myths and Alchemy*, pp. 89, 90, 100, 150, 214, 231.

[78]   R. Fawcett, 'St Mary at Wiveton in Norfolk, and a Group of Churches Attributed to its Mason', *The Antiquaries Journal*, 72 (1982), 51–3 and pl. XI.

side of the nave, and to extend back in the time the narrative of the adjacent east window of the Harling Chantry dedicated to the Virgin Mary with a cycle which would have included scenes of the birth and childhood of the Virgin. Anne may have planned such a window as a thanksgiving for a (late-born) child; since no such child was born, the window was never made.

The clerestory, which now has the remains of angels in some of the tracery lights on the north side, had an extensive display of family heraldry relating to Anne and her first two husbands. This probably dates to c.1467–90, but further work is needed to make this more precise. It is possible that some shields were added later.[79]

Anne married for the third time, imitating her name saint, in 1491, once again moving up the social hierarchy, this time to a lord, John 5th Lord Scrope of Bolton, K.G.[80] It was after this marriage that the east chancel window at East Harling was glazed. At the base of the window were five panels of donor figures of knights and their ladies. They were Anne's parents and Anne herself with each of her three husbands, and Sir John Ratcliff, K.G with his wife, Cecily Mortimer, Anne's grandparents.[81] Radcliff's direct descendant, John Ratcliff, Lord Fitzwalter, was attainted for treason in 1495 and later executed.[82] We do not know for certain what Anne's attitude to Henry VII was; a legacy in her will of 1498 may throw some light on where her inclinations lay.[83] She leaves to 'my lorde of Suff. my godsone' a piece of jewellery and 'a primer whiche kynge Edward gauffe me'.[84] Edmund de la Pole, at that time Earl of Suffolk, had been since the death of his elder brother, John de la Pole, Earl of Lincoln, in 1487, the leading Yorkist claimant to the throne. He had remained loyal to the Tudor Henry VII after his accession in 1485, but found his position increasingly intolerable. In the year following Anne's death he fled to Picardy and was eventually executed in 1513 after returning to England. Thus the choice of an object given to Anne by Edward IV as a legacy to the Yorkist claimant, who was a relative and a godson (Edmund's wife was a Scrope), at a time of tension between him and Henry VII, suggests that a political point as well as a gift was

---

[79] On the south side the heraldry focuses mainly on Wingfield alliances, with those of Chamberlain on the north. Each side began at the east end with donor figures of Anne and her husband either side of a shield. See BL, Lansdowne MS 260, f. 185r–v; Norfolk Record Office, MS DS. 594 (352 × 3).

[80] *Oxford DNB*, vol. 49, pp. 557–9.

[81] BL, Lansdowne MS 260, f. 183v. Interestingly, the sixteenth-century antiquarian made some attempt to characterize the figures, which he calls 'statewes'. Sir Robert Harling is 'smoth fased'; Sir William Chamberlain has 'long gray hare'; Lord Scrope is 'young & smoth fased', and Sir Robert Wingfield is 'ould & bar(de)d'.

[82] *Oxford DNB*, vol. 46, pp. 87–8.

[83] Henry VII is recorded as planning to stay with her en route to Norwich in 1489. See J. Gairdner (ed.), *The Paston Letters* (Gloucester, 1986), vol. 6, p. 121.

[84] PRO, PROB 11/11.

being made. The inclusion of the earlier Ratcliff in the East Harling glass may have occurred at the time of his successor's rupture with the king and could also have been intended as support by Anne for her troubled cousin, but, in view of Fitzwalter's rather unpleasant character, may instead have been to remind viewers of her more heroic step-grandfather, killed fighting on the Yorkist side at the battle of Towton.[85]

Some fragments now in the east chancel window including texts from the *Te Deum* can be assigned to this work on the grounds of style, date and iconography (Plate 22). Representations of the *Te Deum* at this time were in effect complex depictions of the Holy Trinity, a very suitable subject for the east window of the chancel. The text of the *Te Deum*, as well as invoking the name of the Holy Trinity, also mentions angels and martyrs, and fragments of both are found together with the *Te Deum* inscriptions.[86]

In 1503, five years after Anne's death, John Aylward, parson of East Harling since 1474, died. In his will, as Roger Greenwood has shown, he asked for a marble stone and brass to be ordered from William Heyward of Norwich.[87] Heyward was the leading glazier in Norwich at this time, having become a freeman of the city in 1485 and later becoming the only other Norwich glazier apart from John Wighton to be made an alderman. Evidence from his will makes clear his dual role as producer of both glass and brasses. Greenwood proposed that Heyward was responsible for the N3 series of brasses, which correspond in date range to his career (he died in 1506), and that there were strong stylistic links with the glass at Mancroft and the similar glass at East Harling.[88] This glass, however, is too early for a link with Heyward, and is now attributed to the Wighton workshop. However, the above-mentioned panel of fragments is here tentatively attributed to the Heyward workshop, the first glass it has been possible to identify as being perhaps by

---

85   *Oxford DNB*, vol. 46, p. 87.

86   Woodforde, *The Norwich School*, pp. 49–51. See also P. Sheingorn, 'The *Te Deum* Altarpiece and the Iconography of Praise', *Early Tudor England: The Proceedings of the 1987 Harlaxton Symposium*, ed. D. Williams (Woodbridge, 1989), 171–82. The central place of the Trinity in representations of the *Te Deum* suggests that Anne's choice of iconography may have been influenced by her Yorkist background. Before Edward IV went to the Palace of Westminster on March 4th, 1461, to take the oath of accession, he heard the *Te Deum* sung in St Paul's Cathedral. Ross, *Edward IV*, p. 34. The west window of the church of Yorkist dynastic mausoleum at Fotheringhay contained a large representation of the *Te Deum*. R. Marks, 'The Glazing of Fotheringhay Church and College', *Journal of the British Archaeological Association*, 131 (1978), 79–109.

87   R. Greenwood and M. Norris, *The Brasses of Norfolk Churches* (Woodbridge, 1976), pp. 28–30. See also D. King, 'A Multi-Media Workshop in Late Medieval Norwich: a New Look at William Heyward', *Lumières, formes et couleurs: Mélanges en hommage à Yvette Vanden Bemden*, ed. C. De Ruyt et al. (Namur, 2008), 193–204.

88   Greenwood and Norris, *Brasses*, p. 30.

him. There are style connections with N3 brasses. The clearest example is with the brass of William de Grey and family at Merton of 1495, very close in date to the glass (Plate 23). The slightly later patronage of Heyward by the parson of East Harling is another piece of circumstantial evidence pointing to the identity of the glazier, and it may be significant that another N3 brass, that of Henry Spelman and wife at Narborough, 1496, portrays a close friend of Anne Harling and a third of 1499 at Ketteringham depicts Thomas Heveningham, Esq., the son of Sir John Heveningham, one of the nineteen friends of Anne mentioned in her 1479 will.[89] As in the case of the earlier glass from the east window of the Harling Chantry, Anne again chose the leading Norwich glazier of the time to carry out her work.

She had earlier glazed other windows in the church with figures and heraldry of her family, and her will leaves many legacies for the provision of glass and liturgical items bearing her arms and those of her husbands.[90] Although her childlessness haunted her until late in her life, as the endowment of Dame Anne's children at Rushworth in 1490 attests, it would appear that she compensated for this lack by adopting a policy of conspicuous display to memorialise the members of her wider family, and also by the breadth of her social connections, as demonstrated by both her extant wills.[91] One hopes that in later life she achieved the spiritual comfort which she obviously sought.

---

[89] For the Henry Spelman and Thomas Heveningham brasses , see Greenwood and Norris, *Brasses*, pp. 29, 49. The de Greys and Heveninghams were related at this period, although there is some confusion as to the details; see Blomefield, *History*, vol. 5, pp. 91–3. A document of 1474 assigning property to Rushworth College mentions Sir Robert Wingfield and Anne his wife, Henry Spelman, Sir John Heveningham and Laurence Gerard, the previous rector of East Harling; see Bennett, 'Rushworth College', p. 365.

[90] Thirty-six such legacies were left to seventeen churches, two chapels and seventeen colleges, friaries and monastic institutions. PRO, PROB 11/11.

[91] In her 1498 will she leaves legacies to over 150 individuals from a wide range of social strata ranging from villagers to nobles. A detailed analysis of the interconnections between these figures would throw much more light on Anne's affinities. PRO, PROB 11/11.

Ordinary Lives: Medieval Personal Seal Matrices

RICHARD A. LINENTHAL

Let me begin with a very brief autobiographical record which will explain my choice of topics. I am an antiquarian bookseller and have been for the past twenty-seven years. As a bookseller one must respond to the market – what is available to buy and sell – and it is in this way that I first became acquainted with medieval seals, the sort to be found in wax hanging from medieval documents, and more specifically the engraved metal dies or matrices which were used to make wax seals. For as long as Bernard Quaritch Ltd has been in business – now more than one hundred and fifty years – it has bought and sold medieval documents as part of its business in the broader field of medieval manuscripts. In many cases the documents have wax seals attached, in other cases they are missing. We also encounter medieval documents in huge quantities as part of our activity in advising buyers and sellers of whole archives which might stretch in time from the middle ages to the present day. Seal matrices, on the other hand, whether they be made of brass, lead, silver, or ivory are a more recent phenomenon for us. About twenty years ago I first became aware of these chance survivals which were being found by a growing number of metal detector enthusiasts working on the foreshore of the River Thames, on soil waste heaps from building sites in the city of London, and elsewhere in the country. At that time there was no established trade in these small archaeological objects – and there hardly is now – but as things were brought to us we bought them because they seemed interesting and they were not far removed from the sorts of medieval documents with which we are familiar.

I cannot claim that we have many customers for seal matrices. But early on we did sell a group of examples to the British Museum, which was a huge boost to my confidence. This, together with regular advice and great encouragement from John Cherry, set us on our way. We collected matrices over a number of years eventually forming a group of some four hundred examples which was acquired by the collector Martin Schøyen. A catalogue prepared by William Noel of the Walters Art Museum and myself was published in 2004.[1] The Schøyen Collection of medieval seal matrices ranges from the very grand to the very ordinary. There is the splendid thirteenth-century matrix for the equestrian seal of the Norwegian knight Finn

---

[1]   Richard Linenthal and William Noel (eds), *Medieval Seal Matrices in the Schøyen Collection* (Oslo, 2004).

Gautsson, the large gothic seal of the Bishop of Man, the heraldic seal of Thomas de Ros who fought in the War of the Roses, seals for the Chancellor of Chichester and the Court of Pleas of the County Palatine of Durham, and the eleventh-century ivory matrix of Wulfric, one of a tiny number of seal matrices surviving from Anglo-Saxon England.[2]

The strength of this collection, however, is in its great number of non-heraldic personal seals. They are the sort of thing most often found by metal detectorists; they are in complete contrast to the grand seals of kings, bishops, noble men and women often reproduced in books on medieval art and social history, and they have only just begun to receive serious scholarly attention. The material in the Schøyen Collection represents what is probably the largest collection of personal seal matrices assembled in Britain.

In his article on thirteenth-century personal seals in England, Paul Harvey, focussing principally on the wax impressions, describes these artefacts as a 'virtually untapped source of historical information'.[3] So they are, and so too are the matrices on which this article concentrates. Seal matrices were intimately personal objects which could serve not only as badges of identity but also as items of jewellery or good luck charms. They are the only inscribed medieval archaeological objects other than coins found in this country in significant numbers. Furthermore, for a great number of otherwise forgotten medieval men and women, they are the only surviving memorials, albeit accidental ones. In brief, they seem an appropriate subject for the theme of this symposium.

A few words on the subject of medieval English documents will help to provide the appropriate context for any discussion about seals. When we are asked to value a medieval archive comprising – as they usually do – large quantities of documents for property transactions, the first thing to do is to organize them chronologically. How many are of the twelfth century? How many are from the thirteenth century, the fourteenth century, and the fifteenth century? The next stage in assessing them is to see how many of these documents still have their wax seals. As a generalization you can usually expect to find a small number of twelfth-century documents; if you are lucky there will be a few with seals, and if you are very lucky there could be some rather grand looking ones, with knights on horseback, tall standing ladies wearing elegant robes, and bishops with staffs. It is very, very unlikely that there will be any eleventh-century documents, from the few decades following the Norman Conquest. And there is no point in even hoping for a document from the Anglo-Saxon period because there just never are any.

---

2   Schøyen Collection: nos. 16, 11, 368, 12, 13, and 14 respectively.

3   P. D. A. Harvey, 'Personal Seals in Thirteenth-Century England', Ian Wood and G. A. Loud (eds), *Church and Chronicle in the Middle Ages. Essays Presented to John Taylor* (London, 1991), p. 117.

For the thirteenth century the situation quickly changes and suddenly there will be many more documents, often still with their attached seals which are small or small-ish lumps of wax, and by the end of the thirteenth and into the fourteenth century there will be a considerable quantity of vellum and wax. The numbers for the fifteenth century will also be large, but perhaps no more than for the preceding century and a half. What are they all worth? When dealing with an archive numbering many hundreds or even thousands of documents, the key is to find a set of reasonable multipliers. Starting with the most common and therefore the cheapest: if a fourteenth- or fifteenth-century document missing its seal is worth 'X' (which might be not much more than £10, £20, or £30), an example with a nice seal is worth ten times that; thirteenth-century examples are worth more but fall along similar lines. For the twelfth century, though, the commercial picture changes dramatically and you can add a nought to the price and double or triple that if there is a good seal. For anything earlier there are no rules. Conquest era and earlier documents are desperately rare: the last example on the market that I know of was the charter of Godwine, c. 1013–1020, written in Anglo-Saxon, which Quaritch bought at Sotheby's in 1989 for well over £100,000.[4]

The point of what otherwise may seem a crass commerical exercise is to demonstrate that historically there was a proliferation of documents in medieval England in the centuries following the Norman Conquest. This is obvious from the vellum documents in archives which still survive, and probably most have not survived. It is also obvious from the metal seal matrices which are all chance survivals and are still being discovered by metal detectorists.

Michael Clanchy describes the period between the Norman Conquest and the death of Edward I (1066–1307) as a 'distinctive period in the development of literate ways of thinking and of doing business', and a 'formative stage in the history of literacy' in England,[5] during which English society underwent a transition from an oral one to a written culture. Documents were produced and kept on an unprecedented scale. They were a landmark in written records, and by the late thirteenth century they had reached every village in England. From Anglo-Saxon England there are about two thousand surviving charters and writs, and from the thirteenth century there are tens of thousands.[6] Assuming – and it seems reasonable to do so – that for most medieval objects of any kind more have been lost than have survived, Professor Clanchy suggests that as many as eight million documents were produced in England in the thirteenth century.[7]

[4]   Sotheby's, Western Manuscripts and Miniatures, 20 June 1989, lot 27, £115,000 (hammer price); now Schøyen Collection MS 600.

[5]   M. T. Clanchy, *From Memory to Written Record, England 1066–1307*, 2nd edn (Oxford, 1993), p. 1.

[6]   Clanchy, pp. 1–2.

[7]   Clanchy, p. 50.

Did they all have seals? The answer appears to be yes they did. During the twelfth century, and most obviously in the thirteenth century and later, a wax seal was a prerequisite for most sorts of vellum documents, representing the individual parties involved in the transaction. Clanchy characterizes the use of seals as an 'accelerator of bureaucracy' and 'harbinger of literacy' at all levels of society.[8]

Earlier customs, however, appear to have been different. The small number of vellum documents from the Anglo-Saxon period and the tiny number of surviving seals or seal matrices (there are only five of the latter) are unlikely to be just the result of a poor survival rate. The types of transactions in question would have been very much at the local level – say, for instance, the sale of a field or perhaps the rights to the produce of that field. They were not of importance to anyone beyond those involved in the transaction. The person selling was probably well known to the person buying, there would have been an agreement made publicly, probably before witnesses, locals from the village known to all parties. And in the event of a dispute these witnesses could be called upon to intervene. There was hardly a need to write it all down.

But at some point, historically, things began to change. Whether or not this reflects the insecurities of a conquered people and the changes imposed by a new administration I will leave to historians. There may at first have been a reluctance to trust written records, and it is probably significant that most documents included lists of witnesses – essentially translating the village assembly into written form. In the earliest examples the witnesses often signed with a cross next to their names – not necessarily because they were illiterate but rather to confirm a solemn oath made in the presence of Christ. Later, the personally inscribed cross was replaced by a wax seal bearing the person's name usually preceded by a cross. This was the standard form of inscription on personal seals as well as on seals of office. A so-called 'deed' was no longer the physical act of conveyance of land, but rather the sealed document made by the donor.

Another relevant question is whether at this time there were suddenly more land transactions. It is unlikely to be coincidental that this was the great period of newly founded monastic establishments in England. There must have been competition between houses to acquire and retain lands, and it would have been in the interest of all monasteries to create records and preserve them. Whereas previously it was not uncommon to find details of a monastery's possessions written out on the blank flyleaves of its own liturgical books, sacred and secure but not particularly sophisticated, there came to be well organized and indexed archives of documents. It is probably relevant that the first cartularies, which do not have early origins in England, also date from this period.

Within this context of proliferating documents, what role had personal seals and seal matrices? These were the seals of most seal users and represent as much

[8]   Clanchy, p. 115, and p. 317.

as eighty percent of all that survives. They obviously existed in huge numbers and were familiar to men and women at all levels of society. It would be a mistake to think of most of them in terms of social pretension; they should be considered rather as instruments of legal necessity. The matrices rarely display fine craftsmanship or artistry, and some are positively crude and ugly. Nevertheless they do provide us today with a glimpse of medieval individuals, people with ordinary lives who have been entirely forgotten by history. But curiously they have hardly been studied, and this may be because of the difficulties presented by the sheer volume of them.

Of the four hundred and three entries in the catalogue of the Schøyen Collection as many as three hundred and fifty are non-heraldic personal seal matrices. In general terms the earliest date from the second half of the twelfth century and these early ones are the rarest. They are noticeably more common from the thirteenth and fourteenth centuries, and are at least partly replaced in the fifteenth century by signet rings which are outside the scope of the collection. In all cases the standard form is for a pictorial or decorative device to be in the centre, and a legend around the edge, engraved backwards to be read from an impression, in different scripts depending on the date (Roman capitals; Lombardic capitals – a variety of gothic majuscule letter forms; and black-letter).

In more specific terms, personal seals tended to name their owners and were clearly custom-made until the end of the thirteenth century. The matrices at the lower end of the quality spectrum were usually flat lead discs, either round, pointed ovals or shield-shaped, with pierced tabs or loops which could serve as a handle or be used to suspend the seal. The size could vary but something close to our modern fifty pence coin was not unusual. The better quality examples tended to be made of copper alloy or bronze and were of similar form. The central devices were often lions, birds, human figures, fleurs-de-lis, sun bursts, and so forth. Thereafter, bronze replaced lead as the standard material, a new trumpet shape was introduced, and they tended to become smaller in size. Alongside personalized seals with an increasing variety of devices including particular saints, lambs of God, lions, stags, birds and other animals, there emerged in the early fourteenth century a whole group of standard off-the-shelf types. Here there was no mention of the owner's name, but rather a variety of predictable devices accompanied by banal mottoes often of a playful nature.

The range can be illustrated with some examples in the Schøyen Collection: William the son of Aveline is represented by a seal showing an eagle with spread wings. He lived in the early thirteenth century and probably at King's Lynn – at least that is where his lead seal matrix was found (Plate 24). John the son of Godiva lived at about the same time, also in East Anglia, and opted for a variant on the eagle device. But what of one Roger? Unfortunately his seal is imperfect obscuring part of the legend. Although like the others he is represented by an eagle which was quite a common device he stands out for having a matrix made of silver rather than the usual lead or copper alloy. It has been pierced through the centre suggesting that it may have been worn on a chain as a piece of jewellery, perhaps by Roger or someone after him.[9] The devices sometimes offer clues to an owner's profession: there are the scissors of Martillus the tailor (Plate 25); the axe of Vicart, the carpenter; the cross bow of Master Jacques, a crusader who was probably a Frenchman – his seal was found in Cyprus. I am reluctant to draw conclusions about Robert the son of William who chose for his device an unpleasant beetle-like insect.[10] But perhaps this is just another instance of how difficult it is to judge earlier times with modern eyes.

Nor was the ownership of seals confined to men. There are many women's names on surviving impressions and matrices. Take for instance Alice the daughter of Hervicus; Johanna of Alvesgan (a place name we have not been able to identify, but the matrix was found in Northumberland); Aileve the daughter of Levericus who lived near Ipswich; Margery Lambard from East Anglia; Elene the wife of Robert from Grimsby; and Alice the daughter of Richard Halvernist from Midhurst in Sussex.[11] These were all real people, and we know of them only because their seal matrices have survived by accident. They are probably otherwise unrecorded in history.

This is an appropriate place to pause for a moment and make an observation about linking seal matrices with wax seal impressions on surviving documents. To be able to do so would be extremely satisfying and very sentimental, but in fact it never happens. There are probably two reasons for this: firstly, most medieval documents have probably been lost, and what survives is just a small fraction of the original output; and secondly, there are not yet comprehensive databases recording information about wax seals gathered together from local record offices and other collections around the country.

The individual seal owner I would most like to have met of all those represented in the Schøyen Collection is Roland Oisun. He lived around the year 1200 but we do not know where – the find spot for his seal is unfortunately not recorded. The Anglicized form of his name would probably have been Roland Bird, and sure enough this is the device he chose for his seal. But what makes Roland truly remarkable is that he is one of only two people known in England to have had his seal matrix engraved on a reused classical Roman sestertius.[12] The bronze

9   Schøyen Collection: nos. 197, 199, and 198 respectively.
10   Schøyen Collection: nos. 382, 386, 384, and 277 respectively.
11   Schøyen Collection: nos. 80, 246, 299, 312, 332, and 333 respectively.
12   Another similar matrix was exhibited at Gloucester in 1860 during the meeting of the Archaeological Institute of Great Britain and Ireland. It was also engraved on a bronze sestertius of Antoninus Pius, the device was an eagle with wings spread, the legend was +S. CONSTANTINI. S. MARTINI, and it then belonged to C. Faulkner of Deddington, Oxfordshire. See *Gloucester and Gloucestershire Antiquities. A Catalogue of the Museum*

coin minted at Rome still shows the head of he Emperor Antoninus Pius (emperor 138–161 AD) on the obverse, and the reverse has been flattened and re-engraved with the device of a bird and legend of the seal. A small bronze suspension loop has been attached at the top (Plate 26).[13]

It is fascinating to imagine what Roland thought of his seal and how he understood the Roman coin which was used to make it. The engraver had to decide which side of the coin to engrave and he chose to preserve the bust of the emperor which may have endowed the seal with added authority. Did the owner know something about ancient Rome – Britain certainly had many ancient remains – or did he misinterpret the image in a Christian context? Did he think it was the head of Christ, for example? There are such misunderstandings recorded in the literature: two thirteenth-century ecclesiastical seals, one of the Abbot of Selby in Yorkshire, and the other of the Archbishop of York, were published as early as the mid-eighteenth century.[14] Both are interesting up-market types set with engraved classical Roman gem stones which served as the device for the seals. The legends were engraved on the surrounding silver mounts, and one of them misidentifies the head of the Emperor Honorius – and even so named on the stone – as the head of Christ ('Capud hoc Cristus est'). On the other, three classical heads are described as the Trinity.

We will never know what Roland Bird thought of his seal, but it does raise an important question about the various functions of a medieval seal matrix. The most obvious use was to stamp soft wax leaving the owner's mark of authority – essentially his or her signature – thereby authenticating or authorizing a transaction or piece of correspondence. A seal matrix may also have served its owner as a badge of identity or authority, perhaps not unlike a modern passport, or they may have been thought of as personal talismans or good-luck charms. Consider, for example, the common findings today of papal bullae – the actual lead seals – in English churchyards suggesting that sealed documents were buried in graves, or the placing of a papal bull in the tower of St Albans Abbey in the thirteenth century to protect it from lightning.[15]

The evidence of the matrices themselves suggests that they were intended to be carried on the person. They always have small handles or tabs attached to them which were necessary when pressing the engraved face into wax, and these handles are usually pierced for suspension by a chain. They commonly may have been

---

Formed at Gloucester during the Meeting of the Archaeological Institute of Great Britain and Ireland ... July 17th to 26th, 1860 (Gloucester, 1860), p. 31.

[13] Schøyen Collection: no. 245.

[14] J. Lewis, *A Dissertation on the Antiquity and Use of Seals in England* (London, 1740), p. 26.

[15] P. D. A. Harvey and A. McGuinness, *A Guide to British Medieval Seals* (London, 1996), p. 2.

worn on a belt or attached to a purse. It would be interesting to gather any contemporary references to this and I would be grateful to hear of them.

There is one bronze matrix in the Schøyen Collection still with a complete chain which is also made of bronze which I suggest is the reason for its survival.[16] There are quite a few others without a chain but with corroded iron filling the hole in the suspension loop or handle. If iron rather than bronze was the more common material for chains, its susceptibility to corrosion may be why very few chains have survived.

Two other matrices in the collection are oddities which suggest their function as identity badges. One is quite crude but the device of several curlicues is individualistic and the whole thing, in my opinion, has pizzazz (Plate 27).[17] What is unusual is that the legend is not engraved backwards, which is to say that it must be read from the matrix itself rather than from an impression. Lest this be dismissed as a careless mistake, the same thing occurs on another example, this one with a very common fleur-de-lis device, but unusual for being made of ivory. This is the seal of Baldun a thirteenth-century man of whom we know very little.[18] His seal, however, must have been an object of importance to him.

The year 1300, give or take a couple of decades, is significant for the understanding of English personal seals. Around this time a type of matrix appeared which on the one hand is appealing for the great variety of devices and legends, but on the other hand is puzzling because they were produced as duplicates and the name of the owner is not given. The existence of these so-called motto seals in huge quantities – they dominate the fourteenth century – throws into question the function of a seal and the practice of sealing documents. The seal seems to have been demoted from an authoritative to a more symbolic role.

Two lovers clasp hands with the legend 'Je su sel damour', or 'Love me and I the' – note the use of the vernacular. A squirrel has the generic legend 'crede michi' (Believe in me) or 'Prive su' (I am private), or more appealingly 'I crake notis'. A cockerel distinguished by its crested plumage, although very crudely engraved, announces the dawn with the odd legend 'Crov me dai'. A lion sleeps under a tree with the warning 'Wake me no man'. A hare rides a hound and holds a hunting horn with the legend 'Sohou Robin', a hunting cry. A grotesque human figure with a tail and long feet says 'I was a man'.

There are saints, the sacred monogram 'IHC', pelicans in piety, Lambs of God, stags, birds, owls, fish, dragons, and griffins. The legends can be ribald and coarse such as a farting monkey, or elevated to the level of a reference to Virgil's *Eclogues*, 'Amor vincit omnia', a popular medieval motto found on small lead tokens and jewellery such as the brooch worn by Chaucer's Prioress. The most unlikely pair-

[16] Schøyen Collection: no. 230.
[17] Schøyen Collection: no. 303.
[18] Schøyen Collection: no. 328.

ing is that found on one particular seal matrix in an American private collection: 'Amor vincit omnia', Love conquers everything, with the device of a severed boar's head.[19] It must be the case that these motto seals could be bought off the shelf ready-made, and even though we know very little about their production and distribution, it is interesting that towards the end of the thirteenth century craftsmen specifically called seal-makers ('sigillarii') are recorded.[20] In the Schøyen Collecton there are even two 'twins', one a pelican in piety, and the other a hard riding a hound, which are so close in all aspects of design, engraving and style that it is tempting to imagine that they were produced by the same maker; yet they were found at different sites.[21]

If seal production had moved into the hands of professionals who then had made the earlier personal matrices, the ones often engraved in lead, and usually recording the names of their owners? The most likely answer is probably within the bureaucracy of monastic record keeping. Matrices may have been engraved more or less on the spot and used for a particular transaction, a particular act of sealing. Lead was a relatively easy and soft material to work, and the likely place of production was a monastic workshop. It was, after all, in the monastery's own interest to keep track of its gifts and purchases of land, record them properly, certify the documents with seals, and preserve them for future evidence in the event of a dispute. If the smallholding vendor or donor had no seal of his own one would be supplied, and it may have become customary for the person to keep the seal as a perk or souvenir.

This might explain how some individuals came to own more than one seal – there is an example in the Schøyen Collection, and others are described by Paul Harvey.[22] It also suggests that a lead blank engraved with seals for two different people, one on each side – also in the Schøyen Collection – was nothing more than a convenient economy.[23] It would also explain how a series of thirteenth-century land grants to St. Peter's Abbey in Gloucester were sealed with different matrices for different people, but they were all of very similar style.[24]

In spite of the proliferation of anonymous seals with mottoes in the fourteenth century it would be a mistake to believe that the individual had been forgotten. There were still many matrices which were custom-made, and they usually recorded the names of their owners. It may be that the question of ready-made versus customized was a social distinction. This must have been so with the large number of relatively modest heraldic seals which appeared during the fourteenth

[19]   Collection of John Rassweiler, Princeton, New Jersey.
[20]   Harvey and McGuinness, p. 15.
[21]   Schøyen Collection: nos. 224 and 225, 176 and 177.
[22]   Harvey, 'Personal Seals ...', pp. 126–7.
[23]   Schøyen Collection: no. 330.
[24]   R. H. Hilton, 'Gloucester Abbey Leases of the Late Thirteenth Century', *The English Peasantry in the Later Middle Ages* (Oxford, 1975), pp. 154–5.

century. These were not the grand and well-engraved designs reserved for the top ranks of the English aristocracy. They were often no larger than a common motto seal and no more impressive. There was a spread of heraldry socially downwards and it has been observed that by 'the mid-fourteenth century many people had coats of arms whose predecessors a hundred years earlier did not,'[25] and those not entitled to bear arms often adopted quasi-heraldic devices.

Consider too the needs of the merchant class. It is probably a fair assumption that most commercial traders used their seals far more often than the average man or woman. Given the risk of loss from theft, piracy, shipwreck, or other disaster, it was common to commit only a small consignment of goods to a single carrier or vessel, and every such cargo might have contained the properties of many individuals. Around the year 1300 so-called merchants' marks first began to appear on English seals. They were the forerunners of modern trade-marks and were intended to be easily recognizable and unambiguous. The designs of the devices were usually built around an upright stem and incorporated other components such as a cross, streamers, a symbol like a numeral 4, a ball or orb, a shield or initials. Bibliographers will be most familiar with William's Caxton's mark which he used as a printer's device. In the Schøyen Collection there are twelve seal matrices with various such devices.[26] All except one name their owners. In several cases they seem to be continental European, and yet the matrices were discovered in England. This would not be surprising for a travelling merchant. We will never know why he lost his seal, but once again we are offered a tiny insight into an individual's life.

The increasing scholarly interest surrounding seals in recent years is encouraging, witness a British Museum exhibition in 2007,[27] and various international conferences. The avenues of enquiry stretch from the grand seals of the aristocracy, traditional disciplines of art historians and others, to the more humble survivals which are the subject of this paper. Medieval personal seals, the very ordinary as much as the unusual, are gradually achieving recognition but as yet are still under appreciated for the fascinating glimpses they offer into lives otherwise forgotten.

---

[25] Harvey and McGuinness, p. 56.

[26] Schøyen Collection: nos. 370–81.

[27] *Good Impressions: Image and Authority in Medieval Seals*, 11 January–20 May 2007; conference papers published by N. Adams, J. Cherry and J. Robertson (London, 2008).

The Biographical Brass

NICHOLAS ROGERS

In his study of tomb sculpture Panofsky singles out the introduction of the biographical element as one of the markers for the advent of the Renaissance. He cites the tomb of Cangrande de la Scala, d. 1329, at Verona, which incorporates scenes from Cangrande's life on the base, and other early fourteenth-century examples, but notes that this type of commemoration does not become at all widespread until the early sixteenth century.[1] The aim of this paper is to provide a survey of biographical elements in pre-Reformation English monumental brasses, to see to what degree these 'biographical brasses' can be viewed as fitting within the category noted by Panofsky. The monumental brass in England has the merit of providing information about the commemorative priorities of a wide range of people, from the higher aristocracy to tradesmen and yeomen and their wives, from archbishops to chantry priests. There are limitations to the scope of the evidence. It is weighted towards the south and east of England. In some areas religious objections resulted in the systematic removal of inscriptions in the seventeenth century; East Anglia, for example, has a markedly higher proportion of anonymous figures.[2] There has been a disproportionate loss of the more elaborate iconographies, which were to be found especially in cathedral and conventual churches, and in the City of London. The loss occasioned by the Great Fire is, however, offset by the recording of epitaphs by Weever and by Stow and his continuators.[3]

The majority of brasses embody some biographical information, even if it is only the date of death. Brasses are sometimes the sole documentary evidence for family members, such as fourteen of the seventeen children of Nicholas Carew of Beddington, Surrey, including a sad sequence of four Johns.[4] Brasses also provide

---

[1]   E. Panofsky, *Tomb Sculpture: Its Changing Aspects from Ancient Egypt to Bernini*, ed. H. W. Janson (London, 1964), p. 75, fig. 386.

[2]   On the removal of inscriptions from brasses in the 1640s, see *The Journal of William Dowsing: Iconoclasm in East Anglia during the English Civil War*, ed. T. Cooper (Woodbridge, 2001), pp. 101–03.

[3]   John Weever, *Ancient Funerall Monuments* (London, 1631); John Stow, *A Survey of London*, ed. C. L. Kingsford (Oxford, 1908; repr. with adds. 1971); John Stow, *A Survey of the Cities of London and Westminster*, ed. John Strype, 2 vols (London, 1720).

[4]   On this brass, see M. Stephenson, *A List of Monumental Brasses in Surrey* (Guildford, 1921; repr. Bath, 1970), pp. 23–5. See also J. Page-Phillips, *Children on Brasses* (London, 1970), fig. 8.

useful information about the appointments of minor royal officials. But these references to family and status are not the subject of this paper. By 'biographical brass' is meant a brass which either iconographically or textually refers to the deeds, experiences or personality of the deceased.

Before considering the form and content of these 'biographical brasses', the question of 'authorship' needs to be considered. Most monuments were the responsibility of executors, usually members of the immediate family or of the same institution as the deceased. On occasion they would be guided by testamentary instructions. The will of the London mercer Thomas Muschamp (d. 1472) is exceptional in the care with which he specifies the design and inscriptions of his brass.[5] But there are several instances of particular, and even peculiar, iconographies being specified by the deceased, such as 'the pattern of the organ of the choir of St Paul's, London, which I constructed in my lifetime', on the brass of the organ builder John Killyngworth, formerly in St Paul's Churchyard.[6] There is a class of inscription in which the deceased seems to address the spectator. But this is a literary convention, the inscriptions being *post mortem* statements provided by the executors. An early example of a truly 'autobiographical' inscription is that on Richard II's tomb, commissioned in 1395, following the death of Anne of Bohemia on 7 June 1394, in which the personal qualities and achievements singled out for mention provide a unique insight into the way in which the king viewed himself.[7]

The narrative iconography of the Wyvil brass at Salisbury (Plate 28) is unparalleled among medieval English episcopal brasses, although it should be noted that what may well be biographical subjects occupy the spandrels of the tomb of Giles de Bridport (d. 1262), also at Salisbury.[8] Robert Wyvil is shown half-length within the tower of a castle, the gate of which is guarded by his champion, holding a distinctive battle-pick and shield. At the base are rabbits in a warren. The image is explained by the marginal inscription, which uses annalistic vocabulary. After the familiar phrases 'bone memorie', 'pacifice et laudabiliter rexit', 'pastor vigilans', it specifies that he recovered the castle of Sherborne after it had been alienated for more than two hundred years and also regained Bere chase. Sher-

5   M. Norris, *Monumental Brasses: The Craft* (London, 1978), p. 90. Muschamp was buried in St Mary Magdalen, Milk Street.

6   N. Rogers, 'John Killyngworth, alias Gloucester, "Orginmaker"', *Transactions of the Monumental Brass Society*, 13, pt. 4 (1983), pp. 343–6.

7   On Richard's tomb and its inscription, see P. Lindley, 'Absolutism and Regal Image in Ricardian Sculpture', in *The Regal Image of Richard II and the Wilton Diptych*, ed. D. Gordon, L. Monnas and C. Elam (London, 1997), pp. 62–74; S. Badham, 'Cast Copper-alloy Tombs and London Series B Brass Production in the Late Fourteenth Century', *Transactions of the Monumental Brass Society*, 17, pt. 2 (2004), pp. 108–11, fig. 3. I am grateful to Nigel Saul for reminding me of the importance of this inscription in the chronology of 'biographical' monuments.

8   M. E. Roberts, 'The Tomb of Giles de Bridport in Salisbury Cathedral', *Art Bulletin*, 65 (1983), pp. 559–86, especially pp. 575–84, figs. 35–42.

borne Castle had been seized by King Stephen from Bishop Roger. It was when Edward III granted the castle to the Earl of Salisbury that Bishop Wyvil brought a writ of right for its recovery. The case was referred to trial by battle, of which there is a fascinating account in the Year Book for Hilary Term 1355, including the allegation that Robert, son of John de Shawell, the bishop's champion, had various rolls of prayers and charms concealed about him. Eventually the Earl agreed to surrender the property for 2500 marks.[9] The image of the bishop housed within the castle, where the inscriptions records he died in 1375, is perhaps derived from a sigillographic motif of the church enshrining its patron saint or founder. An example of this is the obverse of the 1258 seal of Norwich Cathedral, where Herbert Losinga stands in a porch under the central tower of a conventionalised cathedral.[10] It has also been suggested that the design of the Wyvil brass may owe something to Castle of Love imagery.[11]

Until 1684 the Wyvil brass was situated in the middle of the choir, a traditional position for the tombs of founders and major benefactors. The most common iconographic type, traceable back to twelfth-century continental examples, is that of the founder holding the model of a church.[12] The 3rd Lord Cobham chose to be represented in this guise in the chancel of his new collegiate foundation.[13] At Cowthorpe, Yorkshire, Sir Brian Roucliffe was shown supporting the church he rebuilt together with his wife Joan (Plate 29).[14] However, most commemorations of benefactions are simply textual. It is noticeable that they are frequently in the vernacular. Early examples are the 1393 brass at Wanlip, Leicestershire, commemorating Dame Katherine Walsch, 'whiche in her tyme made the kirke of Anlep and halud the kirkyerd in wurchip of god and oure lady and seynt Nicholas',[15] and

[9]   E. Kite, *The Monumental Brasses of Wiltshire* (London, 1860), pp. 14–19, pl. I.

[10]   G. Pedrick, *Monastic Seals of the XIIIth Century* (London, 1902), pp. 114–18, pl. XXXIII.

[11]   Norris, *Craft*, p. 78.

[12]   The earliest example would appear to be the tomb of King Childebert at St-Denis, of the 1170s (K. Bauch, *Das mittelalterliche Grabbild* (Berlin, 1976), p. 41, Abb. 49). Another early example is the tomb of Henry the Lion in Brunswick Cathedral, made in the late 1230s (Panofsky, *Tomb Sculpture*, fig. 222). The earliest brass of this type is Yso von Wölpe (d. 1231) in St Andreas, Verden, who is shown holding the cathedral and city of Verden (Bauch, *Grabbild*, p. 293, Abb. 440). This iconography is adapted for the incised slab of the architect Hugues Libergier (d. 1263) at Reims Cathedral (Panofsky, *Tomb Sculpture*, fig. 205).

[13]   N. Saul, *Death, Art, and Memory in Medieval England: The Cobham Family and their Monuments, 1300–1500* (Oxford, 2001), p. 90, fig. 11.

[14]   Other examples are the anonymous ecclesiastic of c. 1510 at North Creake, Norfolk (Norris, *Memorials*, I, p. 189, II, fig. 212) and Sir John de la Rivière at Tormarton, Glos. (H. F. Owen Evans, 'Tormarton, Glos.', *Transactions of the Monumental Brass Society*, 11, pt. 4 (1972), pp. 288–90, fig. 1).

[15]   M. Stephenson, *A List of Monumental Brasses in the British Isles* (London, 1926), p. 278.

the verse inscription of *c.* 1405 at Holme-next-the-Sea, Norfolk (Plate 30),[16] which is worth citing in full:

> Herry Notingham & his wyffe lyne here
> þat maden this Chirche stepull & quere
> two vestments & belles they made also
> crist hem saue therefore fro wo
> ande to bringe her saules to blis of heuen
> sayth pater & aue with mylde steuen.

The phraseology of these commemorations echoes that of bede-rolls, and the brasses are to be seen as further guaranteeing the annual remembrance of good works.

Even non-narrative images can possess a biographical value. Although portraits are unknown on English brasses before the Reformation, and are of extreme rarity in the period afterwards, there are several cases where the image of the deceased is individualised. The most common type of individualisation is the depiction of a person as bearded in an unusual fashion, such as Sir William Tendring, d. 1408, at Stoke-by-Nayland, with his long forked beard,[17] or as bearded at a time when a beard was unfashionable, such as John Knyvet, d. 1418, at Mendlesham,[18] and Nicholas Canteys, d. 1431, at Margate (Plate 31). It could be that in the latter instances the beard is a signifier of age, functioning in the same way as the representation of the elder Swynborne at Little Horkesley, Essex, in an appropriately antiquated suit of armour.[19] Only in two cases has it been possible to determine age at death. John Knyvet was 59 or 60, which, while a respectable age, is not remarkable.[20] Robert Greyndour, d. 1443, at Newland, Gloucestershire, with his idiosyncratic spatulate beard, was, if his father's *Inquisition Post Mortem* is to be believed, 52 years old.[21] The individuality of his beard suggests a particular request from an executor.[22] Nicholas Carew, d. 1432, at Beddington, Surrey, is described as 'senex et plenus dierum', a biblical phrase used of the patriarch Isaac, and although Nicholas Carew did not match Isaac's 180 years he lived to be about 76 at the time of his death.[23] But his image does not reflect the great age referred to in the inscription, and this holds true for the generality of brasses, where the con-

[16] *Monumental Brasses: The Portfolio Plates of the Monumental Brass Society 1894–1984*, intr. M. Norris (Woodbridge, 1988), pl. 105.

[17] J. Page-Phillips, *Macklin's Monumental Brasses* (London, 1969), ill. on p. 64.

[18] *Portfolio Plates*, pl. 125.

[19] W. Lack, H. M. Stuchfield and P. Whittemore, *The Monumental Brasses of Essex*, 2 vols (London, 2003), I, p. 361, illus. on p. 362.

[20] J. S. Roskell, L. Clark and C. Rawcliffe, *The House of Commons 1386–1421*, 4 vols (Stroud, 1992), pp. 534–6.

[21] *A Series of Monumental Brasses, Indents and Incised Slabs from the 13th to the 20th Century*, ed. W. Lack and P. Whittemore, II, pt. 1 (2005), pp. 2–3, pl. III.

[22] Post-medieval concern with the question of portraiture is documented for the Llanrwst brasses (Norris, *Craft*, p. 94).

ventional figure contrasts with the injured, diseased, or arthritic body interred beneath.[24]

In this light the depiction of physical disability on the brass of William Palmer, d. 1520, at Ingoldmells, Lincolnshire, made by a Bury St Edmunds marbler, is all the more remarkable (Plate 32). Crippled bedesmen occur as weepers on sculpted tombs[25] and on the recycled brass of a lady of c. 1410 at St Stephen, Norwich[26] but they are generalised images, serving as a reminder that acts of charity can relieve purgatorial suffering. It has not been possible to find out anything about the man commemorated at Ingoldmells beyond the fact that that he was the uncle of William Palmer of Winthorpe,[27] but the way in which he is called 'William Palmer wyth ye Stylt', suggests that the crutch was a long-established part of his personality, perhaps even from childhood. The inscription records that Palmer died on 'Holy Rode Day'. This suggests that the crutch can be viewed as a tau cross of redemptive suffering. Even in a wider European context, Ingoldmells is unusual. Indeed, the only other medieval depiction of disability on a monument that I have found is the blind composer Francesco Landini, d. 1397, whose tomb-slab clearly shows sunken, sightless eye sockets.[28] Even purely textual references to infirmity, such as the 'longo tempore cecus erat' of the Blodwell brass, to be considered later, are decidedly uncommon.

Another remarkable class of individualised image is that where the traditional canine foot-support is given a name. At Deerhurst Lady Alice Cassy is accompanied by a dog labelled 'Terri'[29] and the lost figure of Sir Brian de Stapulton, d. 1438, at Ingham, Norfolk, rested his feet on a lion and a ?terrier named 'Jakke'.[30] The symbol of fidelity has been turned into a lady's pet and a man's hunting companion. This naming of animals can be regarded simply as a manifestation of the traditional love of dogs. But there may be an implicit evocation of the canine companions of romance, such as Tristan's Houdain.[31]

---

[23] Stephenson, *Surrey*, pp. 27–31; Roskell, Clark and Rawcliffe, *The House of Commons 1386–1421*, II, pp. 482–5.

[24] On the pathology of Sir Hugh Hastings at Elsing, see B. Hooper et al., 'The Grave of Sir Hugh de Hastyngs, Elsing', *Norfolk Archaeology*, 39, pt. 1 (1984), pp. 93–8.

[25] A bedesman on an alabaster tomb at North Aston, Oxon., c. 1490, is shown holding a walking stick (A. Gardner, *Alabaster Tombs of the Pre-Reformation Period in England* (Cambridge, 1940), fig. 34).

[26] Norris, *Craft*, fig. 48.

[27] PRO, PROB 11/27, ff. 182–183v. It was the nephew (d. 1538) who paid for the south porch at Winthorpe, rather than the uncle as stated in N. Pevsner and J. Harris, *Lincolnshire*, 2nd edn, revised N. Antram (London, 1989), pp. 406, 806.

[28] B. Santi, *San Lorenzo: Guide to the Laurentian complex* (Florence, 1992), pl. on p. 18.

[29] C. T. Davis, *The Monumental Brasses of Gloucestershire* (London, 1899), p. 13, fig. 8.

[30] Norris, *Craft*, p. 72, fig. 44.

[31] L. Gnädinger, *Hiudan und Petitcreiu: Gestalt und Figur des Hundes in der mittelalterlichen Tristandichtung* (Zürich, 1971).

Literary models of bountiful lordship lie behind the description of the 2nd Lord Cobham, on the brass commissioned by his son in the late 1360s, as 'le cortays viaundour'. As Nigel Saul has noted, a similar virtue is ascribed to Reginald, 2nd Lord Cobham at Lingfield, Surrey (d. 1403), who is described as 'dapsilis in mensis'.[32] This echoes the description of St Edmund in Abbo of Fleury's Life as 'egentibus dapsilis'.[33] The qualities of a gentleman are celebrated on the well-crafted epitaph on the mutilated brass of Thomas Frowyk (d. 1448) at South Mimms, which has been attributed since the time of Weever to that compulsive versifier Abbot Whethamstead.[34] Frowyk, a member of the London merchant family, is documented as a friend of Whethamstead, so the attribution is a sound one. It reads, in Cameron's translation: 'He who lies buried here was called Thomas Frowyk. He was a noble man in character and in birth, bearing, life-style and moderation, and cultivated noble pursuits; for he greatly delighted in what noble men are accustomed to like and pursue with relish; that is catching wild birds and hunting wild beasts. He deprived foxes of their holes and badgers of their sets; in short whatever creatures had brought damage to his neighbours, he put to flight to the best of his ability. Moreover if he ever saw the torches of strife being kindled among those neighbours he acted as mediator and extinguished them and so restored the peace. May God now grant him the peace and rest which endures for ever. Amen.' Whethamstead links the secular task of pest control with the more exalted aim of extirpating causes of conflict.

The date of death is usually recorded, or at least a space is provided for it, primarily with the intention of providing a reminder of the date on which an obit is to be held. This function is made explicit in some instances, such as the sequence of Stathum brasses at Morley, Derbyshire.[35] However, this essential record is occasionally expanded in ways that bring it within the definition of the biographical brass. The death-bed words of the godly are sometimes encountered on post-Reformation monuments, especially those of children, but to the best of my knowledge the only pre-Reformation instance where the voice of the deceased is memorialised in this way is a 1525 inscription at Barnston, Essex, which tells us that Petyr Wood 'departyd the xxx day of Maye Beseching Ihu y^t was crusifid on the rood to Bryng hys sowle to ye blys y^t schall last aye'.[36]

[32] Saul, *Death, Art, and Memory*, pp. 96–7.

[33] *Three Lives of English Saints*, ed. M. Winterbottom (Toronto, 1972), p. 71.

[34] H. K. Cameron, 'The Brasses of Middlesex. Part 23: South Mimms', *Trans. of the London and Middlesex Archaeological Soc.*, 34 (1983), pp. 215–19; Norris, *Memorials*, I, p. 98. Another Whethamstead inscription occurs on the brass of his father, Hugh Bostock, at Wheathamstead, Herts.

[35] On the Stathum and other obit brasses, see A. R. Dufty, 'The Stathum Book of Hours; an Existing MS. Mentioned on a 15th-Century Brass', *Archaeological Journal*, 106 (1949), Supplement, pp. 83–90.

[36] M. Christy, W. W. Porteous and E. B. Smith, *The Monumental Brasses of Essex. Part I*,

The cause of death serves as a memento mori, although it can also convey a sense of shock at sudden bereavement. Death in childbed, an all too common occasion for seventeenth-century monuments, is mentioned in two instances. At Blickling, Norfolk, Anne a Wode, the second wife of Thomas Asteley of Melton Constable, is shown holding swaddled twins, a boy and a girl, to whom she gave birth on the feast of St Agapitus 1512, 'et post parturiendi periculum subito migravit ad dominum' (Plate 33).[37] Elizabeth, the wife of John Prout, merchant of the staple of Calais, at Streatley, Bucks., 'obiit in parturiendo' on the feast of the Epiphany 1440.[38] The cause of death can be suspected in monuments of 1348–9 and 1361, but only one brass is known to have referred to the plague. Gough records the inscription at Braceborough, Lincolnshire, to Thomas and Joan le Wasteneys 'le quel morust en le graund pestilence l'an de grace 1349'.[39] The mysterious sweating sickness is recorded on several brasses: Robert Incent, servant to Cecily, duchess of York, at Great Berkhamstead, Hertfordshire, died 'at the grete swetyng sykenesse' in 1485;[40] Christopher Jackson, fellow of St John's Cambridge, succumbed in 1528 (Plate 34);[41] and an inscription at Lanteglos-by-Fowey notes that John and Anne Mohun died of it in 1508 within twenty-four hours.[42]

A sense of shock at a grave act of sacrilege infuses the verses recorded by Weever on the brass of Robert Haule, who was slaughtered in the chancel of Westminster Abbey, where he sought sanctuary in 1378.[43] This epitaph, like that of Bishop Wyvil, can be viewed as part of the local chronicle tradition. Death in battle, at Barnet, is the subject of another set of verses at Westminster Abbey, on the tomb of Sir Humphrey Bourgchier.[44] Death while on campaign is usually referred to obliquely. Of Sir John Phelip at Kidderminster it is recorded 'fortis apud Harffleu … bene gessit', but that he died of the flux in France in 1415 is not mentioned.[45] Simple statements of death abroad are usually associated with military service. On the brass to Symond and Roger de Felbrig and their wives at Felbrigg,

ed. R. H. D'Elboux (Ashford, 1948), p. 36.

[37] R. Greenwood and M. Norris, *The Brasses of Norfolk Churches* (Holt, 1976), pp. 12, 46; Page-Phillips, *Children on Brasses*, fig. 31.

[38] W. Lack, H. M. Stuchfield and P. Whittemore, *The Monumental Brasses of Berkshire* (London, 1993), p. 138.

[39] J. Bertram, *Lost Brasses* (Newton Abbot, 1976), p. 177.

[40] Stephenson, *List*, p. 181.

[41] N. Rogers, 'Cambridgeshire Brasses', in *Cambridgeshire Churches*, ed. C. Hicks (Stamford, 1997), p. 315.

[42] W. Lack, H. M. Stuchfield and P. Whittemore, *The Monumental Brasses of Cornwall* (London, 1997), p. 67, illus. on p. 69.

[43] Weever, *Ancient Funerall Monuments*, pp. 483–4; J. S. N. Wright, *The Brasses of Westminster Abbey* (London, 1969), p. 42.

[44] Wright, *Westminster Abbey*, pp. 25–6.

[45] Roskell, Clark and Rawcliffe, *The House of Commons 1386–1421*, IV, pp. 68–70. For the Phelip inscription, see Norris, *Memorials*, I, p. 98.

Norfolk, it is recorded that Roger died and was buried in 'Prus', having probably perished while on a *Reyse* against the pagan Lithuanians.[46] Of Sir Reginald Braybrooke at Cobham we are just informed that he died at Middelburg in Flanders in 1404, not that this was the result of wounds sustained during an unsuccessful attack on Sluys.[47] Lingering death from infected wounds and the squalor of camp dysentery are below the dignity of epitaphs.

At the Hospital of St Cross, Winchester, under a bench in the nave, is an English inscription to one John Newles, d. 1452, a brother of the hospital, esquire and servant for more than thirty years to Cardinal Beaufort (Plate 35).[48] We are told that he was born in 'beame', that is Bohemia. This is probably just local colour, but in the case of Margaret, the wife of Sir Simon de Felbrygge, 'nacione et generoso sanguine Boema', her Bohemian origin is part of her status, since, as her heraldry makes clear, she was the daughter of Premislaw I Noszak, Duke of Teschen, and a distant relative of her mistress Anne of Bohemia.[49] Similarly, Agnes Salmon's Portuguese origin is mentioned in the context of her status as lady-in-waiting to her compatriot Beatrice, countess of Arundel.[50] The virtually complete loss of the friars' churches in London and elsewhere, where foreigners tended to worship, has certainly deprived us of further examples of such statements of origin.[51] In such instances, expressions of nationality would have been a means of attracting the prayers of fellow nationals in a strange land.[52] Some references to place of birth may echo bequests to the testator's original parish.

Lengthy verse inscriptions are most frequently found on monuments to higher clergy. A common motif, as on the brasses of William Tybard and John Perch at Magdalen College, Oxford, is the celebration of academic achievement.[53] Panofsky points out that the Bolognese professors of the fourteenth century were

---

[46]   E. M. Beloe, *A Series of Photo-lithographs of Monumental Brasses in Norfolk* (King's Lynn, 1890–91), pl. 4.

[47]   Saul, *Death, Art, and Memory*, p. 27, fig. 18.

[48]   W. Lack, H. M. Stuchfield and P. Whittemore, *The Monumental Brasses of Hampshire and the Isle of Wight* (Stratford St Mary, 2007), p. 370, illus. on p. 371.

[49]   Beloe, *Norfolk*, pl. 21.

[50]   Mrs. Davidson-Houston, 'A List of Monumental Brasses in Sussex. Part I', *Sussex Archaeological Collections*, 76 (1935), pp. 65–7.

[51]   Among the numerous Italian merchants buried in the London Greyfriars were 'Maners Francisci, valens mercator Florencie', d. 1342, under a large stone; 'Gerardus Danyzys [i.e. Gherardo Davizzi] de Florencia, mercator, d. 4 February 1457; and the curiously named 'Baynort Welliam de Luca, valens mercator', with his wife Suibilla and daughter Johanna (C. L. Kingsford, *The Grey Friars of London* (Aberdeen, 1915), pp. 92, 98 and 124).

[52]   Stow records the monument of John van Glave, Easterling, d. 1413, at All Hallows the Great, Haywharf, near the Steelyard (Stow, *Survey*, ed. Kingsford, II, p. 397(xii)).

[53]   R. T. Günther, *A Description of Brasses and other Funeral Monuments in the Chapel of Magdalen College* (Oxford, 1914), pp. 6–7, 10–11.

at the forefront of the revival of the funerary celebration of fame.[54] Several clerical epitaphs, both in verse and prose, take the form of a curriculum vitae. Christopher Urswick's brass at Hackney, after rehearsing his service as almoner to Henry VII, ambassador, dean of York and Windsor, and archdeacon of Richmond, even throws in the titbit that he refused the bishopric of Norwich.[55] But the 1462 brass of John Blodwell at Balsham, Cambridgeshire, which is modelled on that of an earlier rector of Balsham,[56] subverts this mode of commemoration. The twelve-line foot inscription begins promisingly, with its record of achievement (in translation): 'Wales gave me birth; Bologna taught me the science of law; Rome gave me the practice; five nations taught me to speak', but then a second monitory voice, perhaps that of death, chips in: 'All this pompous exhibition of yours is a bore'. To Blodwell's query: 'Praise, fame, good health, strength, rank, long life, surely these things can be offered to God?', the response comes: 'You might as well think of them as vain and transitory.' Similarly, in the marginal inscription, the title of 'egregius doctor' is juxtaposed with references to his blindness and advanced age. W. N. C. Girard, in his excellent article on the Blodwell brass,[57] demonstrates that although his plurality of appointments is not listed, they are alluded to in the choice of saints on the brass: St Asaph, for his Deanery at St Asaph, St Andrew for his Canonry at Wells, and so on.[58]

A more positive account of a career is provided by the brass of Sir Hugh Johnys, at Swansea, which survived the 1941 blitz.[59] In rather breathless prose it recounts his knighting at the Holy Sepulchre in Jerusalem in 1441, his five years fighting against the Turks and Saracens in the parts of 'troy grecie and turky' under the Emperor John Palaeologus, his service as knight marshal of France under John, Duke of Somerset, and his service in the same role in England under John, Duke of Norfolk. This is the world of the Beauchamp Pageants, which on a grander scale recall the experiences of pilgrimage to Jerusalem and military service in France. But the retrospective aspect of the Johnys brass is balanced by the prospective element of the Resurrection scene. Sir Hugh's real journey is one towards the resurrection of the body. The Johnys brass was laid down about 1500, some fifteen years

54   Panofsky, *Tomb Sculpture*, p. 70.
55   H. K. Cameron, 'The Brasses of Middlesex Part XI. Hackney', *Transactions of the London and Middlesex Archaeological Society*, 20, pt. 4 (1961), pp. 175–7.
56   Rogers, 'Cambridgeshire Brasses', pp. 309, 311.
57   W. N. C. Girard, 'John Blodwell, Rector of Balsham', *Transactions of the Monumental Brass Society*, 15, pt. 2 (1993), pp. 119–36.
58   Similar allusions to clerical appointments can be discerned in the choice of saints on the brasses of John Byrkhed (d. 1468) at Harrow and William Porter (d. 1524) at Hereford Cathedral.
59   W. R. B. Robinson, 'Sir Hugh Johnys: a Fifteenth-Century Welsh Knight', *Morgannwg: Transactions of the Glamorgan History Society*, 14 (1970), pp. 5–34; J. M. Lewis, *Welsh Monumental Brasses: A Guide* (Cardiff, 1974), pp. 42–3.

after Sir Hugh's death. The early sixteenth century sees a sharp increase in such accounts of interesting experiences. Two other examples are Sir John Clerk (d. 1539) at Thame, Oxfordshire, who took Louis d'Orléans, duc de Longueville, prisoner 'at ye jorney of Bomy by Terouane' on 16 August 1513,[60] and William Wetherden at Bodiam, a southern equivalent of Sir Peter Legh, who after the death of his wife gave himself to study and took holy orders.[61]

If we did not have the inscriptions of the Johnys, Clerk and Wetherden brasses they would have seemed unexceptional iconographically. Funerary monuments are, of their essence, conservative in nature, and brasses have a narrower range of iconographic expression than the more prestigious sculpted monuments. It is in their inscriptions that brasses provide the most reliable indicator of the measure of the development, which was to be accelerated by the doctrinal changes of the sixteenth century, of the retrospective aspect of the funerary monument as 'a thing erected, made, or written, for a memoriall of some remarkable action, fit to bee transferred to future posterities'.[62]

[60]   Stephenson, *List*, p. 423.
[61]   Davidson-Houston, 'List of Monumental Brasses in Sussex. Part I', p. 87, pl. on p. 86. The inscription reads: Hic iacet dominus Wilelmus Wetherden nuper vicarius istius ecclesie qui quidem non literatus uxorem duxit qua mortua se dedit studio liberali et sacerdocij ordinem suscepit et obijt xxvj februarij Anno M Vc xiij Multa huic bona dedit ecclesie.'
[62]   Weever, *Ancient Funerall Monuments*, p. 1, cited in R. Rex, 'Monumental Brasses and the Reformation', *Transactions of the Monumental Brass Society*, 14, pt. 5 (1990), pp. 376–94 at p. 379.

The Image of the Writer in Medieval English Manuscripts

PAMELA TUDOR-CRAIG

The lecture on which this essay is based was devised and delivered with the assistance of the late Stephen Medcalf. As an art historian I could not have had the temerity to venture so far as I have here into the field of medieval literature and its antecedents, had it not been for the encouragement and support of that remarkable scholar, who died in September 2007. Having greeted my observation of the group of images of reclining writers as a new and important aspect of a change in attitude to the mysterious source of inspiration, he coaxed my ventures into the material with generous loans of his own precious and rare books. We discussed this paper at every stage of its evolution, and as colleagues will remember, he enhanced its delivery by reading himself the quotations he helped me to select. This has not been the only subject where I have benefited greatly over the last decade from his collaboration, and where the Harlaxton Symposium enjoyed his readings. However, it is the paper where my own enquiries have taken me most deeply into his field. It is a cheerless thought that his guidance and his love of interdisciplinary medieval studies will not be with us any more. This paper is dedicated with my gratitude to his memory.

How to record the recorder, to perceive the perceivers? How are those who write presented? The answer is for the most part straightforward. Writers are shown at their desks, whether in the case of John Rous working on his rolls,[1] or of the scholar penning a depressing text reminding us of our end in the charming stained glass roundel in Andrew Rudebeck's collection (Plate 36).[2] Where the matter is exalted, as in portrayals of St Augustine writing to St Jerome about the condition of the soul after death, Botticelli, for example, shows the author seated as

---

[1] In the so-called 'Lancastrian' version of the roll in the College of Arms (produced before 1485), and the later 'Yorkist' version, London, British Library, MS Add. 48976; for a brief account of both see A. Gransden, *Historical Writing in England, II, c. 1307 to the Early Sixteenth Century* (London, 1982), pp. 309–12, and for reproductions of the images of Rous, W. Courthope (ed.), *Thys rol was laburd & finished by Master John Rous of Warrewyk* (London, 1859), reprinted with an introduction by C. Ross (London, 1980).

[2] I am grateful to Andrew Rudebeck for allowing us to use a photograph of his roundel.

usual, pen in hand, but looking upwards towards a sudden shaft of light.[3]

The most directly inspired of all writers, from the medieval viewpoint, were the Evangelists. In the heroic Gospel books of the earlier Middle Ages they take dictation from their symbols. In the Northumbrian Lindisfarne Gospels, Matthew (on account of a confusion of sources) rejoices in two symbols: one (a winged man blowing a trumpet and carrying a book) worn as a scarf, so to speak, and the other (an unidentifiable figure) peeping round the prompt curtain.[4] In the Copenhagen Gospels of approximately three hundred years later, the same eccentric idea is repeated.[5] The suggestion that the figure half-hidden behind a curtain is intended to represent Christ is not convincing. Why should Matthew, and not the three other Evangelists, have had a special hot line to Christ?

Throughout the Carolingian and Ottonian periods industrious Evangelists scribble fervently as they try to keep up with the flow of revelation. One version of the theme stands out, however, in the early eleventh-century Grimbald Gospel book.[6] A lot of silver was used in the sumptuous decoration of this supreme example of medieval illumination, and since silver oxidizes, some of the decoration has gone black and spread. St John, gold quill in hand, looks up almost startled as his eagle thrusts a now illegible silver scroll towards him. What it must say, however, is beyond dispute, since the opposing page carries the opening words of his gospel: *In principio erat verbum.* The borders of the double opening illustrate the text. The insistence upon 'light' in the opening was probably the reason for using so much gold and silver, themselves light-refracting, in its illustration. Tiny figures around the margins represent the multitude of hosts, earthly and heavenly, adoring the figures in the upper roundels. Those roundels on the left-hand page contain seated figures of the three persons of the Trinity. Along the sides are groups of the twelve Apostles, of priests with acolytes, and along the borders the elders of the Apocalypse with their crowns. The central roundel at the bottom has a great gathering of souls held in a napkin by two angels. On the right-hand or incarnational page the top centre is occupied by a Virgin and Child, flanked by a cherub and a seraph, and around them more elders, priests, a Benedictine monk,

---

3   The Botticelli, now a detached fresco, in Ognisanti in Florence, was painted for the Umilitati in 1480 as a pendant to Ghirlandaio's St Jerome; see R. Lightbown, *Botticelli: Life and Work*, 2 vols (London, 1978), I, pp. 49–52, for a reproduction (plate 22) and further discussion.

4   BL, Cotton Nero D. IV, fol. 25v; this page is illustrated in J. Backhouse, *The Lindisfarne Gospels: a Masterpiece of Book Painting* (London, 1995), plate 23 (facing p. 41).

5   Copenhagen, Royal Library GKS 10 2°, fol. 17v; see J. Backhouse, D. H. Turner, L. Webster (eds), *The Golden Age of Anglo-Saxon Art, 966–1066* (London, 1984), p. 48, plate XII. Both the Copenhagen and Lindisfarne Gospels were probably in Durham c.1000; the Copenhagen may have copied from the Lindisfarne Gospels.

6   BL, Add. 34890, fols 114v–115; for a reproduction, see the British Library website at http://www.bl.uk/catalogues/illuminatedmanuscripts/TourLitMass.asp.

and two groups of holy women. So within the framework of two pages appears an entire ordering of the company of Heaven gazing at 'the true Light which lighteth every man that cometh into the world.'

With the fourteenth-century flowering of imaginative literature in the vernacular came new ways of portraying the author. The fifteenth-century *Desert of Religion* includes a relatively straightforward drawing of Richard Rolle, seated in a sparse landscape with a book open on his knees, and his right hand indicating the monogram IHS emblazoned across his heart.[7] This is striking enough, but there is an earlier and almost alarming drawing of Rolle at the beginning of his mystical treatise, *Incendium Amoris,* given to Lincoln Cathedral Library by the great collector and builder of their Wren Library, Bishop Michael Honeywood (Plate 37).[8] Rolle, the hermit of Hampole, died in 1349, but his writings were translated into Middle English by Richard Misyn, himself a canon of Lincoln Cathedral, probably in the 1380s.[9] In this copy of his works, probably originally belonging to Misyn himself, Rolle is represented receiving the divine fire of which he writes, in the form of red rays down which swoops a most urgent Holy Spirit. As with the eleventh-century Grimbald Gospels and the 1480 painting by Botticelli, we know precisely the moment of illumination represented in the illustration. There is one point in the text where Rolle breaks into verse, modernized from Misyn's translation as follows:

O my God! O my love! Into me glide; with they charity thirled; with thy beauty wounded:
Slide down and comfort me, heavy; give medicine to me, wretched; show thyself to thy lover.
After thee my heart desires; after thee my flesh thirsts… .[10]

Rolle was a hermit, so it was perhaps appropriate to show him standing, carrying no book, and clad in his Carmelite habit, rather than seated at a scholarly desk. St Jerome was often represented as a hermit, translating the Vulgate at the entrance to a cave, his lion curled up at his feet. But Jerome sits, on however rudimentary a rock, and uses a contrived book desk. And unlike Rolle, the recipient of

7   BL, Cotton Faustina B. VI, part II, fols 3–23v; the image of Rolle is on fol. 8v and reproduced in M. Comper, *The Life of Richard Rolle. Together with an Edition of his English Lyrics* (London, 1928; repr. New York, 1969), frontispiece; for a description of the manuscript, see K. Scott, *Later Gothic Manuscripts, 1390–1490*, 2 vols (London, 1996), ii, 192–4.

8   Lincoln Cathedral Library MS 218; see R. M. Thomson, *Catalogue of the Manuscripts of Lincoln Cathedral Chapter Library* (Cambridge, 1989), pp. 177–9 and pl. 57. I am most grateful to the staff for letting me spend an afternoon examining this manuscript.

9   Richard Copsey, 'Misyn, Richard (d. 1462)', *Oxford Dictionary of National Biography*, Oxford University Press, 2004 [http://0-www.oxforddnb.com.catalogue.ulrls.lon.ac.uk:80/view/article/18823, accessed 7 Aug 2008].

10   Comper, *The Life of Richard Rolle*, pp. 119–20.

the holy dove in a ray of light from the Father descending is normally the Virgin Annunciate.[11] Other than this Richard Rolle, I have seen no representation where so intimate a contact is made with anyone of less stature than Our Lady until the 1528 screen panel of St Bridget in the church of Horsham St Faith's in Norfolk.[12] Here the rays proceed from a blessing God the Father in a cloud. However, the Virgin kneels, and St Bridget sits at her writing desk. Only Richard Rolle stands, clutching the bar of the letter 'A'.

All the great religions describe divine inspiration received either in a dream or at the moment of waking, in the hypnagogic state between the worlds of sleep and consciousness, whose particular value is known to those who work from the imagination. The opening of the *Corpus Hermeticum* puts it thus:

> Once, when mind had become intent on the things which are, and my understanding was raised to a great height, while my bodily senses were withdrawn as if in sleep, when men are weighed down by too much food or by the fatigue of the body, it seemed that someone immensely great of infinite dimensions happened to call my name and said to me: 'What do you wish to hear and behold, and having beheld what do you wish to learn and know?' 'Who are you?' said I. He said, 'I am Poimandres, the Nous of the Supreme. I know what you wish and I am with you everywhere.'
> 'I wish to learn,' said I, 'the things that are and understand their nature and to know God. O how I wish to hear these things! . . .'[13]

Boethius's *De consolatione Philosophiae*, written shortly before his execution in 524 or 525 AD, and translated into Anglo-Saxon in a version ascribed to King Alfred, into Middle English by Chaucer and John Walton, and into sixteenth-century English by Queen Elizabeth I, opens with the sufferer in his bed, lamenting in the company of the muses of poetry his dire misfortune. Of a sudden Philosophy herself appears to him, 'of awe-inspiring appearance, her eyes burning and keen beyond the usual power of men.'[14] Sumptuous copies from the twelfth to the sixteenth

---

[11] For the most part the dove aims at her womb, although in few examples in a great swoop towards her face. On a frequently illustrated alabaster relief flanking an unidentified fifteenth-century tomb of a cleric, in the chapel of St Calixtus off the north transept of Wells Cathedral, the dove appears to be about to kiss the Virgin on the mouth; see L. S. Colchester, *Wells Cathedral* (London, 1987), p. 110.

[12] See E. Duffy, *The Stripping of the Altars: Traditional Religion in England, c.1400–c.1580* (New Haven and London, 1993), p. 86 and pls. 61 and 62. Duffy associates the image with a woodcut in a printed book of 1520, Wynkyn de Worde's *The dyetary of ghostly helthe* (STC 6833).

[13] *The Way of Hermes, the Corpus Hermeticum and the Definitions of Hermes Trismegistus to Asclepius*, trans. by C. Salaman, D. van Oyen, W. D. Wharton, and J.-P. Mahé (London, 1999), p. 19. This text has been known in the West since 1460, when one of Cosimo de Medici's agents brought a copy in Greek to Florence.

[14] V. E. Watts (ed. and trans.), *Boethius: The Consolation of Philosophy* (Harmondsworth, 1986), p. 35.

centuries open with an illumination of Boethius in bed in his prison and Philoso-phy standing before him.[15] Writers from Malory to Bunyan have vouched for the frequency with which she visits prison cells.

For the most part, however, the awakening from sleep or reverie to inspira-tion comes to the seeker in a sylvan setting, a dark wood, probably with a stream running through it, or on a rugged hill top. The father figure of this new way of introducing the story has to be Dante. In the opening of the *Divina Commedia*, probably written by 1330, Dante enters the dark wood. Numerous illuminated copies show the first steps of his journey, with the author walking through, or crouching in the wood. They culminate in Botticelli's drawing, where Dante is almost overwhelmed by a forest of trees, an interpretation which is not carried through into the earliest printed versions.[16] One of the first illuminated versions, however, by a Sienese illuminator, is now in the Biblioteca Augusta in Perugia.[17] It shows the poet lying down asleep in the dark wood, on the threshold of his vision:

> In the midway of this our mortal life,
> I found me in a gloomy wood, astray
> Gone from the path direct: and e'en to tell,
> It were no easy task, how savage wild
> That forest, how robust and rough its growth,
> Which to remember only, my dismay
> Renews, in bitterness not far from death ...
> How first I enter'd it I scarce can say,
> Such sleepy dullness in that instant weigh'd
> My senses down, when the true path I left;
> But when a mountain's foot I reach'd, where clos'd
> The valley that had pierced my heart with dread,
> I look'd aloft, and saw his shoulders broad
> Already vested with that planet's beam,
> Who leads all wanderers safe through every way.[18]

Dante's education was steeped in the works of Virgil, who is the key to the under-standing of this new way of presenting the writer: as scholar not at his desk, but seeking, and finding, inspiration in a lonely and often woody setting. The signifi-cance of Virgil throughout the Middle Ages is attested by all. In addition to his

[15] For some reproductions, see the plates in H. R. Patch, *The Tradition of Boethius* (Mew York, 1935), and M. T. Gibson (ed.), *Boethius: His Life, Thought and Influence* (Oxford, 1981).

[16] The drawings are divided between the Vatican Library and Berlin; see R. W. Lightbown, *Sandro Botticelli*, 2 vols (London, 1978), i, 147–51, and ii, 172–205, and, more gener-ally, H.-T. Altenkappenberg, *Botticelli: The Drawings for Dante's Divine Comedy* (London, 2001).

[17] Perugia, Biblioteca Comunale, Augusta L. 70, fol. 1v; see the reproduction in M. Camille, *Gohic Art* (London, 1996), p. 145.

[18] H. F. Cary (ed. and trans.), *The Vision, or Hell, Purgatory, and Paradise of Dante Alighieri*, 3rd edn (London, 1844): *Hell*, canto I, lines 1–17.

innate qualities as a poet, and his Christ-like hero Aeneas, he had the added credential of authorship of the fourth *Eclogue*, where his prophecy of the birth of a child who would usher in the Golden Age was accepted as applying to the birth of Christ, who was in fact born approximately 20 years after the poet's death.[19] In her powerful account of the continuity of pagan literature throughout the early Middle Ages, Helen Waddell quoted St Jerome: 'The very Priests of God are reading comedies, singing the love songs of the Bucolics, turning over Virgil.'[20]

The pastorals wind their gentle way among sleepy fields and shaded groves through all the poetry of Europe. Wherever there is the growth of cities and the pressure of war there springs the need to seek nature and solitude.[21] Witness Petronius Arbiter, struggling to serve the Empire under Nero, who drove him in 66 A.D. to suicide:

> Small house and quiet roof tree, shadowing elm
> Grapes on the vine and cherries ripening,
> Red apples in the orchard, Pallas' tree
> Breaking with olives, and well-water'd earth
> And fields of kale and heavy creeping mallows
> And poppies that will surely bring me sleep ...[22]

The same spirit breathes through the fragment from the Priscian manuscript from St Gall:

> A hedge of trees surrounds me: a blackbird's lay sings to me, praise which I will
>   not hide,
> Above my booklet the lined one, the trilling of the bird sings to me,
> In a grey mantle the cuckoo chants to me from the tops of the bushes.
> May the Lord protect me from doom! I write well under the greenwood.[23]

In the classical renaissance of the twelfth century, the classical texts originally transcribed at St Riquier for Charlemagne and his successors were recopied in monastic libraries. In that century the Cistercians, like the Irish monks before them, saught wild and unfrequented places for their monasteries, and in the thirteenth century St Francis taught Europe to love again and to communicate with the natural world. Dante probably owed part of his education to the Franciscans at Santa

[19] See especially B. Reynolds, *Dante: The Poet, The Political Thinker, The Man* (London, 2006), pp. 108–09.
[20] H. Waddell, *The Wandering Scholars* (Glasgow, 1927), p. xviii, quoting Jerome's *Epistle* xxi, from P. Migne (ed.), *Patrologiae Cursus Completus, Series Latina*, 22, cc. 385–6.
[21] For illustrations concerning the eighteenth to the twentieth centuries, see S. Martin, M. Butlin and R. Meyrick, *Poets in the Landscape: The Romantic Spirit in British Art* (Chichester, 2007).
[22] H. Waddell (ed.), *Medieval Latin Lyrics* (London, 1929), pp. 7–8.
[23] Waddell, *Wandering Scholars*, p. 35.

Croce in Florence.[24] The nature of his classical grounding is expressed in his choice of Virgil to lead him through the Inferno and to be his companion through Purgatory.

The Sienese illuminator of the *Divina Commedia* now in Perugia did not make a profound mark on the language of illustration. That honour fell to another Sienese painter, working for Petrarch, another admirer of Virgil. Simone Martini's illumination for the head of Petrarch's copy of Servius's commentary on Virgil's *Bucolica* was painted in Avignon between 1338 and 1344, the year of Martini's death.[25] Petrarch had owned the book, on and off, since 1326, and he commissioned the image from Simone Martini probably in 1340 when they were both in the court at Avignon. Petrarch still had the book by him in Parma in 1348, when he noted on a flyleaf the death of Laura.

Martini's painting does not illustrate any specific passage of Virgil's text, but rather the commentary on it by the fourth-century grammarian, Sestius, who is shown drawing back the curtain that had veiled Virgil, in order to reveal him. The soldier behind Sestius is Aeneas himself; the *Eclogues* are represented by a farmer pruning, and the *Georgics* by a shepherd milking his ewe. Three couplets are transcribed on the banderols, praising in turn Virgil, Sestius and Simone Martini. This honouring of Virgil resolutely places the poet not at his desk but reclining at his ease, pen in hand in a sylvan setting: Virgil is seen primarily not as the poet of the great epic but as the greatest exponent of the pastoral. Martini's image of Virgil, reclining as he writes in a wood, could have been based on an antique river god. The example still on the Capitoline Hill was conspicuous throughout the Middle Ages, and if Simone Martini, as has often been suggested, served an apprenticeship under Giotto at the Vatican, he was working within a stone's throw of this figure.[26] On the other hand, a readier source could have been to hand in Avignon, in the form of the Vatican Virgil itself (MS Vatican Lat. 3225, produced in Rome c. 400 CE, but seemingly in France for part of its medieval existence, probably with the papal entourage).[27] Since only a third of the text is now extant and most of the illuminations are missing we cannot now hope to find an exact source for Martini's image; but surviving pictures show that the artist or artists of the Vatican Virgil

[24] Reynolds, *Dante*, pp. 7–8.

[25] The manuscript is Milan, Bibliotheca Ambrosiana A. 49. inf, fol. 1v; see A. Martindale, *Simone Martini* (Oxford, 1988), pp. 50–51, 191–2, and plates 113–14; and C. Martindale (ed.), *The Cambridge Companion to Virgil* (Cambridge, 1997), frontispiece and p. x.

[26] A. Martindale, 'The Knight and the Bed of Stones: A Learned Confusion of the Fourteenth Century,' *British Archaeological Journal*, 142 (1989), 66–74, and pls xvi–xix. River gods were to be found elsewhere: in the late nineteenth century fragments of one were dredged from the Thames; F. Haverfield, 'On Two Marble Sculptures and a Mythraic Relief of the Roman Period Found in London,' *Archaeologia*, 60 (1907), 43–8.

[27] D. H. Wright, *The Vatican Vergil: A Masterpiece of Late Antique Art* (Graz, 1984).

could have furnished recumbent figures as well as sylvan settings. Simone's illustration may reflect the 'Ego ille' preface to the *Aeneid* that was in the Middle Ages attributed to Virgil himself:

> That man am I who having once played his song on a slender reed, emerging from the woods compelled neighbouring fields to submit even to the greediest farmer, a work welcome to husbandmen...[28]

This later introduction points up the emphasis placed in the Middle Ages on Virgil's voice in the field of husbandry rather than his chronicles of war; that is clear in the passage which most nearly approximates to this profoundly original illumination: the opening of the first *Eclogue*, upon Tityrus stretched at ease, entertaining his sylvan muse. Virgil resides here in an idyllic woodland, whereas Dante's dark wood is threatening: but both authors are represented far from their desks.

In a c. 1378 copy of *Le songe du vergier*, the author portrays France as an earthly paradise as he beseeches the papacy to return to Avignon: 'Le terre de France est comme le Paradis de dieu' (Plate 38).[29] On the right in the illumination sits Charles V in a Franciscan habit, with the personification of Puissance Spirituelle and Clement VII, who did indeed come back to Avignon in 1379. In the middle ground an academic is disputing with a knight, suggesting France as the home of all the sciences, and beneath them the poet lies dreaming on the flowery mead. About four years later Jean Gerson wrote his *Pastorium Carmen* evoking the *Eclogues* of Virgil and the *Buccolicum Carmen* of Boccaccio; Gerson was happy to quote Virgil, Ovid and Terence in his sermons as Chancellor of the University of Paris.[30] The author of *Le songe du vergier* could have taken his pastoral scene from Virgil himself, or from Dante.

We have come now to the cluster of English poets who took up, and in two cases developed, the Virgilian ambiance immortalized by Simone Martini. They do not appear to have included Chaucer, for all Chaucer's vaunted classicism. Chaucer was among the first to render Virgil in English verse, but he chose (in *The House of Fame* and *The Legend of Good Women*) Aeneas's arrival in Carthage and meeting with Dido, rather than a pastoral subject. The famous representation of Chaucer reading *Troilus and Criseyde* to the elegant company of which Richard II was obviously the central figure could hardly present a sharper contrast to the

---

[28] See Elena Theodorakopoulos, 'Closure: The Book of Virgil', in *The Cambridge Companion to Virgil*, ed. Martindale, pp. 155–65 (p. 160).

[29] BL Royal 19 CIV, fol. 1v; reproduced in E. Taburet-Delahaye, *Paris 1400: Les arts sous Charles VI* (Paris, 2004), p. 51, n. 11.

[30] Patrick de Winter, *La Bibliothèque de Philippe le Hardi, Duc de Bourgogne (1364–1404)* (Paris, 1985), pp. 25 and 28; de Winter also notes (p. 283, n. 16) that the French royal library, like the libraries of the Duc de Berry and of Gian Galeazzo Visconti at Pavia, had copies of Virgil in the late fourteenth century.

meditative and retiring contexts we have been examining.[31] The country setting has a castle and what has been assumed to be the procession of Criseyde and her entourage meeting Troilus and his company in the background, while in the foreground a fashionable audience clusters round the author in his outdoor pulpit. This luxurious picture seems to illustrate the following passage:

> Criseyde, whan she redy was to ride,
> Ful sorwfully she sighte, and seyde 'Allas!'
> But forth she moot, for aught that may bitide;
> Ther is non other remedie in this cas.
> And forth she rit ful sorwfully a pas.
> What wonder is, though that hire sore smerte,
> Whan she forgoth hire owen swete herte?
>
> This Troilus, in wise of curteysie
> With hauk on honde and with an huge route
> Of knyghtes, rood and did hire companye
> Passyng the valeye fer withoute,
> And ferther wolde han ridden, oute of doute,
> Ful fayn, and wo was hym to gon so sone;
> But torne he moste, and it was ek to done.[32]

This scene shows Chaucer as courtier and entertainer, reciting rather than composing his poem. At the opening of 'The Franklin's Tale' Chaucer has his narrator declare 'I sleep nevere on the Mount of Pernaso'.[33] Some of his contemporaries, however, opened their poems with verbal images of the writer doing just that. First among them might be *Summer Sunday*, a lament for Edward II:

> Opon a somer soneday se I the sonne
> Erly risinde in the est ende;
> Day daweth ouer doune, derk is in towne,
> I warp on my wedes, to wode wolde I wende.
> ... I hiede to holte with honteres hende.
> So ryfly on rugge roon & raches ronne
> That in launde vnder lynde me leste to lende –
> And Lenede.[34]

---

[31] Cambridge, Corpus Christi College MS 61, fol. 1v; see the introduction to the facsimile ed. by E. Salter and D. Pearsall (Cambridge, 1978).

[32] L. D. Benson (ed.), *The Riverside Chaucer* (Boston, 1987), p. 561: *Troilus and Criseyde*, Book V, lines 57–70.

[33] 'I never slept on Mount Parnassus', *The Canterbury Tales*, V, line 721; Benson (ed.), *Riverside Chaucer*, p. 178.

[34] Lines 1–9 in R. H. Robbins (ed.), *Historical Poems of the XIVth and XVth Centuries* (New York, 1959), pp. 98–102; for a translation, see J. Gardner (ed.), *The Complete Works of the Gawain Poet* (London, 1965), pp. 16–19: 'On a summer Sunday I saw the sun | Rising up early on the rim of the east | Day dawned on the dunes; dark lay the

There he witnessed a vision of a hunt, and later he walked a river, took a boat, 'And wandered away in the woods to find who I'd find | I lounged awhile and listened – on a slope I lay', and met with an allegorical assembly.

Gardner thought, with good reason, that the Gawain-poet may have known this prototype; and not only he – what of Langland?

> In a somur sesoun whan softe was the sonne
> Y shope me into shroudes as y a shep were;
> In abite as an heremite, vnholy of werkes,
> Wente forth in the world wonders to here,
> And say many sellies and selkouthe thynges.
> Ac on a May morning on Maluerne hulles
> Bi biful for to slepe, for werynesse of-walked;
> And in a launde as I lay, lened y and slepte,
> And merueylousliche me mette, as y may telle.
> Al the welthe of the world and the wo bothe
> Wynkyng, as hit were, witterliche y sigh hit;
> Of treuth and tricherye, tresoun and gyle,
> Al y say slepynge, as y shal telle . . .[35]

As Dante's dark wood at the opening to the *Divina Commedia* derives from Virgil, so the English poets may hark back to Dante, but there were native forerunners as well.[36] The pastoral mode has always come naturally to English poets. A French cleric wrote to Nicholas of St Albans, about 1178:

> Your island is surrounded by water, and not unnaturally its inhabitants are affected by the nature of the element in which they live. Unsubstantial fantasies slide easily into their minds. They think their dreams are visions, and their visions to be divine ...[37]

---

town; | I caught up my clothes, I would go to the groves in haste; | ... I went at once to the woods ... | I liked to loll under limbs in the cool glade | And lie down.'

[35] Derek Pearsall (ed.), *Piers Plowman, by William Langland. An edition of the C-text* (London, 1982), pp. 27–28, lines 1–13. For a translation of the equivalent passage from the B-text, see *Piers Plowman. The Vision of a People's Christ by William Langland. A Version for the Modern Reader by Arthur Burrell* (London, 1912), p. 3: 'But on a May morning, on Malvern hills, | A marvel befell me – sure from Faery it came – | I had wandered me weary, so weary I rested me | On a broad bank by a merry-sounding burn; | And as I lay and leaned and looked into the waters | I slumbered in a sleeping, and looked into the waters | And I dreamed – marvellously. | All the world's weal, all the world's woe, | Truth and trickery, treason and guile, | All I saw, sleeping ...'.

[36] Echoes of *Wynnere and Wastoure* have been heard by T. Turville-Petre, 'An Anthology of Medieval Poems and Drama', in *Medieval Literature: Chaucer and the Alliterative Tradition*, ed. B. Ford (Harmondsworth, 1982), pp. 387–602 (p. 411).

[37] Quoted by P. Ackroyd, *Albion: The Origins of the English Imagination* (London, 2004), p. 47.

The single opening medieval illustration to *Piers Plowman*, in the form of an historiated initial 'y' on the opening recto of the copy of the C-text in Bodleian MS Douce 104, shows a recumbent dreamer-figure, although lacking any form of pastoral setting.[38] Iconographical conventions appropriate to dreamer-seers seem to have been established by this period, but not obviously reflecting Virgilian influence. After the two precious late Roman illuminated manuscripts of Virgil's writings, his work does not appear to have been illustrated before the fifteenth century.[39] Finely written copies of his works were produced between the fifth and fifteenth centuries, but with nothing more than historiated initials.[40] Liversidge observed that the visual tradition of the *Georgics* and *Eclogues* devolved into the roundels of the labours of the months that accompany the calendar pages of richly illuminated manuscripts. It was only in Italy in about 1450 that the visual equation was made between Virgil and the Golden Age, with reverberations that have echoed down to our time.[41]

It is a boon therefore that the only text of the four poems *Sir Gawain and the Green Knight*, *Pearl*, *Cleanness*, and *Patience* has not only flourishes and ornamental initials, but twelve illustrative pictures, four for each of *Sir Gawain* and *Pearl*, two each for *Cleanness* and *Patience*.[42] I cannot agree with Edward Wilson's suggestion that one of the wash drawings of the *Pearl*-maiden's father is a representation of the author.[43] The formula suggests a less prosperous layman but of similar type to the courtier behind the shoulder of Richard II in the *Epître de Philippe de Mézières* of c.1395.[44] On the other hand, the learning displayed in *Pearl*, where some have detected the influence of the *Divina Commedia* – may suggest that the author's educational background led to minor orders.

---

[38] See the facsimile intro. by K. L. Scott and D. Pearsall, *Piers Plowman: A Facsimile of Oxford, Bodleian Library MS Douce 104* (Cambridge, 1992); the image, and wider context of dream-illustrations, are discussed by Scott on p. xxxviii.

[39] The early manuscripts are Rome, Vatican Library Codex Vat. Lat. 3867, with nineteen illustrations, and Codex Vat. Lat. 3225 with fifty illustrations.

[40] M. J. H. Liversidge, 'Virgil in Art,' in *The Cambridge Companion to Virgil*, ed. Martindale, pp. 91–103 (esp. p. 91).

[41] Liversidge, 'Virgil in Art', p. 95.

[42] BL, MS Cotton Nero A. X; all the illustrations are reproduced in D. Brewer and J. Gibson (eds), *A Companion to the Gawain-Poet* (Cambridge, 1997). For some analysis of the illustrations and the extent to which they reflect the texts they illustrate, see Scott, *Later Gothic Manuscripts*, ii, 66–8, and A. S. G. Edwards, 'The Manuscript: British Library MS Cotton Nero A. x', in Brewer and Gibson (eds), *Companion*, pp. 197–219.

[43] Edward Wilson, 'Gawain Poet (*fl. c.*1375–1400)', *Oxford Dictionary of National Biography*, Oxford University Press, 2004 [http://0-www.oxforddnb.com.catalogue.ulrls.lon.ac.uk:80/view/article/52804, accessed 7 Aug 2008].

[44] BL, Royal MS 20. B. VI, fol. 2, illustrated in D. Gordon, L. Monnas and C. Elam, *The Regal Image of Richard II and the Wilton Diptych* (London, 1997), p. 191, fig. 112.

The opening of *Pearl* is set in an 'erbere' (arbour) which may be a greensward or a herb garden. The plants described are both medicinal, and, through their fragrance, narcotic and trance-inducing. The illustration in no way suggests a tidy garden (Plate 39). The poet describes how his pearl had slipped from him:

> Allas! I leste hyr in on erbere;
> Thurgh gresse to grounde hit fro me yot.
> I dewyne, foredolked of luf-daungere
> Of that pryuy perle wythouten spot .

> That spot of spysez mot nedez sprede
> Ther such rychez to rot is runne;
> Blomez blayke and blwe and rede
> Ther schynez ful schyr agayn the sunne ...

> To that spot that I in speche expoun
> I entred in that erber grene,
> In Auguste in a hygh seysoun,
> Quen corne is coruen with crokez kene.
> On huyle ther perle hit trendeled doun
> Schadowed this wortez ful schyre and schene ,
> Gilofre, gyngure and gromylyoun,
> And pyonys powdered ay bytwene ...

> I felle vpon that floury flaght
> Suche odour to my hernez schot;
> I slode vpon a slepyng-slaghte
> On that precios perle wythouten spot.

> Fro spot my spyryt ther sprang in space;
> My body on balk ther bod in sweuen.
> My goste is gon in Godez grace
> In auenture ther mervaylez meven ...[45]

The hill or mound is flower-strewn indeed, with a conjunction of plants impossible not only in one season but in one climate. The setting of *Pearl* invites comparison with Patmos, or with the opening of the *Divina Commedia*, or with Mount Parnassus: all rugged and unkempt places, thresholds of visionary experience.

In the cases of the *Gawain*-poet and Langland we have small idea of their literary resources, and we can be sure that even if they had seen texts of Virgil's pastoral poems, these would not have been illustrated.[46] The openings of their dream sequences upon the hills followed literary convention. The background of John

---

[45] E. V. Gordon (ed.), *Pearl* (Oxford, 1953), lines 9–64.

[46] For details of Langland's biography, see G. Kane, 'Langland, William (c.1325–c.1390)', *Oxford Dictionary of National Biography*, Oxford University Press, 2004 [http://0-www.oxforddnb.com.catalogue.ulrls.lon.ac.uk:80/view/article/16021, accessed 7 Aug 2008], who suggests that he was a married clerk in minor orders, living in Cornhill.

Lydgate is better charted.[47] As a monk of the great abbey of Bury St Edmunds he had access to one of the best medieval libraries, with over 2,000 books. In about 1430 Abbot William Curteys, like so many of his contemporaries, had built a more extensive library over one of the walks of the cloister, and in Lydgate's time it boasted many standard classics, including Ovid, Juvenal, Cicero, Horace and Seneca, as well as Virgil (although apparently no Plato or Aristotle). We may suspect that Lydgate took little advantage of the opportunity offered to him: it would seem he had read Ovid, but had a smattering only of Cicero and Virgil.[48] An *Aeneid* in twelve books, of about 1200, was on the shelf beside him,[49] but the main source for his *Troy Book*, written for Prince and then King Henry V between 1412 and 1420 was Guido de Columnis's thirteenth-century *Historia Destructionis Troiae*, of which there was also a copy in the Bury library.[50]

John Lydgate is perhaps a pedestrian heir to the traditions of the Virgilian world, but nevertheless a collection including a number of his minor poems is headed by a drawing, once more of the poet dreaming in a woodland setting (see Plate 40). A miscellany of Middle English prose and poetry made between 1471 and 1483, belonging to the London mercer Roger Thorney and later to John Stow, opens with this piece:

> Here bigynnyth a treatise | of *Parce miche domine*
>
> By a forest side walkyng as I went,
> Disport to take in o morning
> A place I fond shadid with boughis bent
> Isette aboute with flowris swete smellyng
> I laide me doun vpon that greene
> And cast myn eyen me abowte.

[47] See D. Pearsall, *John Lydgate* (London, 1970), pp. 32–3.

[48] Pearsall, *John Lydgate*, p. 15.

[49] Now Cambridge, Trinity College MS R 3 50 (623); see N. R. Ker, *Medieval Libraries of Great Britain: A List of Surviving Books*, 2nd edn (London, 1964), p. 19; and M. R. James, 'On the Abbey of St Edmund at Bury, I. The Library,' *Cambridge Antiquarian Society*, octavo publications 28 (Cambridge, 1895).

[50] D. Gray, 'Lydgate, John (*c.* 1370–1449/50?)', *Oxford Dictionary of National Biography*, Oxford University Press, 2004 [http://0-www.oxforddnb.com.catalogue.ulrls.lon.ac.uk: 80/view/article/17238, accessed 7 Aug 2008]. Lydgate's later acquaintance with Humphrey, Duke of Gloucester presumably brought him access to a new kind of humanist library. There is no record that Humphrey had a copy of Virgil's complete works, but as the most substantial list of his holdings is the record of those he gave to Oxford in 1444, it is always possible he held back the books he valued most highly. See R. Weiss, *Humanism In England during the Fifteenth Century* (Oxford, 1967), pp. 39–70; D. Rundle, 'Habits of Manuscript Collecting: the Dispersals of the Library of Humphrey Duke of Gloucester', in *Lost Libraries: The Destruction of Great Book Collections since Antiquity*, ed. J. Raven (Chippenham and Eastbourne, 2004), pp. 106–24.

I fond ther briddes with fethirs sheene ...[51]

As a Virgilian, if flat-footed, tribute in both verse and image to the pastoral tradition it is one of a number of late Middle English poems which depict writers finding inspiration as they recline in bosky settings. 'I write well under the greenwood', the topos noted in the Priscian manuscript, remained alive.[52]

[51]   Cambridge, Trinity College, MS R 3 21 (601), fol. 34, text transcribed from the manuscript; for a full version of *Parce Michi Domine,* from MS Bodley 596, see C. Brown (ed.), *Religious Lyrics of the XIVth Century*, 2nd edn revised G. V. Smithers (Oxford, 1952), pp. 208–15. The illustration is reproduced in Scott, *Later Gothic Manuscripts,* i, fig. 20; for discussion see ii, 337–9.

[52]   Cf. for example the anonymous lyric beginning 'As I walked me this endurs day | to the grene wode for to pleye ...', in C. Brown (ed.), *Religious Lyrics of the Fifteenth Century* (Oxford, 1939), pp. 2–3.

Richard of York: Books and the Man

LIVIA VISSER-FUCHS

Richard, Duke of York (died 1460), was a political figure and his intellectual life has not received much attention from modern commentators.[1] This paper hopes to fill part of the gap left by historians[2] by focussing on his books. A book collection resembles an autobiography and books, through their contents *and* the manner in which they were acquired, reveal things about their owner not found in narrative and documentary sources. They confirm or contradict what we think we know about their owner's life and personality. There are many well-known fifteenth-century book owners on whom such a theory can be tested:[3] Richard III,[4] and his contemporary Philip of Cleves, Lord of Ravenstein, a German/Burgundian nobleman;[5] Humphrey, Duke of Gloucester, or Louis de Bruges, Lord of Gruuthuse, two of the most prolific book collectors of their day,[6] and in a different category, Richard Neville, Earl of Warwick, who was rich and influential, though only one book survives for him, or the Burgundian chronicler of England, Jean de Wavrin, whose library is so distinctive that an illustrator was named after him.[7]

---

[1] Except J. Rosenthal, 'Richard, Duke of York: a Fifteenth-Century Layman and the Church', *Catholic History Review*, 50 (1964–65), 171–87.

[2] P. A. Johnson, *Duke Richard of York, 1411–1460* (Oxford, 1988); T. B. Pugh, 'Richard Plantagenet (1411–60), Duke of York, as the King's Lieutenant in France and Ireland', in *Aspects of Late Medieval Government and Society*, ed. J. G. Rowse (Toronto, 1986); R. Griffiths, 'Richard of York's Intentions in 1450', *Journal of Medieval History (JMH)*, 1 (1975), 187–209; J. Watts, *Henry VI and the Politics of Kingship* (Cambridge 1996) and the same *Richard of York, Oxford DNB*; M. K. Jones, 'Somerset, York and the Wars of the Roses', *EHR*, 104 (1989), 285–307, M. Hicks, 'From Megaphone to Microscope: The Correspondence of Richard, Duke of York, with Henry VI in 1450 Revisited', *JMH*, 25 (1999), 243–56.

[3] A. F. Sutton and L. Visser-Fuchs, 'Choosing a Book in Late Fifteenth-Century England and Burgundy', in C. Barron and N. Saul (eds), *England and the Low Countries in the Late Middle Ages* (Stroud, 1998); the same, *Richard III's Books. Ideals and Reality in the Life and Library of a Medieval Prince* (hereafter *Richard III's Books*) (Stroud, 1997), pp. 14–16, 19–20, 21–39, 265–77.

[4] *Richard III's Books*; A. F. Sutton and L. Visser-Fuchs, *The Hours of Richard III* (hereafter *Hours of Richard III*) (Stroud, 1996).

[5] J. Haemers, C. Van Hoorebeek and H. Wijsman (eds), *Entre la ville, la noblesse et l'Etat: Philippe de Clèves (1456–1528), homme politique et bibliophile* (Turnhout, 2007).

[6] L. Visser-Fuchs, 'Lodewijk vand Brugge', *Oxford DNB*.

How many books do we need, to draw conclusions? For some collectors, Gruuthuse for example, we can prove, above all, bibliomania: over many years he acquired almost any book available in his time. Similarly Gloucester's collection presents problems concerning his real interests and his 'mere' patronage.[8] For Philip of Cleves, Richard III and Wavrin a perfect number of manuscripts seems to survive: sufficient to create a picture, and not so many as to suggest that the manuscripts were acquired automatically, without any real interest. For Warwick the one surviving manuscript reveals what the people who gave it to him thought of him.[9]

For Richard of York's 'bio-bibliography' we have a tiny 'collection' of, at the most optimistic count, six surviving texts. Most of these were dedicated to him, all are interesting.[10] First his book of hours, fortunately not a standard one; two books of history: John Hardyng's *Chronicle* and one volume of the *Grandes chroniques* of France; one literary work, Christine de Pisan's *Cité de(s) Dames*, and finally two unusual texts: the one a genealogy of the lords of Clare, Suffolk, the other a classical Latin text, with parallel English translation. Most of these texts have been studied, but not together as York's 'library'.

The most interesting item is the edition with parallel translation of part of Claudius Claudianus' poem 'On the consulate of Stilicho'.[11] The historical Stilicho

[7]   L. Visser-Fuchs, 'Jean de Waurin', *Oxford DNB*; the same, *History as Pastime: Jean de Waurin and His Collection of Chronicles of England*, forthcoming.

[8]   An iconoclastic view of Humphrey's bookishness and humanism: D. Rundle, 'On the Difference between Virtue and Weiss', in D. Dunn (ed.), *Courts, Counties and the Capital in the Later Middle Ages* (Stroud, 1996), 181–203, esp. 194–8.

[9]   L. Visser-Fuchs, 'The Manuscript of the *Enseignement de vraie noblesse* made for Richard Neville, Earl of Warwick, in 1464', in G. H. M. Claassens and W. Verbeke (eds), *Manuscripts in Transition* (Louvain, 2006), 337–62.

[10] Not included: **(1)** Giles of Rome, *De regimine principum*, London, Lambeth Palace MS Arc. L 40.2/L 26, as the heraldry contradicts York's ownership claimed by e.g. P. Tudor-Craig, *Richard III* (London, 1977), item 157, and C. F. Briggs, *Giles of Rome's De regimine principum* (Cambridge, 1999), pp. 68–9, 164; comp. A. F. Sutton and L. Visser-Fuchs, 'Richard III's Books: V. Aegidius Romanus' *De regimine principum*', *Ricardian*, 8 (1988–90), 61–73, esp. p. 70, and *Richard III's Books*, pp. 118, 283–5; **(2)** books Cicely Neville owned of which only titles survive, C. A. J. Armstrong, 'The Piety of Cicely, Duchess of York', in his *England France and Burgundy in the Fifteenth Century* (London, 1983), 135–56, esp. pp. 144–50; **(3)** the so-called 'York Psalter', Rennes, Bibliothèque municipale MS 22, K. Scott, *Later Gothic Manuscripts 1390–1429*, London 1996, no. 38, probably belonged to York's sister Anne, Duchess of Exeter; **(4)** the so-called Kerdeston Fragments, Sotheby's 12 March 1946; B. Danielson, 'The Kerdeston "Library of Hunting and Hawking Literature"', in *Et Multum et Multa*, ed. S. Swenk et al. (Berlin, 1971), 47–59, esp. p. 50; Scott, ibid., no. 91.

[11] BL, Add. 11814. Edited E. Flügel, 'Eine mittelenglische Claudian-übersetzung (1445)', *Anglia*, 28 (1905), 255–99, 421–38. For more detail on text, author, protagonist, translation, and the MS, see my '"Honour is the Reward of Virtue": the Claudian Translation made for Richard, Duke of York, in 1445', *Ricardian*, 18 (2008), 66–82.

(died 408) was a politician and general who rose to power under Emperor Theodosius at whose death the Roman Empire was divided between his two sons, the West to the infant Honorius, the east to the weak minded Arcadius. In the struggle for power that inevitably ensued, Rufinus, the strongest man in the east, was murdered and Stilicho ruled unchallenged. The best known commentator on the period, the poet Claudian, was a fanatic supporter of Stilicho and his view, supported by his talent for brilliant praise and deadly invective, shaped the later historiography of the period.

In the 'Consulate of Stilicho' the poet praises his hero in glowing terms for his achievements and pleads with him by means of various 'personages', Spain, France, Britain, Africa and Rome itself, to take on the consulship and save the empire. He focuses on Stilicho's virtues, his clemency, loyalty, justice, temperance, prudence and constancy; avoiding greed, ambition, lust, pride and even 'idle talk'. The presentation of so many virtues and vices in a small compass made the text a perfect 'mirror for princes',[12] but its main merit to the translator was the fact that it described a man about to overcome his temporary troubles because of his many virtues – as Richard of York was in 1445.

Since 1905 commentators have assumed that the translation encouraged York either to assume the protectorship of the realm or the throne itself. Others have put this in perspective, considering that York's problems in 1445, when he was accused of mismanagement of funds and favouritism while king's lieutenant in France, were enough to explain the translator's expressing his confidence in the duke and assuring him that virtue will inevitably carry the day.[13]

The translation bears the subscription 'Translate and wrete at Clare 1445' and the style of the decoration relates the manuscript to productions made in and around Bury St Edmunds.[14] The author was probably an inmate of the Augustin-

[12] Emphasised by W. Fahrenbach, 'Vernacular Translations of Classical Literature in Late-Medieval Britain', PhD thesis (Toronto, 1975), pp. 150–82, not an expert on English politics of the 1440s, and approaching the text with an open mind.

[13] Previous note and S. Moore, 'Patrons of Letters in Norfolk and Suffolk', *PMLA*, 27 (1912), 188–207; 28 (1913), 79–105, esp. pp. 93–5; Fahrenbach, 'Vernacular Translations', pp. 150–82; A. Goodman, D. Morgan, 'The Yorkist Claim to the Throne of Castile', *JMH*, 11 (1985), 61–9; J. Watts, '*De Consulatu Stiliconis*: Texts and Politics in the Reign of Henry VI', *JMH*, 16 (1990), 251–66; S. Delaney, 'Bokenham's Claudian as Yorkist Propaganda', *JMH*, 22 (1996), 83–96; the same, *Impolitic Bodies. Poetry, Saints, and Society in Fifteenth-Century England* (New York, 1998), pp. 133–43; A. S. G. Edwards, 'The Middle English Translation of Claudian's *De consulatu Stilichonis*', in A. Minnis (ed.), *Middle English Poetry: Texts and Traditions* (York, 2001), 267–76; the same, 'Duke Humfrey's Middle English Palladius Manuscript', in J. Stratford (ed.), *The Lancastrian Court*, Harlaxton Medieval Studies, XIII (Donington, 2003), 68–77, esp. pp. 74–7; D. Wakelin, *Humanism, Reading and English Literature 1430–1530* (Oxford, 2007), esp. pp. 70–80.

[14] K. Scott, 'Lydgate's Lives of Saints Edmund and Fremund', *Viator*, 13 (1982), 335–66, esp. pp. 362–3.

ian friary, usually called Clare Priory at Clare, which had a long history of patronage from Richard of York and his ancestors.[15] Eight initials in the Claudian manuscript are historiated in colour with York's heraldic devices: a closed fetterlock, a falcon, a white rose and a white hind.[16] The translator's additional texts mention Richard of York by name.

The translator made a conscious selection, for the whole of the original poem *and* Claudian's other verse were probably known to him and he explains that Claudian's 'othir boke clepid Claudianus in Ruffinum' contains 'the vicious lyfe of Ruffyn'.[17] The surviving manuscripts of Claudian's work, from the eleventh century on, contain all his political poems and a copy could be found, for example, at Bury St Edmunds, fifteen miles from Clare.[18] Britain occurs rarely in Claudian's work and the lively personification of the island would have been noticed long before 1445. The translator realised that here was the story of a great man falsely accused; it also offered the high moral tone and the allegorical material so much appreciated in his day. The figures of Spain, Gaul, Britain and Africa pleading with Stilicho in all their 'national' splendour are among the most attractive sections of the poem. Britain, dressed in wool, her cheeks covered with 'iron', her feet hidden in the water and her cloak resembling the waves of the ocean, declares that thanks to Stilicho she no longer fears battle in Scotland or in Picardy. The fact that the original text has 'the skin of a Caledonian wild animal', not wool; that her feet are covered by her blue cloak, not the sea; and that she no longer fears the Picts, not Picardy, makes the English version the more fascinating.[19]

The translator made a conscious selection *and* had no precedent to direct him; no one had re-used the text as a panegyric. The only precedent, probably not known to the Clare translator, was the *Anticlaudianus* of Alain de Lille.[20] Alain wrote his book as a positive mirror image of Claudian's *In Rufinum* (*Against Rufinus*), a stunning piece of abuse against Stilicho's dead enemy, describing in a way Chaucer would have appreciated how all the vices and evils of this world, discord, famine, disease, lust, greed, gathered together to discuss how they could best injure mankind. Eventually they decided to introduce Rufinus, their most talented pupil, into the imperial court to pervert the prince. The description of Rufinus is malign caricature and Alain de Lille turned it round to create his own hero, whom he called 'Antirufinus', a man blessed with every Christian virtue. Alain composed an original work to make his point, the Clare author managed to use one of Claudian's own texts to create his picture of the perfect man.

[15]   VCH, *Suffolk*, ii (London, 1907), pp. 127–9.
[16]   Add. 11814, ff. 5v and 6, 9v and 10, 13v and 14, 17v and 18.
[17]   F. 4v.
[18]   R. Mynors, 'The Latin Classics known to Boston of Bury', in D. Gordon (ed.), *Fritz Saxl 1890–1948. Knowledge and Learning* (London, 1957), 199–217, esp. p. 215.
[19]   F. 17, lines 269–78.
[20]   W. F. Cornog, *The 'Anticlaudian' of Alain de Lille* (Philadelphia, 1935).

The undoubted theme of the Clare translation is the certainty that virtue will be rewarded, and the reward of virtue is 'honour' or 'worship', unspecified. That 'honour is the reward of virtue' was a Aristotelian concept,[21] summarised and passed on by St Thomas Aquinas,[22] who used the word *merces* for 'reward', which was picked up by the Clare translator. He used it seven times in the refrain of his final dedicatory poem and the crucial words, *honor est merces virtutis*, are also written in large lettering across the cover of the book.[23]

It is difficult to gauge how well informed the translator really was and how able to use the material correctly. It is not clear whether his Latin was not particularly good, or whether his 'mistakes' were not mistakes, but conscious changes. And what did the Clare author know about Roman life, culture and history?[24] If he had known more about the historical Stilicho he would probably not have used him as an exemplum,[25] but he simply had no other information at his disposal, and he would probably not have been interested if he had. It has been pointed out[26] that he had no problem accepting pagan gods and goddesses and mythological heroes, and must have been quite familiar with them.[27] He used words such as 'Phebus', 'the Muses ix', 'Mownte Palatyne' easily,[28] and was able to explain the temperate zone of the earth,[29] who 'Tritonia' was,[30] that *elevacio manuum* means 'praying' (*devocio*),[31] and that Latin *fasti* means public records, 'the volume of Rome which conscript fadris shewith'.[32]

More significant than his learning and his learned notes, however, is the fact that his notes are most numerous in one section: where Stilicho seems to claim

[21] *Ethica Nicomachea*, 1, 8 (1099a); 4, 3 (1123b).
[22] *Summa Theologiae*, q. 2, art. 2, q. 4, art. 1; *Treatise On Happiness*, trans. J. A. Oesterle (Englewood Cliffs, N.J., 1964), pp. 15, 41.
[23] No previous commentator has remarked on this.
[24] It has been pointed out that the learned comments in the margin are in a hand different from that of the text itself (*ex inf.* Simon Horobin); the comments could be by the author, the text by a scribe.
[25] Stilicho's death resembled York's, at least in some versions of the story of the latter's end: he was tricked into leaving sanctuary and executed!
[26] Fahrenbach, 'Vernacular translations', pp. 161–2.
[27] Compare Bokenham's use of classical figures, e.g. the quotation from his life of St Mary Magdalen given by Wakelin, *Humansim*, p. 67, where he says he will pray for God's support only and than proceeds to mention all the classical deities on whom he will *not* call.
[28] However, the temple of Janus of which the doors were closed only when peace reigned throughout the Roman empire, is translated as if the Italian town of Genua 'is bounde to peese', f. 19, line 313.
[29] Add. 11814, f. 6, opposite line 10.
[30] Add. 11814, f. 21, opposite line 367: *Pallas Tritonia Minerva > dea sapientie*, 'Pallas Tritonia Minerva = the goddess of wisdom'.
[31] Add. 11814, f. 23, opposite line 410.
[32] Add. 11814, f. 17, line 266.

he has been slandered. The original text mentions terrible portents and evil deeds and the figure of Rome comforts Stilicho, explaining those things affect the east of the empire only and that no report has reached her. Claudian's references are all to the 'unmentionable' consulship of Eutropius, a eunuch and ex-slave. His holding office created a scandal at the time and tainted the consulship itself and *this* was the reason why Stilicho tried to excuse himself: he did not want to share a title with such a man. Rome praises him for not mentioning this horror to Roman ears, and not polluting the senate by such stories.

The translator, perhaps through ignorance but more likely deliberately, assumed that Stilicho was complaining that *he himself had been slandered*. Rome answers she has no report of that, 'of credens nevir cam letter | the to accuse',[33] and she praises him for keeping silent about the slight done to him and not taking revenge. These lines are highlighted by the marginal note *deo gracias Ricarde* opposite the first one and repetition marks opposite the next six.[34] The emphasis on this section indicates that the only thing the translator had in mind was York's reputation – not his dynastic claims. The words 'steyned my worshippe' and 'sclaunder' are his own, interpreting the Latin very freely. York himself, when protesting against the accusations – about mismanagement of funds, favouritism while he was the king's lieutenant in France and others – called them 'slanderous language' (sclaindereux langaige),[35] and spoke of 'his worship hurte' and 'his grete hurt and sclaundre'.[36]

By the nature of the text its intended audience was limited. Claudian's language is not easy to follow and who would have been interested to read *in extenso* about the duke's virtues and the comforting maxim that the 'good ones' will be rewarded? York himself, perhaps some friends and relations, and the inmates and visitors of Clare Priory? Commentators have theorised about the existence of an East-Anglian circle of neighbours and relatives, including York, which shared an interest in religion and literature.[37] In the 1440s this circle could have been served by a single copy of the Claudian translation and it is likely that we possess this copy: the manuscript appears not to have left Suffolk.[38] The Latin text was perhaps included not so much as an 'authority' to support the translation, but as a demonstration, or perhaps merely a suggestion, of the cleverness of the translator and a semblance of 'proof' of what he had done with the original. He must have known that most people – except perhaps his learned brethren – would not be able to

33 F. 19, lines 324–5.
34 F. 19, lines 325–31.
35 Petition to Henry VI, December 1445(?), Johnson, *York*, 52.
36 Against Bishop Moleyns, 1446(?), M. Kekewich et al. (eds), *The Politics of Fifteenth-Century England: John Vale's Book* (Stroud, 1995), pp. 180–83, esp. 180, 181.
37 *Richard III's Books*, pp. 28–9.
38 Acquired by the BL from the antiquary William Stevenson Fitch, of Ipswich, in 1841.

understand the Latin properly or realise that his translation was excessively 'free' at times, but it suited his purpose; he was not a learned editor working for a university press.

There is no doubt that Richard of York and his supporters, the translator among them, felt strongly about the accusations of 1445, but there is no reason to believe that 'Rufinus' refers to a specific individual, as scholars have tried to prove. The text should not be taken that literally. There was no Theodosius, Honorius or Arcadius in mid-fifteenth-century England, there was a merely prince that 'Stilicho' had been loyal to. Rufinus is not the duke of Suffolk or Somerset or Bishop Moleyns, but the 'enemy', every opponent of York. Rufinus was evil incarnate, not a real person – and so Alain de Lille had used him. The situation of 1445, however unpleasant, was a short-lived crisis, dwarfed by the events of the next decade, and the Claudian translation lost its immediacy and with it much of its meaning.

The theory that the book had a limited audience is supported by another poem produced at Clare Priory, in 1456, the 'Clare Roll', also called the 'Dialogue between a Layman and a Friar', because the latter is telling the former about the history and sights of the house.[39] This text, too, sings the praises of Richard of York, and at the same time celebrates York's family, the friary itself and the earlier lords of Clare. This text, too, is cleverly composed and edited in Latin and English on one sheet of vellum.[40] This text also has no political content, even though by the time it was made York had been protector twice. The Clare Roll follows the line of the lords of Clare from the foundation of the friary to the 1 May 1456. When explaining York's descent from Lionel of Clarence, 'Kyng Edwardis son the third was he', its tone is merely informative: Lionel is included because he married Elisabeth, daughter of William de Burgh, Earl of Ulster and Lord of Clare. York himself receives high praise; the Latin reads (my translation):

> Richard was born, sweet smelling like spikenard, who is called duke of York by right of his father. His sword shines forth, he is glorious in his titles and war triumphs. Nature gave him many talents, and fortune adorned him with great gifts. May he also have the blessing of a long life, happy and virtuous, and be redeemed at the end.

The English has:

> But hir son Richard which yet liveth, is
> Duke of Yorke by discent of his fadir
> And hath Marchis londis by right of his modir.

---

[39] The illustration was painted in the same area as the Claudian decoration; Scott, 'Lydgate's Lives', p. 356n.

[40] *A Manual of the Writings in Middle English 1050–1500*, iii (New Haven, 1972), VII [38]; the edition by W. Dugdale, *Monasticum Anglicanum* (1835) viii, 1599–1600, is the best; A. F. Sutton and L. Visser-Fuchs, '"Richard liveth yet": An Old Myth', *Ricardian*, 9 (1991–3), 266–9; *Richard III's Books,* pp. 3, 23, 25, 146n, 148, fig. 50, pl. III.

The Latin is more elaborate because the flowery words came easily to the author in that language – at least one phrase is borrowed directly from a classical source.[41] There is no political double meaning, neither in the Latin (where it would be hidden from the illiterate), nor in the simpler English.

The Clare Roll's close 'relative' is the so-called Rous Roll, made by John Rous (c. 1411–91), chaplain of Guy's Cliff near Warwick, 1477 to 1485,[42] another antiquarian who wished to inform people about the place he loved. He collected historical material and brought it together in a twenty-four-feet roll with sixty-six pictures and accompanying text. There was a Latin as well as an English version and part of the information celebrated the earls of Warwick, Rous' patrons. It is unnecessary to conclude that the makers of these two rolls ever met, but they did share a love of the place they lived in, an interest in history, an admiration for the Latin language and a healthy desire to please their patrons.[43] Though the Clare Roll and other such rolls[44] were politically 'innocuous' York undoubtedly, in due time, owned genealogical rolls that proved his claim to the English crown, emphasising his descent from Brutus, the founder of Britain, his position as heir of the princes of Wales, as well as his claims to England, France and Castile. Edward IV was later to possess similar manuscripts, some of them highly sophisticated and the result of years of research.

Two history books survive for York, but it is likely he had many more, like most aristocratic book-lovers in his lifetime.[45] The two books can be seen as representing larger categories: English history and 'foreign' history, but also books presented to York and books inherited by him.

The first version of John Hardyng's verse chronicle of England[46] covers the history of England from Brutus to 1436 and was dedicated to Henry VI. The second,

[41] *praefulgurat ensis*, Statius, *Thebais*, 7, lines 501–02, Valerius Flaccus, *Argonautica*, 3, line 119.

[42] *Manual*, ix (New Haven, 1993), XXI [78]; *A Catalogue of English Medieval Rolls of Arms*, ed. A. R. Wagner (London, 1950), pp. 116–20.

[43] A. F. Sutton and L. Visser–Fuchs, 'Richard III's Books: Ancestry and 'True Nobility', *Ricardian*, 9 (1991–3), 343–58, esp. 350–52, nn. 41, 45.

[44] E.g. New Haven, Beinecke Library, MS 323 (*c.* 1440), sets out the lordship of Clare; the genealogy showing York's right to England and Spain was inserted later. Cambridge, Corpus Christi College, MS 98, French and Latin, is linked to Wigmore Abbey and the Mortimers; York was the thirteenth 'founder'; M. R. James, *A Descriptive Catalogue of the Manuscripts in the Library of Corpus Christi College, Cambridge*, 2 vols (Cambridge, 1912) i, pp. 184–5. BL, MS Add. 46354, ff. 59–61, *Richard III's Books*, p. 26.

[45] *Richard III's Books*, p. 153, and ch. 7.

[46] *The Chronicle of Iohn Hardyng*, ed. H. Ellis (London, 1912); F. Riddy, 'John Hardyng's Chronicle and the Wars of the Roses', *Arthurian Literature*, 12 (1993), 91–108; C. L. Kingsford, 'The First Version of Hardyng's Chronicle', *EHR*, 27 (1912), 462–82, 740–53; A. S. G. Edwards, 'The Manuscripts and Texts of the Second Version of John Hardyng's *Chronicle*', in *England in the Fifteenth Century*, ed. D. Williams (Woodbridge 1987), pp. 75–84; H. Summerson, 'John Hardyng', *Oxford DNB*.

shorter, version ends in 1463, probably cut short by the author's death, and was dedicated to York but not finished when the duke died in December 1460. The second version was adapted to York's interests and sets out his descent from Edward III via the female line, listing every claim York could lay to any lordship or kingdom, including Spain, Portugal and Jerusalem. It would be helpful to know when Hardyng started to think it worth his while to rewrite his chronicle, as it would pinpoint the moment York's claims became known to people with an interest in such matters. It has been argued that Hardyng's second version matches the 'new genealogy' used by York, the 'old' one being the one which emphasised his descent from Edmund of Langley, Edward III's fifth son, the male line, the 'new' one tracing his female descent from Lionel of Clarence, Edward III's third son[47] – but as we have seen this descent could also be used 'innocently'. The 'new' genealogy is supposed to have come into use between 1455 and 1458. Hardyng presented his first version to Henry VI in 1457, so – it has been argued[48] – he must have started his new text very soon after. But as no manuscript of before 1465 survives, we have no way of knowing how Hardyng went to work. 800 stanzas into the book, in the story of Cadwallader, he again addresses York, who must therefore have been alive, but this does not mean that all preceding stanzas had already been written. This story also makes it less likely that York turned to Hardyng for information,[49] for Hardyng depicts Cadwallader, the last British king, as a bad ruler, while Edward IV later took him as a symbol of his ancient and native descent: Edward was the Red Dragon of the British, Cadwallader reincarnated, the opponent of the evil and degenerate Saxons and their White Dragon, Henry VI.[50]

Equally interesting for our present purposes are the often-used statements about York in Hardyng's 'Proheme'. The first claims that the duke liked chronicles:

Yet wyll I use the simple witte I have
To your pleasaunce and consolacion,
Most noble lorde and prince, so God me save,
That in chronicles hath delectacion.[51]

The second states that York knows Latin well:

Well I wote your great intelligence,
That in Latyn hath good inspeccion,
Will pleased bee of your hie sapience;[52]

---

47   Riddy, 'Chronicle', 100, and R. Griffiths, 'The Sense of Dynasty in the Reign of Henry VI', in *Patronage, Pedigree and Power in Later Medieval England*, ed. C. Ross (Gloucester, 1979), 13–30; they give no examples.
48   Summerson, 'Hardyng'.
49   Riddy, 'Chronicle', 101.
50   *Richard III's Books*, p. 201n.
51   Ellis edn, p. 16.
52   Ibid., p. 23.

The third is the implication that the book will be shared with York's wife, Cicely, who 'in Latyn hath litell intellect', and York's son.[53] This may be flattery and wishful thinking, but it could be correct: the assumption that York was well versed in Latin is supported by the existence of the Claudian translation and the Clare Roll and there was no need for Hardyng to mention the duke's expertise in Latin if it was not true.

New research on the stationers of medieval Paris has revealed how York acquired his volume of the *Grandes chroniques de France*, covering the years 1270–1380, written in France 1380–1400 and illustrated there 1400–10.[54] This manuscript's history, showing how English collectors acquired their books in France before the conquest by Henry V, is buried in the documents of the trial for treason of a canon of Notre-Dame, Paris, in 1415–16. They describe the comings and goings at the Hotel de Bourbon in 1414, where English ambassadors were daily besieged by booksellers, goldsmiths, illuminators, and doctors, all trying to sell their wares, among them the *libraire* Regnault du Montet, a witness at the trial. Regnault admitted that he had been to England, many years ago, 'when King Richard was alive'. He had gone to see the *conte de Rothelain* – Edward, earl of Rutland, later duke of York[55] – to receive 60 *écus* for *un livre des Croniques de France* which he had sold to the earl. We know that Rutland was ambassador to France on several occasions and given the scene at the Englishmen's lodgings in 1414 it is likely his purchase took place in similar circumstances in the 1390s. From Rutland the book must have passed to Richard of York, his dead brother's son and his heir. York's son, Richard of Gloucester, is known to have owned it: he signed it himself.

As far as the *Cité des dames* is concerned, Christine de Pizan's famous defence of women, one would be pleasantly surprised if there was proof that it was shared by York and his wife, as Hardyng envisaged his own book would be, but the *Cité* was the most popular book in women's libraries in the fifteenth century[56] and we must assume it was Cicely Neville's, one of the texts she preferred before she 'retired' to a semi-religious life after the death of her husband.[57] The

---

53   Ibid.

54   BL MS Royal 20 C vii; R. H. and M. A Rouse, *Manuscripts and their Makers. Commercial Books in Medieval Paris 1200–1500*, 2 vols (Turnhout, 2000), i, pp. 258–88, ii,. pp. 123–5, ill. 176; A. F. Sutton and L. Visser-Fuchs, 'Richard III's Books: IX. The *Grandes chroniques de France*', *Ricardian*, 8 (1988–90), 494–514; 15 (2005), 114–16; *Richard III's Books*, ch. 7.

55   Earl of Rutland 1390, duke of Aumale 1397, duke of York 1402, *CP*, XI, 252; XII/2, 899–905.

56   *Histoire des bibliothèques françaises. Les bibliothèques médiévales du VIe siècle à 1530*, ed. A. Vernet ([n.p.], 1989), p. 252.

57   C. Meale, '"alle the bokes I haue of latyn, englisch, and frensch"', in the same (ed.), *Women and Literature in Britain 1150–1500* (Cambridge, 1993), pp. 128–58, esp. 135.

manuscript[58] was produced in France between 1430 and 1450, the right date for it to have been acquired during York's governorship of France. The readership of the *Cité* can be illustrated by the will of a lady at the Burgundian court, Marguérite de Boncourt, widow of Hue de Lannoy, courtier, counsellor and author. She died in 1460 and left many books to friends, relatives and servants, often a book to the husband and a piece of devotional jewellery to the wife. In one case the wife is given *le livre de la Cité des dames*; her husband was to keep himself amused with a chess set and board.[59]

The York copy of the *Cité des dames* bears his devices of the closed fetterlock and the white rose added to the decoration of the first page on either side of a little pot of flowers, a so-called 'Garden of Adonis', which was part of the original decoration.[60] The 'Garden' was a *memento mori* emblem, symbol of the transitoriness of life: its plants or flowers grew quickly into beauty, but as quickly faded. A version of the 'Garden', showing the authentic wheatears of the classical tradition, was the device of Humphrey of Gloucester.[61] Cicely's device is not known and as pots of flowers or plants were generally popular with illuminators, no conclusion can be drawn from its inclusion in the manuscript.

Finally the most intimate of Richard of York's books: his book of hours. It is a tiny, fat pocket book of about nine by six centimetres, 152 folios, eighteen lines to a page.[62] The larger part, folio 24 to the end, constitutes a standard book of hours, produced in Flanders in the 1450s – the dating is based on art historical evidence.[63] The first three gatherings were added and decorated in England after the book had been imported. There is nothing unusual about this production: Nicholas Rogers has shown that between the 1390s and 1520s thousands of books of hours were made in the Low Countries for use in England and more than 250 survive.[64] The

58 BL MS Royal 19 A xix, parchment, 172 ff., *c.* 28.5 x 20 cm.
59 B. de Lannoy, *Hugues de Lannoy, le bon seigneur de Santes* (Brussels, 1957), pp. 281–95, esp. 292.
60 F. 4, illustrated *Richard III's Books*, fig. 17.
61 T. D. Kendrick, 'Humphrey, Duke of Gloucester, and the Gardens of Adonis', *Antiquaries Journal*, 26 (1946), 119–22.
62 Durham, Ushaw College MS 43. I am grateful to Nicholas Rogers for pointing out this MS to me long ago. N. R. Ker, *Medieval Manuscripts in British Libraries*, iv (Oxford, 1992) pp. 549–51.
63 Use of Sarum: Calendar (Edward, martyr, Cuthbert, Edward, confessor, added in the 15th century), Fifteen Oes, Hours of the Virgin with Hours of the Cross (memorials to Holy Spirit, Trinity, Cross, Michael, John the Baptist, Peter and Paul, Andrew, Laurence, Stephen, Thomas of Canterbury, Nicholas, Mary Magdalene, Katherine, Margaret, All Saints, Peace and the Cross), *Salve regina*, Seven (Penitential) Psalms, Fifteen (Gradual) Psalms (first twelve lines only), Litany, *Vigilia mortuorum*, *Commendaciones animarum*; for all these: *Hours of Richard III*.
64 N. Rogers, 'Patrons and Purchasers: Evidence for the Original Owners of Books of Hours Produced in the Low Countries for the English Market', *Corpus of Illuminated Manuscripts*, xi, xii, *Low Countries*, series 8, ed. B. Cardon (Louvain 2002), pp. 1165–81.

added leaves were decorated by an artist connected to the so-called Caesar Master, a foreigner working in England around this time. Several manuscripts have been linked to him, but their owners can rarely be identified: Richard of York is one, Anne Neville, Duchess of Buckingham (died 1460), is another; the artist's oeuvre suggests he worked in London and for both universities from 1447.[65]

The contents of the additional pages start, unusually, with two prayers to the Guardian Angel.[66] The first has only the first two verses of a longer text, sometimes described as a prayer 'to be said every morning' which probably does not predate the fifteenth century.[67] The second, in prose, is included in full; it may date back to the tenth century and is often ascribed to St Anselm.[68] These two prayers were often linked together and like most prayers to the guardian angel they ask for his protection, day and night, waking and sleeping, from all the temptations of the devil, and from one's own digressions. The longer one begs to be allowed to know the hour of one's death, and that the soul will ascend to heaven, in the Angel's company; this text is marked by a 6-line initial showing York's coat of arms: France modern and England quarterly, a label of three points argent, each point charged with three roundels gules.[69] Prayers to the Guardian Angel are not common, and to have them in such a prominent position is rare. The cult became popular in England in the fifteenth and sixteenth century, but it remained very *private* and no official feast was instituted in this country.[70]

The Guardian Angel is followed immediately by a suffrage, or memorial, to St Edward the Confessor, not marked by a decorated initial, perhaps because the craftsman who looked after the lay-out of the additional pages did not understand its significance.[71] It begins: 'You are among the lilies of heaven and you are an ornament to those who rule in glory, lead all of us who love you to true happiness'.[72]

---

[65]   K. Scott, *The Mirrour of the Worlde* (London, 1980); the same, *Later Gothic Manuscripts*, ii, 278–9, nos 100, 106, 108; Sotheby's catalogue, 22/6/1982, lot 72.

[66]   A. F. Sutton and L. Visser-Fuchs, 'The Cult of Angels in Late Fifteenth-Century England', in J. Taylor, L. Smith (eds), *Women and the Book* (London, 1996), pp. 230–65.

[67]   Ushaw 43, f. 1: *Oracio ad proprium angelum*. Angele qui meus es custos pietate superna, me tibi commissum salva, defende, guberna. A. Wilmart, *Auteurs spirituels et texts dévots* (Paris, 1932), pp. 554–7, esp. 556n (1); Sutton and Visser-Fuchs, 'Cult', p. 249.

[68]   Ff. 1–2v: *Item oracio*. Obsecro te, angelice spiritus, cui ego ad providendum commissus sum, ut indesinenter protegas me, visites et defendas ab omni incursu diaboli. ... ; Wilmart, *Auteurs*, pp. 540–43.

[69]   F. 1, illustrated *Richard III Books*, pl. I.

[70]   Sutton and Visser-Fuchs, 'Cult', pp. 233–4.

[71]   He was not very efficient: the elevation prayer *Domine Ihesu Chrste qui hanc sacratissimam carnem* and its rubric occur on f. 12r–v and on 19v–20, see n. 91, below.

[72]   F. 2v: *Antiphon. De sancto Edwardo*. Ave sancte rex Edwarde, inter celi lilia, meritis tuis exornans regnantes in Gloria; *Analecta hymnica medii aevi (AH)*, ed. C. Blume et al., 55 vols (Leipzig, 1886–1922), xxviii, no. 292.

Edward is the most 'royal' of English saints; he was the first English king to touch for King's Evil, a kingly rather than a saintly gift,[73] and he represented pre-Conquest royalty. His cult had thrived under Henry III; he was replaced by St George as national saint, but greatly venerated again by Richard II.[74] He was to English kings what St Louis was to the kings of France: the saintly ancestor that helped to legitimate their rule. It was the laws and customs of the Confessor, among others, that English kings had sworn to uphold in their coronation oath since the time of John.[75] From the reign of Richard II, Edward the Confessor's fictional coat of arms[76] became part of kingly heraldry; a banner of his arms was carried at coronations, battles and royal funerals. Richard II took it on campaign in Ireland, Henry V displayed it at Agincourt, the duke of Bedford at Verneuil in 1424. In Edward IV's most elaborate genealogical roll St Edward's arms appear opposite those of St Louis.[77] The Confessor appealed especially to kings and his cult never enjoyed general popularity.[78]

St George, well established as the national/royal saint in York's lifetime, is honoured with a 4-line decorated initial and marginal decoration. He was the counterpart of St Denis in France, but with a much more military and chivalric image.[79] His memorial, *predotatum milicia,* is a standard one in hours of Sarum use, asking for protection against visible and invisible enemies.[80] The inclusion of St Christopher among these special prayers is not significant, but his memorial is very long;[81] he protected against virtually everything, particularly physical disasters such as famine and disease.

St Anthony the Hermit was one of the favourite saints of Richard III, but Richard's father also selected him. In York's hours his prayer is the only one honoured with a large historiated initial, showing the bearded saint holding his Tau-cross, a pig at his side, with marginal decoration on both this page and the opposite one.[82] It is another simple prayer, asking for protection against the fires of disease as well as a hell, and to obtain the glory of heaven with body and mind

---

[73] M. Bloch, *Les rois thaumaturges* (Paris and Oxford, 1924), pp. 43–9, 159–83.

[74] *Making and Meaning: The Wilton Diptych*, ed. D. Gordon (London, 1993), 54–5; S. Mitchell, 'Richard II: Kingship and the Cult of Saints', in *The Regal Image of Richard II and the Wilton Diptych*, ed. D. Gordon et al. (London, 1997), pp. 115–18.

[75] P. E. Schramm, *A History of the English Coronation* (Oxford, 1937), p. 200.

[76] Azure, a cross patonce or, between five martlets of the same.

[77] Philadelphia Free Library, Lewis MS 201.

[78] B. Spencer, *Pilgrim Souvenirs and Secular Badges* (London, 1998), 182–3.

[79] S. Riches, *St George, Hero, Martyr and Myth* (Stroud, 2000).

[80] Ff. 3–3v. Georgi martir Christi, te decet laus et gloria.

[81] The page between f. 4v and 5 was cut out. Ff. 4–5. Tu Ihesus es testis; *AH*, xxxiii, nos 67, 68.

[82] Ff. 5v–6. Salve pater heremita, infirmorum spes et vita.

intact. St Anthony is followed by a long, formulaic prayer,[83] sometimes called merely 'a prayer to the Trinity' and promising incredible benefits to whoever says it daily. In its traditional piety and charm-like power it resembles the long devotion that York's son, Richard, had added to his personal book of hours when king.[84]

The next item of interest is the suffrage to St Anne, highlighted by a 4-line decorated initial. Her only 'companion' in this part of the manuscript is St Barbara, and St Anne's presence in such a prominent position in a man's book of hours is undoubtedly unusual. Her feast had been officially instituted in England in 1383,[85] but her cult did not become widespread until the end of the fifteenth century. At the time York's hours were made this development was only starting and her popularity was never as great in England as it became in other European countries. St Anne was particularly venerated as the mother of the sacred dynasty, and as the link between Christ and his royal forebears.[86] Her worship was often linked to people who bear her name; Richard of York's principal claim to the crown derived from his mother, Anne Mortimer; his first daughter was named Anne.

St Barbara is the only other female saint selected by York.[87] She was also one of the saints that Richard, Duke of Gloucester, had 'a special devotion unto', but for York she is not joined by St Katherine, her usual companion in series of prayers to individual saints.[88] When depicted together they symbolised the 'mixed life', the attempt of educated Christians, conscious of their spiritual obligations but not in religious orders, to lead a life that was both active and contemplative.[89] On her own Barbara protected against lightning and was invoked by those fearing sudden death, gunners, miners and people with similar professions.[90]

After a series of standard prayers, a levation prayer,[91] *Deus propicius esto michi peccatori*,[92] and the *O intemerata et in eterna benedicta*[93] follows the last memorial of saints in this section: to the Three Kings,[94] who represented, through

[83] Ff. 6–8. *Oracio devota ad Trinitatem.* Domine deus omnipotens pater et filius et spriritus sanctus, da michi, famulo tuo N, victoriam; see next note.
[84] *Hours of Richard III*, pp. 67–78.
[85] The date of the establishment of the feast and its association with Richard II's queen are open to discussion, R. W. Pfaff, *New Liturgical Feasts in Later Medieval England* (Oxford, 1970), pp. 2, 3.
[86] T. Brandenbarg et al., eds, *Heilige Anna, Grote Moeder* (Uden, 1992), pp. 12, 16–17.
[87] F. 11r–v. *De sancta Barbara*. Veni, sponsa Christi, accipe coronam.
[88] St Katherine is included among the memorials after Lauds of the Hours of the Virgin in the main part of the book.
[89] *Richard III's Books*, p. 64.
[90] R. Nemitz and D. Thierse, *St. Barbara* (Essen, 1995), pp. 191–9, esp. 216–17.
[91] Ff. 11v–12v. *Omnibus confessis* ... Domine Ihesu Christe, qui hanc sacratissima carnem ...; *Hours of Richard III*, p. 52 and n. 151.
[92] Ibid., p. 53 and n. 153.
[93] Ibid., pp. 55–6 and n. 166.
[94] *Die Heiligen Drei Könige,* catalogue of an exhibition of the Wallraf-Richartz Museum,

the Epiphany, the closeness of royalty to the Christ child, and the God-given nature of kingship, and enjoyed popularity with reigning kings. Once their relics had been moved, through the agency of Emperor Barbarossa, from Milan to Cologne in 1164 their shrine became a focus of pilgrimage for people from all over Western Europe, including English kings and princes. It is said that Edward II visited the relics in 1322. Edward III went in 1338 and spent 58s. 6d. at the shrine; a decade later he had himself and his sons incorporated in a two tier Epiphany scene in the murals of St Stephen's Chapel at Westminster.[95] Richard II, who was born on 6 January, continued the cult of the Three Kings and had himself represented in an Epiphany-like scene together with SS Edward and Edmund in the Wilton Diptych.[96] In York's book of hours the prayer itself gives no hint of royal connotations, simply asking for the intercession of the Three Kings for a safe journey through life, as they were led safely to the sacred manger and brought home again.

The additional folios continue with a number of standard texts: five levation prayers,[97] followed by the Venerable Bede's devotion on the Seven Words of Christ on the Cross.[98] The added section ends with a brief prayer for the peace of the souls of York's father and mother and all the faithful departed: *Anime patris et matris meorum ac omnium fidelium defunctorum per misericordiam dei requiescant in pace. Amen.*

For the soldier/author Jean de Wavrin it is hard to find overlap between his books and what we know about his life, but there are clues. In his case it is obvious, for example, that the acquisition of his manuscripts started after he retired from military life and came into some money through marrying a wealthy widow. For Philip of Cleves and Richard III connections can be made between their reading interests and their attitude to family, learning and military matters. Louis de Gruuthuse acquired a Boethius *De consolatione philosophiae* in his mother tongue late in life, when he was in deep political trouble and spent time in prison.

For Richard of York we have evidence that he inherited at least one volume of French history from his uncle, and no doubt that was not the only 'family' book. York and his wife bought books while they were in France and were presumably

---

Cologne, Dec. 1982–Jan. 1983 (Cologne, 1982), pp. 34, 37, 44–5, 46 (fig. 7); H. Hofmann, *Die heiligen Drei Könige* (Bonn, 1975), pp. 130–34, 163, 299–300, 310.

[95]   *Age of Chivalry*, catalogue of an exhibition at the Royal Academy of Arts, London (London, 1987), no. 681.

[96]   Mitchell, 'Richard II', in *The Regal Image*, pp. 122–3

[97]   *Ave principium nostre creacionis*: U. Chevalier, *Repertorium hymnologicum*, 6 vols (Louvain, 1892–1912), no. 2059; *Ave domine Jhesu Christe verbum patris*: Wilmart, *Auteurs*, p. 412; *Ave verum corpus natum*, ibid., pp. 373–6; *Domine Jhesu Christe qui hanc sacratissimam carnem*: *Hours of Richard III*, p. 52; *Anima Ihesu Christi sanctifica me*: Chevalier, *Repertorium*, no. 1090.

[98]   *Hours of Richard III*, p. 52.

in touch with the cultural life of the French nobility and the upper ten of a city like Rouen. We have learned that in the 1440s, possibly within the literary circle of local gentry and intelligentsia which flourished in East Anglia, York was considered learned enough to appreciate an unusual edition *cum* translation of a difficult Latin text. His person and his patronage of Clare priory inspired scholarly writers in the 1440s and 1450s to sing his praises in a unique way – for what he had achieved, not for what he should have been. The neat little book with the Claudian translation, decorated with York's devices and full of praise and comfort, may have been the focus of a formal visit to Clare Priory,[99] or perhaps it was a New Year's gift in 1445–6 – it is not known where York spent the Christmas period, but he was in England.[100] Both the Claudian and the Clare Roll may have remained in Clare Priory to inform and amaze visitors.

In the late 1450s York seemed about to claim his full birthright and this period of expectation was apparently long enough for Hardyng to overhaul his book and hope that his flattering new 'edition' would bear fruit. Also in the 1450s Richard of York acquired a fashionable but simple book of hours for personal use – it contained many prayers he could say while mass was celebrated by his own priest at his own portable altar and it offered private, but clear and conscious references to important 'royal' saints. While praying to them he could think his own thoughts, but, as always, decision making was a slow process and even in his most private book he did not go as far as changing his coat of arms to the 'hole armys of Inglonde with owte any dyversyty',[101] which he did openly and deliberately display when he returned from Ireland in 1460 and proceeded to claim the crown itself.

Among York's books there are two that offer particularly interesting evidence. The Claudian translation gives us a flash picture of one specific moment in time; a brief glimpse of the fears and troubles of one short period, a glimpse of the kind that is difficult for later commentators, with their hindsight and too great knowledge, to interpret correctly and simply. In a similar way York's small and very private book of hours represents one of the very few ways in which we can gain an insight into the workings of the mind of a person long dead, his or her ambitions and doubts, however temporary.

---

[99] The Rous Roll was perhaps shown to Richard III and his family in Warwick in 1483, *Richard III's Books*, p. 146; Pietro Carmeliano's Latin 'Life of St Katherine' was presented to Richard in 1484/5, as a New Year's gift, ibid., pp. 69–71.

[100] Johnson, *York*, p. 51.

[101] *Gregory's Chronicle*, ed. J. Gairdner, Camden, n.s. 17 (1876), p. 208; Johnson, *York*, 214.

Historical Novels and Medieval Lives

SHAUN TYAS

The historical novel is an old, large and influential branch of literature, with medieval settings less numerous than those for later periods, but still substantial. This paper attempts to describe the scale and range of the subject with specific reference to medieval settings in the English language.

Quantities

My project began with a personal interest in the early medieval period, and a collecting interest in the historiography of Anglo-Saxon England. It became apparent from this collecting that the sheer number of historical novels indicates that they have an important role in the popular reception of history,[1] and even an influence on scholarly studies, not least because all historians have read some.

There are well over 5,000 medieval historical novels. This figure is based on my own systematic searching and the ongoing creation of a database which currently stands at 5,092 entries. There are no bibliographies of historical fiction but there are several readers' guides.[2] The largest and most recent, by Adamson, lists

---

[1]   Before my general collecting ceased, the medievalism section of my catalogue, which also included poetry, plays and eccentric writings, had 1,725 entries out of a total number of 7,534, = 22.88%. Of course, much scholarly literature exists in journals rather than books, but it seems not impossible that nearly a quarter of the books on any historical period are literary rather than factual.

[2]   In alphabetical order, the largest and latest appearing first: Lynda G. Adamson, *Recreating the Past. A Guide to American and World Historical Fiction for Children and Young Adults* (Westport, 1994) and eadem, *World Historical Fiction. An Annotated Guide to Novels for Adults and Young Adults* (Phoenix, 1999). Both Adamson titles suffer from seemingly meaningless inclusions and exclusions; there are many overlaps between the two books. Ernest A. Baker, *A Guide to Historical Fiction* (London, 1914) is an early attempt at a comprehensive survey, building on the author's 1903 *A Guide to the Best Fiction in English*, though still incomplete and opinionated. J. A. Buckley and W. T. Williams, *A Guide to British Historical Fiction* (London, 1912) is a short early survey with schools in mind. Lesley Henderson (ed.), *Twentieth-Century Romance and Historical Writers* (Chicago and London, 1990) is arbitrarily selective for the authors it includes, surveys only nine-tenths of the twentieth century, and makes no attempt to record the periods in which the novels are set: its use is therefore limited to checking the entries on the included writers; historians will rightly find the combination of these two genres in one survey as quite bizarre. Daniel D. McGarry and Sarah

273

only 795 medieval entries in total, less than 16% of what really exists. Even the fifteenth-century settings, seemingly well-covered by the Ricardians and other enthusiasts, show as only 131 entries in Adamson, against 305 entries in the Barton collection catalogue,[3] 344 novels in the specialised bibliography,[4] but currently 925 entries in my growing survey.

What uses can be made of such a pile? It can certainly be used to research medievalism, the sociology of the middle ages, because the books were intended for a mass readership. Historical novels also make a subtle contribution to mainstream historical knowledge, in influencing historians who have read them and sometimes where pioneer research has only been presented in a novel; but the subject is also an entirely valid area of the humanities in its own right. As in prosopography, which studies individuals through evidence for communities, a collection takes on an extra dimension of meaning, revealing an overall shape with internal relationships and traditions, something one cannot understand from studies which are selective or confined to the content of individual novels.[5]

Definitions

In natural history, the definition and classification of life forms (taxonomy) is deliberately and accurately inclusive, in order to embrace the reality of what is out there. There is perhaps a tendency in the humanities for definitions to be deliberately exclusive, to limit the subject to the researcher's own interests, but this is not scientific or particularly meaningful. A novel is therefore defined by the present writer as an extended prose fiction, and just that. The three words are important. Short stories are different from novels only in size and there is no frontier between them. Short stories are therefore included in my survey, as, indeed, they

---

Harriman White, *World Historical Fiction Guide. An Annotated, Chronological and Topical List of Selected Historical Novels*, 2nd edn (Metuchen, 1973) is openly selective but sensible. Mary S. Moffat, *Historical Fiction for Children. A Bibliography* (Darlington, 2000), despite the title, is a compilation of the author's reviews, mostly of recent titles. Finally, Jonathan Nield, *A Guide to the Best Historical Novels and Tales*, 5th edn (London, 1929) is an openly selective, but intelligent, classic survey, first issued in 1902; it also includes a rare bibliography of criticism.

[3] See Carolyn Hammond, *The Barton Library Catalogue. Fiction* (Richard III Society, 1998) for a catalogue of the Society's collection, at the time some 305 titles. The American and British branches of the Richard III Society also offer lists on their websites.

[4] Roxane C. Murph, *The Wars of the Roses in Fiction. An Annotated Bibliography, 1440–1994* (Westport, 1995), which includes plays and poetry as well as 344 novels. I am also grateful to Kenneth Hillier for stimulating discussions and a view of his own collection of Ricardian fiction.

[5] I call this the bibliographical approach to knowledge. Some of the ideas in this essay are also discussed in my thesis 'Towards a Rutland Bibliography. A Study of the Concept, Practice and Purpose of County Bibliographies with Specific Reference to Research for a Rutland Bibliography' (unpublished Ph.D. thesis, Department of Information and Library Studies, Loughborough University of Technology, 1997).

are in most scholarship on the historical novel. Indeed, some short stories are longer than works classed as novels: whether the work is printed and bound as a separate item or not, does not seem enough to justify a different approach to it.

'Prose' is in the definition to distinguish the novel from poetry, drama and cartoons. There are, of course, many thousands of post-medieval epic poems or dramas or screen plays or operas or comic strips concerning the middle ages which are just as important as the novel for the study of medievalism, but these are different forms of text so they can and should be excluded if the subject in hand is the novel rather than 'literature'. Mischievously, the phrase 'Graphic Novel' is now being used by the book trade for cartoons. They have always been popular on the continent (*Asterix the Gaul* is only the most famous of many),[6] but if the dialogue is in a word balloon, the real physical difference makes for a different category.

The word 'fiction' is there to distinguish novels from non-fiction works. The separation is not always obvious, of course. Plato used the fictional style in *The Republic*, and in the middle ages itself the distinction between history and fiction was hardly conscious. (In modern French the word *histoire* can still be used for both stories and histories, and English usage is often ambiguous.) Most medieval historians included made-up dialogue, and many actually wrote in verse. These texts sit awkwardly with modern desires to distinguish history and literature. It could be argued that the Icelandic sagas, Geoffrey of Monmouth's *History of the Kings of Britain*, and secular biographies like the *Vita Haroldi* are novels. In the case of Geoffrey of Monmouth, his work is not only a novel, it's a family saga.

There is one important controversy here, which is the desire of literary historians to claim that the English novel begins in the 1740s, with Henry Fielding's *The History of Tom Jones, a Foundling* (1749) and Samuel Richardson's *Pamela* (1740–1);[7] but there are hundreds of examples of extended prose fictions written before then, with over five hundred titles by 1700.[8] It is the quality of realism in these novels of the 1740s which is considered to set them apart from their antecedents, but if the quality of the writing is taken as the defining element rather than the literary form, not only is an element of prejudice introduced but also a serious contradiction. Soon after the publication of *Tom Jones* appeared Horace Walpole's pioneer Gothic novel, *The Castle of Otranto*, in 1764, and over a thousand Gothic novels were published before 1938 when Montague Summers issued

---

[6]   Seemingly a first-century setting, but the Goscinny and Uderzo canon includes *Asterix and the Normans* (London, 1978).

[7]   The publication of *Pamela* would appear to be the justification for the starting point of Andrew Block's useful *The English Novel 1740–1850. A Catalogue including Prose Romances, Short Stories, and Translations of Foreign Fiction* (London, 1939), though he dates it to 1741–2.

[8]   See, for example, the appendix list in Paul Salzman, *English Prose Fiction 1558–1700. A Critical History* (Oxford, 1985).

The Gothic Quest.[9] Since then there has been a huge growth in science and fantasy fiction, all called novels and most of them lacking in realism. Logically, if the definition is blurred after the novel appeared, then it must be blurred beforehand as well. In English we even call them novels,[10] suggesting that they are something new, the antecedents being called romances, allegories or even histories. In French and German there is a more accurate sense of continuity because they are all called *romans* or *romane*, but that is another contradiction, suggesting that the English novel is somehow unique or superior to those written in other languages.

The desire to include short stories sits comfortably alongside the obvious inclusion of multi-period historical novels. These cover a place, or a family, over a long period, so their medieval setting may be just one chapter. Edward Rutherford has made a speciality of this type with *Sarum. The Novel of England* (1987), *The Forest* (2000) and *London – the Novel* (1997), but there are earlier examples, such as J. P. True's *The Iron Star, and What it Saw in its Journey through the Ages from Myth to History* (1899), concerning a meteorite passed from one community to another. Multi-period novels also include ones which concern a relationship between two periods only. Medieval examples are Daphne du Maurier's *The House on the Strand* (1969) and Ronald Welch's *The Gauntlet* (1951). Cartoons are excluded, but the illustrated short story, issued as a separate book, often for children, should be included because the text is in the same physical format as a short story. An entertaining medieval example is *Master Snickup's Cloak* by Alexander Theroux (1979).

A definition is also needed of the *historical* extended prose fiction. The Historical Novel Society[11] defines it as a novel which is set in the past at least fifty years before the time it was written. The border is arbitrary, but necessary. In theory, it means that a historical novelist must be writing about the time before he was born, of which he has no personal experience. This means that new Second World War settings are historical novels but ones written in the 1950s are not. And it also means that novels from the past, set in their own times, are not historical novels, however useful they may be to historians. To accept *Pride and Prejudice* as an his-

---

9   Montague Summers, *The Gothic Quest. A History of the Gothic Novel* (London, 1938). Chapter IV of this large study is 'Historical Gothic' (pp. 153–201). The author also issued *A Gothic Bibliography* (London, n.d. [British Library copy 1940]). Both these works are compromised by their lack of any explicable inclusion or exclusion policy.

10   The word does ultimately mean 'new', but it descends into English in the middle ages themselves from the Italian *novella* for a short ephemeral work of fiction (as the pieces in Boccaccio's *Decameron*). It is perhaps ironic, though quite typical of terms in the humanities, that the term now taken to mean something allegedly specific, originally meant the exact opposite (serious/traditional vs superficial/new).

11   The organisation publishes two important journals, *Historical Novel Review*, a quarterly which seeks to review new novels, and *Solander*, a biannual journal of discussions, interviews and ideas.

torical novel would mean accepting *all* novels as historical.[12] In a few cases, it also means that a novel widely accepted as historical, but which is set fewer than fifty years before it was written, is excluded. The border is indeed arbitrary.

This definition encounters another controversy. Many historians have asserted that the historical novel begins in 1814 with the publication of *Waverley, or 'Tis Sixty Years Since*, by Walter Scott, and for the same reason which makes for the argument that the English novel began in the 1740s. It was Scott's achievement of convincing realism which gave the historical novel new life, made it world-famous and a huge influence on culture and society. But the arbitrary beginning does not work here either. There were literary antecedents to Scott, notably *Longsword, Earl of Salisbury* by Thomas Leland in 1762, and immediate influences upon Scott, notably the novels of Maria Edgeworth,[13] but also the novel by the historian Joseph Strutt, *Queenhoo Hall*, which Scott edited for publication in 1808. There were also earlier Scottish medieval titles, such as Elizabeth Helme's *St. Clair of the Isles* (1804), set in the fifteenth-century Hebrides, and Jane Porter's *The Scottish Chiefs* (1810), set in the days of Wallace and Bruce.[14] The term 'historical novel' is also applied to plenty of works which lack a sense of realism, including Scott's own *Ivanhoe*, and even the phrase occurs much earlier. The first Ricardian novel is the anonymous *Amours of Edward IV. An Historical Novel*, published as early as 1700. So, the fifty-year definition of the historical novel has value, but not the idea that there were none before 1814.

These, then, are the broad definitions: English historical novels are extended prose fictions, written in or translated into English, and set in a period no fewer than fifty years before the time of writing. That definition sounds simple enough, but every word in it has been the subject of different opinions.

The History of the Historical Novel
One way of studying the history of any genre is to analyse it for categories: here the chronology of the setting and subjects covered are obvious possibilities but these would not produce an analytical typology. The scholarly literature on the his-

[12]   This difficulty, however, is assumed by Adamson in her *World Historical Fiction*, which does attempt to include novels that are not 'historical' but are of interest to subsequent historians. The attempt is unsatisfactory, not least because it is so selective.

[13]   The Gothic novelist Ann Radcliffe even wrote an important historical novel in about 1812, her *Gaston de Blondeville; or, The Court of Henry III Keeping Festival in Ardenne*, but this was not published until 1826 because she had been upset by the criticisms of her Gothic works. See the informative essay by David H. Richter, 'From Medievalism to Historicism: Representations of History in the Gothic Novel and Historical Romance', *Studies in Medievalism*, IV (1992), 79–104, and the same for a discussion of *Longsword*, pp. 83–6.

[14]   There is a study and edition of Porter's novel in volume 4 of Gerry Kelly (ed.), *Varieties of Female Gothic*, 6 vols (London, 2002).

torical novel does not include any real attempt at categorisation,[15] however, so this paper now offers one. Indeed, it is only the experience of building a collection which allows the opportunity to reflect on such an exercise. One cannot attempt it in a university or copyright library.

In that important textbook of English constitutional history, *1066 and All That*,[16] all historical events are divided into two categories: good things and bad things. Remarkably, the critical literature contains a similar attempt to divide historical novels into two categories, but never the same two, and never on a systematic basis.

Helen Cam[17] offers novels that recreate a sense of past societies and those that recreate a sense of past personalities (ignoring those that do both or neither). Alfred Duggan[18] has those which make our ancestors odd and those which make our ancestors 'people like us', but who lived in a different environment. He prefers the latter. However, the older the novel is, the more likely the characters are going to appear to be like the novelist's contemporaries rather than the later reader's: different, but far from odd. We might still feel some sympathy for the oddest of ancestors. In fact, it is not the people in *The Castle of Otranto* who are odd, but the events, which would be odd in any setting.

C. H. Firth[19] has those that are over-rich in historical detail (and therefore boring or unconvincing) and those which are over romantic at the expense of historical accuracy. John Tebbel[20] offered those which are well researched and those which are not (regardless of whether they are well-written or not). Harold Orel offers a distinction between those which are authentic reconstructions of the real past and those which reconstruct a 'felt past', presenting it how the contemporary

---

[15]   Some accounts are, alphabetically: Avrom Fleishman, *The English Historical Novel. Walter Scott to Virginia Woolf* (Baltimore, 1971); Richard Humphrey, *The Historical Novel as Philosophy of History* (London, 1986); John MacQueen, *The Rise of the Historical Novel*, The Enlightenment and Scottish Literature, 2 (Edinburgh, 1989); J. A. R. Marriott, *English History in English Fiction* (London, 1940) [mainly a bibliographical review arranged by period]; Harold Orel, *The Historical Novel from Scott to Sabatini. Changing Attitudes to a Literary Genre, 1814–1920* (Basingstoke, 1995); Andrew Sanders, *The Victorian Historical Novel 1840–1880* (London, 1978); and Alfred Tresidder Sheppard, *The Art and Practice of Historical Fiction* (London, 1930) [rambling, but with many good points].

[16]   Walter Carruthers Sellar and Robert Julian Yeatman, *1066 and All That. A Memorable History of England Comprising all the Parts you can Remember including 103 Good Things, 5 Bad Kings and 2 Genuine Dates* (London, 1930). The Folio Society 1990 edition contains an informative introduction by Ned Sherrin, exploring the sources of inspiration.

[17]   Helen Cam, *Historical Novels*, Historical Association pamphlet (London, 1961).

[18]   Alfred Duggan, *Historical Fiction* (Cambridge, 1957).

[19]   C. H. Firth, *Historical Novels*, Historical Association pamphlet (London, 1924).

[20]   John Tebbel, *Fact and Fiction: Problems for the Historical Novelist* (Michigan, 1962).

audience feels it ought to be (though one cannot help thinking that the majority will belong in the second category and the novels selected for the first will only sit there temporarily).[21]

In an early, but little-known, study, the Italian writer Alessandro Manzoni[22] concluded in 1850 that the genre was inadequate because it combined two contradictory modes in a way which could satisfy neither and which also failed to supply an alternative unique mode of its own. The conflicting modes were those of fact and fiction, or truth and 'invention', so he was concerned with the difference between those novels which came close to accuracy and those which fell far short; in the end he believed none of them should exist at all.

The sizeable study by George Lukács[23] also considered the fact and fiction divide, albeit with a Marxist perspective which emphasised the value of novels which concentrate on ordinary people, and their ability to cope with class struggle. In other words, there are those novels which confirm Marxism, and those which do not.

None of these dualities runs through the entirety of the literature. The critics have selected two characteristics which refer only to a minority of novels, and there are plenty of inbetweens and other possibilites. There is, however, a duality which does run through the entirety of the literature, and on a factual basis. It is the obvious one between those novels intended for adults and those intended for children, and it is on this division that a general history of the historical novel can be hung.

The graph is based on my growing database of medieval settings. For convenience I have confined it to 4,795 examples published between 1756 and 2005 (virtually the whole survey, but starting in the decade of *Otranto* and omitting the first four years of the unfinished decade 2006–15), and there are separate lines for novels for children (1,590) and adults (3,205).

The graph shows that the historical novel has gone through different phases. The first might be called the classical period, before 1850, when few were pub-

21   Harold Orel, op. cit.
22   Alessandro Manzoni, *On The Historical Novel. Del romanzo storico*, translated and introduced by Sandra Bermann (Lincoln, Nebraska, 1996).
23   George Lukács, *The Historical Novel*, translated by Hannah and Stanley Mitchell (London, 1962). Richter has criticised this study for its failure to acknowledge the antecedents to Scott, due to the Marxist belief that the 'realistic' historical novel first needed an educated bourgeoisie for it to come into being (Richter, op. cit., pp. 94–5). Citing these continental discussions highlights how the historical novel soon became a world-wide phenomenon. A parallal case to its political importance in Scotland and Italy is that of Finland, on which there is now an excellent study, in English, by Derek Fewster: *Visions of Past Glory. Nationalism and the Construction of Early Finnish History*, Studia Fennica Historica, 11 (Helsinki, 2006). Concentrating on medievalism in all its branches, the work cites novels frequently and lists examples in Appendix 2 (pp. 408–30).

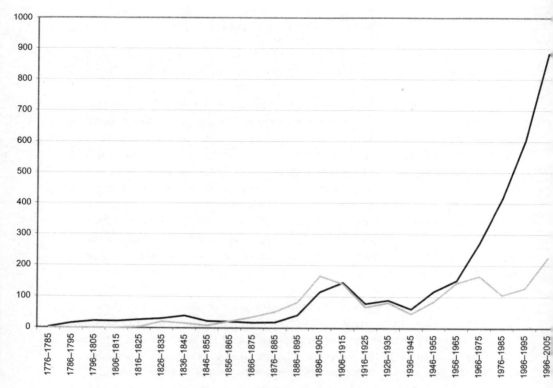

Graph: First-publication dates for 4,795 medieval historical novels
gathered in ten-year periods between 1756 and 2005, and
separated into settings for adults (black line) and children (grey line).

lished, virtually all of them for adults, but most enjoyed a widespread readership
and cultural influence. Many of these early works are the Gothic novels listed by
Montague Summers. In 1850 Manzoni published his pessimistic conclusions pre-
dicting the genre's demise and many other writers at the time also thought the historical novel was finished. Even those who wrote later, like George Saintsbury[24]
and James Simmons,[25] talked of the decline in quality after 1850. However, this
observation seems simply to be based on published comments around 1850,
which have entered the literature and survived without being questioned.[26] What
actually happened is that the historical novel continued to flourish in the second
half of the nineteenth century, entering a golden age.

[24]   George Saintsbury, 'The Historical Novel' [in 3 parts], *Macmillan's Magazine* LXX
       (1894), 256–64; 321–30; and 410–19.
[25]   James C. Simmons, *The Novelist as Historian. Essays on the Victorian Historical Novel*
       (The Hague, 1973).
[26]   Bulwer Lytton's *Harold* received some harsh reviews in 1848. The graph indeed shows
       a slight dip after 1845, but this dip has more to do with the declining popularity of the
       Gothic novel than a decline in the quantities of the mainstream historical novel.

Two things happened which Manzoni could not have predicted. The first was the professionalisation of history. It became a formal part of the curriculum at Cambridge in 1848 and at Oxford in 1852.[27] Before then, most historians actually worked outside academic institutions and the historical novel played a leading role in the spread of historical knowledge, and novelists in research. But after the rise of the professional historian, the novelists were free to concentrate on good story telling, and they survived by doing just that.

The second was the sudden popularity of children's books. After a slow start, they first exceed the quantity of adult settings in 1863, and they lead until the First World War. The education acts, the spread of public libraries, and the confident national atmosphere led to this growth. The damage caused to the market by the wars is clearly apparent. After 1918, there was a disillusionment with history. Nationalism was blamed for the conflict, and the market did not fully recover until after the 1950s, perhaps in the context of a new pride in history.

Something very strange then happens to the genre in the year 1968. The two lines had run in tandem throughout, but in that year they separate in a remarkable way. Children's settings fail to stay with the new popularity of the adult settings, they actually decline in quantity in the 1970s and they only begin to increase in number again in the 1990s, in the context of a new fashion for short humourous children's books like the *Horrible Histories* series. Adult settings, however, go through a period of rapid expansion, in which the previous decade's production figures are repeatedly exceeded. Adults and children now appear to be pursuing different interests. This is all the more remarkable because the young people who stopped reading historical novels in 1968 have become the adults who are reading them today.

Identifying the earliest children's historical novel is difficult because the early ones are slightly ambiguous, not quite obviously historical novels, not quite definitely intended for children. The novels of Scott, and his antecedents, were certainly read by younger readers as well as adults. Captain Frederick Marryat's *Mr Midshipman Easy* (1836), was important for creating a demand for children's historical novels, and is often cited as the first, but because it is set in the recent past, based on the author's own experience, it breaks the fifty-year rule. There are also earlier contenders. Mrs Bary's *The Protestant* (1828) and Grace Aguilar's *The Days of Bruce* (1834) are labelled as juvenile by the reader's guides, but neither *feels* like a children's book when it is handled. The earliest are certainly volumes of short stories: Maria Hack's *English Stories, Illustrating Some of the Most Interesting Events and Characters, between the Accession of Alfred and the Death of John* (London, 1820) was soon followed by a second series covering Henry III to Henry VI (1820), and a third, *Illustrating the Progress of the Reformation under the Tudor Princes* (1825). Sir Walter Scott's *Tales of a Grandfather...* is also early (3

---

[27]   Dates and point from Simmons, op. cit.

vols, 1828–30), but is non-fiction. Emily Taylor's *Tales of the Saxons* (1832) and Agnes Strickland's *Historical Tales of Illustrious British Children* (1833) and *Tales and Stories from History* (1836), continue the short story tradition. The earliest unequivocal English medieval juvenile novel appears to be J. M. Neale's *Agnes de Tracy: a Tale of the Times of S. Thomas of Canterbury* (1843, quite late in fact). However, by the time of Captain Marryat's *Children of the New Forest* (1847), the market for children's historical novels was established and soon there were thousands.

A new phenomenon appeared soon after the advent of children's fiction: the emergence of the specialist children's historical writer. W. H. G. Kingston was the first, and his first effort was *Peter the Whaler* (1851) (Marryat himself wrote for both age groups). Soon there were hundreds of such writers, producing one title after another to meet the insatiable demands of a market that wanted history for pleasure, history for education and history for school prizes. R. M. Ballantyne, Tom Bevan, G. A. Henty, Eliza F. Pollard, and Charlotte M. Yonge are well-known, but just as interesting are A. D. Crake, Mary Debenham, Gertrude Hollis, Sarah Holt, Emma Leslie, and Charles W. Whistler.

Naomi Mitchison put an end to the use of pseudo-archaic language, with the publication of *The Conquered* in 1923. Henceforth, the dialogue would usually be in modern English. Geoffrey Trease, Henry Treece and Rosemary Sutcliff became immensely popular in the 1960s. They were prolific, and they set standards. Ronald Welch and Cynthia Harnett were less prolific but their standards were also high.[28]

There is an unrealistic element in children's novels which makes it difficult for us to regard them as authentic reconstructions of medieval or modern lives. Children value, perhaps more than anything else, friendship. It is a common theme of children's literature that a lad leaves home for the first time and is immediately in the thick of things, performing a pivotal role in some great event and relishing the friendships made during it. In Cynthia Harnett's *The Wool-pack* (1951), Nicholas solves the mystery of the smuggled wool and earns the thanks of his father and the Staple. In *The Load of Unicorn* (1959), Benedict solves the mystery of Caxton's disappearing paper supplies and earns the printer's respect. In C. W. Whistler's *Dragon Osmund*, Osmund soon becomes a friend of King Athelstan, even on first-name terms. I know of no medieval incident where this sort of thing actually hap-

---

[28] Many of the classic histories of children's literature state the importance of historical novels, though no general history of the children's historical novel has yet appeared. A useful volume of conference essays, however, is Fiona M. Collins and Judith Graham (eds), *Historical Fiction for Children. Capturing the Past* (London, 2001), and Rebecca Barnhouse has written a short study, *Recasting the Past: the Middle Ages in Young Adult Literature* (Portsmouth, New Hampshire, 2000), and a short bibliographcal guide, *The Middle Ages in Literature for Youth* (Lanham, Maryland, 2004); both these cover fiction and non-fiction.

pened – it is implausible even in our own more socially-mobile times, let alone a period as class-conscious as the middle ages – but it is interesting that friendship between princes and paupers is a common theme of medieval literature itself, and that medieval stories about children frequently involve a similar coming-of-age experience, albeit one which often took the form of discovery that one's real parentage was different from what one thought it to be.[29]

Today, fantasy fiction and humour have come to dominate the children's market, with writers like J. K. Rowling, Roald Dahl, and Jacqueline Wilson and their emulators. The children's historical novel has an uncertain future, and the medieval period represents a negligible proportion of those still published. The graph suggests a slight increase in the 1990s, but few of these are substantial works like those before 1968, and many of the new titles are short rewrites of traditional tales rather than new explorations of the past.[30]

For adults, however, the genre has never been more popular than it is today. Mitchison and Trease wrote for both adults and children, so the new taste for modern dialogue entered both sides from the same pioneers. Bernard Cornwell, Alfred Duggan, Dorothy Dunnett, Georgette Heyer, Nora Lofts, Ellis Peters, Jean Plaidy, Anya Seton, Mary Stewart, Nigel Tranter – and many more, have been prominent and prolific contributors of well-researched medieval novels since the War. Robert Graves and Mary Renault were prominent for their ancient history settings, and there has even been a growth in prehistoric settings since the 1920s.

In the early period, a small number of writers had dominated with Sir Walter Scott being by far the most successful and the most influential, arguably ever. His success inspired others to be career historical novelists, most famously Harrison Ainsworth, Bulwer Lytton, Charles Kingsley, and G. P. R. James. Overseas, too, his early emulators enjoyed a world-wide influence: Alexandre Dumas and Victor Hugo in France; Manzoni in Italy; Harriet Beecher Stowe and James Fenimore Cooper in the USA.

---

[29] As in the Parzifal and Arthurian romances, even the story of Jesus. This is a good metaphor for self-discovery, but it must have been a very rare experience in real medieval lives.

[30] *Historical Novel Review* covers new titles for both adults and children. The children's are often subject to two reviews, by both an adult and a younger reader. The reprint of Cynthia Harnett's *The Wool-pack* in 2001 was greeted with joy by the adult reviewer (29 August 2004, p. 48) and dismissed as 'boring ... slow ... long-winded' by the 12-year-old. Of the 202 children's titles reviewed in the 8 issues of 2004–5, 17 were medieval, but all of these were early medieval except for two which were Cynthia Harnett reprints, i.e. there was a preferance for the semi-historic heroic age. It is worth mentioning some of the great exceptions to the apparent 'dumbing down' of the children's middle ages, however, such as Kevin Crossley-Holland's 12th-century 'Arthur' trilogy (2001–3) and Elizabeth Laird's *Crusade* (2007), which is topically subtitled on the dust-wrapper 'Two Boys, Two Faiths, One Unholy War'.

After these pioneers, and until after the Second World War, 'career' historical novelists are almost entirely only on the children's side, but adult production nevertheless flourished because mainstream novelists, many of them giants of English literature, contributed many historical novels even if they did not exclusively specialise in them: writers like Joseph Conrad, Arthur Conan Doyle, George Eliot, Charles Dickens, H. Rider Haggard,[31] Thomas Hardy, Rudyard Kipling, Robert Louis Stevenson, William Makepeace Thackeray, Anthony Trollope and H. G. Wells. Standards improved with greater realism, less romance. Fewer aristocratic heroes, more ordinary lives. The genre flourished and the oft-repeated claim that it declined is simply untrue.[32]

After the First World War, fewer new historical novels appeared, but the genre survived, exploring new subject areas and language, and finding new popular markets, for this period saw the appearance of the mass-market publishing of paperbacks and low-cost hardback novels, intended to be bought primarily by their readers rather than by lending libraries.[33] In addition to Mitchison, Trease, Graves and Renault, great writers who contributed historical fiction between the wars include John Buchan, John Cowper Powys and Virginia Woolf.

Sir Walter Scott's achievement was considerable. It made the historical novel a popular and influential literary form in many other languages and it is interesting that many of the novels which have achieved 'international' status, world-famous cultural ambassadors for their countries, have been historical novels. *War and Peace*, *Ivanhoe*, Manzoni's *The Betrothed*, *The Three Musketeers*, *Gone with the Wind*, *Roots*, *The Name of the Rose* are obvious examples.[34] Moreover, it is no exaggeration to say that, within the cultural and political life of many countries, the historical novel has played an important role in building a sense of nationhood, and even of healing divisions. In the case of Manzoni, his novel even helped construct a national language for Italy. Walter Scott's *Waverley* novels celebrated Scottish nationality, certainly, but Scott also recognised that the country's best interests, at least at that time, were in unity with England. *Ivanhoe* consciously described the blending of Saxon and Norman, but it also reconciled Victorian England with its medieval past. Catholic emancipation was completed in various stages by 1829, and the Gothic Revival in architecture and ritual[35] was already in full flow.

---

[31]   See Jóna E. Hammer, 'Eric Brighteyes: Rider Haggard Rewrites the Sagas', *Studies in Medievalism*, XII (2002), 137–70.

[32]   The 1850–1914 period also witnessed the regular reprinting of the classics of the genre, but the difficulty of tracing reprints means they have not been included in my survey.

[33]   The Victorian period, of course, also had its popular paperbacks and its important popular magazines with serialised novels. It is the scale of print-runs which was revolutionary between the wars.

[34]   It must be acknowledged that all 'Westerns' are also historical novels and they have made the experience of cowboys, together with their jeans and their revolutionary attitudes, a world-wide phenomenon.

If *Ivanhoe* did not bring about these developments, it certainly expressed the national mood; and that mood was one of reconciliation. The injustices of the past were not glossed over, but opened. We think of Henty as self-confidently nationalist, even jingoistic, but his novels include the pro-Celtic *In Freedom's Cause: a Story of Wallace and Bruce* and *Both Sides the Border: a Tale of Hotspur and Glendower*. Even in the titles there is apparent an understanding, a sympathy for the opinions of medieval people and a desire to be fair to opposing sides, just as Scott's *Waverley* had acknowledged and helped heal the Jacobite wound. Far from representing a prejudiced one-sided view of history, the historical novel is often mature in its critical balance.[36]

Of the 5,092 novels listed so far, 3,462 are for adults, 1,630 for children, approximately 68% and 32%, but the figures are 1,094 adults', 1,032 children's for the 2,126 novels before 1969 (51.46%, 48.54%); and 2,368 adults', 598 children's for the 2,966 novels published 1969–2009, or 79.84% and 20.16%, and the children's proportion in recent years is even smaller when the survey is more strictly confined to 'serious' historical settings, as the following table shows.

			to 1968		1969–	
			adults'	children's	adults'	children's
5th century	257	6.41%	54	74	112	17
6th century	98	2.44%	26	25	38	9
7th century	72	1.79%	7	20	35	10
8th century	64	1.60%	9	25	19	11
9th century	141	3.52%	19	70	37	15
10th century	167	4.16%	29	56	64	18
11th century	546	13.61%	123	141	245	37
12th century	635	15.84%	121	83	374	57
13th century	500	12.47%	129	70	263	38
14th century	605	15.09%	147	109	298	51
15th century	925	23.07%	328	128	433	36
	4,010	100.00%	992	801	1,918	299

Table: 4,010 medieval novels arranged according to the century of the settings.

In the table, 4,010 of the titles are presented according to the century of the setting. This is a smaller sample because it excludes titles which do not have a clear historical setting (several hundred Arthurian[37] and fantasy titles, for example), and

35   The movement has a huge literature. A new general survey by Michael Alexander, *Medievalism. The Middle Ages in Modern England* (New Haven and London, 2007) emphasises the literary thread through the modern reception; see the essays in Christopher Webster and John Elliott (eds), '*A Church as it Should be*'. *The Cambridge Camden Society and its Influence* (Donington, 2000), for the architectural.

36   One study is Nicholas Rance's *The Historical Novel and Popular Politics in Nineteenth-Century England* (London, 1975).

37   One review, of many, is Alan Lupack, 'Modern Arthurian Novelists on the Arthurian Legend', *Studies in Medievalism*, II (1983), 79–88.

those which are set in modern times with a medieval theme. Titles which crossed two or more centuries have been subsumed under the earlier century. It reveals the popularity of certain key figures in the early middle ages, such as Alfred the Great,[38] William the Conqueror[39] and Robin Hood,[40] and the popularity of the fifteenth century in adult settings. It also shows how balanced the spread of titles is through most of the middle ages, with the exception of the centuries between Arthur and Alfred.

Further Categories

It is entirely appropriate to hang a brief history of the mainstream historical novel on the adults'–children's duality, because this divide embraces the entire genre and both sides have an interesting, slightly different sociology; but if we also describe the categories where historical fiction overlaps with other genres, we will see how historical fiction relates to the novel in general. In most of these categories, the child–adult duality is also present. The majority of novels have a clear historical setting and a general-interest subject content (4,010 of 5,092). The fringe categories are each much smaller in quantity, but they cannot be ignored, not least because the categories are rarely exclusive: the detective titles, for example, are also in the mainstream category because they have a genuine historical setting.

First, the overlap with **contemporary settings**. These novels are not actually set in the past but are concerned with historical matters, and there are 160 of them in my list. Josephine Tay's *The Daughter of Time* (1951) is a good example. Important for the rehabilitation of Richard III, the novel is set entirely in modern times and concerns a London detective recovering from an injury in hospital, who starts to explore the historiography of Richard because he is bored. The arguments which Tay advanced are convincing ones, even if the evidence is circumstantial, and the novel holds one's attention, though the plot is implausible. Nevertheless, it cannot be ignored by those researching Ricardian fiction even if it is not strictly an historical novel.

Angus Wilson's *Anglo-Saxon Attitudes* (1956) is another example. Common themes in this category are buried treasure, archaeology, the discovery of ancient manuscripts, historical mysteries, including invented ones as in *The Da Vinci Code*, and there are also some novels where the main theme is nostalgia for the

---

[38] Alfred is the subject of many historiographical reviews; a recent one is Joanne M. Parker, 'The Day of a Thousand Years: Winchester's 1901 Commemoration of Alfred the Great', *Studies in Medievalism*, XII (2002), 113–36 [the content is far broader than the title suggests].

[39] Carl I. Hammer, 'Harold in Normandy: History and Romance', *Studies in Medievalism*, XII (2002), 79–112, explores six novels set in 1066, though there are several hundred.

[40] R. B. Dobson and J. Taylor, *Rymes of Robyn Hood. An Introduction to the English Outlaw* (London, 1976) has a select guide to 'Robin Hood in Literature' from 1377 to 1956 (pp. 315–19).

past. One of the most famous novels of all, *Don Quixote*, belongs here.[41]

Modern rewrites of medieval stories make for a category of their own, and there are 651 in my list. Here, the novelist is reinterpreting the imaginative literature of the past rather than the historical events of the past, which can be a very interesting exercise. Beowulf, the Arthurian legends, the Robin Hood stories (there is a prose rewrite of Robin Hood as early as 1560; Thomas Love Peacock's *Maid Marion* is 1822, and Robin also appears in *Ivanhoe*), the Viking sagas, *Havelock the Dane*, Chaucer's Tales ... have all been rewritten many times.[42] Interestingly, all the novels and films about Robin Hood have traditionally been on his side, but, post '9/11', we will soon have a treatment which brands him a terrorist and sides with the Sheriff of Nottingham.[43]

Rewrites might be considered to include the specialist area of fairy tales. These are mostly, however, given a timeless or non-medieval presentation. The Cinderella story is originally medieval, but is nearly always presented as vaguely Regency (essential for Austenesque balls). Only where the setting is specifically medieval have such works been included. Tales of Dick Whittington and the Pied Piper of Hamelin are in this category.[44]

If **science fiction** involves time travel, it becomes historical at that point, and therefore of interest; but sometimes a sci-fi novel can be set entirely in the past. One such is *The High Crusade* by Poul Anderson (1960), which has an alien space craft landing in the Lincolnshire village of Ansby in 1345. The locals go on board and kill the aliens and then fly off for an adventure in space, leaving their village behind. This is a hypothesis which reconsiders the evidence for deserted villages and places it in a new context.

The benefit of time-travel settings is that they allow for a stark contrast between past and present attitudes side-by-side. In Ben Sapir's *The Far Arena*

---

[41]   Miguel de Cervantes's *Don Quixote* entered English in a translation by Thomas Shelton, published in two parts in 1612 and 1620. The list of further translations occupies pp. 136–50 of Robert S. Rudder's *The Literature of Spain in English Translation. A Bibliography* (New York, 1975).

[42]   Medieval rewrites for children are the subject of an essay by Velma Bourgeois Richmond, 'Medieval Chivalric Stories for Children', in Joel T. Rosenthal (ed.), *Essays on Medieval Childhood. Responses to Recent Debates* (Donington, 2006), 29–41. Rewrites of Chaucer are briefly mentioned by Stephanie Trigg in Steve Ellis (ed.), *Chaucer. An Oxford Guide* (Oxford, 2005): 'Rewriting Chaucer', pp. 535–9.

[43]   Such a film is under preparation, apparently to be called *Nottingham*. Robin Hood is rewritten every generation. There are also some earlier treatments in which the sheriff is a sympathetic character. Another interesting reversal is John Gardner's *Grendel* (1971), which sides with the monster rather than Beowulf.

[44]   These characters have nevertheless been the subject of sensible mainstream novels as well as children's illustrated short stories: Cynthia Harnett's *Ring Out Bow Bells!* (1953) concerns Dick Whittington; Gloria Skurzynski's *What Happened in Hamelin* (1979) is about the Pied Piper.

(1979), a Roman gladiator, frozen alive in the first century, is discovered and revived in the twentieth. There is much in the novel which criticises the twentieth century. Two things, however, which this approach fails to get to grips with is the sheer terror which both a medieval or modern person would surely feel if they went through such an experience, and the insuperable problem of language. An element of pseudo-science is also needed to explain how the time travel could happen in the first place, though occasionally rational alternative explanations are available.[45] The science fiction section is my smallest, at only 80 entries.

Fantasy fiction frequently embraces the impossible in ways which will always be uncomfortable for historians. There are thousands of fantasy novels and it is often difficult to separate them from the historical because they have similar titles and similar wrappers and they are frequently shelved alongside each other in bookshops. Tolkien's *The Lord of the Rings* series is the most famous, and it does contain certain details based on the author's experience as a professor of Anglo-Saxon.[46] Much medievalism is to be found in fantasy writing, but most fantasies are excluded from my survey because they usually lack the real historical setting. Some titles, however, bring fantasy into history. Freda Warrington's *The Court of the Midnight King* (2003) offers a fantasy about Richard III. The novel has flash-backs between the present and the fifteenth century, but it is not a fifteenth century which will be recognised by historians. There are two religions in England, the established church and a surviving paganism which is not only tolerated by the establishment, it is an organised alternative church and it has Ann Beauchamp as its High Priestess and Richard as its secular supporter. Moreover, this is not a surviving Anglo-Saxon paganism, it is the cult of Isis, the Egyptian goddess, and it is a cult run by women. This preposterous idea denies all we know about the Christianisation of society in the fifteenth century. Richard may have been the last Plantagenet, but the author has got carried away on the idea of 'lastness' and attached other long-lost-last characteristics to him. Richard is also the subject of the equally-fantastic novel *The Language of Stones* by Robert Carter (2004), in which he is associated with Arthurian mythology in a still-enduring Roman and Celtic world.[47] What is interesting about these texts is that they exist at all. Why is there a market for literature which rewrites history, introduces supernatural explanations into

[45] The use of an experimental drug to transport at least the mind of Dick Young back into the fourteenth century lies behind *The House on the Strand*. The possible explanation that it is all a dream, stimulated by the boy's recent reading, lurks in Welch's *The Gauntlet*. The history of science fiction has a huge literature. Two guides are Curtis C. Smith (ed.), *Twentieth-Century Science Fiction Writers*, 2nd edn (Chicago and London, 1986) and *The Cambridge Companion to Science Fiction*, ed. Edward James and Farah Mendlesohn (Cambridge, 2003).

[46] A recent study is by Jane Chance, *Tolkien the Medievalist* (London, 2002).

[47] Fantasy fiction also enjoys a huge critical literature. A starting point is John Clute and John Grant (eds), *The Encyclopedia of Fantasy* (London, 1997).

history, or which transports aspects of European medieval society onto alien planets and into the lives of alien species (as in the *Star Wars* films)? Even with quite rigorous attempts to exclude fantasy, 693 entries are in my list, often because many of the retellings also have a fantasy element, albeit an authentic medieval one.[48]

Gothic novels are entirely relevant if they are also historical.[49] They may overlap with the fantasy but are just as often set in the real world. Horace Walpole regarded his *Castle of Otranto* as the first of 'a new species of romance',[50] and its antecedents are few, and are mostly plays rather than novels. It is not a good read. The novel is nearly all dialogue ... almost as if he originally wrote it as a drama but decided to make it a novel because of the difficulty of staging what happens in the first scene, when the helmeted head on a church statue spontaneously grows to the size of a house, flies into the air and lands on top of Conrad, killing him on his wedding day; and there it stays throughout the book. The setting is vaguely twelfth century but the castle is more eighteenth-century because it has a long gallery. It is Walpole's own Strawberry Hill.

The association with the medieval is why the group is called Gothic, but, once the term was coined, the definition slipped into an emphasis on horror. *Frankenstein*[51] and *Dracula* are the two most famous. The latter has a slight medieval interest, in being an account of an undead fifteenth-century Transylvanian ruler, but

---

[48]   A category which straddles both science and fantasy fiction is that of alternative or 'What If...' history, which is also present in non-fiction writing. There is an essay by Andy Duncan, 'Alternate History', in *The Cambridge Companion to Science Fiction*, pp. 209–18, and such works are reviewed in their own section in *Historical Novel Review*. It seemed to the present author that such writing could be either science or fantasy fiction, depending on whether there is a pseudo-scientific explanation for the event, or whether it is 'set' (just about) in the real world. A medieval example of the type is L. Sprague de Camp's *Lest Darkness Fall* (1939), in which a modern businessman changes history by preventing the downfall of the Roman Empire.

[49]   Summers had a separate chapter on historical Gothic, see above, note 9. Another review is Markman Ellis, *The History of Gothic Fiction* (Edinburgh, 2000), pp. 17–47. A useful guide to early Gothic is Robert Donald Spector, *The English Gothic. A Bibliographic Guide to Writers from Horace Walpole to Mary Shelley* (Westport, Connecticut and London, 1984). See also *The Cambridge Companion to Gothic Fiction*, ed. Jerrold E. Hogle (Cambridge, 2002); this particular series also has *The Cambridge Companion to the Victorian Novel*, ed. Deirdre David (2001), but lacks a volume on historical fiction.

[50]   A useful chronological checklist of early titles appears in Maurice Lévy, *Le roman 'Gothique' anglais 1764–1824* (Toulouse, n.d., 1968), pp. 684–708. The first edition of *Otranto* is labelled 1765 but appears to have been issued on Christmas Eve, 1764. The second of the new species is *The Hermitage, a British Story*, by William Hutchinson (York, 1772). After 1788, several titles appeared every year.

[51]   Mary Shelley, *Frankenstein; or, The Modern Prometheus*, 3 vols (London, 1816). The same author contributed a mainstream medieval novel: *The Adentures of Perkin Warbeck*, 3 vols (London, 1830).

thankfully not for those interested in the English middle ages.[52] The 119 Gothic entries in my list are included because they are acknowledged historical settings which are in the bibliography by Montague Summers. The number should almost certainly be higher, but none of the guides to Gothic fiction make a point of specifying the setting, and the originals are so scarce they are rarely even mentioned on the internet, nor included in the British Library catalogue. One wonders how Montague Summers compiled his list.

Primarily, Gothic fiction is going to interest those who are researching medievalism rather than medieval history, but it has given us a great deal of entertainment and lingering cultural motifs since 1764: the mad woman in the attic;[53] the monster in the basement;[54] the deformed creature in the bell tower;[55] the mad scientist;[56] the sinister housekeeper;[57] the evil monk,[58] the haunted castle, abbey or big house,[59] and a certain frenetic challenge to the traditional male and female roles, whereby the frequently undeserving, terribly self-tortured male is redeemed by a courageous, loving female. It may be called Gothic, but it is of an entirely different world from that of George and the Dragon.

Detective fiction is a huge body of literature,[60] and now we have the phenomenon of historical whodunnits, and they are growing so quickly they threaten to dominate the twenty-first-century historical novel;[61] 368 are already on my list, all but five published since 1977. Fifteen of them are for children, making the adult mysteries over 20% of all adult titles since 1977. The earliest true European medieval whodunnit I know is *The Murders at Crossby*, by Edward Frankland, set in the tenth-century Lake District and published in 1955. It is a good read.[62]

[52]   Bram Stoker, *Dracula* (London, 1897).
[53]   Charlotte Brontë, *Jane Eyre* (London, 1847).
[54]   Frankenstein's monster.
[55]   The hunchback Quasimodo in Victor Hugo's *Nôtre Dame de Paris* (1831). It has been translated into English many times.
[56]   Dr Victor Frankenstein *et al*.
[57]   As Mrs Danvers in Daphne du Maurier's *Rebecca* (London, 1938).
[58]   Possibly pre-Gothic as one appears in Leland's *Longsword*. The modern fear of 'hoodies' seems not unconnected with this Gothic motive.
[59]   Ghost stories, which may overlap both the fantasy and the contemporary categories, are relevant if the ghost is medieval. One of the attractions of the stories of M. R. James to medievalists is that they are written by a fellow scholar; a comprehensive bibliography by Nicholas Rogers appears in Lynda Dennison (ed.), *The Legacy of M. R. James. Papers from the 1995 Cambridge Symposium* (Donington, 2001), pp. 239–67.
[60]   A starting point is the survey by Allen J. Hubin, *Crime Fiction II: A Comprehensive Bibliography 1749–1990* (London and New York, 1994).
[61]   Of the 98 adult medieval titles reviewed in 2004–5 by *Historical Novel Review*, 37 were detective. This fringe category is expanding.
[62]   *The Daughter of Time* is earlier, 1951, but it is set in modern times. Before the modern popularity of the genre there was also a series of fourteen whodunnits by Roberts Hans Van Gulik, starting with *The Chinese Bell Murders*, 1958, all set in seventh-century

Brother Cadfael was not the first medieval sleuth but he was the first success-ful one, in a marketing sense, and now there are so many competing sleuths out there in all historical periods that one wonders they have not run out of cases. Brother Cadfael is a twelfth-century monk at Shrewsbury who frequently finds himself solving murder mysteries. Ellis Peters' historical details are so good that one Domesday historian told the present writer 'she has got the twelfth century down to a T'. Nevertheless, the genre emphasises plot before all else, so both the background details and relationships are few. The first Cadfael was *A Morbid Taste for Bones* in 1977 and another 20 titles followed.[63] The imitations include Sister Fidelma, a young seventh-century Irish nun; the first of these, by Peter Tremayne, was *Absolution by Murder* (1994) and there are now fifteen titles. Alys Clare, Paul Doherty, Susanna Gregory, Michael Jecks and Candace Robb have produced large series in this genre, and we must not forget the international bestseller, Umberto Eco's *The Name of the Rose*.[64]

One thing which is entirely implausible about medieval whodunnits is the very idea that there could be a professional detective in the middle ages. Moreover, sudden death is still common today, and suspicion is not automatic. Are we really expected to believe, as in Robb's *The Apothecary Rose*, that the death of two peo-ple, seemingly from natural causes in fourteenth-century York, would have prompted the despatch from London of a retired mercenary to check for foul play?[65] Even in the cases of obvious murder, justice was performed by courts hear-ing denouncements, rather than by the search for evidence. Trials were over and done with quickly, even as late as the nineteenth century. The detective novel had little chance of birth until society had first produced the professional detective. Edgar Allen Poe's *The Murders in the Rue Morgue* (1841) is considered to be the earliest detective story, and it followed soon after the creation of professional police forces in France, the UK and the USA. So, medieval whodunnits are formu-

China. Remarkably, historical whodunnits have even spread into prehistory, with the publication of *Primal Skin* by Leona Benkt Rhys (2000). Skin is a bisexual Neanderthal hybrid. I am grateful to Carole Watkin, who is researching prehistoric settings, for bringing this one to my attention. Given the extraordinary rise in the popularity of detective novels between the world wars, it is perhaps surprising that historical who-dunnits are a comparatively recent phenomenon. Equally surprising is the fact that some writers, such as John Buchan and H. C. Bailey, wrote in both genres but never seem to have combined the two.

63   There is a study by Edwin Ernest Christian and Blake Lindsay, 'The Habit of Detection: The Medieval Monk as Detective in the Novels of Ellis Peters', *Studies in Medievalism*, IV (1992), 276–89.

64   *Il nome della Rose* appeared in 1980. William Weaver's translation is 1983. The book is unusual in detective fiction for its substantial philosophical content. The same author has also written *Baudolino* (2000, Weaver translation 2002) and a slim volume of *Reflections on The Name of the Rose* (1983, Weaver translation 1985).

65   Brother Cadfael is also a former mercenary.

laic nonsense, but they are perfectly good entertainments, and perfectly good introductions to the period so long as disbelief is first suspended. Their reputation for historical accuracy, even after a good start with Ellis Peters, is ever-improving. In *The Apothecary Rose*, however, one is rather taken aback to read the four-teenth-century sleuth buying some herbs and offering a shilling for them, when the first shilling was not minted till 1497, by Henry VII.[66]

Finally, there is the erotic, or **women's romantic fiction**. Because of the ambiguity of the word 'romance', the genre is better referred to by the name of its most notorious publisher, Mills & Boon, a general publisher in the early twentieth century, but one which made the decision to publish only this type of fiction in 1957.[67] Like the whodunnit, this area shows a major growth in production since the late 1970s (now 602, 11.82% of the whole, but rising to 31% of adult titles since 1968); like the whodunnit, they have spread into all historical periods and loca-tions, and this alone would make them an interesting phenomenon, but their con-tent can also be thought-provoking. In *Proxy Wedding* by Belinda Grey (1982) the heroine attends the coronation of Richard III. She has a coronation pass. The idea that entrance to a coronation in the fifteenth century was controlled by the issue of passes is unconvincing. Were the guards literate? It is an error of detail, but it does make one wonder how attendance at such a complex event was managed. Presumably summons would be by royal writ, but what about seating arrange-ments? How many guests could you bring? How were the uninvited excluded? In the same book, I laughed out loud when the heroine visits the Tower of London *as a tourist* and she has to queue for a ticket.

There is another quality of Mills & Boons which makes them interesting for the medievalist, however. This is what happens in them (all of them): mature man and woman meet (no teen romances here) and are attracted to each other. Woman has an independent and outspoken character. Man is slightly older, hand-some, strong, fiercely independent and treats the woman with utter contempt. He is abominable. Woman swings between anger and self-hatred, but in the course of the plot she manages to find the key to his heart, discovering an explanation for his behaviour, and after one or two further misunderstandings, they form a pas-sionate, life-long bond. Is this not the plot of Jane Austen's *Pride and Prejudice*?

---

66   Another criticism one can make of the multi-volume whodunnit series is that the main characters never seem to develop a reputation from one novel to another. Surely, after twenty successful solutions to murder mysteries, Cadfael would have been accused of witchcraft? Surely he would have come to be regarded as the source of the problem rather than its solution?

67   See the entry for 'Romance Fiction' in Claire Buck (ed.), *Bloomsbury Guide to Women's Literature* (London, 1992), and many essays in Corinne Saunders (ed.), *A Companion to Romance from Classical to Contemporary* (Oxford, 2007), including Richard Cronin, 'Victorian Romance: Medievalism', pp. 341–59.

Mills & Boons are indeed 'Gothic romances'[68] in new packaging. Perhaps it is co-incidental, but there seems to be an unconscious salute to their Gothic origins in the favourite choice of the Regency period for a setting.

It is said that Daphne du Maurier is responsible, in *Rebecca*, for establishing this genre in the twentieth century, but *Rebecca* is from 1938. It has plot features in common with *Jane Eyre*, from 1847. The first Barbara Cartland novel, *Jigsaw*, appeared in 1925. Florence Barclay wrote such romances slightly earlier.[69] Mills & Boon themselves produced a medieval novel approaching this type as early as 1910.[70] Mills & Boon man and redeeming Mills & Boon woman are found in *The Castle of Otranto* and Wagner's operas *The Flying Dutchman* (1843) and *Tannhäuser* (1845). In fact, they are everywhere. This is not a new genre but one that descends in continuous tradition from the eighteenth century. Those who wish to dismiss Mills & Boon novels, even to deny their existence, need to be aware that they are rejecting something which is much more mainstream than they might think.[71]

Despite the large number already listed, I am aware that there are many more medieval Mills & Boons to find, but one can rarely identify the historical period from the title and it is rarely given in on-line listings, so one has to handle them, and that means being prepared to do so in public ...[72]

---

[68] The expression, of course, is a contradiction in terms, meaning something like 'Anti-Roman Roman-like'.

[69] Florence Barclay's *The White Ladies of Worcester. A Romance of the Twelfth Century* (London, 1917) was her last major novel. Her first appeared in 1891.

[70] *Jehanne of the Golden Lips* is by Frances G. Knowles-Foster. The heroine is Queen Joanna of Naples (1343–82).

[71] For this reason it might be considered that Mills & Boons are not a separate category. The border with the Gothic is difficult to draw, but the Gothic has a horror element and is intended for both sexes to read, whereas Mills & Boons lack the supernatural and are consciously intended for women only.

[72] The difficulty involved in needing to handle the books to compile accurate information is present in all branches of historical fiction, and bibliography. Whether a novel is for children or adults is immediately apparent on handling it, but the reader's guides frequently label as juvenile works which are not, or leave unspecified (therefore adult), works which are clearly for children. The compilers cannot have examined every book. One cannot research historical fiction for long before one welcomes those with clear explicable titles and a text which starts with a date. Novels are frequently given meaningless and deceptive titles by their foolish publishers, and equally misleading cover designs by the miserable hacks who work for them. My favourite 'misleading' title is a perfectly sober novel of 1951 set at the time of the Norman Conquest, by Noel Langley and Hazel Pynegar. It is called *Cuckoo in the Dell*. There is no subtitle. Seemingly, neither authors nor publisher wanted the book to be found, but they are not alone; there are thousands of historical novels which do not express their content in their title, including a 1952 Ricardian one called *The Song of a Thrush*... My own collection includes the misfit *Beowulf, Guide Dog*.

Medieval Lives Reconstructed?

These seem to me to be the categories of historical fiction, and describing them has allowed us to describe briefly the size, age, importance and diversity of the genre. What, however, about the quality of the genre and its use to historians?

Historians are concerned with factual truth, and it seems entirely appropriate to refer back to Manzoni and use factual accuracy as the main basis for assessment, because a good read is entirely a personal matter. First, though, we can disagree with Manzoni because human beings have a need for art in their lives, and our love of story-telling has to be one of the most elemental characteristics of our species. Manzoni used logic to reject historical novels in a way which would also have dismissed painting after the invention of photography. Indeed, it was around the same time and such an idea was suggested by some, but art also continued to flourish after it lost the need to be documentary. There is a value in historical novels as art. They can leave you with a useful general understanding after the details are forgotten, and they may leave you with evocative images which prey on your mind, as do films. When Edward I murders his son's friend by casual defenestration in the film *Braveheart*, the truth of it seems less important than the shocking lesson that Edward I was a monster.[73] In Prescott's novel *The Man on a Donkey*, we are given an evocative image of colourful pages from manuscripts, torn from the books in the nunnery's library during the Dissolution, with the phrase '...when the pages were strewn about the garth it looked as if flowers were blooming in November.' These images are meaningful and powerful whether they are literally true or not.

Manzoni was right that the mixture of truth and fiction is uncomfortable and I have felt it myself. When I sought knowledge about Sir Walter Scott, I read Allan Massie's historical novel about him, *The Ragged Lion* (1994), and I found a great many potentially useful quotes, but, without more research, I just did not know which were Scott's, and which were Massie's. Nevertheless, after reading it, I felt that I knew Sir Walter.

Historical novels are valid as reconstruction exercises, as valid as the building of working Roman water wheels or fifteenth-century printing presses, to test whether the model we have works in practice, and frequently to revise theory in the light of what we find. The myth of primitive Germanic democracy is extremely difficult to deploy in a novel, where it soon clashes with the brutal reality of a warrior society. *The Daughter of Time* was not the first pro-Richard novel, but it was deliberately written to reject the traditional view. Others accept the tradition as factual, but make Richard into a sympathetic character all the same. Each contri-

---

[73] Most successful films, and television series, get 'novelised', and often in the same year as the film. Randall Wallace provided the novel *Braveheart* in 1995; *Alfred the Great* was novelised by Victor Hastings [sic] in 1969 and *The Fall of the Roman Empire* was novelised by Harry Whittington in 1964.

bution offers us an interpretation, a suggestion that it might have happened *this way*... In this respect, even the badly-done novel has a value because mistakes are challenging, forcing us to think *why* it is wrong.

The educational value of historical novels has long been recognised. They are useful not only as a general introduction to a period or event, but they can even be used as a more sophisticated educational tool, by offering the well-read student an exercise in analysis (in some respects, the worse the novel, the more opportunities for the student to criticise).

Nevertheless, some historical novels really are ground-breaking, either because they explore an idea which would normally only be a footnote, giving it a book-length exposition, or because they present the results of meticulous pioneer research. Examples of excellence are Alfred Duggan's *Conscience of the King* (1951), which explores the idea that Cerdic of Wessex was a Romano-Briton rather than a Saxon from overseas – interesting; Brian Bates' *The Way of Wyrd. Tales of an Anglo-Saxon Sorcerer* (1983), an attempt to reconstruct the essentials of Old English paganism – interesting; Tay's *The Daughter of Time*, already mentioned; Anya Seton's *Katherine* (1954), a bestseller which evocatively restored Katherine Swynford to the twentieth century; Hilda Prescott's *The Man on a Donkey* (1952), doing the same for Robert Aske; and Irving Stone's *The Agony and the Ecstasy* (1961), the fictional biography of Michelangelo which took ten years to write and which involved the author in commissioning pioneer translations of fifteenth-century texts which had never been published before. These novels are often cited in scholarly footnotes. They have performed their task well.

Deliberate factual error remains incomprehensible to the present writer, and something which should always leave the reader distrustful. In *The Wool-pack*, Cynthia Harnett based her smuggling conspiracy on a real event, but the real event was in 1458 and she set the novel in 1493. Why? There is not a single detail in the plot which required the leap in time, marvellous book though it is.

When one recalls that half the population of Europe died from a disease in 1348–9, that a fifteenth-century king (Henry VI) would suffer from insanity, and his court would practice alchemy to try to cure him, or that in the seventeenth century the Tsar of Russia (Peter the Great), of all people, would travel, as if in a *Boy's Own* adventure, incognito through Europe, learning things like shipbuilding techniques before returning home to westernise his country, then one should be very suspicious of novelists who think history needs improving. History is exciting enough.

Often, of course, it is enthusiasm which makes an author deliberately blur chronology in order to get all his favourite subjects in. Scott did it in *Kenilworth*, introducing Shakespeare as an experienced character when he was a child at the time of the setting, but one is right to feel distrustful. Minor factual errors, however, can be forgiven. Candace Robb's slip on the shilling in fourteenth-century

York does not mean that the whole book is invalidated. Nevertheless, a factual matter which historical novelists have no excuse for getting wrong, but which they frequently do, is the really important subject of names.

The study of place- or personal-names may be a difficult linguistic science, but its conclusions are readily accessible and widely circulated. Many names in novels are simply impossible and the foolish publishers are just as guilty as the authors here. Mills & Boon novels are by far the worst offenders. In Leslie Burbank's *To Tame a Viking* (2005), a heroine of c.1000 AD is called Queen Silke Thorganson of Iceland. Iceland was a republic, and Scandinavian names take a gender (it would have been Thorgansdottir). Ivanhoe takes his name from the Buckinghamshire place-name Ivinghoe, misspelled, and in a form which denies the actual meaning of the word. In the book, Ivanhoe is a locative surname but in typical nineteenth-century public-school style it was used as if it were a forename, and, after the book was published, it became a real one. There are eight in the 1881 on-line census.[74]

Children's books, too, are often quite mischievous here. In Cynthia Harnett's *The Load of Unicorn*, Benedict is given the affectionate diminutive 'Bendy', but Bene't is the form this name would have taken and Bene't is better.

In Karen Cushman's *The Midwife's Apprentice* (1995), a children's novel which uniquely examines some of the difficulties of medieval childbirth, there are the personal names Grommet, Tansy, Figtree and the absurd place-name Gobnet (all impossible). Names are not funny sounds, they have a meaning. Authors who play games in this Dickensian manner cannot be said to be attempting to reconstruct medieval lives with any conscience. Such failure on the part of the novelist also betrays an ignorance of the humourous potential of real medieval names, for surnames now extinct, but based originally on some all-too-human characteristic, offer the historical novelist a great opportunity for entertainment.[75]

There are no naming problems in a recent novel by the place-name scholar Simon Taylor, whose *Mortimer's Deep* (1992) imaginatively constructs a story for the intriguing Fife place-name of the title, set in the twelfth and thirteenth centuries. This novel also makes a rare contribution to historical fiction in exploring the feelings and experiences of a sensitive soul, forced into a life of brutality as a

---

[74] One name scholar who has made literary onomastics a specialised study is W. F. H. Nicolaisen; see his recent essay 'On Names in Literature', *Nomina* 31 (2008), 89–98.

[75] See for example the two articles by Peter McClure in *Nomina*, journal of the Society for Names Studies in Britain and Ireland: 'The Kinship of *Jack*; I, Pet-forms of Middle English Personal Names with the Suffixes -*kin*, -*ke*, *man* and -*cot*', *Nomina* 26 (2003), 93–117; and 'The Kinship of *Jack*; II, Pet-Forms of Middle English Personal Names with the Suffixes -*cok* and -*cus*', *Nomina* 28 (2005), 5–42. Criticisms of naming problems in novels appear irrelevant when compared to the achievement of the Italian composer Donizetti. In his opera, *Alfredo il Grande*, the Viking leader is not called Guthrum, which would have made both historical and musical sense. He is called Atkins. One cannot even sing 'Atkins' in a threatening manner.

warrior before he makes his escape to the sanctuary of a monastery, where other problems await him. Medieval people were like us, and there must have been many such difficult lives, involving dilemmas and fears and desires and isolation for those who did not fit with their families' plans, but such seriousness does not necessarily make for an entertaining read, so it does not appear very often.

One method which can be used to convey a sense of authenticity is to suggest that the story is taken from a source, just as the twelfth-century Arthurians did. It was a commonplace of early novels to pretend that the text was a translation of a unique manuscript, or lost letters. At the start of *The Castle of Otranto* we have: 'The following work was found in the library of an ancient catholic family in the north of England. It was printed at Naples, in the black letter, in the year 1529...' To some extent any novelist who uses the first person singular is doing the same thing. From a literary point of view it is very effective, but historians will be aware that the resulting text is completely different in length and style to any surviving medieval autobiographies.[76] *Mortimer's Deep* adopts instead the solution of conversation where one aged character tells the story of his life to a visitor. The reader can imagine he is present, listening to the dialogue, without having to accept the inherent implausibility of the long written text in a modern style.[77]

In fact, books themselves often appear in medieval novels, but rarely with the understanding that they do in *The Name of the Rose*. In *Proxy Wedding*, the young heroine reads *alone* in her bedroom, tossing a book to one side in casual boredom. It doesn't ring true. We know that there was more literacy in the fifteenth century than we used to think. Some historians even suggest that 50% of the population could read by then; but, when most books were worth the equivalent of a car in today's society, can we really expect fairly ordinary households to contain much light reading? Literacy in itself does not mean that literature was read, but none of the novels I have read express surprise that a household should contain any books at all.[78]

---

[76] Alan Massie's *The Ragged Lion* pretends to be the text of the lost memoir of Scott, the one allegedly quarried and then destroyed by Lockhart. There is a study of this approach, though the content of the book does not particularly include historical fiction: Gwendolyn A. Morgan, *The Invention of False Medieval Authorities as a Literary Device in Popular Fiction. From Tolkien to* The Da Vinci Code (Lewiston [New York] and Lampeter, 2006).

[77] An example of the unconvincing is Paul Watkins, *Thunder God* (London, 2004), pretending to be a long memoir by a tenth- and eleventh-century Viking.

[78] See Nicholas Orme, *Medieval Children* (New Haven, 2001), chs 7 and 8. The existence of surviving popular literature, including printed fiction, would appear to contradict this, but early print-runs were extremely limited, books remained remarkably expensive until the mid-nineteenth century, and reading was often a public rather than a private activity. It remains difficult to accept that medieval readers had a casual relationship with books.

If, in the future, an as-yet-unborn historical novelist writes about the Harlaxton Symposium, would they, one wonders, get it right? Would it reconstruct our lives? One rather thinks that the results would not be recognised by those who attend the symposium now. I see the title, *Congress*, to give the text a racy feel. The names and the sequence of events would be realistic, but the papers would be based on their published versions, and in order to make some entertainment for the reader, the writer would have to provide difficulties and personality clashes and domestic situations which would be entirely invented. Even worse, our dialogue would probably be based on surviving news reports and media interviews, so we would all be made to speak Newspeak. Our conference chat would be cluttered with expressions like blue-sky, cascade, history (meaning recent track record), moving forward, the strange verbs book-end, progress, privilege and showcase, the preposterous use of Russian Emperors as policy co-ordinators, and the campest and most misused word of all, *issues*.[79] It is obvious that the historical novel cannot accurately reconstruct medieval lives. The project is always going to be compromised by the needs of the readership and market, let alone the inadequacies of the writer's understanding.

Nevertheless, the range of subjects covered in the five-thousand titles is astonishing. Although there are some medieval lives and subjects covered many times, many pioneering works cover rarer themes such as embroidery,[80] building,[81] printing,[82] the wool trade,[83] childbirth,[84] disease,[85] football,[86] abandoned children,[87] paganism,[88] heresy,[89] pacifism and same-gender relationships,[90] sculpture,[91] paint-

[79]   They are indeed ridiculous even when used today. A future novel which used them would be truly incomprehensible and create the misleading impression that the intelligentsia of the early twenty-first century had nothing of any substance to say.

[80]   Peter Benson's *Odo's Hanging* (London, 1993) and Sarah Bower's *The Needle in the Blood* (2007) are about the Bayeux Tapestry.

[81]   William Golding's *The Spire* (London, 1964) is, probably, about the building of the spire of Salisbury Cathedral.

[82]   Cynthia Harnett's *The Load of Unicorn* [American title *Caxton's Challenge*], already mentioned, and Blake Morrison's *The Justification of Johann Gutenberg* (2000).

[83]   Cynthia Harnett's *The Wool-pack*, already mentioned.

[84]   *The Midwife's Apprentice*, already mentioned.

[85]   Leprosy is covered by Geoffrey Trease, *The Red Towers of Granada* (London, 1966), the 1348 plague by Reuben Merliss, *The Year of the Death* (London, 1965).

[86]   Rob Childs, *Time Rangers 1: A Shot in the Dark* (London, 1997); ten adventures of these time-travelling footballers appeared between 1997 and 1999.

[87]   Jill Paton Walsh, *Knowledge of Angels* (Cambridge and Boston USA, 1994).

[88]   *The Way of Wyrd*, already mentioned.

[89]   Adam John Munthe, *A Note that Breaks the Silence. The Story of Peire Carcasse and Little Beast* (London, 1977) is about the Cathars, and there are many novels featuring the Lollards.

[90]   *Mortimer's Deep*, already mentioned, whereas lesbianism is more dubiously covered by the werewolves at the court of Charlemagne in two novels by Alice Borchardt, *The*

ing,[92] attitudes to animals[93] ... you name it, there's a novel about it. The opportunities for scholars to explore their favourite subjects in fiction, and to recommend novels as student reading, are only compromised by the lack of an informative bibliography, which I hope, one day, to supply.

The common-denominator of all historical writing is that it illustrates the reception of the past in a different subsequent society. E. H. Carr, in *What is History?* (1961), concluded that history was a continuous dialogue between the past and the present. Novelists and scholars share in this. Of course, the real evidence of medieval lives in archaeology and the source material is far more precious to us, but it is also far more precious than all the history books ever written about the middle ages since their close. Scholarly works and historical novels share not only their research methods and something of their narrative literary style, but also their ultimate fate as ephemeral commentaries. Each generation studies, uses and celebrates medieval lives according to its own needs.[94]

Silver Wolf (1998) and *The Wolf King* (2001).

[91] Francis Mary Peard's *Prentice Hugh* (1887) concerns sculpture at Exeter Cathedral.

[92] *The Agony and the Ecstasy*, already mentioned.

[93] Henrietta Branford's *Fire, Bed and Bone* (1997) delightfully considers the Peasants' Revolt of 1381 from the perspective of a dog.

[94] I am grateful to the editors for their encouraging feedback and for accepting the paper for the conference. I have also benefited from conversations with Mark English, the late Andor Gomme, Martin Hamlyn, Kenneth Hillier, Rebecca Redmond, David Roffe, Kevin Troop, my brother Ian Tyas, Livia Visser-Fuchs, Paul Watkins (not the novelist), Ann Wilkins and countless and often anonymous delegates at conferences at my publisher's bookstall, who greeted news of the paper with encouragement and suggestions.

INDEX

1 (Barron) A marginal illustration by the scribe, found in the registered copy of Salter's will, showing Salter's executor holding a money bag and preparing to hand over bequests to the five children (three men and two girls) of Robert and Elizabeth Symonds. John Symonds, who was to act on behalf of his brothers and sisters is named. TNA, PROB, 11/42a fol. 103v (copyright: The National Archives)

2 (Barron) A marginal illustration by the scribe, found in the registered copy of Salter's will, showing the six glasses and the earthenware bottle with a funnel belonging to it, together with Salter's urinal glass and case, and a drinking 'cruse' (bottle) of earthenware, which Salter bequeathed to John Busshope, the parish clerk of St Nicholas Acon. TNA, PROB, 11/42a fol. 104v (copyright: The National Archives).

3 (Barron) The first page of Thomas Salter's original will, drawn up 31 August 1558, showing the heading 'Jesus aductor meus' and the side headings 'The Wax Chandeler' and 'The Salters almesmen'. Salter decided that it should be the curate of St Michael Cornhill, rather than of St Nicholas Acon in Lombard Street, who was to accompany his body to the burial in St Magnus' church, and this alteration can be seen in line 21.

TNA, PROB 10/38, fol. 1 (copyright: The National Archives).

4 (Barron) The fourth page of Thomas Salter's will showing where Salter ceased to write the will himself and it was continued in the hand of the notary, Thmas Bradforth, who is also the first witness. The two smudged marks (one a cross) at the end of the will may be the marks made by Thomas Salter when he was no longer able to write. TNA, PROB 10/38, fol. 4 (copyright: The National Archives).

5 (Barron) Thomas Salter's letter to Thomas Cromwell, dated 7 August 1534. The letter is written by Salter himself: the distinctive handwriting can be identified again when Salter drew up his own will twenty-four years later (see Illustration 3). TNA, SP1/85 (copyright: The National Archives).

6 (P. King) The tomb of Ralph Woodford, Ashby Folville (copyright: Meg Twycross).

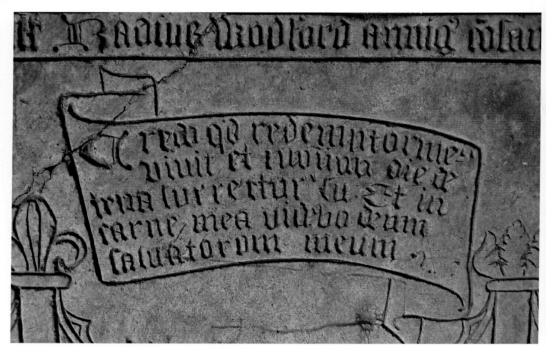

7 (P. King) The tomb of Ralph Woodford, Ashby Folville (detail) (copyright: Meg Twycross).

8 (P. King) The tomb of Ralph Woodford, Ashby Folville (detail) (copyright: Meg Twycross).

9 (P. King) The arms of Ralph Woodford, Ashby Folville (copyright: Meg Twycross).

10 (Meale) The Morley tomb, St Andrew's Church, Hingham (copyright: Carol M. Meale).

11 (Meale) The Morley tomb, St Andrew's Church, Hingham, detail showing the donors flanking Christ (copyright: Carol M. Meale).

12 (Meale) St Andrew's Church, Hingham, Carving of St Michael (copyright: Carol M. Meale).

13 (D. King) Parish church of East Harling, east chancel window (copyright: David J. King).

14 (D. King) Parish church of East Harling, Annunciation, c. 1461–7, east chancel window, originally in east window of Harling Chapel (copyright: David J. King).

15 (D. King) Parish church of East Harling, Vistation, c. 1461–7, east chancel window, originally in east window of Harling Chapel (copyright: David J. King).

16 (D. King) Parish church of East Harling, Nativity, c. 1461–7, east chancel window, originally in east window of Harling Chapel (copyright: David J. King).

17 (D. King) Parish church of East Harling, Presentation, c. 1461–7, east chancel window, originally in east window of Harling Chapel (copyright: David J. King).

18 (D. King) Parish church of East Harling, Harling Chapel (Lady Chapel) and screen
(copyright: David J. King).

19 (D. King) Parish church of East Harling, Harling Chapel, carving in north-east spandrel (copyright: David J. King).

20 (D. King) Parish church of East Harling, Harling Chapel, tomb of Sir Robert Harling (copyright: David J. King).

21 (D. King) Parish church of East Harling, tomb of Sir William Chamberlain and Anne Harling, with view into Chapel of St Anne (copyright: David J. King).

23 (D. King). Parish church of Merton, brass of Sir William Grey and family, 1495, detail
(Copyright: David J. King).

22 (D. King) (opposite). Parish church of East Harling, east chancel window, fragments of *Te Deum* window, c.1491–98 (copyright: David J. King).

24 (Linenthal) Seal matrix of William, son of Aveline, early thirteenth century, found at King's Lynn, Norfolk (copyright: Richard Linenthal).

25 (Linenthal) Seal matrix of Martillus the tailor, fourteenth century, found in Kent (copyright: Richard Linenthal).

26 (Linenthal) Seal matrix of Roland Oisun, engraved on a reused Roman bronze Sestertius, c. 1200 (copyright: Richard Linenthal).

27 (Linenthal) Seal matrix of Agnes Decniftu, thirteenth century, the retrograde legend engraved to be read from the matrix rather than from a wax impression (copyright: Richard Linenthal).

28 (Rogers) Robert Wyvil, bishop of Salisbury, d. 1375, Salisbury Cathedral (copyright: Lack, Stuchfield and Whittemore, County Series).

29 (Rogers) Brian Rouclif, d. 1494, and wife Joan, Cowthorpe (before theft of portions in 1850s, from Mill Stevenson) (copyright: Lack, Stuchfield and Whittemore, County Series).

30 (Rogers) Henry Notingham and wife, c. 1405, Holme-next-the-Sea, Norfolk (copyright: Lack, Stuchfield and Whittemore, County Series).

Herri notingham & hys wytte hine here,
þat madñ this churche stepull & quere,
two vetmentz & belles they made also,
crist hem saue therfore fro wo,
and to bringe her saules to blis of heuen,
sayth pater & aue with mylde steuen.

31 (Rogers) Nicholas Canteys, d. 1431,
Margate, Kent (copyright: Lack, Stuchfield and Whittemore, County Series).

32 (Rogers) William Palmer, d. 1520,
Ingoldmells, Lincs. (copyright: Lack, Stuchfield
and Whittemore, County Series).

33 (Rogers) Anne Asteley, d. 1512, Blickling, Norfolk (copyright: Lack, Stuchfield and Whittemore, County Series).

Christophorus Iacsonus socius huius collegii
et artium ac medicae Lectionis a d Linacro instituta
professor, e sudore britannico adhuc iuuenis mo
ritur atqȝ hic sepelitur An 1528 die 2 Iulii

34 (Rogers) Christopher Jackson, d. 1528, St John's College, Cambridge (rubbing by Nicholas Rogers)
(copyright: Nicholas Rogers).

35 (Rogers) John Newles, d. 1452, St Cross, Winchester
(copyright: Lack, Stuchfield and Whittemore, County Series).

36 (Tudor-Craig) Grisaille stained glass roundel of clerical writer at his desk. Mid fifteenth century Collection Andrew Rudebeck.

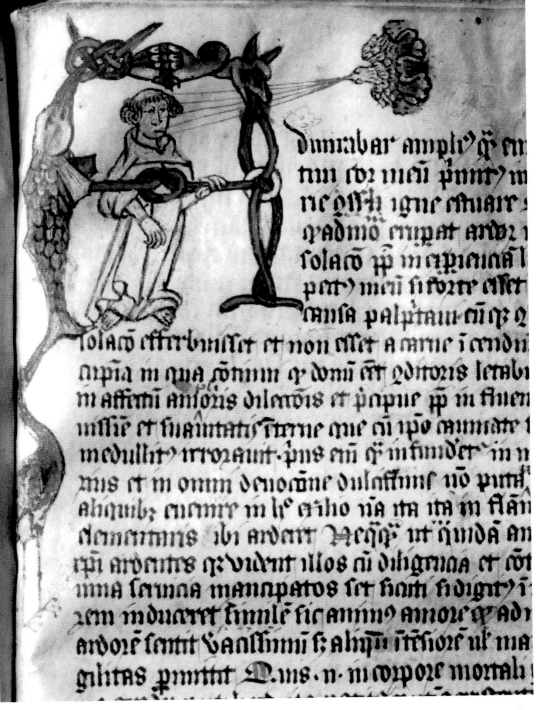

dunabar ampli q̄ er
tum for meū pmr) m
ne gīſſi igne ẽuiart
q̄admō erupat ardor
ſolacō ꝓ mapiciuū
prt) meū ſi forte eſſet
cauſa palpitaui cū cā q
ſolacō efferbuiſſet et non eſſet a carne i cendu
cipia in qua ſomun q̄ domū eſt qdītoris letabu
m affectu amoris dilectois et papue ꝓ m fluen
uiſſie et ſuauitatis ſtirne cuie cū ipo cauinate t
medullitꝰ irroꝛauit. ꝑns enī q̄ mſundet in n
mus et m omm deuocōne dulaſſunif uō pirit
ahquibꝫ cuenrt in hꝰ criho uia ita ita m flām
demcicinuus ibi ardeit Reſꝗꝛ ut q̄uidā an
tpū ardentus q̄vident illos cū dilignicia et cō
nima ſcunoa mancipatos ſet hoū ſi dignr) i
zem mduarrt ſimilē ſic amino amoie q̄ adu
ardoie ſentit vaullimi ſ: ahitū irrſioie ut ma
gilitas pmittit Deus. n̄ m coꝛpoꝛe moꝛtali

37 (Tudor-Craig) Richard Rolle receiving inspiration from the Holy Spirit. Initial from copy in Latin of Rolle's *Incendium Amoris*, c. 1400. Lincoln Cathedral Library MS 218, fol. 101 (copyright: Lincoln Cathedral Library).

38 (Tudor-Craig) *Songe du vergier,* from a French manuscript of just before 1379, London, British Library, Royal 19 C IV, fol. 1v (copyright: British Library Board).

39 (Tudor-Craig) *Pearl*: the dreamer lying on a mound, from the unique manuscript of c. 1400, London, British Library, MS Cotton Nero A. X, fol. 41 (copyright: British Library Board).

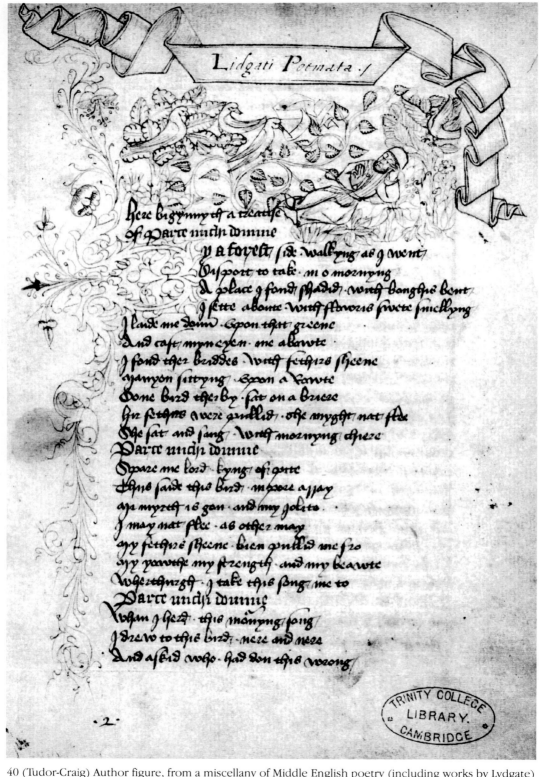

40 (Tudor-Craig) Author figure, from a miscellany of Middle English poetry (including works by Lydgate) and prose compiled between 1473 and 1483, Cambridge, Trinity College MS R 3 21, fol. 34 (reproduced with kind permission of the Master and Fellows of Trinity College Cambridge).